EMOTIONS, CRIME AND JUSTICE

The return of emotions to debates about crime and criminal justice has been a striking development of recent decades across many jurisdictions. This has been registered in the return of shame to justice procedures, a heightened focus on victims and their emotional needs, fear of crime as a major preoccupation of citizens and politicians, and highly emotionalised public discourses on crime and justice. But how can we best make sense of these developments? Do we need to create 'emotionally intelligent' justice systems, or are we messing recklessly with the rational foundations of liberal criminal justice?

This volume brings together leading criminologists and sociologists from across the world in a much needed conversation about how to re-calibrate reason and emotion in crime and justice today. The contributions range from the micro-analysis of emotions in violent encounters, to the paradoxes and tensions that arise from the emotionalisation of criminal justice in the public sphere. They explore the emotional labour of workers in police and penal institutions, the justice experiences of victims and offenders, and the role of vengeance, forgiveness and regret in the aftermath of violence and conflict resolution. The result is a set of original essays which offer a fresh and timely perspective on problems of crime and justice in contemporary liberal democracies.

Oñati International Series in Law and Society

A SERIES PUBLISHED FOR THE OÑATI INSTITUTE
FOR THE SOCIOLOGY OF LAW

General Editors

Judy Fudge   David Nelken

Founding Editors

William LF Felstiner   Eve Darian-Smith

Board of General Editors

Rosemary Hunter, University of Kent, United Kingdom
Carlos Lugo, Hostos Law School, Puerto Rico
Jacek Kurczewski, Warsaw University, Poland
Marie-Claire Foblets, Leuven University, Belgium
Roderick Macdonald, McGill University, Canada

Recent titles in this series

Legal Institutions and Collective Memories edited by Susanne Karstedt

Changing Contours of Domestic Life, Family and Law: Caring and Sharing
edited by Anne Bottomley and Simone Wong

Criminology and Archaeology: Studies in Looted Antiquities edited by
Simon Mackenzie and Penny Green

*The Legal Tender of Gender: Welfare Law and the Regulation of Women's
Poverty* edited by Shelley Gavigan and Dorothy Chunn

Human Rights at Work edited by Colin Fenwick and Tonia Novitz

Travels of the Criminal Question: Cultural Embeddedness and Diffusion
edited by Dario Melossi, Máximo Sozzo and Richard Sparks

*Feminist Perspectives on Contemporary International Law: Between
Resistance and Compliance?* edited by Sari Kouvo and Zoe Pearson

Challenging Gender Inequality in Tax Policy Making: Comparative Perspectives
edited by Kim Brooks, Åsa Gunnarson, Lisa Philipps and Maria Wersig

For the complete list of titles in this series, see
'Oñati International Series in Law and Society' link at
www.hartpub.co.uk/books/series.asp

Emotions, Crime and Justice

Edited by
Susanne Karstedt, Ian Loader
and
Heather Strang

Oñati International Series in Law and Society

A SERIES PUBLISHED FOR THE OÑATI INSTITUTE
FOR THE SOCIOLOGY OF LAW

·HART·
PUBLISHING
OXFORD AND PORTLAND, OREGON
2014

Published in the United Kingdom by Hart Publishing Ltd
16C Worcester Place, Oxford, OX1 2JW
Telephone:+44 (0)1865 517530
Fax: +44 (0)1865 510710
E-mail: mail@hartpub.co.uk
Website: http://www.hartpub.co.uk

Published in North America (US and Canada) by
Hart Publishing
c/o International Specialized Book Services
920 NE 58th Avenue, Suite 300
Portland, OR 97213-3786
USA
Tel: +1 503 287 3093 or toll-free: (1) 800 944 6190
Fax: +1 503 280 8832
E-mail: orders@isbs.com
Website: http://www.isbs.com

© Oñati IISL 2011

First printed in hardback in 2011. Reprinted in paperback in 2014.
Hart Publishing is an imprint of Bloomsbury Publishing plc.

British Library Cataloguing in Publication Data
Data Available

ISBN 978-1-84946-161-0 (Hardback)
ISBN 978-1-84946-683-7 (Paperback)

Typeset by Compuscript Ltd, Shannon
Printed and bound in Great Britain by
Lightning Source UK Ltd

Preface to the Paperback Edition

When this volume was first published, it entered a small but flourishing field of inquiry into emotions, crime and justice. Since then it has expanded into new areas as scholars from history, philosophy or genocide studies started to analyse their subjects through the lens of emotions. The emotional paradigm has invigorated historical studies of violence as well as philosophical inquiries into the essence of justice such as Martha Nussbaum's 'Political Emotions'. The emotional turn promoted in this book has reshaped the understanding of phenomena ranging from mass atrocities and terrorism to the mechanisms of justice in everyday life, as well as raising awareness for the justice needs and interests of victims of crime.

The fundamental questions that are addressed in this volume, however, still loom large. How can we make sense of the paradoxes and tensions that arise from the emotionalisation of criminal justice in the public sphere? Do we need to create 'emotionally intelligent' justice systems? Are we endangering the rational foundations of liberal criminal justice? This set of original essays offers insights into the problems of crime and justice in contemporary societies that are as foundational as they are timely.

As the field of emotion studies in criminology expands, there is increasing demand for such foundational texts for teaching and learning. This volume has been highly recommended by reviewers as such a text for students and researchers entering the field. The editors are therefore delighted to present a paperback edition, and we are grateful to Hart Publishing for offering the opportunity. We hope that it will encourage ever more students and researchers from all disciplines to engage with a fascinating field of inquiry into crime, justice and human nature.

Acknowledgements

The papers published in this volume were first presented in a workshop at the International Institute for the Sociology of Law (IISJ) in Onati, Spain, in 2004. The workshop was supported by the IISJ and by a generous financial contribution of A$10,000 from the Regulatory Institutions Network (RegNet) at the Australian National University. In addition, preparations for the workshop were supported by a Visiting Fellowship to RegNet and the ANU for Professor Susanne Karstedt, as was the editorial work of Dr Heather Strang. The editors and organisers of the workshop wish to express their gratitude to the IISJ, in particular Malen Gordoa Mendizabal for the flawless organisation of the workshop, and to RegNet, in particular Professor John Braithwaite, for generous support. Thanks are also due to all our contributors for their hard work and patience, and to Sophie Palmer, of the University of Oxford, for her assistance with the preparation of the final manuscript.

Contents

List of Contributors

Eliza Ahmed was a research fellow in the Regulatory Institutions Network at the Australian National University, when this paper was written. Eliza's research interests include regulation and governance in a range of contexts such as bullying in schools and workplaces, bystander intervention, higher education loans and tax compliance. Her publications focus on identifying institutional practices that promote adaptive management of emotions and compliance. Currently Eliza is practicing as an educational and developmental psychologist in Canberra, Australia.

John Braithwaite is an Australian Research Council Federation Fellow and a Distinguished Professor in the College of Asia and the Pacific at the Australian National University. His current project is a 20-year comparative study of recovery from armed conflict called Peacebuilding Compared. Its first product is a 2010 book with Valerie Braithwaite, Michael Cookson and Leah Dunn, *Anomie and Violence: Non-Truth and Reconciliation in Indonesian Peacebuilding*. His other recent book is *Regulatory Capitalism: How it Works, Ideas for Making it Work Better*. He has long had an interest in the emotions in criminal justice, restorative justice, business regulation and peacebuilding.

John D Brewer is Professor of Post Conflict Studies at the Institute for the Study of Conflict, Transformation and Social Justice, Queen's University Belfast and Honorary Vice-President of the British Sociological Association. He is a Member of the Royal Irish Academy (2004), a Fellow of the Royal Society of Edinburgh (2008), an Academician in the Academy of Social Sciences (2003) and a Fellow of the Royal Society of Arts (1998). His latest book is *Peace Processes: A Sociological Approach* and he is currently writing up an ESRC-funded project on the role of the churches in Northern Ireland's peace process. He is Principal Investigator on a cross-national, five-year project on compromise amongst victims of conflict, funded by the Leverhulme Trust.

Adam Calverley is a lecturer in Criminology at the Department of Social Sciences at the University of Hull where he teaches Policing and Criminal Justice at undergraduate and postgraduate levels at Hull and HKU SPACE Centre for International Degree Programmes in Hong Kong. He has previously worked as a researcher for the University of Glamorgan and the University of Keele. Publications include *Understanding Desistance from Crime* with Dr Stephen Farrall and he was a co-author of the Home Office Research Study, *Black and Asian Offenders on Probation*. His research interests include desistance from crime and issues surrounding 'life after punishment', ethnicity, crime and criminal justice, and probation. His recent doctoral research investigated the desistance experiences of minority ethnic offenders and is soon to be published as a monograph under the title '*Cultures of Desistance*'.

Randall Collins is Dorothy Swaine Thomas Professor of Sociology and member of the Department of Criminology at the University of Pennsylvania, and President of the American Sociological Association for 2010–2011. He is the author of *Violence: A Micro-Sociological Theory* and *Interaction Ritual Chains*. His earlier books include *Conflict Sociology*, *The Credential Society*, *The Sociology of Philosophies: A Global Theory of Intellectual Change* and *Macro-History*.

Elaine Crawley is Reader in Criminology at the University of Salford. She has conducted extensive prisons research, and is best known for her book *Doing Prison Work*, a study of prison officers. She works closely with a number of prisons, including Dej Prison Hospital and Gherla Maximum Security prison, Transylvania, and at HMP Manchester where she is a member of the prison's Segregation Management Monitoring and Review Group. She is Director of Salford University's Centre for Prison Studies (SUCPS).

Willem de Haan is a Professor-emeritus of criminology at the Department of Criminal Law and Criminology, Faculty of Law, University of Groningen, The Netherlands. Haan is the author of *The Politics of Redress: Crime, Punishment and Penal Abolition*. His current research interests are violence and social and legal reactions to violence in different social contexts. He was President of the Dutch Association of Criminology and is a member of the Social Science Council of the Royal Dutch Academy of Arts and Sciences.

Stephen Farrall is Professor of Criminology at Sheffield University. His research interests focus on why people stop offending and the impact of neo-liberal social policies on citizens' experiences of crime. He is currently undertaking a fifth sweep of interviews with the cases described in his contribution to this collection. His latest book is *Serious Offenders*, co-authored with Barry Godfrey and David Cox, which deals with the sentencing of serious offenders between the 1850s and the early 20th Century.

Nathan Harris is a Fellow at the Regulatory Institutions Network, School of Regulation, Justice and Diplomacy, Australian National University. His research draws on perspectives from criminology and social and community psychology to examine how institutions such as criminal justice and child protection can more effectively respond to social problems. Restorative justice and responsive regulation are one focus of this research; psychological dynamics between social disapproval and shame-related emotions are another, because they explain how individuals respond to interventions.

Susanne Karstedt is Professor of Criminology and Criminal Justice at the Centre for Criminal Justice Studies at the University of Leeds, UK. Her current research and writing focus on transitional justice, on the impact of democratic values and institutions on crime and justice, and on contemporary moral economies. Her recent and forthcoming publications include *Legal Institutions and Collective Memories, Democracy, Crime and Justice* as well as special issues of the *British Journal of Criminology*, and *The Annals of the American Academy of Political and Social Science* (with G LaFree). She is the recipient of the Sellin-Glueck Award of the American Society of Criminology 2007.

Anna King is a Professor at Georgian Court University, New Jersey. Her research focuses on the formation of attitudes towards punishment and forgiveness and on the relationship between culture, self-identity and perceptions of crime and punishment. Her work has appeared in the *British Journal of Criminology, Punishment and Society*, and the *European Journal of Criminal Justice Policy and Research*, and in several books. Previously, she held a post-doctoral NIH fellowship at the Center for Mental Health Services and Criminal Justice Research at Rutgers University and a lectureship at Keele University.

Ian Loader is Professor of Criminology and Professorial Fellow of All Souls College. His books include *Crime and Social Change in Middle England* (with E Girling and R Sparks), *Policing and the Condition of England* (with A Mulcahy), *Civilizing Security* (with N Walker) and *Public Criminology?* (with Richard Sparks). He is currently researching and writing about the commodification of security.

Shadd Maruna is the Director of the Institute of Criminology and Criminal Justice at the School of Law, Queen's University Belfast. Previously, he has been a lecturer at the University of Cambridge and the State University of New York. His book *Making Good: How Ex-Convicts Reform and Rebuild Their Lives* was named the 'Outstanding Contribution to Criminology' by the American Society of Criminology in 2001. His more recent books include: *Fifty Key Thinkers in Criminology* (2010), *Rehabilitation: Beyond the Risk Paradigm* (2007), *The Effects of Imprisonment* (2005), and *After Crime and Punishment: Pathways to Ex-Offender Reintegration* (2004).

Kristina Murphy is an Associate Professor at Griffith University's School of Criminology and Criminal Justice. She was a Research Fellow at the Australian National University's Regulatory Institutions Network at the time of writing this chapter. Her research integrates psychological theory with regulatory theory, arguing that effective regulation depends on being responsive to individuals' needs, values and behaviours. Her major research interest centres around procedural justice in the contexts of law enforcement, environment, taxation, and social security.

John Pratt is Director of the Institute of Criminology, Victoria University of Wellington, New Zealand. He has published extensively in the area of the history and sociology of punishment, including *Punishment and Civilization* and *Penal Populism*. He is currently involved in comparative penological research that involves Anglophone and Scandinavian societies. In 2009 he was awarded the Sir Leon Radzinowicz Memorial Prize by the British Journal of Criminology for his published work on Scandinavian penal systems.

Meredith Rossner is an assistant professor of criminology at the London School of Economics. She received her PhD in Sociology and Criminology from the University of Pennsylvania in 2008. She has conducted extensive research on the emotional dynamics and crime reduction potential of face-to-face restorative justice meetings with offenders and victims of serious crime. Her research interests include restorative justice, criminology theory, social interactions, and the sociology of emotions.

Thomas Scheff is Professor Emeritus at the University of California, Santa Barbara. He is past president of the Pacific Sociological Association, and past chair of the Emotions Section of the American Sociological Association. Some of his publications are *Being Mentally Ill, Microsociology, Bloody Revenge, Emotions, the Social Bond and Human Reality*. Two recent books are *Goffman Unbound!: A New Paradigm* and *Easy Rider* and *What's Love Got to Do with It? The Emotion World of Pop Songs*. He is interested in creative teaching and integration of the social, behavioural and clinical human arts and sciences.

Lawrence W Sherman is the Wolfson Professor of Criminology and Director of the Jerry Lee Centre for Experimental Criminology at Cambridge University, where he is also a Fellow of Darwin College. He also serves as Distinguished University Professor in the Department of Criminology and Criminal Justice at the University of Maryland. He has conducted field research and experiments in over 30 police agencies in the US, UK and Australia. Publications of the results have appeared in the *American Sociological Review, Law and Society Review, Criminology, Journal of the Royal Statistical Society (Series A), Journal of Experimental Criminology*, and the *Journal of the American Medical Association*. His work covers a wide range of issues, from predicting crime locations and serious offences by individual offenders to historical analyses of the control of police corruption.

Wesley G Skogan holds joint appointments with the Political Science Department at North Western University and the University's Institute for Policy Research. His most recent books report on his empirical studies of community policing initiatives in Chicago and elsewhere. He is also the author of two lengthy reports in the Home Office Research Series examining citizen contact and satisfaction with policing in Britain and co-edited a policy-oriented report from the National Research Council in Washington, DC: *Fairness and Effectiveness in Policing: The Evidence*. Professor Skogan's second line of research concerns neighbourhood and community responses to crime, including fear of crime, the impact of crime on neighbourhood life and crime prevention efforts by community organisations. He has also been involved in research on criminal victimisation and the evaluation of service programmes for victims.

Richard Sparks is Professor of Criminology at the University of Edinburgh and Co-Director of the Scottish Centre for Crime and Justice Research. His main research interests lie in prisons, penal politics, public responses to crime and punishment and criminological theory. His publications include: *Criminal Justice and Political Cultures* (co-edited with Tim Newburn), *Criminology and Social Theory* (co-edited with David Garland), *Crime and Social Change in Middle England* (with Evi Girling and Ian Loader), *Prisons and the Problem of Order* (with Tony Bottoms and Will Hay) and *Public Criminology?* (with Ian Loader).

Heather Strang is Director of Research at the Institute of Criminology, University of Cambridge. She has been involved in several experimental tests of the effects of restorative justice in Australia and the United Kingdom and is currently analysing a ten year follow-up of victims and offenders who participated in the Australian study. She has published extensively in this area, including her victim-focused book, *Repair or Revenge: Victims and Restorative Justice*.

Bas van Stokkom is a lecturer and research fellow at the Criminological Institute, Radboud University, and the Faculty of Social Sciences, Free University Amsterdam, The Netherlands. His research concentrates on the fields of citizenship, deliberative democracy, restorative justice, policing and punishment ethics. He studied emotion-dynamics in local citizen forums and restorative justice conferences. He is secretary of the Dutch-Flemish journal *Tijdschrift voor Herstelrecht* (Journal of Restorative Justice) and co-editor of the studies *Images of Restorative Justice Theory, Reflections on Reassurance Policing in the Low Countries* and *Restorative Policing*.

Handle with Care: Emotions, Crime and Justice

SUSANNE KARSTEDT

I. CROWDING OUT EMOTIONS

IN JUNE 2008, the British Government received a report from an advisor, Louise Casey, on the future of criminal justice and crime prevention, that instantly captured the imagination of the media and the public (Cabinet Office 2008). Although the report did not use the term itself, its propositions on informing the public, and making criminals performing community 'payback' more visible, were widely debated as a return of 'shame'. The report proposed that the visibility of punishment and offenders, and information on crime, are major factors in restoring public confidence in the criminal justice system and the capacities of government to deal with the crime problem. Not entirely without reason, the suggestion of 'naming criminals' was instantaneously transformed into 'shaming' them in the ensuing public debate. This echoed similar demands and practices that had spread in the US, Australia and New Zealand during the past decade (Karstedt 1996; Pratt 2006; see also Elster 2004). But, more remarkably, the report and subsequent debate established a link between individual and collective emotions: that shaming individuals in the public sphere, and the public display of individual shame, should not only attenuate public sentiments on crime and criminals, but also might be capable of dispersing anger and discontent directed towards the government—and thus re-establish a new and stronger emotional bond between the government and its citizens. The relationships between citizens, government and the criminal justice system seemed in need of a strong injection of emotions.

Criminologists watch such debates with disquiet.[1] Emotions are suspicious to them, and criminology's approach to emotions has been cautious and circumspect. Criminology as a science is a descendant of the Enlightenment, and is as such committed to the ideals of reason and reasonable discourse. This

---

[1] For the response of one of the editors of this volume to the Louise Casey report, see Loader (2008).

equally applies to modern penal law, and to the practice of criminal justice and its institutions as they developed since the Enlightenment in the late eighteenth century, and within modern liberal democracies. Just as exuberant emotions in the political sphere of democratic societies threaten to disrupt the whole system (and are typically observed in a breakdown of the political system), so the legal system strives to curb the strong emotions that it routinely and inescapably confronts. Yet for a long time it has ignored their undeniable presence and strength. Consequently, the presence of emotions in public debates about criminal justice has deepened the uneasy feelings of criminologists. Collective emotions and their expressions are seen as capable of being manipulated in the interest of politicians and other groups, and in particular by the media, in an irresponsible way. Criminologists tend to deny authenticity to outbursts of collective emotions, and they are more inclined to perceive them as manifestations of a popular 'false consciousness' (see Burkitt 2005; see also Loader, this volume). Emotions around crime and justice in the public sphere are viewed as the outbursts of a populace that 'does not know better'.

With the Enlightenment, criminology set itself on the same path as jurisprudence, penal law and criminal justice. The conventional story of modern penal law portrays a narrowly delineated list of, and proper roles for, emotions in the legal realm, so that emotions do not intrude into the true preserve of law: reason (Bandes 1999: 2). Such a juxtaposition of reason and emotion, one that is deeply embedded in modern social and political thought, seems to ignore the subtle recognition of the actual role of emotions in crime, law and legal procedures (Douglas 1993). The conventional story is, in other words, thoroughly misleading. As Nussbaum (2004: 46) points out, emotions have entered into the penal law under the disguise of 'reasonable emotions'. They are acknowledged in so far as they represent a reasonable evaluation and reaction, as in mitigating circumstances for crimes of passion (Wiener 2004). In fact, the whole edifice of penal law is erected on the assumption of strong emotions: fear of sanctions should instill compliance, and vengeance has to be channeled by legal procedures (Elster 1999). Both popular wisdom and criminological theory have posited fear of sanctions as a cornerstone and powerful mechanism of the criminal justice system. The institutions of criminal justice thus find themselves in a paradoxical situation. They offer a space for the most intensely felt emotions—of individuals as well as collectivities—while simultaneously providing mechanisms that are capable of 'cooling off' emotions, converting them into more sociable emotions, or channelling them back into reasonable and more standardised patterns of actions and thoughts. Indeed, the range of diversity among institutions of criminal justice throughout human history and across human societies testifies to humanity's efforts to contain the emotions that inevitably flare up in victims, offenders and bystanders.

Criminology's Enlightenment inheritance was thus fraught with contradictions and discrepancies as to the role and importance of emotions, and their relation to reason in the realm of criminal justice. In a recent analysis, Sherman (2003) shows that the Enlightenment model, proposing that law and the collective it represented should (and would) react *rationally* towards the offence of a *rational* offender, was deeply 'irrational' and bound to fail. Criminal justice today is characterised by what Sherman terms 'expressive economics'; this implies emotional reactions by the public and through criminal justice policies towards offenders who are assumed to act rationally (ie, are susceptible to harsh punishment). The report and debate referred to at the start of this chapter are exemplars of 'expressive economics'—based on harvesting expressions of public sentiment and on the assumption that offenders will react 'rationally' to the sanctions that the public demands to assuage its own anger.

How can these contradictions and discrepancies be resolved? The solution, Sherman points out, might be a rational reaction by criminal justice towards an emotional offender, or more precisely an 'emotionally intelligent' reaction. Emotionally intelligent justice would, he argues, acknowledge the emotions and emotional needs of both offenders and victims. It would provide institutionalised mechanisms to deal with these emotions, and design forms of justice and reactions towards crime that prevent the detrimental effects of unacknowledged emotions (Scheff, this volume). Proper acknowledgment of emotions might, in other words, avert some of the more detrimental effects of unrestrained emotions gushing into the arena of criminal justice (see also Walgrave 2008: chs 3 and 6).

II. THE RETURN OF EMOTIONS

Sherman's proposal for a more emotionally intelligent justice is timely. It grasps the essence of a process that started at the beginning of the 1990s, and which has since then signified the surprisingly abrupt end of the secular movement and modern project of the 'rationalisation' and 'de-emotionalisation' of criminal justice (see Pratt 2000, 2002). The 're-emotionalisation of law' (Laster and O'Malley 1996; see also de Haan and Loader 2002) shows itself in several signal events and processes: the return of shame into criminal justice procedures, in particular through restorative justice (Braithwaite 1989); a stronger focus on victims and their emotional needs, as evidenced eg in the US by their presence at executions or statements in courts (Rice, Dirks and Exline 2009); further the return of ostensibly humiliating public punishments as in the US in the 1990s; and finally highly emotionalised public discourses on crime and justice in western democracies (Karstedt 2002). The main trajectories of the return of emotions seem to have been embedded in the major movements that have changed the face of criminal justice over the past two decades: the victims' movement, restorative justice and the emergence of a highly emotional and mostly punitive public and political discourse on crime and justice.

As Pratt (2006: 64) argues, both the restorative justice movement and the simultaneous emergence of a more punitive climate, owe their existence to the 'decline of the welfare state' and 'the particular arrangements of penal power' that were its signature feature. These power arrangements relied on and were shaped by professional elites and a 'criminal justice intelligentsia' who were in charge of penal policies (Garland 2001; Loader 2006). The retreat of the welfare state opened the floodgates for the return of emotions back into the criminal justice system, within restorative justice procedures as well as in the public sphere. It turned the clock back towards those allegedly pre-modern forms of 'ostentatious' and 'emotive' punishment (Pratt 2000) that figure in the accounts of Durkheim and Elias. The fact that restorative justice thrives within a more punitive climate (such as New Zealand, with its strong restorative justice movement and high imprisonment rates) does not testify to opposing developments, but to a subterranean common ground (Pratt 2006: 61; see also Crawford 2006).

The discrepancy between allegedly rational offenders and emotionally charged reactions, as noted by Sherman (2003), seems to have increased concomitantly with the re-emotionalisation of law. Simultaneously, and contrasting with the developments described above, new strategies of situational crime prevention, risk-based sentencing and other procedures emerged that are unambiguously based on the rationality of offenders and victims. The move towards 'actuarial justice' (Feeley and Simon 1994) permeated criminal justice with the rational calculation of risks. However, it seems that this move profoundly miscalculated the impact of perceived risks in terms of their emotional equivalents, namely fear, anger, and blame. Thus, when 'actuarial justice' imposed risk-calculation on criminal justice and risk crowded out justice, criminal justice and crime prevention transmuted into a highly emotionalised sphere, and to just the opposite of what a dominating risk-framework would have created (see Hope and Karstedt 2003). Actuarial justice ends up with a victory of emotions (fear) over rationality (risk), and collective emotions tend to elbow rational reactions in the criminal justice system to the sidelines (Freiberg 2001).

The re-emotionalisation of law seems to be the final stroke for the project of modernisation of criminal punishment, and to signify the end of the modern period which denied emotions and their expressions a proper place and stage. It also seems to indicate the demise of the processes that drove the project of modernisation of punishment, as described by Emile Durkheim and Norbert Elias, the classical writers on the sociology of punishment. This process is embedded and part of a broader movement or 'emotional turn' in post-modern societies (eg Barbalet 2002). Cas Wouters has aptly described the two facets of this process as 'informalization' and 'emancipation of emotions'. Emotions that had been increasingly disciplined and controlled en route to modernity (and ruthlessly exploited by authoritarian regimes), re-entered both individual consciousness and public discussion as 'the long-term process of formalization gave way to a long-term process of informalization' (Wouters 2004: 209). Instead of being repressed and denied, emotions became valuable assets in social exchange, and required recognition as expressions of individual identity. The emancipation of emotions is more demanding in terms of their management, and informalisation nonetheless gives rise to subtle rules of feeling and display of emotions (Hochschild 2003). Consequently, it is a distinctive feature of the 'emotional turn' in societies that expressive values overtake more instrumental orientations. These changes are perfectly visible in large comparative surveys covering the last three decades in several waves. Welzel and Inglehart (2005; 2008) show with data from the World Values Survey that values of self-expression have not only become more prominent in many western countries, but have rapidly gained ground in transitional societies.

The process of re-emotionalisation seems to share some common features with the process of de-secularisation that brought religion back to the fore during the same period. Secularisation did not make religion disappear; to the contrary, religion re-emerged and took new forms when it became a matter of individual choice and thus an expression of individual and cultural identity. Like religion, emotions are defended as expressions of individual identity, and religious choice demands recognition, as does the individual expression of emotions. Simultaneously with religion, emotions emerge as a strengthened force on the post-modern stage.

The process of re-emotionalisation of justice consequently created and was driven by demands for the recognition of emotions that were contrasted with a cold, calculating and 'emotion-ignorant' model of justice. This is succinctly illustrated by statements made in the Willie Horton case in 1988 who while on furlough (temporary release) had kidnapped a couple and raped the woman (Garland 2001; Simon 2007: 57). When confronted with expert testimony and calculations of risk on which the policy of furlough had been based, the partner of the victim simply demanded that their own emotional experience had to take centre stage, not figures and calculations. Justice could only be done if 'real' people and their emotions were to be accounted for, and neither experts nor figures should interfere with that.

The demand for recognition of emotions in criminal justice might be a defining feature of post-modern societies. However, the reasons for acknowledging emotions in criminal justice are often traced back to the very nature of humans. In a recent article in *The New Yorker*, anthropologist Jared Diamond argued that modern criminal justice ignores the 'thirst for vengeance' that is 'among the strongest human emotions'. He deplored that modern states 'permit and encourage us to express our love, anger and grief, and fear, but not our thirst for vengeance' (Diamond 2008). Modern criminal justice dispossesses us of our feelings of vengeance, and alienates us from our deep-rooted feelings, instead of encouraging us to acknowledge them. In a similar vein, Cass Sunstein (2009) has recently argued that (criminal) law is based on 'moral indignation', and as such on the 'intuitive system of cognition' rather than the 'reflective system' through which morality as a system of abstract rules can be understood and is subject to reasoned arguments. Rather than being 'anchored in reasons', moral emotions and intuitions are expressed in 'automatic' responses to crime and (in)justice that people often are unable to justify in a 'rational' way. Anger, disgust and contempt are the main forms of expressing moral indignation and of automated responses to crimes, perpetrators and criminal justice. Notwithstanding that legal institutions aim at moral *reasoning* and at checking moral intuitions, they have to acknowledge the 'compelling demands' that the system of cognition and moral intuitions is making on them. Re-phrasing Sherman (2003), what is needed is an 'intuitively' intelligent system of criminal justice.

III. ENCOUNTERING EMOTIONS

Do these developments in post-modern societies simply reveal the enduring presence of emotions within criminal justice, or did emotions actually become a more powerful force? Do we really need to give more space to vengeance in criminal justice on the grounds that it is one of the strongest human emotions? Are not emotions of forgiveness and regret equally strong, and should they not equally have a proper space in criminal justice (Walgrave 2008; see Sherman and Strang in this volume)? The re-emotionalisation of criminal law and justice indeed is asking tough questions and demands reasoned decisions.

Criminal procedures—particularly in court—provide formal mechanisms that limit and govern emotions. Simultaneously, expectations are defined as to ways in which emotions should be expressed and displayed. 'Feeling rules' and 'display rules' (Hochschild 2003) are both decisive parts of proceedings in court, and they represent a broader culture of emotions and society's expressive values. Judges on the other hand might not be aware of the intuitive nature of their moral judgments and the ways these inform the legal conclusions that they draw (Sunstein 2009). Encounters with criminal justice—in particular with police—are emotionally fraught events, often for both parties involved, and can easily slip out of control (van Stokkom, this volume). Victims require space and recognition for their emotions in the procedures of criminal justice. They express their emotions in victims' statements, which are granted in cases involving violent crime, including capital punishment cases, in the US, in murder cases in the UK and also increasingly in international criminal justice (Sarat 2001; Karstedt 2010; Rose, Nadler and Clark 2006; Rice, Dirks and Exline 2009). The institutions of criminal justice—ranging from the police to prison—are simultaneously objects and representations of collective emotions, and thus provide powerful emotional scripts and iconography.

While there seems to be unanimity that a process of re-emotionalisation has changed criminal justice over the past decades, there is much less clarity as to whether the volume or character of crime actually has changed concomitantly and for the same reasons. It is equally reasonable to assume, as Sherman (2003) argues, that many offences and types of crime have an inherent emotional quality, that offenders are more emotional than rational, and that in fact this has not changed. As Wiener (2004) and Nussbaum (2004) both remind us, 'crimes of passion' have been acknowledged for centuries. We ascribe a particular emotional quality to violent crimes or crimes of honour. But we rarely recognise the emotions involved in property crime. In their seminal research on street robbers in Amsterdam, Willem de Haan and Jaco Vos (2003) found an explosive mixture of fear, anger, feelings of dominance, empathy with the victim, and moral sentiments reported by their subjects. In a similar vein, Jack Katz (1988) has drawn our attention to the highly emotional process of committing property offences. In his most recent books, Randall Collins (2004; 2008) demonstrates ways in which violence develops in interaction rituals that fuel emotions, and how violence is based on the reflection and amplification of individual emotions in and by collectivities (see also Collins, this volume). It is obvious that the 'emotional turn' has sparked renewed interest in the emotional aspect of crime. Such knowledge is indispensable if we are considering 'emotionally intelligent' justice as a way forward to deal with emotional offenders.

IV. INTRODUCING THE VOLUME

For criminologists, the 'emotional turn' raises numerous questions and opens up new perspectives. In which ways could reason and emotion in crime and justice be re-calibrated under the auspices of re-emotionalisation? Can and should professional rationality hold the more punitive sentiments of the public at bay, and can this be justified in a democracy, if at all? What is the 'emotional rationale' or moral intuition that forms the basis of punitive attitudes and its expressions? What does the assumption of emotional offenders actually imply? Is 'emotionally intelligent justice' possible, and what may it look like? What kind of 'emotion work' is presently done in prisons and police forces? How can and should collective emotions of revenge be handled in transitional justice and peacemaking?

The contributions to this volume span topics from the micro-analysis of emotions in violent encounters, to the paradoxes and tensions that arise with the emotionalisation of criminal justice in democracies. They analyse shame and pride in workplace bullying as well as in ethnic conflicts, or the process of desisting from crime; they are based on ethnographic analysis, qualitative, quantitative and experimental methodology; they have been researched in different continents and cultures; and they use a wide range of theories that transcend the borders and limitations of criminological theory.

In order to guide our readers through the range and diversity of the 17 contributions, we have divided them into five sections. Part I brings together contributions that explore emotional experiences in transgressions and crime from different angles, for different situations and processes, and from the perspective of offenders, as well as victims and the general public. Part II focuses on emotional experiences of justice, ranging from vengeance to shame, within a diversity of criminal justice institutions and settings. In Part III, emotion work within the criminal justice system is explored in two contributions, one on police–citizen encounters in the Netherlands, and one on prison officers in the UK. Part IV engages with questions of collective violence, conflict and peacemaking; the two contributions in this section look into the emotional causes of collective violence and conflicts, and how to deal with them in the process of peacemaking. The volume concludes, in Part V, with three contributions that address questions of how democracies deal with penal sentiments and their undercurrent of collective emotional fervour.

Part I: Emotions in Transgression and Crime

The contributions in this section frame emotions within the context of social relationships ranging from those that evolve instantaneously in a situation of conflict and violence, to emotions that are embedded in wider, even cultural patterns of social solidarity and tensions. As Nathan Harris (this volume) argues, 'emotions provide individuals with the motivation that is necessary to translate their beliefs into behaviour'. This applies as much to the involvement into (violent) transgressions and crime, as to the desistance from crime, and it is precisely this which makes them central to the concerns of criminologists. Randall Collins, Willem de Haan, and Elizabeth Ahmed and John Braithwaite select violent incidents for their studies of the emotional dynamics of individual, interactive and 'shared emotions' (Collins, this volume). Collins' and de Haan's approach can best be described as micro-sociological: de Haan analyses in depth a case of seemingly 'senseless violence', and Collins explores the emotional dynamics of 'forward panics', when 'the attackers become engrossed in a rhythm of repetitive, temporarily uncontrolled attack on a helpless victim', often seen in police and war atrocities. Whilst de Haan traces an individual story and life history, Collins tracks down the mechanisms at work in such forward panics. The micro-sociological approach is clearly visible in the account of status degradation, domination and the mechanisms of power that emerge as a leitmotif of de Haan's case study, as well as in Collins' analysis of a number of carefully selected and observed incidents of forward panic, and the dynamics of collective emotions of anger and fear that drive them.

The contribution by Ahmed and Braithwaite takes up the theme of emotions related to degradation and domination and their impact on violent transgressions. They focus on shame and pride, and identify both positive and negative dimensions in these emotions. In this they endorse Scheff and Retzinger's (1991: xix) frame that emotion and social relationships come in 'conjugate pairs', specifically: 'pride is the emotional conjugate of social solidarity, and shame is the emotional conjugate of alienation'. Bullying, they argue, is an exemplary testing ground for the relationship between shame and pride, since both emotions are deeply involved in this behaviour. The results of their empirical study of workplace bullying in Bangladesh show that if shame and pride are managed adaptively in interpersonal interactions, aggressive transgressions can be prevented, as both emotions are linked to the strengthening and repair of social bonds. Their study confirms the multi-faceted character of emotions and the complex relationships between shame, pride and aggressive behaviour.

Adam Calverley and Stephen Farrall follow their subjects through the process of desistance as an emotional journey that is closely linked to changes in social relations and identities. They take a diachronic view on shame and pride as both shape different phases in this process. Emotions, according to Calverley and Farrall, are not 'by-products' of the thorough changes that desistance requires from offenders in terms of their social relations and identity, but causal factors and driving forces in the process of change. The emotional trajectories of desistance start with a first phase dominated by hope, followed by a phase of emotional memories of the past. The next and penultimate phase is characterised by feelings of shame and guilt, with finally trust and pride (in the achieved change) emerging as powerful, and seemingly necessary counterbalances against guilt and shame.

The last two contributions turn from emotional experiences and their role in involvement in crime and transgressions, towards emotive reactions to crimes, namely fear and moral indignation. For a long time, research on fear of crime has rested on the assumption that fear of crime was a kind of rational reaction towards rising crime rates based on everyday risk-assessment. However, it remains one of the 'conundrums of fear of crime … that it does not always appear that the public feels safer when they should' (Skogan, this volume). The complex pattern of emotions related to risk and fear of crime obviously generates reactions that are prima facie 'irrational', but might reveal a kind of 'emotional rationality' in its deeper layers (see Karstedt 2002). For Wesley Skogan (this volume), 'it is an important political question whether or not debates over crime will take place within an ever-mounting spiral of emotionality, regardless of "the facts of the case"—which is taken by some as the condition of late modernity'.

The fact that trends in fear of crime have not reflected real declines in crime in the UK and elsewhere takes on political significance, and crucial in this debate is the answer to the question how much, if at all, fear of crime has changed over time and concomitantly with crime rates. Skogan investigates this question via eight surveys in Chicago neighbourhoods covering the decade from 1994 to 2003. Fear of crime in these communities at least, is an 'emotionally rational' reaction to rising as well as falling crime rates, but also to perceived personal risks and general feelings of insecurity of migrating into a foreign country and unknown environment.

Anna King and Shadd Maruna base their analysis of contemporary moral indignation on Svend Ranulf's work dating from the 1930s. According to Ranulf (1938), the impulse to punish results from resentment, envy and moral indignation, arising from the individual's position within the class structure. In the social position of what Benjamin Franklin called the 'middling sort', moral indignation and the punishment of complete strangers function as powerful mechanisms to improve one's sense of self-worth and pride, in the precarious socio-economic situation between rich and poor. King and Maruna put Ranulf's theory to a test in the UK. One of their most interesting findings is the fact that the strongest punitive attitudes were directed against young people. The theme of lack of respect, anxieties about one's own status as an elderly person, and a felt loss of power over young people are pervasive in their in-depth interviews. Feelings of generational injustice and envy of the young appear as a strong undercurrent in the narratives. King and Maruna's subjects feel the emotional consequences not only of a lack of power, but also of a lack of cohesion between the generations. More than anything else, these interviews reflect a shift in the affective-moral forces connecting young and old, and once again speak to the decisive role of degradation and domination in shaping our moral sentiments.

Part II: Emotional Experiences of Justice

The four contributions in this section question and dissect the emotional dynamics related to justice. Felt injustice and unfair treatment, or humiliation at the hands of authorities, are well-known for triggering strong emotional responses, mainly anger. It seems that this is true universally, independent of specific cultures of justice (see Karstedt 2002). The ways in which criminal justice transforms emotions—not least, those that it creates itself—is a major unresolved question for criminology. How can those who receive sanctions overcome the inherent humiliation, and embark on compliance with the law? How do victims convert their anger and quest for revenge into acceptance of a verdict? Are they in the end capable of forgiveness? The pacifying impact of justice seems to rely on the successful transformation of these and related emotions; however, criminal justice institutions and procedures differ widely as to the ways in which they try to achieve this, and in how successful they finally are.

The contributions address these questions from very different perspectives and within different settings. They mainly explore the relation between emotions and compliance, which according to numerous theoretical accounts is shaped by the 'master emotion' of shame, as well as the role of vengeance in victims' encounters with offenders and justice. Lawrence Sherman and Heather Strang take issue with the results of neuroscience laboratory research that probes into the 'hard-wiring' of revenge, and not only postulates its universal role in all types of justice, but its inevitability. Indeed, the pacifying effects of justice outlined above would be hard to explain if we did not allow for a transformation of revenge, or a change of emotions, in the course of justice. Using interaction ritual as a concept, Sherman and Strang analyse data from 12 rigorous, randomised controlled trials of restorative justice in Australia and the UK. They present eight cases—four from their experimental and four from their control groups. Their case studies show in which ways restorative justice changes the emotions of victims and offenders, and they in particular demonstrate that 'conventional' criminal justice ignores these feelings. Conventional justice, it seems, dispossesses victims and offenders of their emotions, prohibits their expression and thus misses out on productive engagement with victims' and offenders' emotions. Their results confirm that in restorative justice procedures, offenders are more willing to express shame and guilt and to offer an apology to the victim; victims, on the other hand, are more likely to abandon revenge in such settings. The restorative interaction ritual, it seems, is superior to traditional criminal justice in transforming initially negative feelings into more positive emotions and those that enhance social bonds. Sherman and Strang offer an explanation that links to power-status theories of emotions (Turner and Stets 2005; Karstedt 2006). Restorative justice facilitates the 'transfer of power from the once-dominant offender back into the now-victim' (Sherman and Strang, this volume), and thus apologies and forgiveness in exchange.

Meredith Rossner takes a close look at the emotional dynamics in restorative justice settings and opens the 'black box' of Sherman and Strang's experiments. As such, her contribution addresses several desiderata for research on restorative justice. She takes up Braithwaite's challenge to develop a theory of restorative justice that can help to improve its practice, and consequently focuses on the conversational nature of restorative justice (Sparks, this volume). However, by acknowledging its ritualistic character, she situates restorative justice practices much closer to conventional justice than most other proponents would do. Her micro-sociological approach is based on Collins' notion of interaction rituals, and is Durkheimian in spirit. Concurring with Nathan Harris in this part, Rossner does not take for granted the 'shame-model' that Braithwaite introduced to underpin restorative justice in his seminal work *Crime, Shame and Reintegration* (1989). Seeing restorative

justice as interaction ritual, she argues, 'implies that it is successful ritual
that builds bonds and reintegrates an offender, not shame.' The emotions are
embedded in and produced by the interaction ritual, and it is not the *type* of
emotions that matters, but the fact that they are *collectively shared*. Rossner
draws upon a rich material from restorative justice encounters and in-depth
interviews with participants. She shows how emotional energy is built up in
the course of conference interaction rituals. One of her most important findings is that this emotional energy needs to be sustained in order to achieve
reintegration, presumably through a series of conferences.

Nathan Harris also questions a rather unidirectional shame-compliance
model. He argues that instead of being simply a response to the fear of
rejection, 'shame occurs as a result of the individual's perception that what
they have done is wrong', and is connected to the ethical identity and integrity of the individual. Findings that offenders have a weaker commitment
to particular values, and that they are less likely to admit feeling shame
for committing offences, may actually reflect weakly integrated identities.
In line with Calverley and Farrall, Harris sees changes in identity and in
relationships inextricably linked to emotions. Expressing and resolving
emotions seem to be necessary for individuals to repair social bonds with
others and to put past failures behind them.

Research on procedural justice confirms a decisive role for emotions,
including pride, anger and guilt, in the evaluation of both processes and
outcomes of justice. Likewise to Nathan Harris, Kristina Murphy argues
that the seminal role of emotions derives from the fact that they provide the
link between the experience of justice and subsequent behaviour. They are
therefore of utmost interest to all authorities seeking to respond more effectively to resistance and defiance in present and future behaviour. Her findings are based on a survey of taxpayers who had been involved in a dispute
with the Australian Tax Authorities (ATO). Deterrent strategies aiming at
the disallowance of a tax minimisation scheme that had been the subject
of dispute between the ATO and Australian taxpayers generated negative
emotional reactions and subsequent resistance among the taxpayers. Those
who were generally more emotional in their reactions were also more likely
to feel that they were treated unfairly. Her results stress the importance of
'emotionally intelligent' reactions in a broader range of regulatory arenas.

Part III: 'Emotion Work' in Criminal Justice Institutions

If experiences with criminal justice are fraught with emotions for citizens,
we must assume that such encounters also involve emotions for those who
represent the authorities. Encounters between citizens and criminal justice
are particularly status-sensitive, and as such susceptible to intense emotional
dynamics (Turner and Stets 2005: ch 7). 'Emotion work' (Hochschild 2003)

is the other side of the coin of emotionalised justice, part and parcel of 'doing justice' in courts, in the streets, in prisons and other institutions of the justice system. The two contributions to this section address the needs for and patterns of emotion work in two very different criminal justice settings, in police work and in prisons. Bas van Stokkom looks at both sides of contentious and highly emotional encounters between police and citizens which took place following the introduction of a 'zero-tolerance' policy by the Amsterdam police towards minor infringements and loutish behaviour, called 'Streetwise'. He analyses cases when citizens had insulted officers, and complaints by citizens about their treatment by police officers. Conflicts arise when humiliating enforcement styles are used by the police and when police 'mirror' the emotions of citizens—that is, when 'emotional contagion' amplifies the emotional dynamics of the encounter, causing a number of them to spiral out of control. Van Stokkom argues that citizens expect persuasion from the authorities, not strict orders, and to be treated with respect. He diagnoses a higher level of status sensitivity in encounters with the police, and consequently they are more emotionally charged. His results suggest a number of strategies to build 'emotional intelligence' into police work, ranging from emotional awareness, to the strategic expression of emotions by police.

Given the 'compressed' state of social life in prisons—the density of interaction, the intimacy of contacts, the proximity between authorities and 'subordinates', and the vulnerable emotional state prisoners find themselves in—prisons should be seething with emotions. Elaine Crawley looks at the demands that this puts on prison officers in terms of 'emotion work' in their daily life and work. Emotion management is embedded in the culture of prisons and in the practices that prison officers use; it is performed in routines, and defines the role of the prison officer to a considerable extent. In juxtaposing the demands of emotion work involved for 'normal' young male prisoners, and elderly inmates, she teases out deeply ingrained emotional postures of prison officers, and contrasts feelings of disgust (towards elderly prisoners) with those of empathy (towards young men), both of which are supported and reflected by collective sentiments within the professional group.

Part IV: Violence, Reconciliation and Conflict Resolution: Dealing with Collective Emotions

According to Elster (2004), transitional justice is largely an attempt to deal with the urgency and impatience that are symptomatic of collective emotions in the transition period. Channelling 'retributive' emotions, and transforming emotions ('transmutation') into the quest for more peaceful justice are defining characteristics not only of justice in general, but of a transition period after war, conflict and strife in particular. The need to address these emotions reaches far back into the preceding period, when collective and/or state violence were endemic in society. However, this necessity is also a direct result of the transition period, during which existing hierarchies are turned upside down, and the 'defended' and 'defeated' are forced to change place. The transition period is hence rife with emotions like anger, fear, pride and guilt.

The two contributions to this part are situated on either side of the watershed of transition. Thomas Scheff, renowned for his work on individual and collective shame, takes a step back and gives theoretical grounding to the role of emotions in ethno-centrist collective violence. These are emotions which any effort at reconciliation and conflict resolution in the transition period will have to deal with. John Brewer moves on into 'restorative peace-making' and analyses how the emotions aroused by communal violence can be constructively dealt with in such procedures. Scheff's exploration of the emotional and relational underpinnings of ethno-centrist violence starts with the emotions of love and hatred: love of one's country and hatred of the enemy. However, ethnocentrism is a perversion of love; it is infatuation, a 'self-generated fantasy'. Hatred of supposed enemies 'could be a gloss on a complex process of hiding feelings of inadequacy and alienation under the cover of "pride"'. Scheff links hatred of the enemy to unacknowledged shame and feelings of humiliation, as he did in his earlier work, *Bloody Revenge: Emotions, Nationalism, War* (1994). He emphasises the irrationality of violence between groups that is generated by unacknowledged emotions. Rediscovering, acknowledging and addressing the emotional and relational dimensions of the violent conflict bring rationality back into conflicts and restrict the sphere of irrationality.

John Brewer links communal violence to the strong emotions that are aroused by identity, particularly membership of and loyalty to a group. These emotions are embedded in collective memories: 'Past incidents of violence and its forms of resistance, struggle and suffering, can become represented in a tradition of principles, memories, commemorations, symbols and iconography that are shibboleths determining the nature and course of the communal violence.' It is the cleavages between groups and the strong pressures on group membership that make reconciliation after such types of communal violence a difficult task. Individual-based cycles of shame-guilt-reintegration are likely to fail in an environment where victims and perpetrators first and foremost see themselves and each other as members of a group. Nonetheless, Brewer identifies a number of practices of restorative peacemaking, including restorative conferences, truth commissions, shame apologies and restorative diplomacy that might reach beyond group boundaries and loyalties.

Part V: Democracy and Penal Sentiments

The three contributions to this section cast the problems of re-emotionalisation in criminal justice within the wider framework of the institutional regime of democracy. Strong emotions seem to endanger the alleged balance, measured pace and level-headedness of the political process in democracies. But they also pose a problem for the criminal justice process in democracies. A heated emotional climate and debate is the seedbed of populist demands and the attendant impatience and urgent calls for 'action now' which are so inimical to the democratic process as well. The emotions that fuel populism in general are resentment, alienation, anger and fear, that are transmitted into an anti-government and more broadly anti-political impulse. In penal populism this impulse is transformed into demands for punitive criminal justice, but it can also take an unexpected turn towards more leniency (Pratt 2008). While all contemporary democracies seem to be experiencing a certain and rising level of penal populism, they continue to differ widely in the extent to which populist demands can actually shape and have in fact influenced criminal justice policies (Karstedt 2002; see also Zimring and Johnson 2006; Lacey 2008).

Richard Sparks identifies two emotional strands in contemporary societies as being at the heart of the new punitiveness in democracies. Emotive responses to crime and demands for harsher punishments are fuelled by feelings of estrangement from the public and political sphere, and simultaneously by intuitive sympathy and empathy with the victim. Sparks demonstrates the value of linking back to great traditions in arguing for the 'continuing relevance' of the philosopher David Hume. This relevance, as Sparks suggests, emerges from the 'conceptual structure of the *questions* and perhaps the method of inquiry', rather than from the substantive solutions to problems that Hume might offer to us across the centuries. First, David Hume's account of the mechanism of *sympathy,* and its generation in *conversation* (real, imagined or internal), seem surprisingly contemporary. Second, and of utmost relevance for our questions, is his achievement 'to destroy the false opposition between reason and passion, showing passion to penetrate the very heart of the alleged activity of reason'. His and his contemporaries' view of morality 'is neither rationalism, nor egoism', but rather an account of the 'moral sentiments', or 'moral sense' that is achieved in conversation. Sparks argues that restorative justice practices provide such conversation in a Humean sense, and thus are capable of eliciting and nourishing moral sentiments (see also Rossner in this volume). Estrangement, in contrast, signifies a lack of proper conversations in the public sphere, and consequently a loss of moral sentiments among citizens, and moral argument in democracies.

John Pratt shows that for New Zealand, penal populism is not the inevitable fate of contemporary democracies. Initially, New Zealand's institutional regime and recent changes made the country, like a number of others, quite susceptible to penal populism. In response to growing disenchantment, the Government introduced a Citizens' Referendum to its political process, with the aim of giving the citizenry a greater voice. A referendum on a series of measures to adopt harsher penal policies was adopted, and became a point of reference (though non-binding) for government legislation and NGOs. However, when penal populism waned in the following years, it became clear that there were limits to public demands, and that those who presumed to express the sentiments of a majority did not actually do so. According to Pratt, an array of structural, political and temporal conditions make penal populism wax and wane in modern democracies. It is not an inevitable concomitant of post-modern democracy.

Democracies, however, need a certain level of emotional engagement from their citizens, being participatory in nature. Ian Loader explores the question that has worried political scientists when confronted with the emotional turn: how can affect be made safe for democracy? This question translates for criminologists into the problem of how hostile—and seemingly 'primordial' and intuitive—public moral indignation and moral sentiments towards crime and criminals can be transformed from destructive into constructive forces, how they can be addressed properly, and become accepted within the process of politics. Ian Loader identifies three models of discursive engagement with public penal sentiment: a 'deficit model' that focuses on information gaps and the need to educate and inform the public; an 'insulation model', that proposes to install 'buffers', or 'mediating institutions', between public opinion and the operation of the justice system'; and a model of 'redirecting' penal sentiments and collective emotions into institutional frames. The redirection model takes as its starting point the centrality of emotions to the question of how societies control crime and punish offenders. According to this model, it is the acknowledgement of emotions that has to inform public debate and deliberation, not its suppression. Loader aims at transcending the top-down approach of crime policy taken by welfare elites and experts of past decades, and at strengthening a genuinely democratic discourse on crime policy that avoids the fallacy of ever increasing punitiveness. His 'redirection model' requires dialogue and deliberation, and thus facilitates the re-channelling of emotions back into reason.

Taken together, the papers in this volume represent the diversity of engagement with questions of reason and emotion, of deliberation and intuition, and ultimately of the space of emotions in crime and justice. Far from resolving the paradoxes of 'emotional reason' and 'rational emotions' in criminal justice, they are significant contributions to the conversation on a topic of increasing relevance in contemporary criminal justice debates.

REFERENCES

Bandes, S (1999) 'Introduction' in S Bandes (ed), *The Passions of Law* (New York, New York University Press), 1–18.

Barbalet, JM (2002) 'Moral Indignation, Class Inequality and Justice. An Exploration and Revision of Ranulf' 6 *Theoretical Criminology* 279–98.

Braithwaite, J (1989) *Crime, Shame and Reintegration* (Cambridge, Cambridge University Press).
Burkitt, I (2005) 'Powerful Emotions: Power, Government and Opposition in the War on Terror' 39 *Sociology* 679–95.
Cabinet Office (2008) 'Engaging Communities in Fighting Crime: A Review by Louise Casey'. Available at www.cabinetoffice.gov.uk/~/media/assets/www .cabinetoffice.gov.uk/publications/crime/cc_full_report%20pdf.ashx.
Collins, R (2004) *Interaction Ritual Chains* (Princeton, Princeton University Press).
—— (2008) *Violence. A Micro-Sociological Theory* (Princeton, Princeton University Press).
Crawford, A (2006) 'Institutionalizing restorative youth justice in a cold, punitive climate' in I Aertsen, T Dams and L Robert (eds), *Institutionalizing Restorative Justice* (Cullompton, Willan) 120–50.
De Haan, W and Loader, I (2002) (eds) Special Issue on 'Crime, Punishment and the Emotions' 6(3) *Theoretical Criminology*.
De Haan, W and Vos, J (2003) 'A crying shame. The over-rationalized conception of man in the rational choice perspective' 7 *Theoretical Criminology* 29–54.
Diamond, J (2008) '"Vengeance Is Ours": What can tribal societies tell us about our need to get even?' *The New Yorker*, 21 April.
Douglas, M (1993) 'Emotion and Culture in Theories of Justice' 22(4) *Economy and Society* 501–15.
Elster, J (1999) *Alchemies of the Mind. Rationality and Emotions* (Cambridge, Cambridge University Press).
—— (2004) *Closing the Books. Transitional Justice in Historical Perspective* (Cambridge, Cambridge University Press).
Feeley, M and Simon, J (1994) 'Actuarial Justice: The emerging new criminal law', in Nelken, D (ed), *The Futures of Criminology* (New York, Sage) 173–201.
Freiberg, A (2001) 'Affective Versus Effective Justice Instrumentalism and Emotionalism in Criminal Justice' 3 *Punishment and Society* 265–78.
Garland, D (2001) *The Culture of Control* (Oxford, Oxford University Press).
Hochschild, AR (2003) *The Managed Heart. Commercialization of Human Feeling*, 20th anniversary edition with a new afterword (Berkeley, University of California Press).
Hope, T and Karstedt, S (2003) 'Towards a New Social Crime Prevention' in H Kury and J Obergfell-Fuchs (eds) *Crime Prevention. New Approaches* (Mainz, Weisser Ring) 461–89.
Karstedt, S (1996) 'Recht und Scham' 8(4) *Neue Kriminalpolitik* 22–25.
—— (2002) 'Emotions, crime and justice' 6(3) *Theoretical Criminology* 299–318.
—— (2006) 'Emotions, Crime and Justice: Exploring Durkheimian Themes' in Deflem, M (ed), *Sociological Theory and Criminological Research: Views from Europe and the United States*. Sociology of Crime, Law and Deviance vol 7 (Oxford, Elsevier) 223–48.
—— (2010) 'From absence to presence, from silence to voice. Victims in transitional justice since the Nuremberg Trials' 17 *International Review of Victimology*, 9–30.
Katz, J (1988) *The Seductions of Crime. Moral and Sensual Attractions of Doing Evil* (New York, Basil Blackwell).
Lacey, N (2008) *The Prisoners' Dilemma. Political Economy and Punishment in Contemporary Democracies* (Cambridge, Cambridge University Press).

Laster, K and O'Malley, P (1996) 'Sensitive New-Age Laws: The reassertion of emotionality in law' 24 *International Journal of the Sociology of Law* 21–40.

Loader, I (2006) 'Fall of the "Platonic Guardians": Liberalism, Criminology and Political Responses to Crime in England and Wales' 46(4) *British Journal of Criminology* 561–86.

—— (2008) 'The Great Victim of this Get-Tough Hyperactivity is Labour', *The Guardian*, 19 June; available at www.guardian.co.uk/commentisfree/2008/jun/19/justice.ukcrime.

Nussbaum, M (2004) *Hiding from Humanity. Disgust, Shame and the Law* (Princeton, Princeton University Press).

Pratt, J (2000) 'Emotive and ostentatious punishment: Its decline and resurgence in modern society' 2 *Punishment and Society* 417–41.

—— (2002) *Punishment and Civilization* (London, Sage).

—— (2006) 'Beyond evangelical criminology: The meaning and significance of restorative justice' in I Aertsen, T Dams and L Robert (eds), *Institutionalizing Restorative Justice* (Cullompton, Willan) 44–67.

—— (2008) 'When Penal Populism Stops: Legitimacy, Scandal and the Power to Punish in New Zealand' 41(3) *The Australian and New Zealand Journal of Criminology* 364–84.

Ranulf, S (1938) *Moral Indignation and Middle Class Psychology* (New York, Schocken Books).

Rice, SK, Dirks, D and Exline, J (2009) 'Of guilt, defiance and repentance: Evidence from the Texas death chamber' 26(2) *Justice Quarterly*, 295–326.

Rose, MR, Nadler, J and Clark, J (2006) 'Appropriately upset? Emotion norms and perceptions of crime victims' 30 *Law and Human Behaviour* 203–19.

Sarat, A (2001) *When the State Kills. Capital Punishment and the American Condition* (Princeton, Princeton University Press).

Scheff, T (1994) *Bloody Revenge: Emotions, Nationalism and War* (Boulder, Westview).

Scheff, T and Retzinger, S (1991) *Emotions and Violence* (Lexington, Lexington Books).

Sherman, L (2003) 'Reason for emotion: Reinventing justice with theories, innovations and research. The American Society of Criminology 2002 Presidential Address' 41 *Criminology* 1–38.

Simon, J (2007) *Governing Through Crime* (Oxford, Oxford University Press).

Sunstein, CR (2009) 'Some effects of moral indignation on law' 33 *Vermont Law Review* 405–33.

Turner, JH and Stets, JE (2005) *The Sociology of Emotions* (Cambridge, Cambridge University Press).

Walgrave, L (2008) *Restorative Justice, Self-Interest and Responsible Citizenship* (Cullompton, Willan Publishing).

Welzel, C and Inglehart, R (2005) 'Democratization as the growth of freedom: The human development perspective' 6(3) *Japanese Journal of Political Science* 1–31.

—— (2008) 'The role of ordinary people in democratization' 19(1) *Journal of Democracy* 126–40.

Wiener, MJ (2004) 'Homicide and "Englishness": Criminal justice and national identiy in Victorian England' 6 *National Identities* 203–13.

Wouters, C (2004) 'Changing regimes of manners and emotions: From disciplining to informalizing' in S Loyal and S Quilley (eds) *The Sociology of Norbert Elias* (Cambridge, Cambridge Unviersity Press) 193–211.

Zimring, FE and Johnson, DT (2006) 'Public Opinion and the Governance of Punishment in Democratic Political Systems' in S Karstedt and G LaFree (eds), *Democracy, Crime and Justice. The Annals of the American Academy of Political and Social Science* vol 205, 266–80.

Part I

Emotions in Transgression and Crime

1

Forward Panic and Violent Atrocities

RANDALL COLLINS

CONFLICT SITUATIONS ARE first and foremost full of tension and fear. One important way in which this tension/fear can be released is a pattern that I will call 'forward panic'. We see this in most of the widely publicised incidents of police violence and military violence, and also in many instances of ethnic violence. The basic mechanism is that the attackers become engrossed in a rhythm of repetitive, temporarily uncontrolled attack on a helpless victim. It is the piling on and overkill that so shocks outside observers and attracts the label of atrocity to this kind of violence. It is a dynamics of shared emotions which gives these incidents their quality of being out of control. But it is a fully interactional phenomenon: not only are the attackers caught up in each other's mood, but they are also locked together emotionally with their opponents. As we see in the following cases, both sides are tied together in a prolonged build-up of tension and fear, which later becomes released in a one-sided attack on a now-overmatched victim.

In a well-publicised incident in April 1996, two southern California deputy sheriffs chased a pick-up truck crowded with illegal Mexican immigrants. The truck had driven around a checkpoint north of the border, refusing to stop then or later as the patrol car followed it at speeds over 100 miles per hour. During the chase, weaving through freeway traffic, occupants of the truck threw debris at the police car and attempted to ram other cars, to divert their pursuers' attention. After almost an hour and having travelled 80 miles, the truck drove off the side of the road, and most of its 21 occupants climbed out and ran into a plant nursery. The deputies caught up with only two, a women who had trouble getting the front door of the truck cab open, and a man who stayed to help her; these the furious officers beat with their nightsticks. One deputy clubbed the man on the back and shoulders six times, continuing while he fell to the ground. As the woman emerged from the cab, the deputy hit her twice on the back and pulled her to the ground by her hair, as the other deputy hit her once with his baton. The beating took about 15 seconds (*Los Angeles*

Times, 2 April 1996). A television news helicopter had been following the last part of the chase, and its cameras taped the beating. When these tapes were shown on the air, there was a widespread public outcry.

The incident has the character of a forward panic. This is possibly the most frequent kind of police atrocity, and perhaps of police violence generally. A forward panic starts with tension and fear in a conflict situation. This is the normal condition of violent conflict, but here the tension is prolonged and built-up; it has a dramatic shape of increasing tension, striving towards a climax. There is a shift from relatively passive–waiting, holding back until one is in a position to bring the conflict to a head–to fully active. When the opportunity finally arrives, the tension/fear comes out in an emotional rush. Ardant du Picq (1921), who observed the pattern repeatedly in military battles, called it 'the flight to the front'. It resembles a panic, and indeed the physiological components are similar; instead of running away, the fighters rush forward, towards the enemy. They are caught up in an emotional loop in which running and fear feed into each other; the mechanism is that of the James-Lange theory of emotion, in which action intensifies an emotion, rather than an antecedent emotion merely setting off a following action (James 1890). Running forward or backwards, in either case they are in an overpowering emotional rhythm, carrying them on to actions that they would normally not approve of in calm reflective moments.

Most incidents of police violence which create public scandal have the character of forward panic. The Rodney King beating in Los Angeles, 1991 is an archetypal instance (www.law.umke.edu/faculty/projects/ftrial/lapd/lapd.html). Police chased a speeding car at up to 115 miles an hour for eight miles on a freeway and city streets; radio calls for back-up brought 21 officers by the end of the chase, when King was cornered behind an apartment house. A famous amateur video recorded the last three and a half minutes of the arrest. Patrol officers were in a mood of excitement and tension from the high-speed chase, enhanced by anger at King's refusal to obey their sirens and pull off, and determination to win the race and bring him to submission. On emerging from the car, it turned out there were two young black men: one a passenger, who submitted to arrest; the other King, a big muscular man, whom the officers identified as a likely ex-convict from his weight-lifter's 'prison body'; they also thought he was high on the drug PCP. The chase was not yet over. King was uncooperative to his arrest, creating a brief moment of counter-attack by rushing at one of the officers; at this point he was knocked down by four officers using night clubs and a taser (a device sending a high voltage electric shock). Beating with the clubs continued for another 80 seconds–the part captured on the video–until King was completely trussed up, and the police prepared to leave. The most active officer–the one who had been knocked down by King–hit him over 45 times with his stick.

The dynamic of forward panic extends beyond the ambit of police atrocities; but it is useful here to review studies of police behaviour while attempting to make arrests (Worden 1996; Geller and Toch 1996; Alpert and Dunham 2004). Police violence is more frequent when the suspect resists. It is also more frequent following a car chase, apart from resistance. These patterns are borne out in the instances given above of the Rodney King case and the illegal immigrant car chase. Alpert and Dunham (1990) found that in various jurisdictions, 18–30 per cent of vehicles in car chases escape; thus apart from the tension of high-speed driving and anger at defiance of authority, police have a genuine feeling of uncertainty about the outcome. In 23–30 per cent of car chases there is an accident with property damage. In 10–17 per cent of the chases, there is bodily injury, although usually minor (this figure rises to 12–24 per cent of the cases where the pursued car does not get away). In one-third of these cases, the injury happens after the chase stops: that is to say, the injury is not caused by a vehicle accident, but by violence. This is the archetype of the Rodney King beating and similar cases.

Nevertheless, the majority of car chases do not lead to beatings. What additional causes are involved? One pattern is the bystander effect: the more police involved in an arrest (and indeed the more bystanders of any kind), the greater the likelihood of police violence (Worden 1996). Why should this be the case? These patterns are consistent with the model of forward panic.

I. TENSION/FEAR AND RELEASE: HOT RUSH, PILING ON, OVERKILL

Let us consider the emotional sequence in detail. First a build-up of tension, which is released into a frenzied attack when the situation makes it easy to do so. This is not simply tension and release; it is the kind of tension which involves very strong fear.

The tension can build up from various components. Police officers in a high-speed chase have some feelings of the danger of fast-moving vehicles, especially when potentially dodging other vehicles and obstacles; their tension can also be partly excitement, partly frustration at not yet catching one's target. For police officers, this is an exacerbated version of their normal situation when dealing with civilians, and especially civilian suspects: their effort to always control the interactional situation (Rubinstein 1973). The resistance of a civilian to letting the officer control the situation brings about a confrontational tension, raising the possibility of the officer using both official authority and informal pressure to bring about his (or her, but usually his) control. As Rubinstein shows from ethnographic observation, police try to position their bodies to control anyone they stop for questioning; their non-verbal manoeuvring ranges from putting themselves in a position to disarm someone of weapons or overpower them, to brushing against them in casual searches, to more subtle control by aggressive use of eyes in observing the other person in a prolonged and deliberate fashion, contrary to normal civilities of interpersonal looking and eye contact. Thus the police in a chase are experiencing a prolonged situation of being frustrated in what they normally expect to carry out in any interaction. The demeanour of Rodney King when he finally left his car to surrender to the police was it seems not merely threatening; apparently in the very first moments of the arrest he was not so much threatening as insolent. The first arresting officer, a woman officer of the highway patrol, testified that he grabbed his buttock and shook it at her–a gesture which other officers present took as offensive, and which led other, more aggressive Los Angeles Police Department officers to take over the arrest (from court testimony). Thus what turned into a forward panic situation continued to escalate on the micro level even after the end of the car chase.

In a famous case in New York city in February 1999, an African street vendor, Amadou Diallo, was followed into an apartment house hallway by four undercover policemen (*New York Post*, 9–13 February 1999). The police were a special detail, part of a city-wide programme looking aggressively for street criminals; in effect they were something like anti-guerilla soldiers on patrol, suspicious of everyone in the civilian population. In this case the police were looking for a neighbourhood rapist, whose description resembled Diallo. Apparently frightened by their appearance, Diallo made a sudden move back into the building, which the officers interpreted as a furtive sign of guilty flight. They may also have been caught up in chasing whatever runs away; as they rushed forward, they interpreted Diallo's next gesture as pulling a weapon–although it turned out he was reaching for his wallet for identification. All four policemen fired, a total of 41 bullets, of which 19 hit their target. This tremendous overkill was the central point of outrage in the news media and the popular protests which ensued. But consider another point: the policemen fired at a distance of less than seven feet, yet half of their bullets missed. The vestibule was five feet wide; the four officers were thus pressed together, shoulder to shoulder, a single mass of bodies. Two of the officers led the firing, shooting 16 bullets each; the other two were caught up in the contagion, firing an additional nine bullets between them (*USA Today*, 28 February 2000). This situation has all the marks of a forward panic: tension/fear on the part of the police, a sudden retreat of the apparent enemy, a triggering gesture of apparent resistance, a hot rush of attack, more ferocious than accurate. The police are entrained in their own firing, unable to stop.

Compare a case which has a somewhat different build-up but much the same outcome. In Riverside, California in December 1998, a young black woman returning from a party had a car breakdown at 2 am. (*Los Angeles Times*, 2 January 1999; *San Diego Union*, 30 December 1998; *USA Today*

21 January 1999). Believing herself (with some justification) to be in a dangerous neighbourhood, she stopped at a petrol station, locked herself in the car, and used her mobile phone to call her family for help. Family members arrived, but the woman had gone to sleep, under the influence of alcohol and drugs, and they were unable to awaken her. They in turn called the police. Because of her feeling of danger, she had placed a handgun on the car seat next to her. The police, accordingly, approached the car with their guns drawn, and after unsuccessfully attempting to waken her, broke the car window. In the following seconds, the four policemen fired 27 bullets (as indicated by cartridges found at the scene), hitting her with 12 of them. The incident has overtones of absurdity–being killed by one's own rescuers; what was most shocking to both the family and the public was the sheer amount of firing unleashed. Reaction to the news was outrage in the local black community, demonstrations against the police, and investigations launched by political authorities. Here again the elements of forward panic are clear: tension/fear, a sudden trigger, wild firing, overkill.

Numerous incidents show a similar pattern. In Los Angeles, March 1998, a drunken 39-year-old white man was shot 106 times by police. He had been sitting in his car on a freeway ramp for an hour; he then led police cars in a low-speed chase at 20 miles an hour to another location, where he got out of his car, and waved what turned out to be an air pistol, at times pointing it at his head as if to commit suicide (*Los Angeles Times*, 26 July 1999). The large number of bullets fired were due to the very large number of police cars which had accumulated during the long stand-off. During this period, police radio dispatchers spread erroneous reports that a man had been firing at police helicopters and at deputies on the ground. The sheer number of police called in from different jurisdictions no doubt created confusion and magnified the sense of threat. Some of the police bullets hit apartment houses two blocks away. Here we see both wild, inaccurate and bystander-threatening fire; as well as the tendency for rumours to become more inflammatory as the links in the chain grow longer.

After two days of anti-war demonstrations at Kent State University in May 1970, National Guard troops killed four students and wounded nine others. Demonstrators had burned the campus army ROTC (Reserve Officers' Training Corps) building, and were taunting the guardsmen, with some students throwing rocks. In a sudden 13-second burst, the guardsmen fired 61 shots. One of those killed was a student not in the demonstration but passing nearby on her way to class. The rate of casualties to shots fired was 13 of 61, about 20 per cent, typical of wild and inaccurate fire (Hensley and Lewis 1978).

Wild firing is not confined to the police. In a bank robbery in February 1997 in Los Angeles, two robbers wearing body armour, apparently embold-ened to think they were invulnerable, engaged in a 56-minute shoot-out with police. The robbers fired 1100 rounds from automatic weapons; 200

police fired a proportionate number of bullets in return. Eleven officers and six bystanders were wounded, some by friendly fire. The two robbers were killed; one was shot 29 times. Police reportedly shooed away paramedics and let the robber bleed to death while holding a gun at his head (*Los Angeles Times*, 1 March 1997; *San Diego Union*, 20 February 2000). Both sides engaged in tremendous over-firing, most of it inaccurate.

Most of the political outrage at these cases in the 1990s and thereafter has arisen from the perceived racism involved in them. The outrageous behavior–usually focusing on the overkill, the repeated and non-utilitarian acts of violence–is what draws attention to these cases; if there were only one bullet, one hit with a stick or fist, it seems likely the cases would not have attracted as much attention. Once we have publicly defined the cases as outrages, we are quick to attribute as their cause the skin colour of the police and of their victims. But the dynamics of forward panic are central. Racism may sometimes be involved; but it is a contingent factor, which sometimes sets up the initial situation. In the Diallo shooting, the police were operating in a black neighbourhood which they took as a general sign of danger; their stereotyping of Diallo was what created the tension and the sudden chase into the hallway. But the wild firing and overkill is the mechanism of forward panic, which exists very widely and is not confined to racial incidents. Similarly in the Riverside case: the perception of a dangerous black neighbourhood (a perception shared by the victim herself), and the fact that she was perceived as part of it, is what sets up the police outburst. We also find cases of white-on-white forward panic in police shootings, such as the apparent suicide on the Los Angeles overpass, at Kent State, and the bank robbers in body armour.

We see the dynamics of forward panic both across and within a wide variety of ethnic groups. A similar dynamic is visible in an incident in Milwaukee, Wisconsin, in October 2002, in which a 36-year-old black man was beaten to death by a group of children and teenagers ranging in age from 10 to 18. The man was a shabby, dishevelled figure, homeless and usually inebriated, an easy target:

> ... about 16 to 20 young men prodded a 10-year-old to throw an egg at Young. The egg hit the man in the shoulder, and he started chasing the boy. [The encounter begins with a brief threat.] But a 14-year-old got between the two, and Young punched him, knocking out a tooth. [The threat becomes an injury, from the side that was regarded as a weak and despised person.] Several of the youths then banded together to attack Young. They chased him onto the porch of a house and pummeled him, leaving blood splattered from floor to ceiling. [The climax is a prolonged beating.] Young managed briefly to escape into the house, but the mob dragged him back outside and beat him until police responded to a neighbor's 911 call. (AP News report, 1 October 2002).

Here the pattern is: a build-up of taunting, in expectation of aggressive fun; brief counter-attack, creating momentary tension increase; panicked retreat by weak victim, which leads to entrainment of mob in chase mode, enhanced by crowd multiplier.

Such dynamics can happen with the 'good guys' too. In a southern California beach community, a 58-year-old woman had her purse snatched by two teenage boys while loading groceries into her car in a parking lot. 'She called out for help and began running after the boys. A store employee and a bystander followed, and along the way a water-delivery man and others joined the pursuit.' The crowd built up to about 50 people, mostly men, who formed a perimeter and scoured the neighbourhood in cars, on bicycles and on foot, and eventually captured two boys, ages 16 and 17, hiding in the bushes in a back yard. Participants acted with great esprit de corps, proud of themselves for pitching in as a community. But here's the rub: 'An unidentified man on a bicycle became so involved in the manhunt that officers had to restrain him when the arrests were made' (*San Diego Union*, 23 March 1994). In short, the enthusiasm of good-doers in protecting a woman become an emotional rush, and when the target was finally captured, at least one participant did not want to stop the attack. Here, it is easy to label the heroes and the villains; yet the dynamic of solidarity is much the same in any conflict group, making it heroic in its own eyes, no matter how much its violence may be viewed by outsiders as an atrocity.

Forward panics are found in many kinds of violent situations. Most military atrocities have the character of a forward panic; but so do less scandalous, indeed even celebrated combats, since the most decisive victories usually have occurred when the troops on one side have become completely helpless and the other side has then slaughtered them in a forward panic (Collins 2008). Gang fights are mostly stand-offs when the sides are evenly matched; when an isolated victim from the opposing side can be caught, however, and especially if he is knocked down, the other side will go into a forward panic mode of battering and kicking him on the ground, colloquially referred to as rolling on him. Crowd violence has a similar pattern: stand-offs if forces are well-organised and equally matched, until the lines break apart and little groups can find isolated victims to attack in the piling on and overkill mode. Deadly ethnic violence has the same pattern: a build-up of tension, usually with rumours of prior atrocities or threats by the other side, then the isolation of a vulnerable group of victims who are unable to fight back, and a frenzy of overkill in an atmosphere of collective emotional effervescence (Horowitz 2001).

II. CONFRONTATIONAL TENSION/FEAR MAKES VIOLENCE DIFFICULT TO PERFORM

In violence-threatening confrontations, the most widespread emotion is a combination of tension and fear. This affects every aspect of how people behave in such situations. The majority of people avoid violent confrontations; when they are in them, they find ways to minimise the actual violence. Studies of troops in combat have shown that only a minority of them fire their guns, unless forcefully commanded by superior officers; similarly, a minority of police are responsible for almost all police violence; a minority of members of violent crowds carry out virtually all the violence (Collins 2008). Fights are mostly bluster and threat, with relatively little action. Even among the minority (of the order of 5–20 per cent) of any group who are actively violent, tension/fear still pervades their behaviour. We see this from studies of the accuracy of soldiers' firing in combat: ratios of bullets fired per casualty incurred were in the range of 200 to one in the nineteenth century, declining to 50,000 to one by the time of the Vietnam war (ie getting worse in recent years, as guns fire at higher rates); in comparison, the rate of hitting the target is much better in non-confrontational situations of target practice. Because of tension/fear, evenly matched confrontations tend to be stand-offs, whether among troops, crowds or individuals.

It should be emphasised that a forward panic is an interactional phenomenon which encompasses both aggressors and victims. Both sides are emotionally and bodily entrained in the same situation. Violence is successful chiefly when the sides are very unequal, and especially when there is a sudden shift in power after a period of stand-off, for instance if the enemy falls down, gets caught up in a human traffic jam of bodies stumbling over each other, or attempts to run away (Keegan 1977). Then the side which is still intact goes into the forward panic mode. Often the losing side becomes limp, passive, frozen, incapable of defending themselves; this further emboldens and infuriates the attacking side, full of contempt for the abject indignity of the opponent. It also can unleash the hideous joy so often noted in the expressions of the perpetrators of an atrocity; after all, they have come through an emotional transformation from tension/fear to its release, from a feeling of constraint and impotence to one of total domination. Both sides are caught up in an asymmetrical entrainment of emotional dominance and subordination.

Even when confrontational tension/fear is released on one side of an encounter, it continues to pervade the event. The victors are in the immediate aftermath of their own tension/fear, and this makes them incompetent in their violence, unable to control and calibrate their behaviour. The defeated are still in the grip of tension/fear, carried to the extreme of being unable to resist at all, or only in token ways that further infuriates their conquerors. The winners sense the tension/fear of the losers, and are reminded of the emotions they themselves had strongly felt just moments before. The asymmetrical entrainment of winners and losers motivates the former to distance themselves even further from the latter by taking total dominance over the micro-interactional details of the situation. The momentum, initiative and emotional energy of the situation shift one-sidedly to the dominant side and away from the subordinated.

What kind of tension and fear is this? The obvious answer would seem to be fear of bodily injury or death. But there are numerous reasons to believe that such fears are much less important than a tension/fear peculiar to conflict: it is a fear of killing or doing harm, especially at close range and in immediate confrontation with other human beings (Grossman 1995; Collins 2008). Soldiers in combat are more afraid of confronting small-arms fire at close range than they are of objectively more dangerous long-range artillery fire; medics and other non-combatants in combat zones can perform tasks in a high degree of danger, as long as they do not have to try to kill someone else. Even stick-up men, who have control of the armaments in the situation, are in a situation of high tension, and especially dislike being looked in the eyes (Anderson 1999: 127). Soldiers have less difficulty in going forward under heavy fire with a strong chance of being killed, than in actually killing other human beings. Nor is this simply a culturally inculcated inhibition against killing. The behaviour of tribal warriors shows the same pattern of shying away from contact with the enemy except for brief blustering incursions; if a victim has been caught by stealth or forward panic, however, there is no moral inhibition on joyous celebration of the killing. And in modern warfare, the same troops who dislike face-to-face killing have no qualms about operating long-distance weapons. It is not fear of being hurt, nor a philosophical dislike of killing, which is the source of inhibition. It is a specifically interactional emotion. This confrontational tension builds up as persons in conflict come close to each other, and not merely because that is the point at which one might be hurt; it is at the point that one has to face the other person down, to put him or her under one's interactional control, while the other attempts to do the same in reverse.

Confrontational tension/fear arises because it contravenes the most general fundamental properties of human interaction. This is the model of interaction ritual (IR), which is the mechanism of normal sociability (Collins 2004). When persons in face-to-face encounters become involved in a mutual focus of attention, and when also they share a common emotion, processes are set in motion which feed back upon and build up both mutual attention and emotional entrainment. Eyes become locked together in a repeated sequence of checking one another's gaze; bodily postures mirror each other; bodily rhythms become attuned; the shared emotion becomes stronger. A high level of mutual entrainment generates a new, shared emotion in addition to the original emotion: the excitement of collective effervescence. When this condition is reached, there are a series of outcomes in the aftermath: participants come away from the encounter with feelings of solidarity; and on the individual level, a sense of confidence, initiative, or exhilaration which I have called emotional energy. These are the processes of a successful interaction ritual; the degree of success or failure of an encounter varies along a continuum, depending on whether the initiating conditions are present to get the ritual off the ground (ie conditions for generating an initial focus of attention, and an emotion strong enough so that it is shared by participants). Successful IRs are people's most pleasant and attractive experiences; the most basic motivation of social life is to make one's way towards encounters which give the highest success (in terms of emotional energy gains), and to avoid encounters which are failures (and which lose emotional energy).

Confrontations in which violence is threatened have a peculiarly mixed quality as interaction rituals: they involve a high degree of mutual focus of attention, but it is action very strongly at cross-purposes. Whereas in most interactions where people do not share a common emotion and goal, they avoid looking at each other (colloquially, they 'do not see eye to eye'); but in conflict encounters the height of hostility is a mutual stare-down. This is why the facial expression of anger or hate is a hardening of the muscles around the eyes (Ekman and Friesen 1975); it takes muscular effort to keep one's eyes focused on the eyes of a person with whom one is not attuned, where the mutual lack of attunement is both explicitly demonstrated and prolonged. A violence-threatening confrontation is an interaction ritual in which the processes tending towards a feeling of collective effervescence and solidarity cannot occur; the feedback loops are blocked that would bring each other into a mutual entrainment or attunement; instead of a feeling of flowing together of agency into a we-feeling, there is the opposite feeling of having one's own rhythm blocked and another's imposed.

This is the source of the tension of violent confrontation. It is over and above whatever sense there may be that one might be hurt or killed. It is the tension that arises from going against the grain of the normal process of mutual entrainment. That is why I call it confrontational tension/fear. It is specifically the fear or tension of being in a confrontation at cross-purposes.

III. THE ROLE OF GROUP SUPPORT

Group support on one side of the confrontation provides an additional input which can overcome the tension/fear, and escalate the conflict into violence. If there is a group of antagonists on one side, they engage in an IR among themselves. The emotions of anger, excitement, even tension/fear are shared among themselves as a form of solidarity-generating mutual entrainment; this gives them elevated emotional energy, hence the confidence to take the initiative and carry out the fight. Of course, the scene may be divided into two opposing groups, each of which carries out its own IRs and builds its own solidarity; that leaves them in a situation where there is solidarity within groups and confrontational tension/fear between them. In this case, on most occasions, the result is a stand-off; as indicated above, rival armies, gangs, or crowds do not do much damage to each other when

they are evenly matched. I do not mean they have to be just the same in size
or armaments, but rather that when both sides are mobilised by their own
IRs and maintain their own organisation, they present a front to the other
which keeps up the confrontational tension/fear, and prevents either side
from gaining much initiative. This is the formula for stand-off.

Another variant is that there are only two individual fighters, plus a surrounding audience. In this case, the individuals usually stay in the mode of
bluster, until the audience in effect decides what it wants them to do. This
may be illustrated by the pattern in a collection of ethnographic observations of confrontational situations; this consists of all the cases of violent
threat which I have personally witnessed, together with retrospective reports
from students in my class on the sociology of violence. This sampling frame
is unknown, and most of the instances are from school, entertainment or
street situations in middle-class America. My chief methodological concern,
however, is to get detailed observations of the emotional behaviour of all
the persons present in violent situations; this is the material needed to build
a dynamic theoretical model. Thus, in a total of 89 cases, the disposition
of the crowd has an overwhelming effect on what the fighters will do: In
17 cases where the crowd cheers and encourages the fight, 15 have serious
fights (88 per cent), and in eight of these some of the crowd joins in the
fight. In 12 cases where the crowd's expressions are mixed (mildly excited,
part of crowd entertained, laughing, amused), one has a serious fight (8
per cent), and eight have prolonged but mild scuffles, blustering, or other
extended but limited violence (67 per cent); three have very brief fights (25
per cent). In 21 cases the crowd is silent, uneasy, embarrassed, tense, or
afraid; there is *one serious fight* (5 per cent); four cases of prolonged but
mild scuffles (19 per cent); four have brief and mild episodes of violence
(eg one punch or slap) which end abruptly (19 per cent); in 12 cases the
fight aborts (57 per cent). In 11 cases the audience intervenes, mediates,
or breaks up the fight; these include one *case of prolonged scuffling* (9 per
cent); five cases of brief, mild violence (45 per cent); and four cases where
the fight aborts (46 per cent). Overall, there are extremely strong parallels
between the degree of encouragement or opposition by the audience, and
the amount of violence which takes place.

What happens if the audience is neutral? In 28 cases the audience is neutral: ie absent, distant, dispersed, invisible, not paying attention, or tiny in
relation to the number of belligerents. In nine of these (32 per cent) there
are serious fights; three prolonged scuffles or blustering quarrels (11 per
cent); 10 mild and brief fights, stopping abruptly (36 per cent); in six the
fight aborts without any violence (21 per cent). What makes the difference?
Unquestionably it is the number of belligerents; of the nine serious fights, in
all but one case, these are substantial groups (on the order of 10 or 15 on
a side, with the smallest consisting of five versus five); in two of the cases,
there are demonstrators numbering in the hundreds. In almost all the other

cases with neutral audiences and mild or abortive violence, the participants are few (mostly one-on-one, sometimes two or three on the defensive side; the only instance of bigger groups here is six-on-six).

If the fight breaks out where belligerent groups are already large, they override any audience effects; in effect they bring along their own supportive audiences (since in fact only a proportion of the group takes a really active part in the fighting). This helps explain the few anomalies in the prior paragraphs, which are italicised. In one case the audience is fearful but a serious fight occurs nevertheless: this is a popular concert where two rival groups of skinheads invade the mosh pit from opposite sides, scattering the usual moshers; these are groups of 20–30 fighters, ignoring and frightening the crowd of several hundred fans. The audience does not matter when the fighting groups are large, because the groups are their own audience.

Serious violence is chiefly a matter of asymmetrical entrainment. This is not fight or flight, but both at the same time. The victim falls into the passive rhythm, while the aggressor goes into the mode of forward panic. Most successful violence is atrocity, the situationally strong rolling over the situationally weak.

IV. CONCLUSION

The spectacular character of forward panic makes it tempting to see it everywhere. But forward panic is only one pathway from the starting point of tension/fear in conflictual confrontations. Forward panic is set in motion only if the tension is suddenly released, if the apparent threat and strength of the opponent rapidly turns into weakness; there must be a space in that situation into which to rush forward instead of running away, a vacuum into which the encounter is precipitated. If that vacuum does not open up, the situation flows in a different direction. Quite often, the tension is not released, because there is no sign of disproportionate weakness on one side; many conflictual situations–indeed most, if we count all the banal incipient conflicts–become stand-offs, with much posturing, but petering out with little damage done.

There are many kinds of violence. Forward panic is just one kind. Farthest away from the micro-dynamics I have analysed here are long-distance military operations and other kinds of bureaucratised violence; in these, macro-sociological conditions are paramount. If one cannot see one's victims but only know of their whereabouts at the far end of a long-distance artillery or aerial bombardment, confrontational tension/fear does not enter, and violence is impersonal and routine. Closer to the micro-situational end of the continuum, we find other types of violence. Some of these resemble forward panic insofar as the barrier of confrontational tension/fear is successfully breached by finding a weak victim; these types of violence include much of domestic abuse, bullying, as well as mugging and robbery. But not all confrontations involve finding a weak victim; in a very different type of violent interaction, an audience cooperates in the performance of staged and limited fights, often with a rule-bound format of a 'fair fight', in which equally matched individuals fight it out under the appreciative eyes of the crowd. Still another type is carousing violence in an atmosphere of permissive celebration, and related to this sports violence. Some of these kinds of violence are much more legitimated that others. Audience-oriented 'fair fights' enjoy a good deal of popular acclaim, at least locally; so do many fights which break out at festivities or sports events, and which rely on the ebullient emotion of the crowd to energise the small number of individuals who do most of the violence.

Analytically, violence divides into different branches around the question of where it gets its emotional energy from, to carry through a confrontation to the point of doing real harm. Confrontational tension/fear is the baseline of all violence, in the sense that this is the barrier which all hostile action must overcome if it is to turn into actual violence. Where audiences support and regulate the fighting, the violence tends to be contained and legitimated in ways that make it seem more acceptable, less of a breach of our moral sensibilities. Forward panic, on the contrary, is the most extreme of the pathways for circumventing confrontational tension/fear. In these instances the perpetrators themselves–together with their victims comprise a closed universe, impervious to audiences. Forward panic is the epitome of getting carried away in one's own emotional rush; it is this obliviousness to anyone outside the conflict that makes it horrifying to behold, and which makes it an atrocity.

If the different kinds of violence have different etiologies and different interactional mechanisms, it is essential to separate them conceptually. We are a long way from a comprehensive theory of violence. A step in that direction is to understand the mechanisms for different types of violence, one at a time.

REFERENCES

Alpert, GP and Dunham, RG (1990) *Police Pursuit Driving* (New York, Greenwood Press).
—— (2004) *Understanding Police Use of Force* (Cambridge, Cambridge University Press).
Anderson, E (1999) *Code of the Street. Decency, Violence, and the Moral Life of the Inner City* (New York, Norton).
Ardant du Picq, C (1921) *Battle Studies: Ancient and Modern Battles* (New York, Macmillan).
Collins, R (2004) *Interaction Ritual Chains* (Princeton, Princeton University Press).

—— (2008) *Violence: A Micro-sociological Theory* (Princeton, Princeton University Press).

Ekman, P and Friesen, WV (1975) *Unmasking the Face* (Englewood Cliffs, Prentice-Hall).

Geller, WA and Toch, H (eds) (1996) *Police Violence: Understanding and Controlling Police Abuse of Force* (New Haven, Yale University Press).

Grossman, D (1995) *On Killing. The Psychological Cost of Learning to Kill in War and Society* (Boston, Little Brown).

Hensley, TR and Lewis, JM (1978) *Kent State and May 4th: A Social Science Perspective* (Dubuque, Kendall/Hunt).

Horowitz, DL (2001) *The Deadly Ethnic Riot* (Berkeley, University of California Press).

James, W (1890) *Principles of Psychology* (New York, Holt).

Keegan, J (1977) *The Face of Battle. A Study of Agincourt, Waterloo, and the Somme* (New York, Random House).

Rubinstein, J (1973) *City Police* (New York, Farrar, Straus and Giroux).

Worden, RE (1996) 'The Causes of Police Brutality: Theory and Evidence on Police Use of Force' in WA Geller and H Toch (eds) (1996) *Police Violence: Understanding and Controlling Police Abuse of Force* (New Haven, Yale University Press).

2

Making Sense of 'Senseless Violence'

WILLEM DE HAAN[*]

I N THE LATE 1990s, an incident of lethal street violence in a provincial
town in the Netherlands caused great concern among the general
population. In court, the judge described the perpetrators, who were
family men in their twenties, and without criminal records, as 'remarkably unremarkable'. No explanation for their impulsive outburst of violent
behaviour could be found other than that they had 'gone through the roof',
after having consumed a considerable quantity of alcoholic beverages. So-
called 'silent marches' were organised in protest against what was felt to
be an increasing level of 'senseless violence' in Dutch society. As feelings
of anxiety increased, a national public debate was staged to discuss the
causes as well as the prevention of such 'senseless violence'. In the course
of this debate, public discourse showed a tendency toward a 'dramatisation of evil' (Tannenbaum 1938), as almost every form of 'public violence'
(Schuyt 1999) came to be considered as random and irrational, while the
perpetrators/offenders of these violent acts were demonised and socially
rejected and excluded (Schuyt 1995). The idea that acts of violence might
be committed by individuals who cannot easily be distinguished from the
average man-in-the-street is difficult to contemplate, given the consolation
provided by the belief that such murderers must suffer from extreme pathological conditions: psychosis, psychopathy, or some other form of 'mental
disturbance' (Cartwright 2002: 2).

The ensuing discussion about 'senseless violence' was often unrealistic
and sometimes hypocritical. It was unrealistic because the discussion was
more about media images than about what really happened, and because
the notion of 'senseless violence' became subject to inflation as very different events and behaviours were categorised and qualified as such. It was
also because the label of 'senseless violence' was increasingly mentioned
in the same breath as other forms of public nuisance and crime, with the

[*] I would like to thank Sylvia Heijting and Marlene Zwaan for their cooperation, and Kathy
Davis and Tony Jefferson for their invaluable suggestions and comments, even though, within
the limits of this chapter, I could only partially follow their suggestions.

result that 'senseless violence' came to be seen as epidemic. The debate was hypocritical because moral outrage was embraced without considering the extent to which this kind of derailment could be the result of the kind of risky ('masculine') behaviours which are, in fact, widely accepted or tolerated, if not stimulated by the 'night time economy' of entertainment in bars and pubs (Hobbs et al 2005). Initially, all the government could think of in terms of violence prevention was a ban on the so-called 'happy hour' when drinks are offered at reduced prices to stimulate consumption.

In the debate, 'senseless violence' was depicted as random, one-sided and disproportionate, committed in the largely anonymous contexts of night-time entertainment areas with bystanders who tended to remain passive and unwilling to intervene in order to help the victims, who could not understand why they were chosen to be victimised by perpetrators that were both unknown to them and, in their view, had no reason whatsoever for the attack. Within the context of the national debate on 'senseless violence', however, public reactions were primarily moralistic. Unfortunately, moralistic approaches to violence do not have much to offer in terms of understanding the causes and prevention of violence; and, what is worse, some of the moral assumptions about violence may actually inhibit more serious attempts to learn about its causes and prevention (Gilligan 1996: 24). The more forceful violent behaviour is morally condemned, the harder it becomes to seek to understand what 'senseless violence' means to the perpetrators, or what renders this kind of violence justified or particularly attractive to them. Labelling street violence as 'senseless' obscures rather than clarifies matters.

In order to have a more sensible discussion about 'senseless violence' and find more effective ways of combating and preventing public violence, more insight is necessary into the perpetrators' emotional experiences before, during and after committing these kinds of violent acts. To make make sense of 'senseless violence' we need to discover how it feels for men to engage in this type of violence. Only if we put ourselves 'in their shoes' (Goldie 2000), ie take their point of view and try to empathise with their feelings, might we be able to get an understanding of what it really means for them to be violent. In this chapter, I will analyse a single case of what might be considered 'senseless violence'. It is a case in which a seemingly trivial occurrence becomes the occasion for an instance of what, at first glance, seems an incomprehensible and thus 'senseless' violent reaction. However, I will show how by taking the perpetrator's perspective and analysing his account of his emotions, some 'sense' evolves that helps us to understand why he had to do what he had to do. As Scheff (2002) argues, there are relatively few studies that investigate the part that emotions play in the causation of crime and violence. Therefore, in conclusion, I discuss how analysing a single case can not only help to make sense of 'senseless violence', but also provide an explanation of the role emotions play in this type of violent crime.

I. CRIMINOLOGY AND THE STUDY OF EMOTIONS

In the field of criminology there has, unfortunately, been little interest in the affective and expressive aspects of (violent) crime (De Haan and Loader 2002), with most criminologists tending to make a priori assumptions about the emotional dynamics of crime, rather than subjecting them to empirical investigation. Mainstream criminological theories offer general explanations of criminal behaviour by focusing almost exclusively on the backgrounds of crime. These theories fail to do justice to the fact that violence is both a dynamic process and an idiosyncratic experience par excellence. Rather than asking why specific instances of violence occurred, the focus remains more generally on the question of what—directly or indirectly—causes violence. A general lack of interest in the affective and expressive aspects of social action is far from unique to criminology, however (Turner and Stets 2005: 1). In his overview of sociological research in the field of violence, Von Trotha (1997) characterised these causal explanations as narrow-minded quantitative factor analyses in which everything is correlated statistically with everything else. Empirical correlations often are too readily viewed as causal in an attempt to explain a phenomenon that is hardly understood. Not only are such explanations—in the words of Max Weber—'perceptually inadequate'. In his view, theorising in this way can never lead to the development of 'causally adequate' explanations.

A sociology that really wants to understand and explain violence will have to begin by describing the phenomenology, ie the appearances and modalities of various forms of violence (Von Trotha 1997: 20). In his widely acclaimed study, *Seductions of Crime*, Katz (1988) had, of course, already argued that criminological theory should begin by studying the foreground of criminality (see also Katz 2002). By foreground, he meant the substantive aspects of criminal behaviour—that is, what happened exactly when a specific type of crime occurred, and what did the act of committing the crime mean to the perpetrator. How did he experience his involvement in committing the crime? According to Katz, it is only after this foreground of criminal behaviour has been explored that it makes sense to look at other relevant background factors, not to mention having any real chance of discovering new correlations between background factors and foreground characteristics.[1]

The classic assumption that most criminologists make is that human action is aimed at satisfying basic needs and that violence is the outcome of a discharge of emotions which have been frustrated when other needs are

---

[1] For Katz (2002), it is a strategic question that advocates of formal theories, based on so-called 'hard data', regard them as a model for 'big science' and discredit qualitative research as inferior 'soft science'. By referring to the academic prestige of theory, attention is deflected from the major shortcomings in the description of phenomena or behaviours, which are purportedly being explained.

being satisfied. Fights are not intentional, but rather something that 'just happens', while violence is viewed as impulsive and committed 'in passing'. Perpetrators of violence generally seem to possess a temper and to exhibit little self-control, becoming furious at the most minor provocation and immediately attacking a would-be opponent without pausing for a second to imagine what the possible consequences of such violent behaviour might be. Such 'emotional aggression' seems, indeed, 'senseless' and impossible to explain because it appears motivated more by an urge to injure a person than by a wish to achieve some other purpose. The attacks are conducted within the spirit of a quickly developing rage (Berkowitz 1986: 26–27). Explaining and understanding this type of behaviour would require a theory of emotions which operates with a broader conception of practical and discursive consciousness and moral agency—a theory which also does more justice to the feelings of offenders, the normative meanings that they attribute to their own behaviour and the social and cultural contexts within which such meanings are activated. While there has generally been little interest in the affective and expressive aspects of (violent) crime in criminology, there are some notable exceptions. Matza (1964) explicitly deals with the significance of moral emotions for explaining violent behaviour. Becoming violent requires the perpetrator's anxiety and feelings of guilt to be neutralised and his will to act to receive a strong impulse, for example, through an intense emotion. According to Matza, moral emotions in particular provide exactly the kind of strong impulse needed for perpetrators to turn to physical violence.

Scheff (1992), more recently, has also been concerned more specifically with the relationship between emotions and physical violence. According to Scheff, shame is the most relevant of all the emotions that might be involved in the genesis of crime and violence. However, many studies either implicate shame without naming it,[2] or exclude the vast domain of shame which occurs outside of consciousness, ie the kind of shame that may be called bypassed or unacknowledged. Based on this insight, Scheff has developed a theory according to which violence is a reaction to disappointed expectations regarding the display of recognition and respect for a person's identity. Scheff argues that humans are in a constant state of self-feeling, particularly with respect to the emotions of guilt and shame. People feel ashamed when they experience a lack of deference and respect from others. As shame is an extremely painful emotion to experience, individuals often activate their defences against the experience. However, if the shame is unacknowledged, denied, or repressed, a chain reaction starts whereby outbursts of anger and rage invariably result in impulsive, explosive violence. In this way, a

---

[2] One example which Scheff mentions is the study of the key role of insults in generating violence (such as Luckenbill 1977) which implies a shame/anger/aggression sequence, but fails to make it explicit.

highly disruptive cycle of emotion that oscillates between rage and shame is activated. Indeed, individuals can become locked in shame-anger cycles in which each outburst of anger causes more shame, that is then denied or repressed in ways escalating the intensity of the next outburst or anger.[3] Eventually, a person's biography comes to be dominated by such emotional cycles.

More recently, there appears to be a growing consensus that violence is a reaction to shame or 'narcissistic injury'. Gilligan (1996) argues that all forms of violence have shame at their core, and shows how a deep sense of shame is central to understanding the flight into violence. When someone is ashamed because he feels that he has been put on the spot, or because he has been ridiculed, he will be likely to react to such humiliation with violence, because the feelings of shame induce a sudden loss of self-esteem that, in turn, produces desperate defensive action aimed at preventing further humiliation. Thus, the impulsive character of 'senseless' violence can be explained by emotions like shame and rage, while the expressive aspects of violence can be regarded as an attempt on the part of the perpetrator to relieve himself of an 'unbearable state of mind' (Cartwright 2002), by repairing his identity and having it confirmed by others.

Last but not least, Katz (1988) argues along the same lines as Matza and Scheff, but takes the argument a step further by suggesting that, in order for violence to be committed, every (violent) crime requires three conditions to be fulfilled: 1. a path of action—distinctive practical requirements for successfully committing the crime; 2. a line of interpretation—unique ways of understanding how one is and will be seen by others; and 3. an emotional process—seductions and compulsions that have special dynamics.[4] In particular, 'moral emotions' like humiliation, righteousness, arrogance, ridicule, cynicism, defilement and vengeance always play a central role in the commission of violence. According to Katz, these moral emotions not only play an underlying role in violent behaviour, but violence itself must also be seen as the perpetrator's attempt to respond to a moral challenge: 'the attraction that proves to be most fundamentally compelling is that of overcoming a personal challenge to moral—not to material—existence' (Katz 1988: 9). More generally, he reinstates perpetrators of crime as moral subjects, striving reflexively to give meaning to their actions before, during and after the crime.

---

[3] Like Scheff and Retzinger (1991), Sherman (1993) as well as Hagan and McCarthy (1997) suggest that when shame is not acknowledged, it can lead to sequences of anger, aggression and violence (Scheff 2002: 365).

[4] According to Katz, each of these conditions is necessary, but only taken together, are they sufficient in order for a crime to be committed.

II. ANALYSING 'SENSELESS VIOLENCE'

In order to answer the question why perpetrators commit 'senseless' violence, I will analyse a single case of such violence. In the analysis, I will try to demonstrate, more specifically, how we can make sense of violent acts that would otherwise be considered as 'senseless'. Through this analysis, I will also seek to find an answer to the question how a theory of emotions may help us to not only understand, but also explain 'senseless violence'.

We must first of all try to discover how it feels and what it means to them to engage in physical violence. However, people often do not realise at the moment in question what the reasons for their actions are. This seems almost by definition the case with spontaneous, impulsive ('discharge') violence. Violent perpetrators are only able to reflect on why they were violent after the fact. People are then able to think of reasons for their action, which they were unable to come up with at the moment itself. However, these reasons provide retrospectively sufficient explanation (justification) for their behaviour for themselves (and possibly for others as well). In many cases, this explanation will also be an excuse or a retrospective justification for an earlier misdeed.

When perpetrators talk about their behaviour retrospectively in interview situations, and reflect upon it, clues can then be discovered in their descriptions, justifications, and explanations as to their 'sense of motivation'—in other words, what ultimately moved them to become violent. The assumption here is what Ken Plummer (1995: 39) has described as the 'emotional well' from which a person draws in order to explain who he is and why he has behaved in such a way under the circumstances. Narratives of violent perpetrators often centre on topics like compulsive, irresistible inner drives and intense, uncontrollable emotions. One of the core themes (reasons) in perpetrator or victim narratives is the reason that makes the occurrence understandable and explains it retrospectively. This includes the thoughts or fantasies which the violent behaviour symbolically represents. More specifically, he argues that 'in order to understand violence we must interpret *action as symbolic language*—with a "symbolic logic" of its own' (Gilligan (1996: 62). Individuals may or may not be able to state consciously the meaning of their action. In the case of some violent individuals, they may be so orientated toward expressing their thoughts in the form of actions rather than words, that their verbal inarticulateness prevents them from expressing the thoughts which their behaviour expresses symbolically.

In order to uncover exactly what respondents are trying to say, an interpretative analysis is required, which assumes that there is at least some relationship—however unclear at first glance—between people's experiences and their obscure and often contradictory accounts of these experiences (Hollway and Jefferson 2000). Perpetrators' accounts can provide clues to what committing a crime means to them, as well as how they experienced being a criminal. By investigating the facts of the case (the narrative aspect), the occasion and trajectory of the incident (the interactive aspect), how it is perceived (the interpretative aspect), how it was experienced (the affective aspect) and how it is perceived retrospectively (the reflexive aspect), it is possible—at least to some degree—to reconstruct what violence meant to the perpetrator of a violent incident.[5]

A. A Case of 'Senseless Violence'[6]

Pete is a big and strong-looking 55-year old man who presents himself as a successful businessmen and 'self-made man'. He lives and works at an industrial site 'in the middle of nowhere'. His house is sparsely furnished and might be seen befitting a bachelor. The house is attached to the workshop, which can be reached by a connecting door on the inside. On several sides of the building there are agricultural machines parked in the driveways. When he looks at the enormous machines that he himself has designed and constructed, he feels proud of what he has achieved, regardless of his not having a degree. Having left school at age 14, he worked first for his father, then for others and now in his own business, designing and building advanced agricultural machines.

He lives where he works and works where he lives, and does not observe a division between working and leisure time. Seven days a week, he goes between his house and his workshop. That his work is never finished does not bother Pete, because he has no need for free time. Working on his inventions is his joy in life.

Hard work is something he learned while growing up on his parents' farm. 'Work first, then eat' was the golden rule, which has only become more important to him later in life. In fact, his work makes up most of his identity. He explains that his wife did not share his passion for his work, which is why they split up.

One day, when Pete is taking a coffee break with his three employees, sitting outside the workshop on a warm summer's day, they see a young truck driver trying to manoeuvre his truck into the driveway of the company on the other side of the street. The four men watch him and have a laugh

---

[5] Methodologically, it is possible to analyse the perpetrators' accounts and interpret them in the context in which they are given in such a way that a systematic relationship can be established between their actions and their—at first glance—often imperfect, clumsy, and sometimes contradictory explanations (Hollway and Jefferson 2000). How convincing such explanations are depends upon the 'context of justification', which may be hermeneutic or causal (Scheer 2001).

[6] The case is taken from a larger research project that I directed (Beke, de Haan, Terlouw 2002). This particular interview was conducted by Sylvia Heijting.

because 'he can't get it in there'. They go back to work until Pete sees the same truck driving across his property, coming to a standstill half inside his workshop. At this point, Pete feels something needs to be done and walks up to the scene. As soon as the truck driver sees Pete coming, he gets out of his truck and walks up to him with the remark: 'It's all right, isn't it?' Pete, however, gruffly reacts with: 'No, it's not all right. In here, we don't do it like that.' When the younger man responds by saying that he hasn't any argument with him, Pete gets angry, lifts his hammer and summons the driver to either 'Get the f.... out of here', or wait to get hit. When the truck driver quickly moves to get back into his truck, Pete kicks him in the backside. The incident is being watched by employees from the company on the other side of the street.

After the truck driver has nervously left the property, still unable to get his truck into the driveway, Pete takes up his work again and forgets what happened. The next day, the police call Pete and ask him to come to the station to be 'questioned'. The truck driver had filed a complaint because, according to the victim, Pete had kicked him twice, which did not cause any serious injury but had been painful. Pete is prosecuted for threat and assault without injury and has to appear in court. He is convicted and sentenced to pay a 225-euro fine.[7]

At first glance, Pete's violence might appear to be simply a case of over-reaction, rather than an instance of 'senseless violence'. After all, he merely threatened his opponent and kicked him without causing serious injury. But the fact that the violence in this case did not lead to serious injury is irrelevant in terms of whether or not it might be considered a case of 'senseless violence'. After all, injury—even fatal injury—tends to be an arbitrary outcome of this type of confrontational social interaction. The 'senselessness' of the violence rests in the fact that the motivation for it seems incomprehensible. Why would someone become so upset at such a trivial occurrence? What motivates a person to physically attack someone, instead of verbally arguing his case?

B. Justifying Emotions

'Why was I running around with a hammer?' With this rhetorical question, Pete starts his narrative. He explains the incident, arguing that the man was an incompetent driver ('lousy') who did not even have the 'decency' to ask him for permission before trespassing on his premises. 'He should have

---

[7] I should perhaps point out that I have chosen this case in particular because of the length and quality of the interview. In fact, the respondent demanded a second interview because he felt that not all the important aspects had been covered in the first interview. Because his life history was discussed in such detail, this case is particularly suited to an analysis of motives.

asked, but instead he took the law into his own hands.' Pete is angry about the way the driver approached him: 'I did not like the way he did it. If he had been a real man he would have said he was sorry.' But instead, 'He just acted like, "I am smarter than you are." That's the impression he gave me.' In order to ensure that the interviewer not only understands him but also accepts his interpretation, Pete repeatedly completes his line of argument with a questioning: 'Yes?'

He characterises the driver who parked his truck on his property as someone who was acting superior, despite the fact that in Pete's eyes he was a young man who was not even capable of parking his own truck competently. He disqualified him because: 'He is a useless truck driver. We can all see that.' According to Pete, the truck driver, at that moment, displayed a self-confidence which did not correspond with his obvious lack of driving ability. He regarded this kind of assertiveness as 'conceited'. Pete's view of the situation is confirmed by the behaviour of the truck driver, when he got out of the truck. 'He had a big grin on his face. "I am smarter than you are", that's the kind of impression that he made. "I'm the winner here and you can't do anything about it to me."' What really aggravated Pete was the man's grin, that seemed to underline his arrogance. Or as Pete put it: 'That grin in this situation, that was just too much!'

This assertiveness gives Pete the impression that the truck driver feels superior to Pete. The driver's reaction takes him by surprise, and Pete is deeply wounded that he wasn't able to anticipate this reaction and, therefore, is unable to think of a comeback. Smarting from his hurt feelings, he is unable to think calmly: 'It just boiled over.' At that moment, everything span around so fast in his head that he couldn't say anything. Even if he had wanted to negotiate, he would not have been able to. Nevertheless, Pete felt he was fully within his rights. So when the police called him about the driver's complaint, he angrily challenged them with a menacing remark: 'Shall I come over and drive through your backyard, then?'

The background to Pete's moral outrage becomes clearer in the context of several other events, which he recounts during the interview. With great eloquence, he remembers other confrontations where he feels that he was short-changed; his reaction is 'to make sure nobody walks all over him'. Three examples are illustrative of the behavioural pattern in which he repeatedly displays his violent reactions in different contexts and in different relationships.

In one story, Pete is responsible for gritting the local roads in frosty weather. In the course of this work, he often encounters people who obstruct him from doing his job. This irritates him, because he sees himself as working for the safety of the community. Moreover, the work causes him considerable personal discomfort: little sleep, dangerous roads, and working on Sundays and holidays, sometimes for 24 hours at a time. He is working under stress. When other cars are in his way and prevent him from doing his job, he thinks that their drivers are refusing to cooperate on purpose, because: 'They think they own the road.' Quite often, he says, he gets out of his truck and kicks a dent in the other car, or uses his truck to make scratches on their cars or push them off the road. 'I get so mad because I just cannot stand their aggression. I am working seven days a week for them.'

In another story, Pete describes delivering a machine to one of his clients. After urging the client several times to settle the account, it becomes clear to him that he must either take back the machine or lose money. Pete is convinced that the client has refrained from paying on purpose in order to upset him and, of course, for his own financial gain. He feels betrayed, makes a visit to the client, and tells him 'in no uncertain terms' to pay up. In order to make his point even more decisively, he 'grabs him by his shirt front'.

Similar emotions arise in the course of another incident. When his business goes bankrupt, Pete refuses to cooperate with the court-appointed trustee because he feels being talked down to about what he can and cannot do. When the trustee requests him to hand over his passport, Pete refuses. After he proceeds to call the trustee an 'asshole', Pete ends up in court. In the interview, Peter explains why he could not stomach the lawyer's behaviour: 'I am not going to listen to an asshole like that. I am not going to let myself be put down by someone like that.'

It might seem that Pete is overly sensitive about his treatment by people in authority. His work requires him to negotiate projects with people who have had more formal education than he had. In these situations, there are often differences of opinion about technical matters, which Pete describes as situations where his 'arguments were ignored'. It infuriates him when he feels he is not taken seriously and his 'opponents' pretend a status, which he thinks they should not have, on the basis of a degree. Even minor irritations may lead to violent conflict. In his view, his opponents lack his own true technical understanding. As he puts it: 'I may not have any diplomas, but I am still a very good craftsman. Making a big point out of official papers pisses me off.' He perceives their behaviour as 'authoritarian' and intended to make him feel 'worthless'.

Pete draws upon these stories to explain what the 'real' problem is: a power struggle. It is very important to him that everyone knows that he is not just anybody, and that you can't make a fool out of him. But Pete also occasionally displays another side: he presents himself as a man who is uncertain in some situations and doesn't always find the right words during confrontation needed to keep things on an even keel. By using physical force, he tries to restore the balance of power which, in his view, has been disrupted. Thus, in conflict situations, Pete especially wants to make clear two things: that he is smart, because he understands the game, and that he won't let anybody walk over him.

From a psychiatric point of view, Pete's violent resolution of interpersonal disputes would probably be viewed as rooted in hidden and repressed feelings of shame, which probably developed in his primary interactions with his parents. According to Goldberg (1996), a perpetrator is someone whose capacity to handle painful experiences is so limited that he believes that his lack of sensitivity, indifference and increasingly destructive behaviour are completely normal. He views them as an acceptable and justifiable way to cope with the difficulties of everyday life. Other ways of dealing with conflicts are no longer even considered, or are experiences so alien that they bear no correspondence to his own practices. Repressed feelings of shame left over from childhood, accompanied by a low self-esteem and indifference toward other people's feelings, creates the risk of excessive reactions like frequent violent responses to stressful situations, in private and in public and in interaction with peers or with authorities.

This explanation is confirmed in the case of Pete, who also accounts for his conduct by drawing upon his cultural background, his family home, the farm and the world of day croppers as an explanation for his shortcomings: 'I come from a world of real rednecks.' He explains that when he had a conflict with his father, it was never possible to work anything out. There was no question about whether Pete would be punished or not. If Pete made a mistake, in the eyes of his father there was only one course of action: immediate punishment. 'I had to bend over with my eyes to the ground and he began hitting me with anything he could get his hands on.' And: 'When you got in too late nothing was said. The bicycle [I used] was immediately taken to the attic and consequently I just had to walk to wherever it was I was going next.' Property and respect for property were of the utmost importance in the farming community where Pete grew up. The boundaries of his father's own farmland provided the social boundaries, which demanded respect. 'There were long straight ditches between the farms. One didn't have anything to do with one's neighbours unless it was absolutely necessary.' Thus, Pete underlines that he had little opportunity at home or elsewhere to learn other ways of resolving conflicts: 'When others are quick tempered, so are you. You are part of that small world.'

As a result of his talent for designing machines Pete now meets other kinds of people who are different from the 'rednecks' he knew as a boy: 'I can see now that the world is different. I have travelled to other countries because of my work and I have seen other things. People do things differently. I like that a lot.'

Based on these experiences Pete tries to see his own behaviour in a different light and to learn how to act differently and think before acting, because: 'With hot-headedness and stubbornness you just create more shit.' He feels that he can judge these situations better because: 'I now have knowledge that I didn't have before.'

Pete talks about how his colleague resolves conflict situations without using violence: 'He pulls the guy out of the cabin of his truck and talks to him, real calmly. I admire that. I think that's fantastic. I would like to be that way too.'

Having come to the end of his stories, Pete returns to the incident with the truck driver and admits to having second thoughts about it. He wonders whether maybe he has judged a little too quickly. 'I get steamed up fast. I fly off the handle.'

It is clear from the above that it is not simply Pete's emotions driving him to a violent response. The reasons, which he draws on in order to account for his behaviour, explain why to him his response was just a 'normal' reaction and why, given the circumstances, he claimed: 'I had to do what I had to do.' Even a cursory analysis of Pete's account shows that repressed rage and shame induce an emotional chain reaction, which often results in Pete's impulsive, explosive use of violence. It is also clear that violence is a way for him to compensate painful feelings of inadequacy. Pete's provocative display toward the truck driver seems to be an attempt on his part to rise to the occasion of a moral challenge. At first glance, Pete's behaviour makes no sense, and seems to be little more than an impulsive act of senseless violence. However, upon closer inspection, moral emotions seem to be providing his will to act with such a strong impulse that he almost cannot avoid resorting to physical violence.

C. Interpreting Emotions

Emotions are reasons that people refer to when they reflect on what compelled them to act in a particular way—reasons with which they can defend, justify or explain their actions. Emotions serve as explanations that make past, present and future actions understandable and justifiable. In order to account for their actions, actors invariably turn to emotions as common-sense explanations that are culturally available in the form of 'vocabularies of motive' (Mills 1940). According to Cressey (1954), emotions are reasons which, indirectly, determine human action in the sense that actors identify with the type of personality belonging to people for whom such reasons are considered typical. In his view, people are well aware ('conscious') that reasons strengthen their will to act. Similarly, McCord (1997) believes that these reasoning styles can give us a handle to understand and explain intentional action and, more specifically, (violent) criminal behaviour. She argues that the reasons we learn to use in justifying our actions become potentiating reasons, because once an individual has developed a set of reasons, that individual will use the set to organise the environment and to act upon it. In this way, the actions of individuals tend to become predictable because, under the circumstances, they will feel an inner compulsion to react in a specific way (Jansz 1996).

On the one hand, this tendency is individually determined because different people learn different potentiating reasons and even though we all go through the same processes, we each do so differently. Nobody shares our unique biographical experiences in all their particularity. It is, therefore, essential that the psychological dimension of subjectivity should not simply be dissolved into the social. On the other hand, however, whatever our particular, biographically unique experiences of early life processes, with their resulting patterns of defences, identifications and orientations, these are always also simultaneously social (Jefferson 2002: 153).

Reasoning styles are no exception. We learn when a certain type of what McCord calls 'potentiating' reasons provides socially acceptable grounds for actions and can be used as motives. Socially, particular circumstances and conditions create systems of more or less durable and culturally transmittable predispositions—that is, tendencies to act in particular ways. Such systems of predispositions can be defined as habitus (Bourdieu 1977), ie a *sense pratique*, which allows a person to immediately understand the meaning of a situation and to find almost instinctively an appropriate reaction, even—as Bourdieu puts it—'in the heat of the moment' of a fight. Habitus can also be understood as a set of specific behavioural repertoires that almost have the quality of a 'second nature'.[8]

One repertoire of activities, which is particularly salient for understanding and explaining public violence, is masculinity. Within criminology, Messerschmidt (1993) and Jefferson (1994) are pioneers in arguing that violence can be regarded as an extreme form of 'doing' masculinity. In their view, violence is a likely outcome when generally accepted notions of masculinity are being disturbed. When additional effort is required to display masculinity, violence can offer a solution. For example, the violence of a youthful perpetrator could be explained by referring to the fact that he became enraged when he was humiliated or treated differently than a normal white heterosexual middle class man could expect to be treated (Gadd 2000). In order to express his moral indignation he used his physical dominance to control the situation. The use of physical violence becomes a means *par excellence* to suppress painful experiences, such as the feeling of constantly being pushed around. It is perhaps in the act of seizing control of a situation where the perpetrator feels that he is a victim that we can find the deeper sense of 'senseless violence'.

In the case of Pete, all of his confrontations were with other men, and all concerned events in which his masculine identity was in one way or another under threat and needed to be restored.

---

[8] In Bourdieu's concept of 'habitus', individual and cultural factors are integrated into an individual biography.

For example, the incident with the hammer can be interpreted as a reaction to another man (the truck driver) who had literally and figuratively trespassed on Pete's territory. By trespassing upon the boundaries of his property as well as his person, his sense of autonomy, crucial to his self-image as man, was damaged. The truck driver diminished the distance between himself and Pete to such a degree that Pete no longer felt 'in control'. His identity was threatened and, therefore, his masculinity was at stake.

Pete's violent reaction can be explained by the fact that he became enraged at being treated differently than he had expected as a successful white heterosexual man.

In order to express his moral indignation and regain control of the situation, he was compelled to use physical strength. Seizing control of a situation in which he felt that he was a victim rather than the perpetrator is, perhaps, the underlying meaning of his act of 'senseless violence'. Given the behavioural repertoires which were available to him, the use of physical violence seemed to be the most immediately effective means for suppressing the painful experience of not being taken seriously, and being treated unfairly.

In the interview, Pete clearly understands that his violent reaction might give a strange impression to outsiders, and that he is expected to provide at least some kind of explanation. He repeatedly attempts to explain his behaviour, insisting that he did not mean to injure the driver or that he certainly did not swing the hammer with the intention of really hitting him. He explains that: 'I just wanted to put a little force behind my words. I was at a loss for words. It was a way for me to say I don't appreciate this.' In his view, Pete was 'forced' into a situation requiring negotiations, for which he is poorly equipped. Because of his lack of self-esteem and his difficulty in understanding the intentions of others, it was almost impossible for him to deal flexibly with the situation. He immediately fell back on his stock behavioural repertoire of using violence. In this sense, he retrospectively experiences and explains his violent reaction to the truck driver as both compulsory and justified.

From an analytical point of view, the most important reason for Pete's violent behaviour seems to have been that he wasn't taken seriously and respected as a man or, at least, as a man in his position should have been. By linking his initially 'senseless' reaction to the somewhat thoughtless behaviour of an inexperienced truck driver in the context of his narrative, we can begin to understand Pete's reaction. His wronged self-respect had to be avenged, and with force. He draws upon the context in which his moral outrage was expressed in order to establish his actions as 'normal'—that is, an appropriate reaction for a man under the given circumstances. His version of 'normal' masculine behaviour is, of course, (sub)culturally determined. Men like Pete have learned that impulsive violent responses can be considered and condoned as unavoidable and irresistible (Baumeister 1997). In this way, the social and cultural conditions for 'doing' normal masculinity create systems of more or less enduring, symbolically transmittable predispositions to respond in a violent way.

Given the almost endless number of possible factors explaining human behaviour, the idea of a general pattern of causal explanation the parameters of which merely need to be determined in order to render violent human behaviour predictable, seems extremely unlikely. Roy (2000) has compared such criminological prediction of a violent outburst with meteorological forecasting: predicting the chances of a thunderstorm occurring somewhere can be done reasonably well, but to predict precisely where and when a flash of lightning is going to strike seems well nigh impossible. With regard to their unpredictability, cases of 'senseless violence' seem to be comparable to flashes of lightning. They can be better understood with hindsight, than predicted in advance.

III. CONCLUSION

The analysis of the single case presented in this paper allows two conclusions to be drawn regarding the question of how 'senseless' violence can be explained and understood. First, the case analysis shows that there are clear reasons for acts which, at first glance, seem to be instances of 'senseless violence'. We may not necessarily condone these reasons, but we can, nevertheless, understand them. From the perspective of the perpetrator, an incident always has a clear occasion, and there are usually several reasons for what to an observer may look like a random and disproportionately violent reaction. In a certain sense, the perpetrator experiences his actions as a necessity, the main reason being that he does not feel he is taken seriously, given the respect he deserves. A case analysis can show why a perpetrator commits a violent crime by showing what it meant to him to become violent and how violence helps him gain control over a situation which threatens to transform him into an object.[9] In specific situations and when overtaken by their emotions, men may act violently as a way to express in the most powerful terms possible, that which they are or would like to be. Such explosions of violence may seem impulsive and beyond control. However, even the most intense emotional reactions are socially constructed and constrained by social norms prescribing when the expression of certain kinds of emotions is acceptable, desirable or mandatory. Put another way,

---

[9] Informants were possibly willing to tell what happened to an interviewer because they were hoping for some recognition for their side of the story. Some element of self-selection seems likely, given that almost half of the informants felt they had been treated unfairly, or did not agree with the official interpretation of what happened.

emotions add an affective component to people's accounts of their actions, with the result that their behaviour lends itself to (causal) explanation and understanding.

Second, the case analysis shows that offender emotions may be much more complex than is usually assumed. Although the analysis of the particular emotions of an individual perpetrator do not immediately allow us to draw firm conclusions concerning the general causes of 'senseless violence', it does provide valuable indications regarding the relative impor- tance of the various personal and situational factors, which bring about 'senseless violence'. Obviously, case-oriented research differs from regres- sion-based approaches. However, it arguably has many advantages when it comes to generating theory by identifying factors and processes that remain otherwise poorly understood. By investigating the ways in which multiple layers of context structure social action, case-based methods not only establish causal chains within individual cases. They also situate a given case, in as much richness of detail as possible, within the wider social field which shapes the processes unfolding in that case (Sullivan 2002: 265).

To the end of contributing to a sensible public debate about disturbing (violent) crimes, criminologists need, first and foremost, to invest in a 'thick description' of what is 'essential' in violent behaviour. Violent behaviour is perhaps best observed in situ, but in lieu of that, perpetrators, victims and witnesses can be interviewed and invited to talk at length about what they experienced and what it meant to them. It is then the researcher's task to analyse their accounts in detail, specifying the necessary and suf- ficient conditions for specific types of violence to occur. Not only the actual interaction and its interpretation, but also the effects of the context on the meaning of violence for those involved need to be empirically grounded, eg individual violent behaviour related to differential opportunity structures and the social genesis of violence related to situational, contextual, socio- cultural and political factors. In this way, more general answers can be provided to questions concerning how institutional social arrangements can generate, but also prevent violent behaviour.

REFERENCES

Baumeister, RF (1997) *Evil, Inside Human Violence and Cruelty* (New York, WH Freeman and Co).

Beke, BMWA, De Haan, WJM and Terlouw, GJ (2001) *Geweld verteld. Verklaringen van daders, slachtoffers en getuigen van geweld op straat* (Den Haag, Wetenschappelijk Onderzoek- en Documentatiecentrum, Ministerie van Justitie).

Berkowitz, L (1986) 'Some varieties of human aggression: criminal violence as coercion, rule-following, impression management and impulsive behaviour' in

A Campbell and JJ Gibbs (eds), *Violent Transactions. The Limits of Personality* (Oxford, Basil Blackwell)

——(1993) *Aggression. Its Causes, Consequenses and Control* (Philadelphia, Temple University Press).

Bourdieu, PF (1977) *Outline of a Theory of Practice* (Cambridge, Cambridge University Press).

Cartwright, D (2002) *Psychoanalysis, Violence and Rage-Type Murder. Murdering Mind* (Hove and New York, Brunner-Routledge).

Cressey, DR (1954) 'The differential association theory and compulsive crime' 45 *Journal of Criminal Law, Criminology and Police Science* 49–64.

De Haan, W and Loader, I (2002) 'On the emotions of crime, punishment and social control' 6(3) *Theoretical Criminology* 243–54.

Gadd, D (2000) 'Masculinities, violence and defended psychosocial subjects' 4 *Theoretical Criminology* 429–49.

Gilligan, J (1996) *Violence. Reflections on a National Epidemic* (New York, Vintage Books).

Goldberg, C (1996) *Speaking with the Devil. Exploring Senseless Acts of Evil* (New York, Penguin Books).

Goldie, P (2000) *The Emotions: A Philosophical Exploration* (Oxford, Clarendon Press).

Hagan, J and McCarthy, B (1997) *Mean Streets. Youth Crime and Homelessness* (Cambridge, Cambridge University Press).

Hobbs, D et al (2005) 'Violent Hypocrisy: Governance and the Night-time Economy' 2 *European Journal of Criminology* 161–83.

Hollway, W and Jefferson, T (2000) *Doing Qualitative Research Differently. Free Association, Narrative and the Interview Method* (London, Sage).

Jansz, J (1996) 'Constructed motives' 63 *Theory and Psychology* 471–84.

Jefferson, T (1994) 'Theorizing masculine subjectivity' in T Newburn and E Stanko (eds), *Just Boys Doing Business* (London, Routledge).

——(2002) 'For a psychosocial criminology' in K Carrington and R Hogg (eds), *Critical Criminology. Issues, Debates, Challenges* (Cullompton, Willan Publishing).

Katz, J (1988) *Seductions of Crime. Moral and Sensual Attractions in Doing Evil* (New York, Basic Books).

——(2002) 'Start here: Social ontology and research strategy' 6(3) *Theoretical Criminology* 255–78.

Luckenbill, DF (1977) 'Criminal homicide as a situated transaction' 25(1) *Social Problems* 176–86.

Matza, D (1964) *Delinquency and Drift* (New York, John Wiley).

McCord, J (1997) '"He did it because he wanted to …"' in D Wayne Osgood (ed), *Motivation and Delinquency*. Nebraska Symposium on Motivation, vol 44. (Lincolna, University of Nebraska Press) 1–43.

Messerschmidt, J (1993) *Masculinities and Crime* (Maryland, Rowan & Littlefield).

Mills, CW (1940) 'Situated actions and vocabularies of motive' 5 *American Sociological Review* 904–13.

Plummer, K (1995) *Telling Sexual Stories: Power, Change, and Social Worlds* (London and New York, Routledge).

Roy, KG (2000) 'The systemic conditions leading to violent human behaviour' 36 *The Journal of Applied Behavioural Science* 389–406.

Scheer, RK (2001) 'Intentions, motives, and causation' 76 *Philosophy* 397–413.

Scheff, T (1992) 'Rationality and Emotion. Hommage to Norbert Elias' in J Coleman and T Fararo (eds), *Rational Choice Theory. Advocacy and Critique. Key Issues in Sociological Theory* 7 (Newbury Park, Sage) 101–17.

——(2002) 'Review of Jack Katz, How Emotions Work' 6(3) *Theoretical Criminology* 361–66.

Scheff, TJ and Retzinger, S (1991) *Emotions and Violence: Shame and Rage in Destructive Conflicts* (Lexington, Lexington Books).

Schuyt, CJM (1995) 'De crimineel als vreemdeling' 25 *Delikt en Delinkwent* 927–30.

——(1999) 'Publiek geweld' 29 *Delikt en Delinkwent* 383–88.

Sherman, LW (1993) 'Defiance, deterrence, and irrelevance: A theory of the criminal sanction' 30 *Journal of Research in Crime and Delinquency* 445–73.

Sullivan, ML (2002) 'Exploring layers. Extended case method as a tool for multilevel analysis of school violence' 31(2) *Sociological Methods & Research* 255–85.

Tannenbaum, F (1938) *Crime and the Community* (Boston, Ginn).

Turner, JH and Stets, JE (2005) *The Sociology of Emotions* (New York, Cambridge University Press).

Von Trotha, T (1997) 'Zur Soziologie der Gewalt' 37 *Kölner Zeitschrift für Soziologie und Sozialpsychologie* 9–56.

3

Shame, Pride and Workplace Bullying

ELIZA AHMED AND JOHN BRAITHWAITE

I. SHAME, PRIDE AND JUSTICE

EMOTIONS ARE INHERENT to human behaviour and social conflict (Lazarus 1991). They are central to understanding how individuals think about and respond to certain situations (Frijda and Mesquita 1994). This is particularly true for self-conscious emotions (eg, shame, pride), which often have been considered disruptive to everyday interactions (Fischer and Tangney 1995; Keltner 1995).

The relevance of shame in explaining wrongdoing has long been supported by a body of psychological, sociological and criminological literature which suggests a link between shame, anger and antisocial behaviour (Ahmed et al 2001; Gilligan 1997; Lewis 1971; Scheff and Retzinger 1991; Tangney 1990). For example, Lewis (1971) has argued that unacknowledged shame provoked anger and angry reactions in her clients during psychotherapeutic sessions. Support for unacknowledged shame in triggering anger can also be found in studies using a variety of methodologies, such as videotaping of facial expressions (Retzinger 1991). While focusing on the non-adaptive aspects of shame, none of these researchers has denied adaptive aspects of shame. Indeed some have conceded the possibility that shame acknowledgement plays a central role in maintaining adaptive interpersonal relationships (see Retzinger 1996).

The emotion of shame/guilt following wrongdoing is an experience with which we are all familiar. According to shame management theory (Ahmed et al 2001), just as shame/guilt can be adaptive, it can also crush people and their relationships. When we acknowledge these feelings, take responsibility for the harm done, and take steps to make amends, it is adaptive. Shame management is not adaptive if we displace those feelings to escape from negative consequences of the wrongdoing. In the latter case, we blame others. This damages interpersonal relationships.

Shame management and bullying is a topic that has attracted research attention in recent years, with a number of studies replicating the result that shame acknowledgment is associated with lower levels of bullying, and that shame displacement into anger, blaming and other externalising reactions is associated with higher levels of bullying (Ahmed and Braithwaite 2005; Braithwaite et al 2003; Morrison 2006, 2007). Pride management, in contrast, has been ignored in terms of its effect on bullying. This is surprising, since many endorse Scheff and Retzinger's (1991: xix) frame that emotion and social relationships come in conjugate pairs, specifically: 'pride is the emotional conjugate of social solidarity, and shame is the emotional conjugate of alienation'. Bullying is the antithesis of social solidarity, so good pride management should be implicated in bullying prevention. Scheff and Retzinger (1991: 175) specifically critique Braithwaite (1989) for his failure to give equal weight to pride as to shame in the study of social control. Scheff and Retzinger supply the revisionist perspective that we bring to this research.

Webb (2003) shows that shame and pride share the feature that people tend to distinguish good and bad forms of shame and pride. Positive pride is seen as about self-esteem and self-respect in our own accomplishments. It encompasses accepting our limitations, knowing we never succeed by ourselves, and promotes collaborative relationships (Cherney, www.team-buildinginc.com/article_ai.htm). Negative pride is about hubris and arrogance, which seems to be the essence of narcissism. It is an excessive pride in ourself as a whole person, instead of pride in a specific competence or a specific performance. Webb (2003: 162) shares this intuition of his subjects, seeing 'authentic pride' as tinged with humility, thereby avoiding the trap of hubris.

While there is research finding an undifferentiated conception of pride to be inversely related to destructive aggression in children (Ornstein 1997), Tangney's (1990) work that distinguishes good and bad pride (beta and alpha pride, respectively) has found healthy pride to be negatively associated with behavioural problems (see Ahmed 2001), and pathological pride to have a positive association. Baumeister (2001) has warned about thinking highly of ourselves in ways that are devoid of modest and realistic self-opinion. He proposes that violent pride has negative ramifications in damaging the balance of power of interpersonal relationships.

This chapter distinguishes narcissistic pride from humble pride. Narcissistic pride, we hypothesise, means putting ourselves above others by status assertion. Humble pride is about self-respect for what we have done and who we are. But it is quiet self-esteem; it is not vaunting pride that projects our sense of superiority over others. It is about respecting oneself as we respect others. With humble pride, superiority above others is not projected to others, because this is not the way the person with humble pride feels. They feel intrinsic pride in what they have accomplished and who they are, not extrinsic pride in being better than others around them. At its most pathological, narcissistic pride, in contrast, means being self-obsessed about one's superiority over others and indeed domination of weaker others. This evokes our hypothesis that narcissistic pride will explain bullying.

Bullying is often defined as an act of domination through an abuse of power (Einarssen and Skogstad 1996; WorkCover Corporation 2004). If narcissistic pride as a perception of self is about feeling dominant over others, then it should conduce to acts of domination. If humble pride, in contrast, involves feeling secure in the face of the strengths of others, then the person with humble pride has no need to affirm their self-esteem by acts of domination. If humble pride is quiet pride, it also does not provoke others to contest status with us. Vicious circles, where they bully us and we bully back, become less likely. The respect and humility that are definitional of humble pride are conducive to building relationships, while the disrespect and arrogance of narcissistic pride threaten social bonds.

II. EMOTIONALLY INTELLIGENT MANAGEMENT OF SOCIAL PROBLEMS

In criminology, the debate around shame and shaming has moved beyond opposed views that shame is a good or a bad thing. There is now considerable agreement that there is good and bad shame; the empirical and normative debates are about what distinguish them. Unfortunately, the debate on pride is not so mature. Delinquency scholars today, just as they did half a century ago, routinely throw a measure of self-esteem into their survey instruments. Their presupposition is that self-esteem is a healthy thing, that therefore must explain delinquency. The argument we develop implies that self-esteem is not necessarily healthy, and this explains why it has not proved a robust predictor of delinquency. When it does predict, higher self-esteem is sometimes associated with higher delinquency (Baumeister, Boden and Smart 1996). Measures of predominantly narcissistic self-esteem predict the latter result; measures dominated by items capturing humble self-esteem should reduce delinquency.

School pride is often presented to our children as unequivocally good. Little thought is given to how the hard core variants of this pride marginalise children who are branded failures according to the value system of the school. Albert Cohen (1955) taught criminology that delinquent subcultures in schools solve the status problem such children suffer. They solve it collectively, by taking pride in values that are the exact opposite of those of the dominant school culture: open expression of aggression instead of impulse control, contempt for property instead of respect for it, and so on. They become successes according to the values of the delinquent subculture, precisely because they are failures in the culture of the school.

National pride is also often viewed as an unmitigated virtue. But if we take vaunting pride in America as a nation with Christian traditions, this may marginalise Muslims. Vaunting pride in Nazi Germany as an Aryan nation marginalised Jews and Roma. So we see the biggest crimes of the past century—genocides, mass terrorism and counter-terrorist crimes against humanity such as Abu Ghraib and Guantanamo Bay—as explicable in terms of our theoretical framework. Narcissistic national pride conduces to humiliation of other peoples. This engenders defiance (Sherman 1993), which can be violent. It need not be, however: Valerie Braithwaite's current work distinguishes the 'dismissive defiance' of the drop-out from the 'resistant defiance' of the angry young man (Braithwaite 2009). Narcissistic white pride, according to the theory, risks both black despair/drop-out and black violence.

But before we become too vaunting about the macro explanatory potential of our theory of shame and pride management, we must do more humble micro work in a context where it is possible to refute or develop the theory on a large sample.

III. THE BULLYING PROBLEM

In recent years, increased incidents of workplace bullying (Hoel 2004) have attracted the attention of not only the media and the general public, but also organisations and researchers interested in investigation of the phenomenon. Despite its importance, scholarly work on bullying in the workplace is only beginning to accumulate, and theoretical propositions and empirical tests of these propositions are only beginning to emerge (Rayner 2004).

Bullying is a serious and continuing problem in many workplaces (see Di Martino, Hoel, and Cooper 2003; Einarsen et al 2003). Its negative effects on employees' well-being are widely documented. These include the risk of a variety of adjustment difficulties, including anxiety, depression, low self-esteem, post-traumatic stress and suicide (Mikkelsen and Einarsen, 2002; Nielsen, Matthiesen, and Einarsen 2004; Quine 1999). Organisational costs are also significant. Sickness, absence from work, high turnover, complaints resulting in lawsuits, and impaired job performance or job satisfaction have been reported in the literature (Glendinning 2001; Kinimäki, Elorainio, and Vahtera 2000; Voss, Floderus, and Diderichsen 2001).

Workplace bullying is a heterogeneous phenomenon, with different styles, intensities, contexts, motivations, and statuses of both the perpetrator and the victim. It ranges from a threat to one's professional status and social exclusion, to the threat of physical injury (Di Martini, Hoel and Cooper 2003; Einarsen et al 2003; for a review, see Rayner and Hoel 1997). Workplace bullying has been defined as negative behaviour arising from the deliberate intent to cause psychological and/or physical distress to others in the workplace (Leymann 1990; Einarssen and Skogstad 1996). It is characterised as persistent, offensive, abusive, or intimidating behaviour which can make the victim feel threatened, humiliated and/or stressed, affecting his/her health, safety, and well-being at work (Di Martini, Hoel and Cooper 2003). The experience of bullying also undermines the victim's self-confidence and dignity (Di Martini, Hoel and Cooper 2003).

The above studies that have demonstrated the adverse consequences of bullying in the workplace certainly have inspired further explorations of the factors that contribute to its occurrence. This work has suggested that adults who bully their co-workers are more likely to have authoritarian parents (eg, Randall 1997), to feel anxiety, aggression, and depression (eg, Quine 1999; Randall 1997), and to perceive hypocrisy in their workplaces (Braithwaite, Ahmed and Braithwaite 2008). Given that bullying is an abuse of power within human relationships (see WorkCover Corporation 2004), and relationships are shaped through emotions (Lazarus 1991), it is surprising that little research has been devoted to the extent to which emotions regulate bullying in the workplace.

IV. THE WORKPLACE BULLYING STUDY

This study aims to investigate the extent to which management of shame and pride affects bullying in the workplace. Bullying is a relational issue. Emotions of shame and pride are chosen for study in this context particularly because these two social emotions arise from viewing one's self from the standpoint of another (Scheff 1990). Both these emotions involve an evaluation of self, and are reflected in a manner of interacting with others. Therefore, they can speak to a deep civility and accountability in relation to everyday interactions in the workplace or of incivility and unaccountability.

We argue that unless these two emotions are managed adaptively in interpersonal interaction, neither of them will realise their full potential in preventing injustice such as bullying at work. Shame is often regarded as clearly linked to social alienation, whereas pride is about social solidarity. Contrary to this, however, we posit that both shame and pride can bring social solidarity on the one hand, and social alienation on the other. Which form they take largely depends on how those emotions are managed. For example, shame can create social solidarity if it is acknowledged. Shame can also create social alienation if it is not acknowledged but rather is displaced. Similarly, pride can create social solidarity if it is felt humbly. Pride can also lead to social alienation if it involves an excessive self-admiration, that is arrogance.

From this point of view, bullying can be explained as a function of an individual's shame displacement and narcissistic pride. According to the

	Shame	Pride
Constructive	**A** Shame acknowledgment (Social solidarity)	**C** Humble pride (Social solidarity)
Destructive	**B** Shame displacement (Social alienation)	**D** Narcissistic pride (Social alienation)

Figure 3.1: A conceptual model of relationship management through shame and pride

model in Figure 3.1, we need Cell A (shame acknowledgment) and Cell C (humble pride) to promote constructive interpersonal relationships. Because shame acknowledgment and humble pride build social bonds through respect, dignity and social inclusion, they should be conducive to less bullying and more justice in the workplace. In contrast, the disrespect and arrogance of Cell B (shame displacement) and Cell D (narcissistic pride) are destructive and thereby damage the social bond. Hence, they should be conducive to acts of social domination, such as bullying.

Neither the idea of shame nor pride is new in the literature. Psychologists and criminologists have long argued over the implications of shame and pride on human behaviour. The most significant contribution this study brings to our knowledge is the empirical examination of the implications of both shame and pride management on bullying at work.

A. Hypotheses

From the foregoing discussion, we derive six hypotheses in total.

> *Hypothesis 1*: pride as a domain of emotion consists of two inversely related pride management factors—narcissistic versus humble pride.

Then we hypothesise that shame acknowledgment reduces bullying, but shame displacement increases it (*Hypothesis 2*) and narcissistic pride may be positively associated with bullying, while humble pride is negatively associated (*Hypothesis 3*).

> *Hypothesis 2a*: shame acknowledgment is negatively related to workplace bullying;
> *Hypothesis 2b*: shame displacement is positively related to workplace bullying.
> *Hypothesis 3a*: narcissistic pride is positively related to workplace bullying;
> *Hypothesis 3b*: humble pride is negatively related to workplace bullying.

Finally, we expect that such pride management effects are robust and have explanatory power over and above the established effects of shame management (*Hypothesis 4*). While correlations confirm our expectation that humble pride is associated with shame acknowledgment (because acknowledging shame tends also to involve humility), and narcissistic pride is associated with shame displacement (because both involve an extrinsic preoccupation with putting others down to defend the self), we predict that pride management will have effects on bullying net of shame management effects.

Hypothesis 4: the pride management variables (narcissistic pride and humble pride) contribute to predicting workplace bullying, above and beyond the effect of shame management variables (shame acknowledgment and shame displacement).

B. Participants and procedure

Some 1500 questionnaires were distributed in workplaces in the large metropolis of Dhaka, Bangladesh, in 2002. A total of 824 completed questionnaires were returned from employees of various organisations (24 per cent from the government sector,[1] 20 per cent the semi-government sector,[2] and 56 per cent the private sector,[3] which is broadly representative of the formal Dhaka economy). Thirty-five per cent of the respondents were coded as lower status (eg, garment employees, clerical employees), 33 per cent as middle status (eg, school teachers, public servants who do not hold supervisory roles, support staff), and 32 per cent as higher status (eg, employees who hold supervisory and professional positions). Sixty-three per cent of the respondents were male, reflecting the disproportionate representation of men in the formal organisational economy of Bangladesh. The average age was 34.4 years. Sixty-eight per cent of respondents had had a university education. Even allowing for the fact that non-university

[1] This comprises of the departments and agencies fully controlled by the Bangladesh Government. The primary function of the government sector is to provide public services for the collective consumption of the community. Examples of government-owned departments are National Board of Revenue, Bangladesh Bank, Bangladesh Post Office, and Power Development Board.
[2] Organisations in this sector are operated by a board of directors appointed by the Bangladesh Government, and receive an annual subvention from the Government. Employers in the semi-government sector are private legal entities. The budget available for part of this sector is decided at central policy level, and thereafter the employers are responsible for pay and working conditions, and for the level of services provided to the employees. Examples of semi-government organisations in Bangladesh are University of Dhaka, Bangladesh Council for Scientific and Industrial Research (BCSIR), and Rural Electrification Board.
[3] This sector is a self-sustaining and non-government entity which aims to improve the effectiveness of social policies, programmes and community initiatives. Employees working in this sector are not entitled to privileges accorded to government employees. Most private organisations by and large have some sort of rules, usually partially based on local labour laws. However, some private organisations have their own rules and regulations governing all the conditions of payment and work. Mostly these are foreign investment entities or joint ventures where the foreign partner usually adopts its home country standards to an extent. Examples of private organisations are Grameen Cybernet, Southeast Bank Ltd, Bangladesh Centre for Advanced Studies, and most garment industries.

educated people in Bangladesh are more likely to be found in the rural and informal urban economies than in the formal organisational sector in the metropolis, there is a substantial bias for the survey to be more likely to be completed by more educated people. The average organisational tenure of respondents was 5.5 years and their average monthly salary was 19,576 taka (US$289.52), ranging from 400 taka (US$5.84) to 280,000 taka (US$4087.77). Such a wide range in income reflects the social and economic inequality existing in Bangladesh.

C. Measures

i. *Dependent Variable—Workplace Bullying*

Workplace bullying was assessed using Quine's (1999) measure, which was originally derived from the literature (eg, Adams 1992; Bassman 1992). In the measure, there were 20 kinds of bullying acts, representing the five categories signified by Rayner and Hoel (1997). The categories are: threat to professional status (sample item: persistent attempts to belittle and undermine your work), threat to personal standing (sample item: making inappropriate jokes about you), isolation (sample item: withholding necessary information from you), overwork (sample item: undue pressure to produce work), and destabilisation (sample item: shifting of goal posts without consulting you). Participants used a five-point rating scale (1 = never, 2 = on occasion, 3 = sometimes, 4 = mostly, and 5 = almost always) to indicate the extent to which they had targeted co-workers with any of the 20 tactics listed (for details on items and construction of the workplace bullying scale, see Appendix below).

ii. *Predictor Variables—Shame Management and Pride Management*

Shame management was measured through the Management Of Shame State-Shame Acknowledgment and Shame Displacement (MOSS-SASD) instrument. Originally, this was developed in the context of school bullying. Since then, the instrument has proved to be psychometrically valid and reliable (for details on psychometric properties of the MOSS-SASD instrument, see Ahmed 2001), and has provided the foundation for further research on rule violation.[4]

---

[4] See Ahmed and Braithwaite (2004[a]) and Morrison (2006) for support for the relationships between shame management and school bullying; see Braithwaite et al (2003) and Ahmed (2005, 2006) for support for the relationships from a follow-up study; see Ahmed and J Braithwaite (2005) for a replication of the relationship in a different cultural context; see Ahmed and Braithwaite (2004[b]) for application of shame management in the context of tax compliance.

MOSS-SASD is a scenario-based self-report measure. In the current study, the items were contextualised by using one of the most common incidents (threat to professional status) that occurs in the workplace. Respondents were asked: 'Suppose you just had voiced a "criticism of work and undervalued the efforts" of a co-worker in front of other staff, including subordinates of the co-worker. How likely is it that you would feel the following ...'.

Respondents were then presented with a list of 12 shame-related reactions. Participants used a five-point rating scale (1 = definitely not, 2 = unlikely, 3 = unsure, 4 = probably, 5 = definitely) to indicate the extent to which they felt they would have felt those shame reactions.

A confirmatory factor analysis (CFA) was performed to test the factor structure underlying the concept of 'shame'. Two conceptually meaningful factors were obtained: shame acknowledgment and shame displacement. The process of factor derivation including item details is given in the Appendix.

Following the CFA, six items were averaged to construct the shame acknowledgment scale (sample item: regretting what you have said). All these six items represented owning shame/guilt, whereby an individual acknowledges wrongdoing and seeks to put matters right. A high score on this scale indicates greater shame acknowledgment.

The second dimension of shame management is shame displacement, which comprises four items (sample item: angry with your co-workers). All these four items represented disowning shame/guilt by displacing it— blaming others. Displacement as disowning is not a new concept. Shame displacement has always been conceptualised as disowning shame by blaming others. We have made a very minor change to the wording here that we hope simplifies the communication. The four items were averaged to produce the shame displacement scale, where a high score indicates greater shame displacement.

Like shame management, pride management was assessed through a scenario-based self-report measure—the Management Of Pride State (MOPS; Cross National Restorative Justice Research Project, www.crj.anu. edu.au/crossnational.html). The MOPS was developed following a thorough review of the relevant literature (eg, Cherney, www.teambuildinginc. com/article_ai.htm; Fischer, Manstead, and Mosquera 1999; Raskin and Terry 1988; Webb 2003). The 22 items that were generated were contextualised using one of the most common incidents that occurs in the workplace. Respondents were asked to imagine that they had been successful in achieving an important task: 'Suppose that you were required (asked) to solve an old and difficult problem at your workplace. You solved it successfully. How likely is it that you would feel the following ...'.

Respondents were then presented with a list of 22 pride-related reactions. Participants used a five-point rating scale (1 = definitely not, 2 = unlikely,

3 = unsure, 4 = probably, 5 = definitely) to indicate the extent to which they would have felt those pride reactions.

A CFA was performed to test the conceptualisation of 'pride' which suggested two conceptually meaningful factors: narcissistic pride and humble pride. The factor derivation procedure including item details is given in the Appendix.

Suffice it for now to say that nine items (sample item: 'feel superior over your co-workers') were averaged to construct the narcissistic pride scale which represented hubris that is not tinged with humility. To construct the humble pride scale, seven items (sample item: 'respect the contribution of others to solving the problem') were averaged that represented one's feelings of pride about the achievement without having an inflated sense of the superiority of one's global self over co-workers.

iii. Control Variables

In previous studies on workplace bullying (for a review, see Rayner and Hoel 1997), gender, age, type of organisation, job status and income were all found to be somewhat important in explaining bullying. They are, therefore, included as control variables for the models to predict bullying in organisations.

The type of organisation was measured by asking: 'What best describes the job you do?' There were three response categories: government sector, semi-government sector, and private sector. Respondents' job status was measured by asking 'What kind of work do you do?' There were three response categories: lower-, middle- and higher-ranking positions. Finally, personal income was measured in taka per month.

D. Results—Outline

The results are reported in three parts. First, we evaluate the hypothesised factor structure of pride management items in the MOPS by using a CFA. Then we test for the correlations between predictor variables and the dependent variable. Finally, we test the multivariate effects of pride management and shame management on workplace bullying through a hierarchical regression analysis.

i. Confirmatory Factor Analysis (CFA)

In order to test the hypothesised two-factor model, we undertook the following two-step procedure (Byrne 2001): (a) separate one-factor congeneric modelling to develop a measurement model with an acceptable fit to the data before putting each factor into the structural equation model; and (b) CFA to test the structural model once an acceptable measurement model was developed.

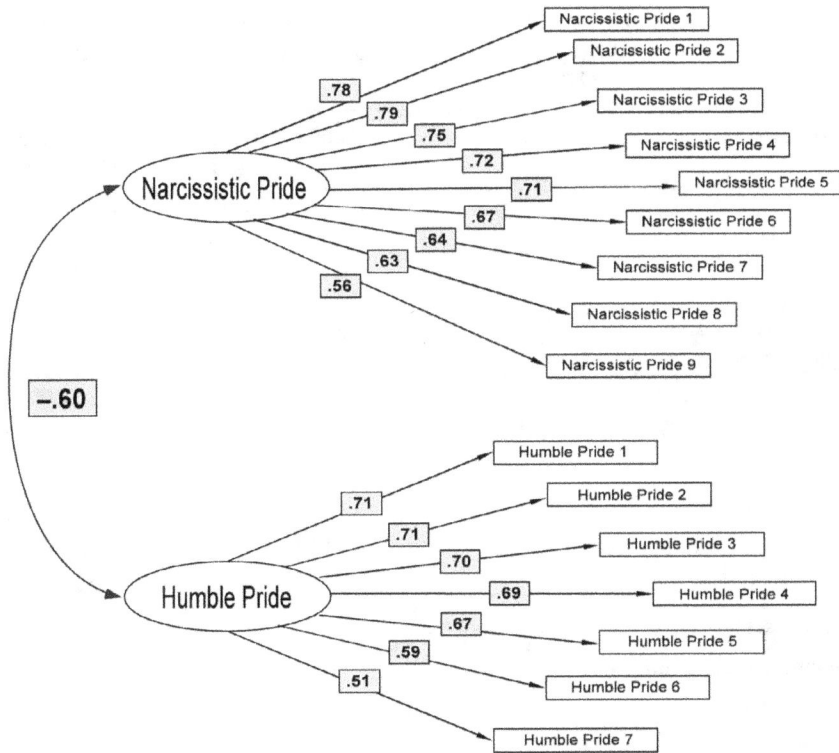

Figure 3.2: Final two-factor Pride management model. The circles designate latent constructs whereas the rectangles are the measured variables. Factor loadings are standardised (all p < .001). Titles of the measured variables should be read in conjunction with MOPS items in the Appendix. [χ^2 = 192.40 (df = 55), CFI = .98, IFI = .98, TLI = .96, GFI = .97 and RMSEA = .05]

The AMOS 4.0 program (Arbuckle and Wothke 1999) was used to perform these analyses. Model testing was done using the covariance matrices and a maximum likelihood estimation procedure. These are detailed in the Appendix.

Figure 3.2 displays the factor loadings of the final two-factor model. It also presents fit statistics of the model. As can be seen, all fit indices supported the hypothesised two-factor model (Hypothesis 1) as best accounting for the conceptualisation of pride management. The factors represented in the final model are narcissistic pride and humble pride.

ii. Correlational Analyses

Table 3.1 indicates that both shame management variables, shame acknowledgment and shame displacement, were significantly correlated

Table 3.1: Correlation coefficients (between bullying and predictor variables), and standardised beta coefficients from a hierarchical regression analysis in predicting workplace bullying (N = 728)

Variables	Correlations	Control Model	Shame Model	Shame and Pride Model
Gender	−.21[b]	−.20[b]	−.09[c]	−.08[c]
Age	.11[b]	−.01	−.02	−.04
Type of organisation[a]				
Type of organisation (government)		−.25[b]	−.11[c]	−.12[b]
Type of organisation (semi-government)		−.11[d]	−.04	−.04
Job status[a]				
Job status (low)		−.12[d]	−.10[d]	−.08
Job status (middle)		−.11[d]	−.03	−.03
Personal income	.21[b]	.14[c]	.04	.06
Shame acknowledgment	−.22[b]	–	−.18[b]	−.15[b]
Shame displacement	.66[b]	–	.61[b]	.44[b]
Narcissistic pride	.63[b]	–	–	.17[b]
Humble pride	−.50[b]	–	–	−.08[d]
Adj R square	na	.13	.45	.47

Notes
[a]These are indicator variables, and hence, an analysis of variance was performed to see their association with workplace bullying. The F value for 'Type of organisation' was 13.31 (p < .001) and for 'Job status' was 15.21 (p < .001) suggesting statistically significant associations.
[b]p < .001
[c]p < .01
[d]p < .05

with workplace bullying. Respondents who reported bullying co-workers were less likely to acknowledge their shame (r = −.22, p < .001) by admitting shame/guilt and making amends, and were more likely to displace shame (r = .66, p < .001) by blaming others and expressing anger at others. These findings support Hypotheses 2a and 2b.

Also as expected (Hypothesis 3a), narcissistic pride was positively related to bullying (r = .63, p < .001). Pride that was vaunting, associated with a feeling of dominance over co-workers, was correlated with higher bullying in the workplace.

As for humble pride, the obtained relationship with bullying was also as predicted in Hypothesis 3b. Humble pride was strongly and negatively related to bullying (r = −.50, p < .001). Employees who took a pride in their achievements that was tinged with humility and a sense of respect for the capabilities of others were less likely to engage in bullying.

2. Prior to conducting the hierarchical regression analysis, initial analyses explored multicollinearity issues. Although the intercorrelations between shame displacement and narcissistic pride were strong (r = .79, p < .001), multicollinearity did not appear to be of major concern. The condition index and tolerance values were all within the acceptable range. Most importantly, our major interest in this article is on the independent effects of pride management variables—narcissistic pride and humble pride. Eliminating variables or creating a single construct to reduce multicollinearity is thus not reasonable options for substantive reasons.

iii. Ordinary Least Square Regression Analysis

An OLS regression analysis was performed to test for the contribution of pride management variables (narcissistic pride and humble pride) above and beyond the effects of shame management variables (shame acknowledgment and shame displacement) as specified in Hypothesis 4 (see Table 3.1).

The variables were entered in three steps. First, five control variables were included in the equation (Control Model). These were respondents' gender, age, type of organisation, job status, and income. Both type of organisation and job status were entered as indicator variables. For type of organisation, government and semi-government types were entered simultaneously leaving out the private type of organisation for comparison. Similarly, for job status, lower and middle status were entered as indicator variables simultaneously leaving out the upper status for comparison.

As can be seen from the 'Control Model', bullying was more prevalent among males. It was also common among private sector employees. Workers with higher job status and higher income also reported participating in higher rates of bullying of their co-workers. Altogether, this set of variables accounted for 13 per cent of the variance in the bullying measure.

In the next step, the shame management variables were entered (see Shame Model). Both shame acknowledgment and shame displacement emerged as significant predictors of bullying (β = −.18, p < .001; β = .61, p < .001, respectively), explaining an additional 32 per cent of the variance in the outcome.

On the third step, the pride management variables were added (see Shame and Pride Model). Narcissistic pride (β = .17, p < .001) significantly increased bullying and humble pride (β = −.08, p < .05) reduced it. Together, the pride management variables accounted for an additional 2 per cent of the variance in workplace bullying.

These results, therefore, show moderate support for Hypothesis 4—pride management variables have a contribution to make above and beyond shame management variables—though the additional contribution is modest. It is of note that adding the pride management variables did not cause a marked change in the contribution of the shame management variables. The final model accounted for a total of 47 per cent of the variance in bullying in the workplace.

V. DISCUSSION

To remedy the neglect of the role of the emotions in explaining workplace bullying, this research adopted an earlier model of shame management, and offered a new conceptual model of pride management. A measurement scale, MOPS, was developed from a thorough literature review to assess how people manage their feelings of pride in the workplace. Then, a CFA was conducted to validate the construct of pride management.

Findings from the CFA have provided strong evidence that MOPS is a psychometrically valid and reliable instrument. Findings have confirmed the two-factor structure (narcissistic pride and humble pride) of the pride management construct. The absence of cross-loadings of items and the existence of significant negative inter-factor correlation indicate that pride management as measured by MOPS reflects two distinguishable domains as consistent with our conceptualisation.

The regression analysis reveals that both shame and pride management variables make significant independent contributions to the explanation of workplace bullying. The integrated shame management/pride management model has formidable explanatory power. While effects of both pride management variables are clearly significant, they do not add hugely to the explanatory power of the shame management model. Obversely, if we put the pride management variables into the regression equation first, the shame management variables add an extra 4 per cent to the variance in workplace bullying already explained by the controls and the pride management variables.

The question that then arises is whether shame management or pride management offers the better emotional intelligence account of bullying prevention. Given the high intercorrelations among the shame and pride management variables, an appealing choice is not to choose between shame management and pride management as a preferred theoretical framework. Some similar skills seem to be involved in both constructive shame management (shame acknowledgment) and healthy pride management (humble pride). They are skills of humility and respect of self and others.[5] Such skills

---

[5] There is evidence that respectful treatment in organisations nurtures pride in membership of those organisations (Tyler, Degoey and Smith 1996), and that disrespectful treatment such as stigmatisation is associated with shame displacement and respectful treatment with shame acknowledgment (Shin 2006).

sustain a healthy, socially interdependent self. This returns us to Scheff and Retzinger's (1991) theoretical framework that shame is the central emotion when social bonds are threatened, pride the central emotion when bonds of solidarity are strengthened.

Shame management and pride management are both about healthy management of our social bonds. Emotionally intelligent people manage shame reintegratively so that connections with others are not permanently severed; they manage pride in being a certain kind of person in a way that protects others from feeling exclusion because they are not that kind of person. They do not externalise shame in a way that creates exclusion, nor do they vaunt inclusionary pride in a way that creates feelings of exclusion among others. Communication with others about the experience of shame and pride is certainly necessary, desirable and hard to avoid. But both can be communicated quietly, without bombast, respectfully, empathically. Humility in the way we experience and communicate shame and pride averts the feeling in others that we are stripping them of honour, humiliating them. Our humility averts their humiliation. This is what we mean by suggesting that humility and respect hold the key to emotionally intelligent management of both shame and pride.

While acknowledging shame/guilt can mitigate the threatened bond and restore social solidarity, displacing shame can escalate a vengeful sense of bitterness in relationships, and create alienation. Similarly, pride can create alienation, if communication is conducted with narcissistic arrogance and disrespect. It can, however, strengthen interpersonal relationships if communication consolidates quiet honour among those sharing in the pride without loudly dishonouring those who do not.

When we learn how to manage shame well, we learn something about how to manage pride well, and vice versa. Nevertheless, healthy pride management has positive effects on our relationships with others over and above the positive effects of healthy shame management, and constructive shame management has good effects on our relationships with others over and above the effects of pride management. The bullying results reported here are consistent with the interpretation that shame and pride management are an emotional intelligence package that together is somewhat more than the sum of its parts. The most important implication about the model and findings concerns a different understanding of workplace bullying that portrays bullying as an outcome of non-adaptive management of shame (low shame acknowledgment but high shame displacement) and pride (low humble pride but high narcissistic pride). By teaching our children and employees, or perhaps more importantly by displaying in our own interactions with them, the values of humility and respect for self and others, we may be simultaneously teaching them the underlying principles of both healthy pride management and healthy shame management. Teaching emotional intelligence is therefore suggested as a promising approach to workplace bullying (see Sheehan 1999).

A more sophisticated design than we have here would be required to test this dynamic account of the relationship between the display of emotional intelligence and bullying prevention. Further progress on the questions raised will require panel designs where changes in behaviour can be observed following shame and pride management interventions, or, as suggested in the last paragraph, educative interventions to display values like humility, respect for self and others—values that are fundamental to healthy management of both shame and pride. For the moment, all we have shown is that pride management has an importance very comparable to shame management, and effects on bullying over and above shame management. If the theory of pride management and bullying is correct, it may have macro implications beyond the micro context of workplace relationships studied here. These results come from an Islamic society. Muslim people, sensitised by Islamic teaching on vaunting pride as a vice, see an association between hubris and bullying, in their view of the world. Our data suggest that this perception is based on a realistic understanding of patterns of bullying internal to a Muslim society. Americans in particular need to be careful that the national pride they have in greater measure than people of any other country (Evans and Kelly 2002)[6] is humble pride, quiet pride—not bombastic, vaunting pride. Americans are exceptional in the extent to which they view pride positively and in the way they see pride as something to wear on the national shoulder. If Americans are seen in the Muslim world as vaunting in their national pride, equally they may be more prone to be seen as bullies. And if Western pride is genuinely humble, the West in general may indeed be less likely to be seen as a bully in its interactions with other people. These are at least hypotheses that the results suggest are worthy of future exploration, both within the Muslim world and in the West.

We hypothesise that Muslim teaching on the dangers of vaunting pride is relevant not only in Muslim societies but to all societies. History's winners are no less vulnerable to its truth; they are, however, less willing to see it. The reason for this is that hubris can be gratifying to human beings who win. This is why bad pride can help win elections. In the short term, many vices such as gluttony, lust, greed and sloth, like hubris, supply short-term gratification. Unless they are tempered by virtues such as kindness, respect, humility and justice itself, they can inflict deep destruction and injustice upon human societies. This is why we persist in the theoretical perspective that virtuous shame and pride management are topics of profound importance for the social sciences and for humanity.

---

[6] See also Sommers (1984) on pride being viewed more negatively in some cultures (eg, Chinese) than others (eg, American).

APPENDIX

Workplace Bullying

The *Threat to professional status* scale (M = 1.91; SD = 1.20; alpha = .93) items:

(1) persistent attempts to belittle and undermine your work;
(2) persistent and unjustified criticism and monitoring of your work;
(3) persistent attempts to humiliate you in front of colleagues;
(4) intimidatory use of discipline or competence procedures.[7]

The *Threat to personal standing* scale (M = 1.82; SD = .91; alpha = .78) items:

(1) undermining your personal integrity;
(2) destructive sarcasm with you;
(3) verbal threats to you;
(4) making inappropriate jokes about you;
(5) persistently teasing you;
(6) threat for physical violence to you;
(7) threat of violence to your property.

The *Isolation* scale (M = 1.77; SD = 1.24; alpha = .94) items:

(1) withholding necessary information from you;
(2) ignoring/excluding; and
(3) unreasonable refusal of applications for leave/training/promotion.

The *Overwork* scale[8] (M = 2.25; SD = 1.13; alpha = .26) items:

(1) undue pressure to produce work; and
(2) setting of impossible deadlines.

The *Destabilisation* scale (M = 1.71; SD = 1.01; alpha = .77) items:

(1) shifting of goal posts without consulting you;
(2) constant undervaluing of your efforts;
(3) persistent attempts to demoralise you; and
(4) removal of areas of responsibility without consultation.

---

[7] This item was dropped, as it led to low alpha reliability of the scale.
[8] This scale was dropped from the study due to low alpha reliability.

Workplace Bullying Scale Construction:

Workplace bullying scale items in the respective categories (see above) were significantly and positively inter-correlated (ranged from .46 to .65, p < .001), and hence, responses were averaged to produce the subscale scores for each participant. Because there were no hypotheses specific to any one bullying form, responses on these subscales (correlations between subscales ranged from r = .47 to r = .81, p < .001) were averaged to produce an aggregated score of workplace bullying (M = 1.80, SD = .93). A higher score indicates greater involvement in bullying in the workplace.

Some might suggest that because of the nature of the bullying variable, using logarithmic/square-root transformations/logistic regression would be appropriate. However, in circumstances where the bullying measure is not skewed, OLS captures more information on variation than logistic regression, and therefore, provides the superior method of analysis. Because the bullying variable in this study was not skewed (1.01), we preferred to use the OLS regression analytical method.

Shame Management

While adapting the MOSS-SASD instrument in the workplace bullying context, the wording of some of the items measuring Shame Acknowledgment and Shame Displacement was modified to suit adult respondents and the workplace context better. In addition, some items were taken from Harris (2001) to extend the measure of Shame Acknowledgment. To obtain a comparable Bengali translation of the MOSS-SASD, the items which have previously been used in our studies were translated and back-translated by a bilingual scholar who was native to the region of Bangladesh where the study was conducted. The translations were then reviewed for accuracy and cultural appropriateness by another bilingual scholar who is also native to the region. Both these scholars had excellent English knowledge and experience with psychological terminology.

A confirmatory factor analysis (CFA) was used to test the hypothesised two-factor model with the Bengali version of the MOSS-SASD. Prior to performing the CFA, two separate one-factor congeneric modellings were completed (one for shame acknowledgment, the other for shame displacement). All these analyses were performed using the AMOS (Analysis of Moment Structures) 4.0 program (Arbuckle and Wothke 1999) with the covariance matrices and a maximum likelihood estimation procedure.

Six items loaded significantly on the shame acknowledgment factor and four loaded significantly on the shame displacement factor. Because of lower squared multiple correlations (less than .30), that is the amount of explained variance, one item ('feel angry with myself') from the shame acknowledgment factor was excluded. Another item ('pretend that nothing was happening') was not included in the CFA because it represents shame avoidance (for details on shame avoidance, see Ahmed, 2006; Ahmed and Braithwaite, 2005). The final standardised regression weight estimates demonstrated excellent convergent validity of the two factors, meaning items that are theoretically supposed to be highly interrelated with the factor are highly interrelated in the data.

MOSS-SASD Scenario and Question Items to Measure Shame Acknowledgment and Shame Displacement

MOSS-SASD Scenario

Suppose you just had voiced a 'criticism of work and undervalued the efforts' of a co-worker in front of other staff, including subordinates of the co-worker. How likely is it that you would feel the following ...

MOSS-SASD Items (Retained in the Final Scale)

Shame Acknowledgment

1. ashamed of yourself
2. you had let down your co-workers
3. regretting what you have said
4. concerned to put matters right and put it behind you
5. you have harmed your professional reputation
6. feel hesitant to come at the office

Scale mean = 2.28 (SD = .83, alpha = .80)

Shame Displacement

1. angry with your co-workers
2. unable to decide, in your mind, whether or not you had done the wrong thing;
3. placing the blame somewhere else for what you said
4. you wanted to get even with someone else

Scale mean = 2.29 (SD = 1.13, alpha = .86)

Pride Management

One-Factor Congeneric Modelling:

Two separate one-factor congeneric modellings were done to test the adequacy of the measurement models for narcissistic pride and humble pride. Twelve items loaded significantly on the narcissistic pride factor and eight items significantly on the humble pride factor.[9] Because of lower squared multiple correlations, three items ('having compliments from everyone', 'yourself very powerful', and 'rule the world to make it a much better place') from the narcissistic pride factor, and one item ('I could have made a mistake') from the humble pride factor, were excluded. Item standardised regression weight estimates demonstrate excellent convergent validity of the two factors—narcissistic pride with nine items, humble pride with seven items. This is an important finding which suggests that unidimensionality for both factors was evidenced by moderate to high range standardised loadings (p < .001) on their intended factors.

Confirmatory Factor Analysis

In this analysis, each item is restricted to load on its prespecified factor, with the two factors allowed to correlate freely. The chi-square for this model is significant (χ^2 = 192.40, df = 55, p <.001). Because the chi-square statistic is over-sensitive to sample size, we also assess additional fit indices: the Comparative Fit Index (CFI), the Incremental Fit Index (IFI), the Tucker-Lewis Fit Index (TLI), the Goodness-of-Fit Index (GFI), and Root Mean-Square Error of Approximation (RMSEA).[10] As is evident from Figure 3.2, the CFI, IFI, TLI, GFI and RMSEA of this model are .98, .98, .96, .97, and .05 respectively. Hence, despite the significant chi-square, the fit indices reveal that the final structural model is an excellent fit to the data.

MOPS Scenario and Items to Measure Narcissistic Pride and Humble Pride

MOPS Scenario

Suppose that you were required (asked) to solve an old and difficult problem at your workplace. You solved it successfully. How likely is it that you would feel the following...

---

[9] Prior to performing one-factor congeneric modelling, two items were excluded from consideration because it was advised that the items represent an extrovert personality instead of a context-based pride reaction. The advice was sought from two experts who had extraordinary experience with psychological scaling. The excluded items are: (1) feel like increasing social encounters; and (2) feel like telling everyone about your achievement. Therefore, 12 items were retained for measuring narcissistic pride whereas eight items were retained for humble pride.

[10] The CFI and RMSEA are generally the preferred indices for assessing adequacy of model fit (Byrne 2001; Loehlin 1998). Values greater than .95 for CFI, IFI, TLI, and GFI are considered to indicate good model fit (Byrne 2001; Hu and Bentler 1999; Loehlin 1998). An RMSEA of .05 or less is suggested as an indicator of acceptable fit (Arbuckle and Wothke 1999; Bollen 1989).

MOPS Items (Retained in the Final Scale)

Narcissistic Pride

1. good about yourself
2. superior over your co-workers
3. dominant over your co-workers
4. admiration from your co-workers
5. you are a very talented person
6. an increased sense of self-confidence
7. you had authority over your co-workers
8. putting down your co-workers
9. Putting your needs over your co-workers' needs

Scale mean = 2.32 (SD = 1.12, alpha = .91)

Humble Pride

1. show humility in all respects
2. respect the contribution of others to solving the problem
3. your co-workers could have solved the problem as well
4. proud of yourself without being arrogant
5. respect all co-workers irrespective of their status
6. considerate to your co-workers' comments on this solution
7. a sense of achievement without being arrogant

Scale mean = 3.05 (SD = 1.00, alpha = .86)

REFERENCES

Adams, A (1992) Bullying at work: how to confront and overcome it (London, Virago).
Ahmed, E (2001) 'Shame management: Regulating bullying' in E Ahmed, N Harris, J Braithwaite and V Braithwaite (eds), Shame Management through Reintegration (Cambridge, Cambridge University Press) 211–314.
—— (2005) 'Patterns of shame management and bullying status' in R De Vitto and C Slakmon (eds), Restorative Justice (Brazilian Ministry of Justice, in collaboration with the United Nations Development Programme) 321–48.
—— (2006) 'Understanding bullying from a shame management perspective: Findings from a three-year follow-up study' 23(2) Educational and Child Psychology 26–40.
—— and Braithwaite, J (2005) 'Shaming, shame, forgiveness and bullying' 38(3) Australian and New Zealand Journal of Criminology 298–323.
—— and Braithwaite, V (2005) 'A need for emotionally intelligent policy: linking tax evasion with higher education funding' 10 Legal and Criminological Psychology 1–19.

Ahmed, E and Braithwaite, V (2004[a]) '"What? Me ashamed?": Shame management and bullying' 41(3) Journal of Research in Crime and Delinquency 269–94.

—— (2004[b]) 'When tax collectors become collectors for child support and student loans: Jeopardizing or protecting the revenue base?' 3 Kyklos 303–26.

Ahmed, E, Harris, N, Braithwaite, J and Braithwaite, V (2001) Shame Management Through Reintegration (Cambridge, Cambridge University Press).

Arbuckle, J and Wothke, W (1999) Amos 4.0 User's Guide (Illinois, SPSS).

Bassman, E (1992) Abuse in the Workplace. (New York, Quorum Books).

Baumeister, RF (2001) 'Violent Pride' 284(4) Scientific American 96–101.

——, Boden, JM and Smart, L (1996) 'Relation of threatened egotism to violence and aggression: the dark side of high self-esteem' 103(1) Psychological Review 5–33.

Bollen, KA (1989) *Structural Equations with Latent Variables* (New York, Wiley).

Bozdogan, H (1987) 'Model selection and Akaike's information criterion (AIC): The general theory and its analytical extensions' 52 *Psychometrika* 345–70.

Braithwaite, J (1989) *Crime, Shame and Reintegration* (Cambridge, Cambridge University Press).

Braithwaite, V (2009) *Defiance in Taxation and Governance: Resisting and Dismissing Authority in a Democracy* (Cheltenham, UK and Northampton, USA, Edward Elgar).

—— Ahmed, E and Braithwaite, J (2008) 'Workplace Bullying and Victimization: The Influence of Organizational Context, Shame and Pride'. 13(2) *International Journal of Organisational Behaviour* 71–94.

Braithwaite, V, Ahmed, E, Morrison, B and Reinhart, M (2003) 'Researching the prospects for restorative justice practice in schools: The "Life at School Survey" 1996–9' in L Walgrave (ed), *Repositioning the Restorative Justice: Restorative Justice, Criminal Justice and Social Context* (Cullompton, Willan Publishing).

Browne, MW and Crudeck, R (1993) 'Alternative ways of assessing model fit' in KA Bollen and JS Long (eds), *Testing Structural Equations Models* (Newbury Park, Sage).

Byrne, BM (2001) *Structural Equation Modeling with AMOS: Basic Concepts, Applications, and Programming* (Mahwah, Erlbaum).

Cherney, JK 'Appreciative Teambuilding: Creating a Climate for Great Collaboration'. www.teambuildinginc.com/article_ai.htm.

Cohen, AK (1955) *Delinquent Boys: The Culture of the Gang* (Glencoe, Free Press).

Di Martino, V, Hoel, H and Cooper, CL (2003) *Preventing Violence and Harassment in the Workplace* (Dublin, European Foundation for the Improvement of Living and Working Conditions).

Einarsen, SE, Hoel, H, Zapf, D and Cooper, CL (2003) *Bullying and Emotional Abuse in the Workplace. International Perspectives in Research and Practice* (London, Taylor & Francis) 3–30.

Einarsen, S and Skogstad, A (1996) 'Epidemiological findings of bullying' 5(2) *European Work and Organizational Psychologist* 185–201.

Evans, M and Kelly, J (2002) 'National pride in the developed world: Survey data from 24 nations' 14(3) *International Journal of Public Opinion Research* 303–38.

Fischer, AH, Manstead, ASR and Rodriguez Mosquera, PM (1999) 'The role of honour-related versus individualistic values in conceptualizing pride, shame and anger: Spanish and Dutch cultural prototypes' 13 *Cognition and Emotion* 149–79.

Fischer, KW and Tangney, JP (1995) 'Self-conscious emotions and the affect revolution: Framework and overview' in JP Tangney and KW Fischer (eds), *Self-Conscious Emotions: The Psychology of Shame, Guilt, Embarrassment, and Pride* (New York, Guilford) 3–22.

Frijda, NH and Mesquita, B (1994) 'The social roles and functions of emotions' in S Kitayama and HR Markus (eds), *Emotion and Culture* (Washington, American Psychological Association) 51–87.

Gilligan, J (1997) *Violence: Reflections on a National Epidemic* (New York, Vintage Books).

Glendinning, P (2001) 'Workplace bullying: Curing the cancer of the American workplace' 30(3) *Public Personnel Management* 269–86.

Harris, N (2001) 'Part II. Shaming and shame: regulating drink driving' in E Ahmed, N Harris, J Braithwaite and V Braithwaite, (eds) *Shame Management Through Reintegration* (Melbourne, Cambridge University Press).

Hoel, H (2004) 'Violence and harassment in European workplaces: trends and political responses'. Paper presented at the Fourth International Conference on Bullying and Harassment in the Workplace, Bergen.

Hu, L and Bentler, PM (1999) 'Cutoff criteria for fit indexes in covariance structure analysis: Conventional criteria versus new alternatives' 6 *Structural Equation Modeling* 1–55.

Keltner, D (1995) 'The signs of appeasement: Evidence for the distinct displays of embarrassment, amusement, and shame' 68 *Journal of Personality and Social Psychology*, 441–54.

Kinimäki, M, Elorainio, M and Vahtera, J (2000) 'Workplace bullying and sickness absence in hospital staff' 57 *Occupational and Environmental Medicine* 656–60.

Kline, RB (1998) *Principles and Practice of Structural Equation Modeling.* (New York, Guilford).

Lazarus, RS (1991) *Emotion and Adaptation* (New York, Oxford University Press).

Lewis, HB (1971) *Shame and Guilt in Neurosis* (New York, International Universities Press).

Leymann, H (1990) 'Mobbing and psychological terror at workplaces' 5 *Violence and Victims* 119–26.

Loehlin, JC (1998) *Latent Variable Models: An Introduction to Factor, Path, and Structural Analysis* (Mahwah Erlbaum).

Maruyama, GM (1998) *Basics of Structural Equation Modeling* (Thousand Oaks, Sage).

Mikkelsen, EG and Einarsen, S (2002) 'Basic assumptions and post-traumatic stress among victims of bullying at work' 11(1) *European Journal of Work and Organizational Psychology* 87–111.

Morrison, B (2006) 'School bullying and restorative justice: Towards a theoretical understanding of the role of respect, pride and shame' in B Morrison and E Ahmed (eds), *Journal of Social Issues*, a special issue on Restorative Justice and Civil Society.

—— (2007) *Restoring safe school communities,* (Sydney, Federation Press).

Niedl, K (1995) *Mobbing/bullying am Arbeitsplatz* (Munich, Rainer Hampp Verlag).

Nielsen, MB, Matthiesen, SB and Einarsen, S (2004) 'When the bully is a leader: The relationship between destructive leaders and symptoms of posttraumatic stress disorder among victims of workplace bullying'. Paper presented at the Fourth International Conference on Bullying and Harrassment in the Workplace, Bergen.

Ornstein, A (1997) 'A developmental perspective on the sense of power, self-esteem, and destructive aggression' 25 *Annual of Psychoanalysis* 145–54.

Quine, L (1999) 'Workplace bullying in NHS community trust: staff questionnaire survey' 318 *British Medical Journal* 228–32.

Randall, PE (1997) *Adult Bullying: Perpetrators and Victims* (London, Routledge).

Raskin, R and Terry, H (1988) 'A principle-components analysis of the Narcissistic Personality Inventory and further evidence of its construct validity' 54 *Journal of Personality and Social Psychology* 890–902.

Rayner, C (2004) 'The boundaries of bullying at work'. Paper presented at the Fourth International Conference on Bullying and Harrassment in the Workplace, Bergen.

—— and Hoel, H (1997) 'A summary review of literature relating to workplace bullying' 7 *Journal of Community and Applied Social Psychology* 181–91.

Retzinger, S (1991) 'Violent Emotions: Shame and Rage in Marital Quarrels'. Newbury Park, CA: Sage.

—— (1996) 'Shame and the social bond' in D Parker, R Dalziel and I Wright (eds) *Shame and the Modern Self* (Victoria, Australian Scholarly Publishing) 6–20.

Scheff, TJ (1990) 'Socialization of emotions: pride and shame as causal agents'in TD Kemper (ed) *Research Agendas in the Sociology of Emotions* (Albany, State University of New York Press).

—— and Retzinger, SM (1991) *Emotions and Violence: Shame and Rage in Destructive Conflicts.* (Lexington, Lexington Books/DC Heath).

Sheehan, M (1999) 'Workplace bullying: Responding with some emotional intelligence' 20(1/2) *International Journal of Manpower* 57–66.

Sherman, L (1993) 'Defiance, deterrence and irrelevance: A theory of the criminal sanction' 30 *Journal of Research in Crime and Delinquency* 445–73.

Shin, HH (2006) 'Workplace practice and shame management' PhD dissertation, Australian National University.

Sommers, S (1984) 'Adults evaluating their emotions: A cross-cultural perspective' in CZ Malatesta and C Izard (eds), *Emotions in Adult Development* (Beverly Hills, Sage) 319–38.

Tangney, JP (1990) 'Assessing individual differences in proneness to shame and guilt: Development of the self-conscious affect and attribution inventory' 59 *Journal of Personality and Social Psychology* 102–11.

Tyler, TR, Degoey, P and Smith, H (1996) 'Understanding why the justice of group procedures matters: A test of the psychological dynamics of the group-value model' 70(5) *Journal of Personality and Social Psychology* 913–30.

Voss, M, Floderus, B and Diderichsen, F (2001) 'Physical, psychosocial, and organizational factors relative to sickness absence: a study based on Sweden Post' 58(3) *Occupational and Environmental Medicine* 178—84.

Webb, T (2003) 'Towards a mature shame culture: theoretical and practical tools for personal and social growth' Phd dissertation, University Of Western Sydney, Australia.

WorkCover Corporation (2004) 'Workplace Bullying'. www.workcover.com/ftp/documents/aeworkplacebullying.pdf.

4

The Sensual Dynamics of Processes of Personal Reform: Desistance From Crime and the Role of Emotions

ADAM CALVERLEY AND STEPHEN FARRALL

I. INTRODUCTION: GETTING EMOTIONAL

ACCORDING TO STANKO (2002: 367), 'criminology, as a discipline, is seeped in the emotionality of its subject matter and the emotions of its subjects'. Indeed, emotions are found everywhere when study- ing crime. This is essentially because people view and experience crime *emotionally*. Furthermore, as Stanko points out, academic criminologists are not exempt from similar subjective forces themselves. Their debates seethe with outrage and they cannot take a neutral stance when asking: 'What is crime?', and 'Why are some crimes more dangerous than others?' It is, therefore surprising that, despite this ubiquity of emotion, the study of emotions has remained largely absent from criminology. This was high- lighted by de Haan and Loader in a recent special issue of *Theoretical Criminology* that sought to address some of the gaps in the literature and provoke debate on the subject. While the contributors focused their atten- tion on the emotions concerned with the social censure of crime, such as those underpinning the law (Barbarlet 2002) and the criminal justice system (Karstedt 2002; van Stokkom 2000), little further light was shed on the emotions or feelings surrounding those who have been involved in crime but have since ceased, or are (at least) beginning to cease from being so.

This is the case too for other studies that have specifically focused on the role played by emotions and crime in terms of their relationship to the offender. Katz argues that in order to seriously address the tricky question of why individuals, who for the most part of their life have not committed crime, suddenly feel driven and propelled to do so, we need to 'under- stand the emergence of distinctive sensual dynamics' (1988: 4) that take place in that moment. Through his study of largely secondary sources, he draws attention to the foreground of action—ie the personal attractions of crime for its participants, what they expect to gain and how they actually feel when doing it—rather than the background 'reasons' favoured by traditional theories of crime. Through a phenomenological approach, Katz highlights the symbolic meanings that criminals give their actions and the actions of others, and argues that their emotions construct and justify these meanings. Their emotions are not just the by-products of criminality, but are in fact causal factors that drive and sustain crime: the sneaky thrill of the petty thief, the kudos of the 'walk' for members of male gangs, the power of the 'badass' stick-up, the thrill of carrying out more and more audacious crimes and getting away with it. As much as this explanation of the role emotions and feelings play in explaining how individuals are 'seduced' into crime is welcome, it leaves, for us, one major question unanswered: how are they 'seduced out' of crime? Why do almost all criminals over their lifetime eventually find that the incentives of danger and thrill cease to be sufficiently desirable to keep them involved in crime? What are the feelings experienced as people leave crime behind them? How do these feelings help them make sense of 'who' they are becoming and how far they have 'travelled'?

In this essay we take a broad-brush approach to the emotions which people report when they stop offending. We are keen to outline not just the emotions, but the feelings, aspirations and experiences that are associated with such emotions. In this respect we attempt to build an understanding of the sensual dynamics of desistance by focusing on the sensual aspects of desistance, as opposed to the more structural aspects associated with desistance, such as employment, marriage, child-rearing and so on. Of course, the two are closely intertwined, as we shall see below. We deliberately refrain from a discussion of which experiences count as 'a feeling' and which 'an emotion'. Often these are too closely entwined for rigid lines of demarcation to be drawn, and this is not the task we have set ourselves.

The remainder of this chapter is constructed as follows. First we will outline our sample, before going on to deal with various technical matters. Following from this, in the main section, we will outline the phases of what we have called the emotional trajectory of desistance. However, this is a slightly misleading title, as we are as concerned with feelings and other sensual matters as we are with emotions. The first phase of our schema is characterised by early hopes for a new life, for example. The next phase (the intermediate phase) is concerned with the feelings brought about by reminiscences of the past and of their actions in the past. The penultimate phase is concerned with feelings of shame and guilt; however, we take two explicit detours at this point, to consider two other feelings which came out strongly in the penultimate phase: trust and pride. Our final phase—normalcy—ends the main section of our essay. We close our contribution with a conclusion which tackles future directions research in this area may wish to take.

II. SAMPLE AND METHODOLOGY

Our present sample is based on a five-year follow-up of a study originally reported in Farrall (2002). In all, some 199 probationers and their supervising officers were recruited into the original sample. The methodology built upon that employed in an earlier study of recidivism among prison inmates who had recently returned to the community (Burnett 1992). Probationers aged 17–35 years old and who were starting probation or combination orders of 6–24 months' duration between the start of October 1997 and the end of March 1998 were eligible for inclusion in the study (see Farrall 2002 and Farrall and Calverley 2006). In September 2003 we commenced on a follow-up of 51 members of the original sample. These interviews, which focused on a range of topics (see Farrall and Calverley 2006) contained a series of questions about how our sample members felt (both at the time of the interview and previously) about their lives and their offending careers. It is these answers that we report herein.

The operationalisation of desistance used herein placed an emphasis on gradual processes. Such an operationalisation both better captures the true nature of desistance from crime, in which lulls in offending are common, and provides a schema in which reductions in offence severity or frequency can be interpreted as the emergence of desistance. This entailed a careful reading of each respondent's reports of their offending at each interview (there were up to four interviews, this being a follow-up study). The desisters in our sample were then rank-ordered in terms of how far they had 'travelled' towards a total cessation of criminal activity (see Figure 4.1, p 100 and discussion below).

III. THE EMOTIONAL TRAJECTORIES OF DESISTANCE

Our schema of the emotional trajectories of desistance is an attempt to classify the sorts of emotions and feelings that our respondents reported having experienced and the approximate point in the process of desisting that they experienced them. This entailed ordering each of our desisters along one continuum, with the recently desisted (ie those who had only recently embarked upon the road to desistance) at one end, and those who had ceased offending several years previously at the other. We then coded each respondent's description of their desistance in terms of the emotions that they said they had felt. All of the emotions and feelings reported to us were reported during the fourth sweep of interviewing; however in some cases these reports refer to earlier episodes. From our schema, four rough 'phases' emerged. It is clear from Figure 4.1 (p 100) that the emotions and feelings which we report could occur for some individuals at any stage in the process of desisting; however, some do appear to coalesce together, and this is the basis of our rough phases. We are not automatically suggesting that there are four emotional phases which any desister 'needs' to go through in order to successfully desist (for each process has its own unique facets). Rather, our use of the term 'phases' is as much an aid to analysis as it is the results of any analysis.

A. The First Phase: Early Hopes

Compared with other phases of the trajectory towards desistance, those respondents who were placed in the early phase, were found to express a narrower range of emotions. The most commonly expressed emotions were that they were now 'happier' than they used to be, and they frequently described themselves as feeling 'better in myself'. These positive feelings were largely seen as the result of no longer having to endure the unwelcome emotions that were associated with offending, such as the fear of impending arrest, the inconvenience and trepidation associated with court appearances, and the general requirement of continually 'having to look over your shoulder'. The following quote from Matthew illustrates this point:

> How am I different? I don't take drugs and I don't commit crime anymore.
>
> AC: How do you feel about this change?
>
> I feel good about it. As I say, I don't have to look over my shoulder, I don't have to appear in court, I don't have to … The only person I've got to answer to is me really.[1]

Matthew later went on to echo these comments in his description of the alleviation of the disadvantages associated with the chaotic and haphazard lifestyle he had endured. This lifestyle had been required to support a long-standing addiction to heroin. The disadvantages included fear of apprehension and arrest, and the consequences of convictions as well as the unpleasant, but ultimately inconvenient and mundane rituals of being processed by the court and criminal justice system. His move away from this towards desistance had meant:

> … not having to worry about getting arrested or the police coming after you or going to prison. … It's the lifestyle that you lead, you know, always looking over

---

[1] As requested by the editors, all quotes have been 'cleaned up' to remove any regional phrases or structures of speech, mixed tenses and to conform to 'standard English'.

your shoulder and missing bail appointments and court appearances and one thing or another, so you're constantly on the run, aren't you?

After identifying working, 'instead of going out and pinching whatever I could get my hands on', as the biggest change in his life since the last interview, another case, Tom, went on to describe the impact of this change:

> It's a lot better, yeah. It's a lot better. I don't have to look over my shoulder. I was only thinking half an hour ago when I was stood over there at court [the arranged meeting place before interview], I could see people going in and out and I just knew what they were feeling. 'Am I going to go to jail or aren't I gonna go to jail?', and it's a horrible feeling, it really is.

Every one of the eight respondents we placed in this phase reported feeling happier (see Figure 4.1, p 100). In fact, feeling good and happier than before was reported by almost our entire desisting sample, regardless of the phase they were in, and 'feeling better in myself', although not quite so universal, repeatedly emerged throughout the schema. Thus, these may be viewed as two of the most common emotions associated with desistance. Many of those who begin to desist from crime automatically reduced or removed altogether the unpleasant aspects and emotions associated with their former lives. Compared to the worst times of their lives, no matter how far along the process of desisting they were, sample members always felt happier. Perhaps this explains this emotion's ubiquity as a permanent rather than temporary feature of the desistance process.

Several of the desisters in the early phase experienced a sense of hope. Often this was the hope that from now on, they would successfully avoid future offending. This is strongly felt by the cases in this early phase of the schema and would appear to be the most noteworthy emotion in this phase. Like other offenders, 'recent desisters' have an aspiration towards 'normal life', in line with society's goals such as family, job and a place to live (Bottoms et al 2004). These desires were regularly encountered in their descriptions of their future ambitions, as here by Frank:

> Just keep going the way I'm going ... and hopefully to get back with [ex-partner] who is, like, the mother of my son and live a proper, proper family life. And carry on the way I'm going and build on everything I've got already.

This journey towards 'normalcy' is not an automatic but rather a gradual process of adjustment and change, and is probably one that is never fully completed (see Douglas 1984). At this initial stage the experience of actually moving in this direction appears to be a conscious one (Maruna and Farrall 2004). Desisters are reminded that desistance is a worthwhile goal, and of the progress they have made, by the fact that the features associated with their lifestyle as offenders often linger. For example, Matthew described the impact on his life of not having used drugs for the previous six months:

> I feel a lot more positive. Getting into what you see as 'normal' society and not be[ing] judged by anyone because I don't have to disclose [his past offending].

Respondents in this early phase were still likely to need to overcome many of the obstacles to desistance, such as heavy drug and alcohol use, or problems with employment. It is this precarious position of respondents at the start of the desistance process that means that there is a greater degree of uncertainty that this desire for normalcy can be achieved. These cases have not only travelled a shorter distance away from the circumstances of their offending, but also have a greater distance still to cover. There is a feeling that they are still moving towards, rather than achieving, a 'normal life' (Goffman 1963). It is this uncertainty that qualifies the aspiration as 'a hope' to continue the journey towards normalcy and to avoid future offending. Ben was aware of this:

> Well, I've settled down with my girlfriend. Although sometimes we do have [our] ups and downs ..., my financial situation is a bit better because I've been working on and off. I'm not always in a steady job though. I just think, you know, I'm getting on a bit better with my life, you know, I've grown up a little bit but I'm still not there you know.
>
> AC: What do you mean by that?
>
> I've got a long way to go, you know, before I think, you know, I'm settled.

He went on to say that he still had 'a long way to go' to overcome his problem with drugs (he was still on a daily methadone prescription) and find regular full-time employment. Being frequently out of work led to times when Ben had no money and felt depressed (which he also attributed to his use of methadone) and which resulted in uncertainty—Ben said he had been tempted 'to turn back to crime' and that 'it's always in the back of my head'. Despite owing its existence to uncertainty, hope provides an important resource to draw on for those at the beginning of the desistance process. It provides them with the vision that an alternative, more 'settled', future is possible, it provides them with both a plan and a motivation to continue in the direction of desistance.

B. The Intermediate Phase

As we move into the next phase of the trajectory, we find offenders who have, by and large, left offending behind for longer periods of time, sometimes for around two to three years. However, in many cases, they had experienced set-backs, and either relapsed and used drugs again or committed isolated offences. These offences were often comparable in seriousness to the ones they were originally convicted for. However, despite this, their identity as non-offenders appears, as a result of their 'backsliding', to have become much stronger, as was their resolve that they would not offend again. As these desisters begin to put more 'distance' between themselves in the present and their 'old' selves, we begin to witness a pattern where they refer back to 'negative' experiences and emotions. The emotional experience of this phase was characterised by a growing sense of internal disquiet when they remembered previous actions and lifestyles. Regrets about the past started to emerge for many around this time. For some, however, merely realising that they were no longer (or were increasingly less) dependent on drugs and alcohol, provided new feelings of self-esteem.

For example, at the time of the first interview, Clive reported his use of alcohol as an obstacle to desistance (Farrall 2002). His proposed solution to overcoming this problem was to isolate himself from other alcoholics. However, he was pessimistic about the possibility of achieving this because, as he saw it, 'it would be an offence to be with them and not to drink. It would mean you are not one of them'. By the time of the fourth interview this sense of obligation had gone. Although he had not solved his drinking problem (he was still drinking daily, and had been arrested for being drunk and disorderly), he now felt capable of avoiding peer pressure. Previously Clive had said that he had given in to this pressure as he felt a debt to his 'community' and did not wish to lose the 'sense of belonging' and support that they offered. However, he now acknowledged that, in fact, his actions owed a lot to his wishing to avoid unwanted feelings of being degraded and humiliated, if he refused to comply with their wishes. Awareness of these feelings can be seen in his explanation as to how he is different currently compared to the time of the offence:

> 'Well I wouldn't put myself in that position. I wouldn't do it. Where I had light fingers[2] before, when I was drinking [with] that sort ... don't tend to do it anymore. I don't put myself in that type of company. I used to drink with a lot of lads and, know what I mean, a lot of it was coached ... You felt degraded if you ... or they made you feel degraded if you didn't do what they wanted you to do. You know what I mean, you just want to be one of the lads, one of the group, and I don't get involved in that anymore. That's not, [I] don't have a problem with any of that. If I do drink, it's my own choice now, you know what I mean. It's not ... I mean people don't force you to. I feel like I've changed such as I don't mix with it. I don't set myself up to fail. I don't put myself in that position.'

In part, then, the changes experienced by Clive were insights that he had gained into his own feelings and about how others had made him feel. George described how not offending was not only good, because it removed the stigma of being labelled as an 'offender', but that it also meant that he no longer had to handle his own feelings of anger generated by what he saw

---

[2] Having 'light fingers' means having a propensity to steal.

as the presumptuous judgements of others. Dominic, a former long-term heroin user, referred to the embarrassment he used to feel about his physical appearance. Stopping heroin had led to an improvement in this and the bonus of improving his interaction with his family:

AC: How do you feel about having stopped [offending?]

Dominic: Feel a lot better, in myself alone and for my family. Like I say, kids have noticed it more, as well. Our lass is a lot happier any way.

AC: You say the kids have noticed a lot more?

Dominic: Yeah, yeah, yeah, and everytime. It's like one time, [they] wouldn't have their photograph taken with me, but it's all over now. I mean kids, fishing and all sorts, you know ... All drawn in face and looked poorly all time and you know what I mean? I were conscious about how I looked. Things like that.

For others such as Barry, there was a more conscious recognition of the existence of these negative feelings and the implications they had on his offending. An awareness of the need to control them emerged over time. Again, talking about how he is different from when he finished his probation order, he said he 'sits back and observes things more'. His assessment of this change was:

It's much better, you know. I feel that I'm not so aggressive and more chilled. So yeah, no, it's better for me really ... I'm still an angry person. I don't think I've ever said that. I've always been an angry person, but I've only realised now, later on, that I am quite an angry person, you know. I get frustrated quite quickly, which is slowing down, but I still do, but I'm finding myself stopping myself, instead of going 'Aaargh!' Do you understand what I mean?

He also identified the maintenance and control of these negative feelings of anger as being the result of his own efforts and conscious changes within himself over time so he didn't 'bottle things up' so much anymore:

I think [probation] helped me to open up, and yeah, part of maturing as well. It also helped me to start talking about ... Before I used to bottle things up, you know. When I was a kid especially. But as I've got older and older, I find it more and more easy to talk about what's going on in my life, you know. Now so many things have happened you know, there's nothing else can happen that'll be as bad as what has happened, you know.

C. The Penultimate Phase

Almost all of the cases placed in this category had managed to stay (largely) crime-free for three or more years. During this phase of the desistance process, more of our respondents started to talk about the shame and guilt they felt about their former lives (see also van Stokkom 2002: 340). For some, despite the temptation to offend remaining with them, the emotions of guilt and personal shame provided a brake on them making a return to their previous offending behaviour. In this respect, guilt appeared to motivate respondents into taking responsibility for their past and future actions (see Retzinger and Scheff 1996, cited in van Stokkom, 2002: 343). For Jamie, thinking about the wider implications of stealing a car again, the potential impact on its owners and the disruption he would cause, created an awareness of the feelings of guilt that pursuing such temptations would cause:

> It's one big playground, isn't? It's just the way it is, isn't? There are plenty of opportunities out there for someone to get into trouble. It's just whether you can walk on by, isn't it? I mean I walk on by ... passed a shop one time when I was with my girlfriend and I said 'Look out there', outside the dentist there was a BMW convertible with the engine running sat in a car park. Back when I was seventeen I would probably have jumped straight in there and gone. I would have loved that but when I walk past now I would say things as 'Look at that, fucking hell!', now I would see it as a sort of ... I could be not like a crime avoider but a sort of a person that avoids the people and not what to do without your fucking car stolen. Because I wouldn't steal a car now because I know [that] the mortgage don't get paid and things like that, but when I was seventeen you don't realise about things like that. I thought it weren't harming no one. It was only a fifty pound Metro,[3] it wasn't worth anything. But now I realise that fifty pound metro is probably someone's wages for a week to get to work in and then you know, the kids don't get fed and shit like that and so ... And that's probably what's changed in me, I've grown up and realised that you can't do things like that no more, because no matter how less things are worth, its always worth more to someone else than what it is to you, isn't it?

This guilt was not confined to feelings about 'direct' victims. For Anthony, although he admitted feeling nostalgic for his 'rogue' days of heavy drinking and fighting, he could not see himself returning to it because of the shame it would bring to those closest to him, adding 'You can't be a pissed-up bum to your kids'. During this phase, the shame felt regarding the suffering their behaviour had caused family members was identified by some desisters as the motivating force behind starting the transformation away from offending.[4] Tony described the biggest change in his life as coming off drugs. He had this to say about what he feels is responsible:

> And my family as well, my mum, my mum hasn't been well. She's always in and out of hospital. They said a lot of that was caused through stress and that. Most of all her blood pressure or something stupid, having heart attacks and that, said they're all caused through stress and that so me dad put that down to me, you

---

[3] A Mini Metro. A small family car typically used as a family's second car.

[4] In this respect, there would appear therefore to be an even earlier phase—perhaps with its own set of emotional drives and aspirations—which 'kick starts' the desire to get away from a particular lifestyle.

know? Her worrying about me, so basically putting my mum in a grave as well as myself in a grave. I didn't think it [continuing to use drugs] were fair really.

For those who suffered setbacks and relapses back into offending and substance misuse, intense feelings of shame were often experienced. Al saw it as 're-labelling' him as a criminal:

AC: How do you feel about that fine [for possession of an unlicensed vehicle]?

Al: Oh it done my head in.[5] It's nothing to do with the fine, it's to do with all the amount ... the length of time I've been out of trouble to getting something else on my record. It's like I've not stayed away from it, you know what I mean, anymore. So now any judge or any policeman or anything like that they'll look at me and say 'he's not changed he's just not been caught'. And it's not right you know what I mean.

But for others, like Peter, the unwelcome re-introduction of guilt provided a further incentive to desist from heroin use:

You know, when I was on drugs, I didn't have a care, everything was great. You know, then when I wasn't on drugs, then just, it was [the] complete opposite. So it was more to do with my moods but I just learnt to deal with it, I just thought 'well, you know, I don't want to get back on drugs'. Because it, it perpetuates, you know, I would go and use drugs and then the following day, one I would feel guilty for using drugs, which that in itself would put me on a downer and make me feel worse, which I'd, you know, there's more a propensity to go out and use again. And two, there's the physical side of it, the cold turkey side of it, and, you know, so I'd have to go use, so I didn't want to get back into that trap.

However, one of the most interesting feelings that emerged from respondents we placed in this phase, was that of trust. Feelings of trust had not been mentioned by respondents in either of the earlier two phases, but were mentioned by six of the 11 respondents in the penultimate phase (see Figure 4.1, p 100).

i. The Emotions Surrounding Feelings of Trust

Respondents in the penultimate phase increasingly described how, having desisted for a period of time, they found themselves increasingly trusted by family members. The feelings engendered by this were important incentives for their continued desistance. While they had been offending, this trust had been lost, but now that they had ceased offending for a reasonable period of time (often over three years), they could start to rebuild this trust. Peter described this as 'building bridges':

I get on reasonably well with my brother. We have, overall, a decent relationship. Although, since then, I've built a lot of bridges, get on a lot better with me family these days.

[5] In this context, to feel annoyed or upset.

He described the struggle he had had to endure in order to rebuild his relationship with his family:

'I think a lot of it at the time was the drugs, there was a lot of mistrust. I mean I've never actually did anything to my family. I mean, like, I know people that have been in my situation and they've robbed their family blind, you know, but I, I've never done anything like that. You know, it's not like I'd give them reason, I think it, a lot of it was, it's just stigma, you know, stigmatised. And there was a lot of mistrust and because of that I, I isolated myself more than them isolating me, you know, because I didn't like going down to visit my brother, or visit my mum and then they'd be following me round the house everywhere I went, you know, and that made me feel bad. So that's why I actually stopped going [to visit them], you know, to save putting myself in that situation because then that put me on a downer, which were pointing more towards drugs and I were trying best I could to avoid triggers like that. Because a lot of the reasoning why I got involved with drugs in the first place was through, through emotional issues, through family and things like that. So I was just trying to box clever[6] and avoid them situations.

The fact that being trusted is an enjoyable sensation, in comparison to the unpleasant feelings that come with being mistrusted, provides an additional incentive. Furthermore, the act of successfully rebuilding trust also meant that they have something to lose, itself an incentive to avoid reoffending (see also Sampson and Laub 1993), sentiments echoed by Bill:

The main thing is, just look at your family first, and see how they'd feel. Because once you've buggered up again then it all comes right back down to trust. And I've got a lovely relationship now with all my family, apart from my dad.[7] And I don't want anything to change that again.

These feelings of being trusted were not confined to relationships with family. Those offenders nearer the point of complete desistance, such as Niall, also described how they were now trusted by the authorities:

My allotment's down there and [the police] take their cars down there to wash them through the car wash. Whenever I'm down there they'll say, 'Oh, come on, Niall, let's have a look in your greenhouse then, what have you got growing?' because, you know, they all know that I like a smoke [of cannabis]. And they all say 'Are you still at it then?' I'll say, 'Well I smoke, but I don't grow it any more.'[8] 'All right then, can we have a look in your greenhouse?' Just having a laugh with me, you know, it's ...

AC: Do they have a look in your greenhouse?

---

[6] Meaning to act in a smart or cunning manner.

[7] Bill and his father had fallen out over one of Bill's former girlfriends. Although Bill and she had split up, he and his father had yet to patch things up.

[8] The UK Government had recently changed the law, so that possession of cannabis and similar 'soft' drugs was permitted for personal use.

No. No, they don't, no. I always offer them some rhubarb. No, they wouldn't do. They just do it as a laugh because I know them. Well I've known them for years, you know.

ii. The Emotions of Pride

Feelings of personal pride and of a sense of achievement also featured strongly towards the end of the desistance process. For the most entrenched criminals, like Al, who admitted to having shoplifted every day of his life from the age of 11 years to 25, just having managed to abstain for two years gave a sense of personal achievement:

That's another thing I'm proud of myself. Because from the age of eleven to twenty-five every single day I was a shoplifter. It was the only thing I knew how to do, after moving to ... I just changed my life. I couldn't even think about pinching a [sweet] or anything man. If I see the kids anywhere near anything picking things I'm like 'move away from there don't touch anything'.

Others were proud about having achieved their goals through the conventional means of legitimate employment, and described the difference between 'now' and when they had started their original probation order:

[I'm] a lot more healthier. I've got a lot more friends, my social life's a lot better. There's no dodgy people coming to the house anymore. I go to work every day, like I earn an honest wage and stuff. I just stay out of bother, that's all I do. [Nick]

There was also a pride in their achievements of 'respectable domesticity':

I'm all right now. I'm happy with myself. I've got a nice house, I keep it that way. Reasonable garden. [Bill]

Ann said owning her own property was the biggest change in her life, and explained why this was important to her:

'Even though I've had all the problems that I've had and illness and ... and stuff ... this place is my own now, I can make it my own. I can change it the way I want it to be. I can have whoever I want in here. Or if I please, not have them here. It makes me feel quite proud. But like I say, it is just a material thing. It's not ... I feel very lonely at the moment being here alone.

The respondents we placed in the both the penultimate and the final phases also experienced an interesting variation in their hopes. Previously, most notably in the early phase, the hopes experienced had been for an 'escape'—from an addiction, or away from a particular lifestyle associated with offending. In the last two phases we see hopes becoming more concrete—people desire specific goals, such as their own businesses, a family (or children if they are in a relationship), a home which they own, and so on. The hopes experienced towards the end of the emotional trajectory of desistance take on a different tone—the future is more certain now, and particular needs and wants can be strived for.

D. The Final Phase: 'Normalcy'

Those cases who had, to all intents and purposes, completed the process of desistance and that we had identified being non-offenders, were placed in the final phase of our schema. For these desisters, 'normalcy' is underlined by two repeating themes that emerged from their responses. First, they see their offending as now being a 'long way away'. They regarded themselves in the present as very far removed from the 'them' at the time of their offending. Furthermore, when they talk about how the emotions of trust, guilt and shame have encouraged their desistance, these emotions were typically referred to in the past tense (a trend that emerged amongst cases placed in the previous stage of the schema). Not just their offending, but the journey of desistance itself, was seen as something that has happened, rather than is still to happen. That six of the eight people we placed in this phase reported regrets about the past suggests that they are indeed rebuilding their 'selves' and strengthening other non-criminal aspects of their identities (van Stokkom 2002: 350). Secondly, where once they were involved in crime, in some cases, such as Ian and Terry, being deeply entrenched in it, starting families, re-building bonds with parents and establishing successful careers has meant they are now more firmly entrenched in 'normality'. This new existence brings with it new feelings of being rewarded, and improved self-esteem and confidence.

While feelings of being rewarded are reported in a few cases in earlier phases of the schema, these exclusively involved persons with histories of either alcohol and/or heroin misuse. Given that addictions to these substances were previously perceived as powerful malign forces responsible for driving their criminal behaviour, it is hardly surprising that those who have managed to desist or, in the case of Clive, control their consumption, feel rewarded and have their self-esteem raised. Moreover, these feelings were specifically related to occasions when they have had the opportunity to offer their experiences for the benefit of others with drug and alcohol problems and to 'give something back' (Maruna 2001). For example, both Dominic and Nick had been invited by local drug agencies to give a talk about their experiences since coming off heroin, and how they were successful. Although they both declined, they said they were 'chuffed actually' (Nick) and 'came home proper buzzing'[9] (Dominic) after being asked.

---

[9] Both 'chuffed' and 'buzzing', in this context, refer to feelings of euphoria or extreme happiness.

Others, such as Sally-Anne, did adopt this role of 'wounded healer' by taking on a voluntary placement as a key worker at the drug rehab she graduated from. For her the experience was a reward and a reminder. She said it was 'really good for me, to see it from another side ... to see the heartbreak, and all the pain that families that have got people that are on drugs, what it does'. Clive, however, took on the role of self-styled local do-gooder, 'passing on information to [the] younger generation', and said 'It's really nice when someone thanks you for something ... when they say "Oh cheers for that", that makes all the difference.' Therefore, what all these cases have in common is not just that they were once heavy addicts and offenders, but that the feelings of reward they experienced were new, surprising, occurred at specific moments in time, and served as reminders of the incentives of continuing their desistance.

However, by the final phase of the schema, these feelings of reward and improved self-esteem were not uniquely confined to those with previous alcohol and drug problems. They are, in fact, much more widespread and included five of the eight cases we placed in this category. Furthermore, these feelings of being rewarded were not merely the result of 'wounded healer' roles, of getting something back in return for giving something, but owed their origins to the more continuous and subtle advantages of 'normal' life. This means, perhaps, that they have vested interests in maintaining the status quo of their current lifestyles, or at least, not acting in such a way as to damage it in the long term. For Richard, falling in love and getting married, and recently becoming a father, had provided him with a completely different outlook and purpose in life:

> I'm 42 nearly, that's a lot different. I'm married, I've got a child ... got a little dog over there ... It's, it's a world, a world of change. Everything is different.

> AC: How do you feel about this change?

> It's brilliant, it's ... that's why I'm alive now ... I'm alive. [Laughs]. And I'm living a life. Whereas before I was just running through life, how it happened, you know, I didn't care how it ended up. Mattered not. 'Dead or alive? Who cares?' But now I want to live, you know, I've got a purpose for stay alive for.

Others, like Mark, also considered that there was an appeal in the 'home comforts' of normalcy. This made even the thought of the behaviour he was previously involved in, such as going out with his friends clubbing, drinking, taking drugs and fighting, now seem unappealing in comparison, and hence for that reason much more unlikely to happen again. This is illustrated in response to the question, 'Is there anything that might make it hard for you to stay stopped?':

> No I don't think so now. I've just sort of grown out of it now. It's like never lurking around at two o'clock in the morning and you know things like that. I'd rather be tucked up in bed. [Laughter]. I don't even, you know, I don't even go

nightclubs anymore, you know. It's just like, it feels as though you're getting a bit old and ... [Yeah] I just can't be doing with it. [Laughter]. It's terrible really ... you know, you come out of a nightclub at two o'clock in the morning and you see people fighting and drunken people just falling all over the place, you know. No I'd rather be at home with the kids, knowing that they're safe and tucked up in bed and, you know, its things like that.

The notion that the distance covered had been too great to make a return to crime likely is seen in the attitudinal shift of Rajeev. He was 19 years old at the time of the first interview and on probation, having been convicted of fraud and deception. Although officially his first offence, he informed us that it was preceded by a list of convictions prior to 17 for theft and drugs. At his fourth interview, he had not re-offended, had completed a university degree, had a 'good job', and was planning to buy a house. He described himself as 'totally different' and with a completely new set of goals. By the fourth interview Terry, the only former drug addict and alcoholic in the 'normalcy' phase, had avoided alcohol and drugs for seven years and, as a Christian, was still an active member of his fellowship.[10] He was now working as a drugs worker for a clinic in the voluntary sector. In many ways his story is similar to the previously cited 'wounded healers' located earlier along the trajectory. However, Terry differs, as the following example illustrates, in that his 'reward' is continually reinforced 'every day', rather than intermittently. Interestingly he also compares the 'high' he gets from his current job to the 'lows' he has suffered in the past, again a reminder of how far he has come:

[Getting a job as drugs worker] made me feel ace,[11] you know. Doing something that, you know, all my life, all my life I've done jobs ... My dad basically tried to mould me into, he tried to mould me into the building trade, because my dad's a bricklayer. And he tried to mould me into himself. And I always come against that, I didn't want to be in the building trade. I didn't want to do that. And I used to do a lot of jobs that I hated. I used to go labouring on a building site and doing different jobs but I didn't like it, you know what I mean. I used to get up on a morning, think 'I don't want to ...' I hated going to work ... a lot of work what I did I just didn't like. I worked in an office, I worked in factory. And doing really, I did some really crappy jobs. But now, the job that I do now, it's been tailor-made for me. It's just unbelievable. It's everything what I've gone through in my life. I'm actually helping people who are going through the same [that I did]. So I love coming to work, every day I love coming to work. To me it's just like me life, you know. And I'm getting paid for it, which is fantastic, you know.

For others, such as Meera, a 'one-off' white collar offender convicted of embezzlement, the journey towards desistance had been one of regaining normalcy rather than trying to gain normalcy. She described herself at the

---

[10] A member of the local church (possibly a 'born-again' Christian group).
[11] As 'chuffed', above.

time of conviction as feeling 'nervous, scared ... like a piece of dirt' and 'to be truthful, [I] was good for nothing.' Once detected she was dismissed from her job and felt intense shame for what she had done, saying that when she went out she had a 'fear that someone would recognise me'. She identified the turning point as her decision to file for bankruptcy, which gave her the confidence to look for work again and to start by applying for a place on a part-time computer course. She said doing this course made her feel:

Better, stronger.

AC: In what way?

Emotionally I felt more stable, as if I was, I suppose as if I was on a high, it was like, you know, 'I know I can do this', so what was stopping me from going out and actually doing it for real, so to speak. Err, there was me previously, like independent, career-minded person, who'd turned into this very weak, insecure person and had no confidence in herself whatsoever. And, like I said, the course was, I suppose confidence-building as well as getting the experience of trying to venture out to do something new.

Meera's experiences suggest that Seidler (1998: 209) is correct when he argues that it is only when a relationship has been lost that individuals realise what they have lost. She later went on to describe her feelings about her current financial situation as follows:

Good, positive. I don't think I've done too badly for myself over the last six years. I've got, like I say, I've got three lovely kids that I'm very proud of. I've got a job now which I thoroughly enjoy and I've been able to study and move forward with my life. And I've learnt that if I can survive on £200 a month, you know, in comparison to what, £900?, I've got myself sorted. So if I can adapt from that difference of figure I know I don't need to spend recklessly etcetera. Because if I can manage that amount then I can manage my monthly salary, without it getting out of hand or anything like that.

Meera has undergone a long, slow journey, from being caught and charged with embezzlement to rebuilding her career. The experience, for all its faults, has been one of learning, and she has managed to obtain something worthwhile. For others, previously painful emotions of shame and guilt were identified as having been responsible for prompting what had been for them a difficult change of direction and the desire 'to make a go of it' and 'to try going straight'. Ian, in talking about such feelings, reported that these emotions were 'painful' and said that he felt that he was 'digging up old bones'.[12] However, he has been able to rebuild trust with his daughter; this too meant he has been rewarded in his 'new life'.

---

[12] Returning to issues which he would rather not look again at.

My oldest daughter is now nine and in '99, when I served my last [prison] sentence, it was very traumatic for her. And I saw the pain she was going through and that is what gave me the strength to think 'Well, I can't put myself in a situation where I ain't there for her because it's affecting her life and upbringing'. Whereas I want to give her a stable family, whereas I didn't have that stable thing and I felt that if I carried on now, then I'm just really showing her the path that I went down, and making history repeat itself maybe with her. Maybe she could, you know, anything could happen, she could be doing drugs or ... You know, there's always, you know, she and I thought to myself 'there's no more'. Whereas before it would be like, you know, 'daddy's away' or 'daddy's away working' or, you know, 'daddy's not here' for whatever reason. Whereas they're not stupid no more and I want to see my kids and if they come in to visit prison to see me, I am there, there, they can know, they know what's going on. They see it, they see it. I mean in '99 'Eastenders'[13] was on, you know, like with that boy in ... [Yeah] You know, there was someone in [prison] without a bib on[14] whereas she's coming to see me with that on. So it was all real for her, do you know what I mean? And so basically I don't want to put her through that anymore and that's what gave me that, the attitude to think 'Well, she can't see that no more'. Then, that's gone and even my youngest, like, she was eight months when I went in and it's like both of my daughters I've been away for both of them at a young age. And I think, you know, to say it's missing them and it took me, I tell you what it took me, I bet it took, it took me eighteen months to two years to actually build some kind of life. No, she loved me but when she's tired she wouldn't want me and that has hurt me that like she wants her mother before me and I've always been the intruder where as now it's not the case.

What Ian draws to our attention here is not only his own feelings and how they structured the process of desistance for him, but that the emotional aspects of desistance are not simply 'contained' within the desister. Like those involved with restorative justice conferences, distress is shared (van Stokkom 2002: 343). The emotional trajectories of desistance are as much a part of the experiences that others around the desister feel (see the experiences related above by ex-substance users, who refer to how their families had felt and how they now felt). Thus the emotional aspects of desistance are part of the feelings experienced by a wider social network of people other than the desister. It appears that, in many cases, the feelings experienced by the wider network were as important to desisters as their own feelings, 'It takes two to trust'. Perhaps, therefore, these individuals were better able to desist than others, because of the emotional ties that they had established (or re-established).

---

[13] A 'soap opera' on the UK's BBC1 television channel.
[14] Prisoners often wear bibs around their tops to distinguish them from visitors during visiting times.

IV. CONCLUSION

Previous studies of desistance have, by and large, focused on the structural factors associated with reform (although Maruna (2001) represents a notable exception to this). It is clear, however, that as well as there being an 'external' world of desistance, there is also an 'internal' world too. How people feel about what they have done, the emotions which they experience as they make the sometimes uneasy transition from 'offender' to 'non-offender', and the sensual dynamics of reform, are as important as the structures which they encounter. Our research suggests that as people previously engaged in crime move further along the road to complete cessation, so their emotional experiences and feelings start to reach out to larger social entities. In the first phase, our would-be desisters talk about what they want for themselves. By the time of the intermediate phase, there is an increase in the discussion of what other people (eg family members) need. In the penultimate phase, the discussion of 'the other' has extended to include non-family members as well, and by the final phase there appears a synthesis of concern for specific family members, 'the other' and oneself (eg Mark or Terry).

The next phase of research into desistance will need to attempt to address how structural impediments to desistance alter an individual's feelings and, vice versa, how emotional states can help individuals overcome practical problems as they try to build their lives afresh. It is becoming increasingly recognised that changes in life events (such as employment status) are not only about objective changes in status but also embody deep felt emotions (see Farrall and Calverley 2006: ch 4). In this respect, providing people with a sense of hope may be the key to unlocking desistance for many men and women whose past lives have been characterised by an involvement in crime. Building societies in which hope is neither rationed nor unevenly distributed may be the way—at a policy level—of uniting individually experienced feelings and wider structural processes.

REFERENCES

Barbarlet, JM (2002) 'Moral Indignation, Class Inequality and Justice: An Exploration and Revision of Ranulf' 6(3) *Theoretical Criminology* 279–98.
Bottoms, A, Shapland, J, Costello, A, Holmes, D and Muir G (2004) 'Towards Desistance: Theoretical underpinnings for an Empirical Study' 43(4) *Howard Journal of Criminal Justice* 368–89.
Burnett, R (1992) *The Dynamics of Recidivism* (University of Oxford, Centre for Criminological Research).
—— (1994) 'The Odds of Going Straight: Offenders Own Predictions', in *Sentencing, Quality and Risk: Proceedings of the 10th Annual Conference on Research and Information in the Probation Service* (Birmingham, University of Loughborough, Midlands Probation Training Consortium).

de Haan, W and Loader, I (2002) (eds) 6(3) special edition of *Theoretical Criminology*.

Douglas, J (1984) 'The Emergence, Security, and Growth of the Sense of Self', in J Kotarba and A Fontana (eds), *The Existential Self in Society* (Chicago, Chicago University Press).

Farrall, S (2002) *Rethinking What Works With Offenders* (Cullompton, Willan Publishing).

—— and Calverley, A (2006) *Understanding Desistance From Crime* (London, Open University Press).

Goffman, E (1963) *Stigma* (Harmondsworth, Penguin Books).

Karstedt, S (2002) 'Emotions and Criminal Justice' 6(3) *Theoretical Criminology* 299–317.

Katz, J (1988) *The Seductions of Crime* (New York, Basic Books).

Maruna, S (2001) *Making Good: How Ex-Convicts Reform and Rebuild Their Lives.* (Washington DC, American Psychological Association Books).

—— and Farrall, S (2004) 'Desistance From Crime: A Theoretical Reformulation' 43 *Kölner Zeitschrift für Soziologie und Sozialpsychologie*.

Retzinger, SM and Scheff, TJ (1996) 'Strategy for Community Conferences: Emotions and Social Bonds', in B Galaway and J Hudson (eds), *Restorative Justice: International Perspectives* (Monsey, Criminal Justice Press) 315–36.

Sampson, RJ and Laub, JH (1993) *Crime In The Making: Pathways and Turning Points Through Life* (London, Harvard University Press).

Seidler, VJ (1998) 'Masculinity, violence and emotional life' in G Bendelow and S Williams (eds), *Emotions in Social Life* (London and New York, Routledge).

Stanko, E (2002) Review of Katz, Jack, 'How Emotions Work' 6(3) *Theoretical Criminology* 366–69.

Van Stokkom, B (2002) Moral Emotions and Restorative Justice Conferences, 6(3), Theoretical Criminology, 339–60.

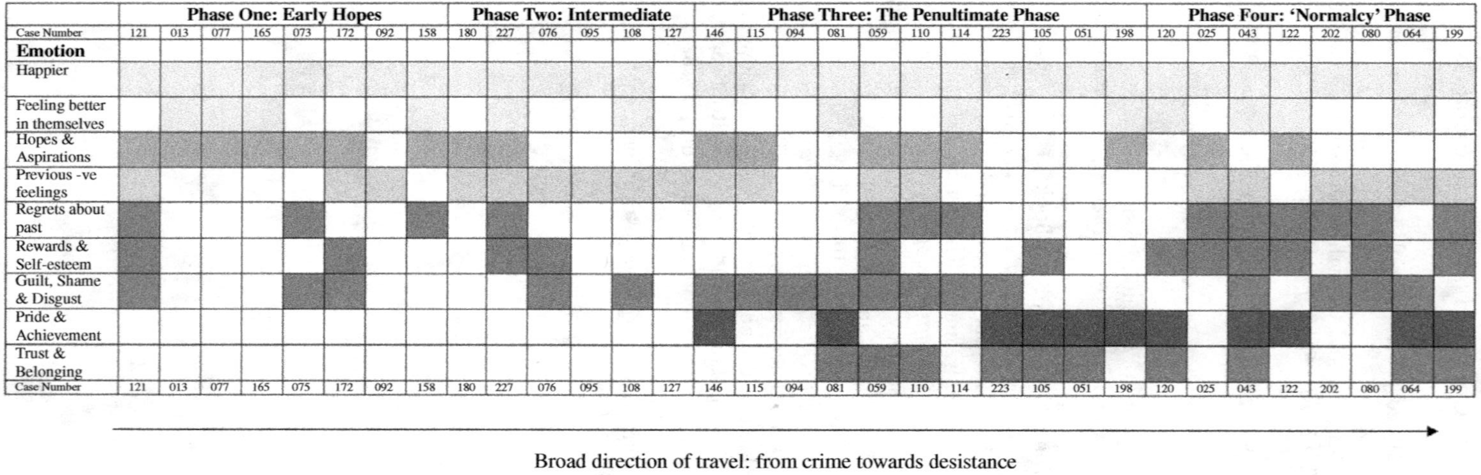

Phase One: Early Hopes | Phase Two: Intermediate | Phase Three: The Penultimate Phase | Phase Four: 'Normalcy' Phase

Case Number	121	013	077	165	075	073	172	092	158	180	227	076	095	108	127	146	115	094	081	059	110	114	223	105	051	198	120	025	043	122	202	080	064	199
Emotion																																		
Happier																																		
Feeling better in themselves																																		
Hopes & Aspirations																																		
Previous -ve feelings																																		
Regrets about past																																		
Rewards & Self-esteem																																		
Guilt, Shame & Disgust																																		
Pride & Achievement																																		
Trust & Belonging																																		
Case Number	121	013	077	165	075	073	172	092	158	180	227	076	095	108	127	146	115	094	081	059	110	114	223	105	051	198	120	025	043	122	202	080	064	199

Broad direction of travel: from crime towards desistance

Figure 4.1: Emotional Trajectory of Desistance

5

Trends in Crime and Fear: Lessons from Chicago, 1994–2003*

WESLEY G SKOGAN

I. INTRODUCTION

F EAR OF CRIME has real consequences for the communities in which we live, as well as for the emotional and social lives of those it afflicts. Fear can confine people to their homes, and it undermines their trust in neighbours and—especially—in their neighbours' children. Fear leads some to withdraw from public life, and it undermines informal and organised efforts by the community to control crime and delinquency. Fear undermines the value of residential property and thus the willingness of owners to maintain it properly, and the viability of small businesses. In the United States, fear of crime has been one of the most important factors driving city-centre residents to the suburbs, encouraging race and class segregation, and undermining the political importance of American cities. Fear of crime is also a 'wedge issue' that is used to divide whites from other Americans, because it is politically useful to some factions (Skogan 1995). The fears of the public also resonate in debates over crime policy, again supporting the positions of some factions over others.

But in the United States, as in some other countries, crime is down. After peaking in 1991, by 2003 the murder rate had dropped by 42 per cent and robbery by almost half, or 48 per cent. Public opinion has followed this trend to a more limited extent. In February 1992, 44 per cent of Americans reported that there was a place within a mile of their home where they would be afraid to walk alone at night, but by October 2004 that figure had fallen in 32 per cent (Gallup 2005). While this is far from being a perfect

* This project was supported by awards from the Illinois Criminal Justice Information Authority; the National Institute of Justice, US Department of Justice; and the John D and the Catherine T MacArthur Foundation. Points of view or opinions contained within this document are those of the author and do not necessarily represent the official position or policies of any of these organisations.

mirror of the extent of changes in national crime rates, crime and fear in the United States have at least moved downward in concert. However, in 2004, 53 per cent of Americans still thought that there was more crime in the country as whole than there was the year before, despite more than a decade of declining crime (Gallup 2005).

As this illustrates, one of the conundrums of fear of crime is that it does not always appear that the public feels safer when they 'should'. As the National Reassurance Policing Programme (2004) website noted:

> Since 1995 the amount of recorded crime in Britain has declined, but this decline has not been matched by a corresponding fall in the public's fear of crime. This divergence of achievement and recognition—the 'reassurance gap'—is a serious concern to the Police, a service that ultimately depends on public support for its funding and legitimacy. It is a concern shared by the Home Office.

Convinced by the British Crime Survey, the National Crime Victimisation Survey and other sources that crime has been falling, some have been puzzled that surveys do not show fear declining in proportion. Ditton et al (2000: 144) propose as a 'criminological maxim' that fear of crime climbs when crime rates climb, but fails to fall when crime falls. Concern about what Innes (2004) calls the resulting 'reassurance gap' between levels of crime and fear has begun to drive government policy in the UK, as witnessed by the launch of the National Reassurance Policing Programme (see www. reassurancepolicing.co.uk), the imposition of an official five-year plan to bring fear down (see www.crimereduction.gov.uk), the official prioritising of anti-social behaviour as well as conventional crime in order to respond to the causes of fear (see www.policereform.gov.uk), and the launching of a spate of research on whether fear is driven by distinctive 'signal crimes' rather than general trends, helping explain this conundrum (Innes 2004).

It is thus an important policy question whether fear inevitably 'ratchets up' and does not decline, and it is an important political question whether or not debates over crime will take place within an ever-mounting spiral of emotionality, regardless of 'the facts of the case'—which is taken by some as the condition of late modernity.

It turns out that little is known about the over-time dynamics of fear of crime. Aside from descriptions of trends presented by pollsters, there has been almost no research on why fear goes up or down. Almost all fear-of-crime research begins with the influence of factors such as gender and age, but demography alone cannot explain the short-term fluctuations in concern that are of such interest to policy-makers.

This chapter addresses the issue of trends in fear, using repeated surveys of residents of the city of Chicago. Like other US cities, over recent years Chicago witnessed a dramatic reduction in recorded crime, and surveys enable us to determine the extent to which this brought down levels of fear. Other factors that might have affected fear were changing as well, and this chapter is able to address the influence of several of them as well. During the time period considered here, the city adopted a community policing programme, for example. In addition, there were substantial changes in the composition of the population: the (safer) white population dropped by about 13 per cent, mostly to be replaced by (more fearful) immigrants from Mexico and their families. The chapter parses out the impact of these components of change, and documents how they explain a substantial—but still only partial—fraction of the very noticeable decline in fear of crime that took place in Chicago during the 1994–2003 period.

II. TRENDS IN FEAR IN CHICAGO

This chapter examines trends in one of the most common measures of fear, responses to the question 'How safe do you feel or would you feel being alone outside in your neighbourhood at night?' Respondents were asked to indicate whether they would feel very safe, somewhat safe, somewhat unsafe, or very unsafe if they found themselves in that situation. This question has been included in surveys conducted by the US Census Bureau, and it is commonly used in research on fear. It is not a behaviour measure. Behavioural measures of fear—such as reports of staying indoors at night or driving rather than walking to avoid being victimised—are sensitive to a host of contingencies and life situations (such as having a night-time job, or not having a car) that make them very complex to interpret. Responses to questions about one's (perceived) risk of being victimised incorporate some of what fearful people have already done to protect themselves (such as staying at home), and they can also miss the mark (Skogan 1993). The fear measure examined here does not hone in on particular 'signal crimes' that can dominate people's views because of their social or even political significance (Innes and Fielding 2002), nor does it count the frequency with which respondents experience instances of dread (Farrall and Gadd 2004). It focuses on the potential for harm that people feel crime holds for them, or what they believe *could* happen to them *if* they exposed themselves to risk. It is a neighbourhood-oriented, close-to-home measure of fear.

The chapter reports findings from eight citywide surveys conducted in Chicago between 1994 and 2003. The interviews were carried out by telephone, contacting households using random-digit-dialing procedures in order to ensure that new households, those that recently had moved and changed their telephone number, and persons who choose to be unlisted (which is more than 50 per cent of Chicagoans) would be included in the sample. When more than one adult lived in a responding household, one of them was chosen at random to represent the family, and extensive callbacks were made to reach selected respondents. During 1994–96 the surveys included 1300 to 1800 respondents. During 1997–99 they involved 2800 to 3000 respondents, in 2001 just over 2500 individuals were interviewed, and in 2003 there were 3140 respondents. The most conservative completion rates for the surveys ranged between 40 and 60 per cent, declining somewhat over time. While the respondents remained anonymous, they were asked to identify the general location of their home by giving the name of their residential street and the nearest cross street, or—failing that—to indicate the name of their neighbourhood. Responses to these questions enabled most respondents (92 per cent) to be identified by their police beat, and data gathered independently at this level are used to describe the geographical context within which each respondent lived.

Figure 5.1 examines trends in fear during the course of the 1990s, and into the 2000s. It presents trends separately for key demographic groups— by age, gender, home ownership and income. The trend lines chart the percentage of respondents who indicated they would feel either somewhat or very unsafe out alone in their own neighbourhood at night.

The surveys reveal that fear of crime has been in general retreat over most of Chicago. By 2003, every group depicted in Figure 5.1 had fallen below the 40 per cent fearful mark, and seven of the nine were at or below 30 per cent. As the figure indicates, divisions remain; even in the twenty-first century, men make themselves out to be less fearful than women.

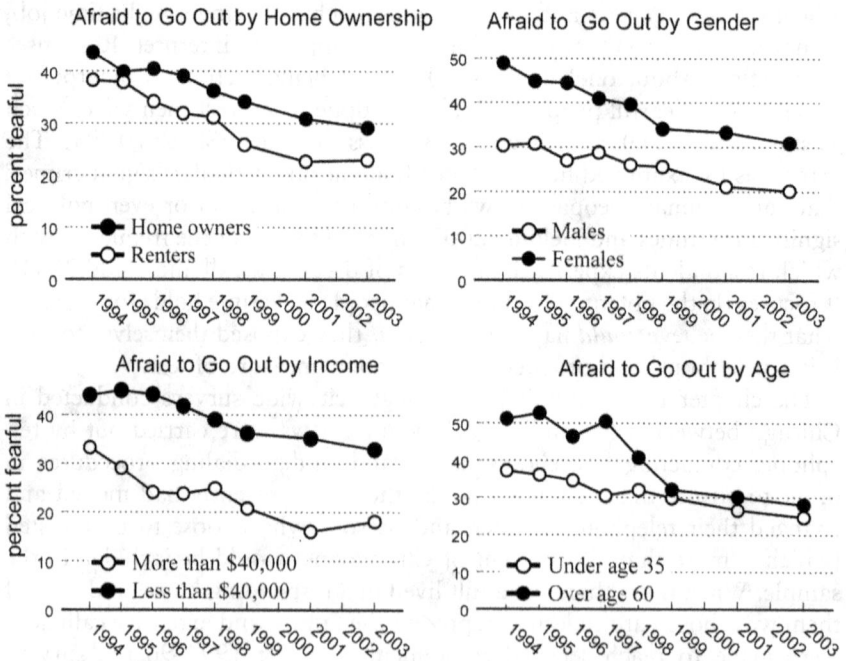

Figure 5.1: Trends in fear, by age, gender, home ownership and income

Among men, fear was down by 10 percentage points or so. However, fear dropped by almost twice as much for women, from 49 per cent to 31 per cent. It was down among both younger and older Chicagoans. Among those over 60 years of age fear dropped from 51 per cent to 28 per cent. In fact, age differences in fear (here comparing the fears of those under age 35 and those 60 and older) virtually *disappeared* in Chicago at the end of the 1990s. This is very surprising, because age has hitherto been one of the most reliable correlates of fear (Fattah and Sacco 1989). In an early study of crime and the elderly, Cook and Cook (1976: 645) concluded that 'the major policy problem associated with the elderly and crime is probably not crime *per se*. Rather, the problem is related to the elderly person's fear of crime and the restrictions to daily mobility that this fear may impose.' They argued that 'the policy response to victimisation of the elderly should be targeted to alleviating fear'. Fear also declined among both home-owners and tenants, and at about the same pace. The lower-left panel documents the more limited gains reported by less affluent residents; in this group, fear dropped from 44 per cent to 33 per cent. By contrast, among better-off Chicagoans the fear index stood at 33 per cent in the first survey, and dropped to just 18 per cent by 2003.

Figure 5.2 documents trends in fear by race and—within the city's large Latino population—by language. By this measure, fear dropped by half among the city's whites, from 34 per cent to 17 per cent. Fear dropped among African-Americans at about the same pace: the percentage of blacks who reported they would feel somewhat unsafe or very unsafe declined from 49 per cent to 25 per cent. The city's Latinos turned out to have made the fewest gains over this period. In comparison to 1994, the 2003 level of fear for the group as a whole was down just a bit, from 43 per cent to 38 per cent. Earlier in the decade African-Americans were the city's most fearful group, but by the turn of the century blacks felt significantly safer than the city's Latinos.

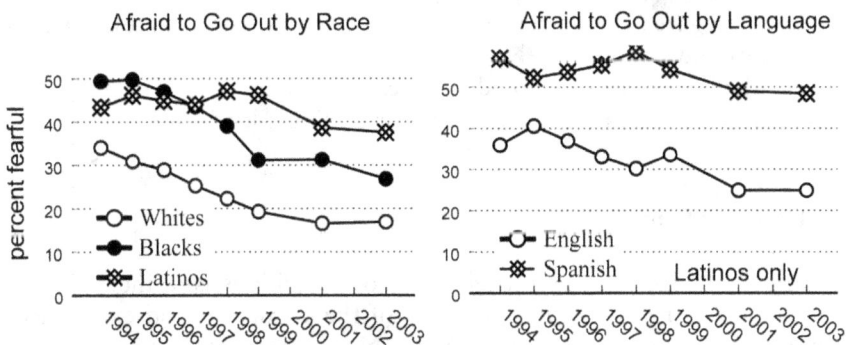

Figure 5.2: Trends in fear, by race and language

The right-hand panel in Figure 5.2 divided Latinos into Spanish-speakers and English-speakers, based on the language in which they preferred to be interviewed when contacted by survey interviewers. It describes the large differences in fear associated with language. Spanish-speakers are a growing group: by 2003 they made up 54 per cent of all the Latinos that were interviewed, foretelling an important demographic shift in Chicago's population (Skogan and Steiner 2004b). In the mid-1990s, Spanish-speaking Latinos were easily the most fearful large demographic group. Over time, fear declined among both English- and Spanish-speakers, but the gulf between them actually widened.

III. EXPLAINING TRENDS IN FEAR

What could account for declining fear? Past research does not provide much guidance for answering this question; most of it examines fear as a static phenomenon. The findings of these studies emphasise the importance of the fairly fixed features of people—their race, age, gender, affluence, education and the like. The Chicago findings substantiate all of the observations on which these inferences are built. In the early 1990s, women, the elderly, the poor, and racial minorities were substantially more fearful than their counterparts. However, these personal attributes take on a different and more limited significance when the goal is explaining *trends* in fear over time. For all of their obvious importance, the fixed personal factors that play such an important role in discussions of fear of crime cannot explain substantial changes in levels of fear over a relatively short period of time. Some demographic features of a city's population change only glacially. This includes one of the strongest predictors of fear, the average age of the population. In addition, the sex ratio in large populations tends to not change at all. Home ownership is also quite 'sticky' and changes only slowly over time. Further, in Chicago, fear was down *within* these groups. The racial composition of American communities is a demographic factor that can change rapidly, but we saw in Figure 5.1 that fear was down among the city's whites, African-Americans and Latinos.

The challenge, then, is to identify causal factors that can and have changed over time, and could account for declining levels of fear.

A. Declining Crime and Disorder, for Many

What can change rapidly is neighbourhood conditions, and they are also linked to fear. Fear is related to many of the conditions and experiences reported by respondents to the surveys. Not surprisingly, Chicagoans are more fearful when they think burglary or assault is a problem in their neighbourhood. They are also more fearful when they can see around them visible signs that social order is breaking down: they report more fear in places where public drinking, loitering and graffiti are common, and they are distressed by the appearance of street drug markets in their community. In Chicago, as elsewhere (see Lane and Meeker 2003), the relationship between neighbourhood conditions and fear is a strong one.

It is thus doubly significant that the problems undermining the quality of life in respondents' neighbourhoods declined substantially in Chicago during the course of the 1990s and into the 2000s. By many measures, including those drawn from data archives and the Census, as well as from the evaluation surveys, Chicago's neighbourhoods became cleaner, safer and more orderly, and fear declined as a result.

Figure 5.3 examines two measures of the extent of neighbourhood crime problems in Chicago, and how they trended over time. More details about all of them can be found in Skogan and Steiner (2004a). The top panels of Figure 5.3 chart trends in officially recorded crime between 1991 and 2003. Incident-level data on all of the crimes that were recorded by police during this period were supplied by the Chicago Police Department. To construct these trend lines, the city's residential police beats (the smallest police administrative units) were grouped by their racial composition, based on

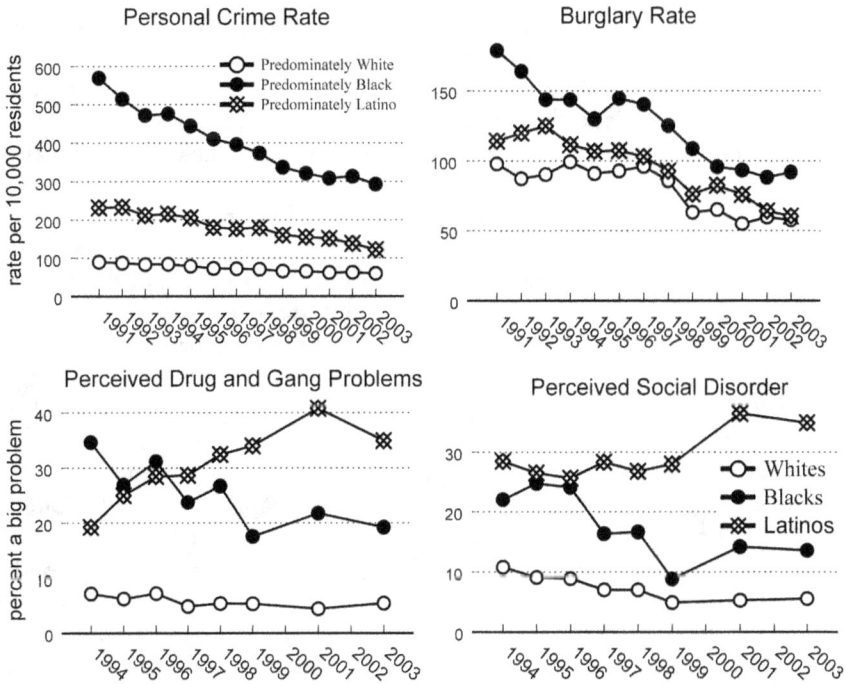

Figure 5.3: Trends in official and survey measures of crime

the 1990 census. Some beats were so racially diverse that it was impossible to classify them in simple fashion, and they are excluded here for simplicity (Skogan and Steiner (2004a) presents all the details). The aggregated groups of beats differed in size, so the analysis here reports rates of crime per 100,000 persons living in each grouping.

As Figure 5.3 illustrates, crime was down in all or most areas, but it declined most dramatically in African-American communities. By 2003, robbery was down in predominately African-American beats by 61 per cent, rape by 43 per cent, murder by 26 per cent. Personal crime rates were not very high in white areas even at the outset, but in percentage terms even they enjoyed significant declines in violent crime. For African-Americans, the biggest decline in property crime was registered in the burglary category, which is depicted in the upper right-hand quadrant of Figure 5.3. Motor vehicle theft rates were also generally down.

In addition to conventional crime, neighbourhoods can be plagued by 'social disorders', which are conditions that are also strongly associated with fear. Elsewhere I described social disorder as 'bands of teenagers deserting school and congregating on street corners, prostitutes and panhandlers soliciting for attention, public drinking, ... verbal harassment of women on the street, street violence, and open gambling and drug use' (Skogan 1990: 2). Others have added fare evasion in the subway (Kelling and Coles 1996), recreational violence in clubs and pubs, and threatening phone calls (Leigh, Read and Tilley 1998), and homeless squatters and 'dumpster divers' searching for food (Finn 1988). In general, most of these activities are illegal, and the others frequently are, but it can be hard to get police interested in them. Albert Reiss (1985) captured the essence of many forms of disorder when he described them as 'soft crimes', lying on the boundaries of traditional definitions of crime and the priorities of police.

This chapter examines the impact of trends in three forms of social disorder: public drinking, loitering, and school disruption. School disruption was assessed by responses to a question about 'disruption around schools, that is, youths hanging around making noise, vandalizing or starting fights', and teen loitering by responses to a question about 'groups of people hanging out on corners or in the streets'. Respondents were presented with a list of these problems, and asked in each case to rate whether they were 'no problem', 'some problem', or 'a big problem' in their neighbourhood. In the eyes of Chicagoans, all three problems were quite common. In 1995, loitering was the most highly rated problem in the survey—22 per cent reported that loitering bands of people were a big problem in their neighbourhood, and another 32 per cent thought they were some problem. In the same survey, 52 per cent indicated that public drinking was a problem in their neighbourhood, and disorder around local schools was identified as a big problem by 16 per cent of Chicagoans. Because responses to these questions were substantially correlated with one another (in 1995, the average inter-item correlation was +.52), they are combined here into one index of perceived neighbourhood social disorder.

Surveys also provide an alternative measure of two hard-core crime problems that are very ill-measured in official data—gangs and drugs. In the case of drugs, police work mostly with records of drug arrests, but this is actually an enforcement measure. Gang activity is even more difficult to track separately from the success of police investigations. In the surveys, respondents were also asked to rate 'drug dealing on the streets' and 'gang violence' in their neighbourhood. In 1995, 23 per cent of Chicagoans rated drug dealing a 'big problem' in their neighbourhood, while 19 per cent gave top billing to gang violence. Responses to these two question were particularly strongly related to one another (+.73 in 1995), and they too are combined here into one index of neighbourhood gang and drug problems.

As Figure 5.3 illustrates, when asked about gang, drug and social disorder problems, people's responses presented a complex picture of trends in neighbourhood conditions in Chicago. In particular, by many measures conditions worsened for the city's Latinos. This was largely because of the impact of massive immigration and the emergence of new, poor and highly segregated Latino neighbourhoods in Chicago (Skogan and Steiner 2004b). At the same time, reports of crime and disorder problems declined substantially among African-Americans, and even among whites, who faced far fewer problems. To the extent to which they are linked to fear, trends in gang, drug and social disorder problems—and differential changes in these factors by race—may help explain declining levels of fear for many in Chicago.

The statistical analysis of fear that is presented below uses another measure of neighbourhood conditions as well, one combining accounts of the extent of three conventional crimes. Officially collected data have substantial limitations, one of which is that police are heavily dependent on the willingness of residents to report crimes. A rule of thumb is that no more than about 50 per cent of crimes are reported (Hart and Rennison (2003) report the details). The police further screen complaints to ensure that they meet legal and bureaucratic requirements before they file an official record, and this also reduces the count. Survey measures of crime bypass these barriers by going directly to the public, who are in a position to report on crime as it is experienced rather than as it is counted. Respondents were quizzed about 'cars being stolen', 'people breaking in or sneaking into homes to steal things', and 'people being attacked or robbed' in their neighbourhood. Trends in these followed the patterns depicted in Figure 5.3. Whites thought things were a bit better, despite their already low base. In the mid-1990s, African-Americans and Latinos reported about the same level of concern for every crime problem. Then, during the course of the 1990s, their experiences diverged. Over time, more and more African-Americans reported that things were not so bad, and by 2003 their scores in these problem indices had dropped by about 10 percentage points. By 2003, the views of blacks had converged toward those of whites, and both groups expressed relatively low levels of concern about these crimes. But there was again little good news for the city's growing Latino population. In the first survey they reported about the same level of crime problems as did African-Americans, but reports of concern by Latinos did not decline during the 1990s. Worse, their ratings jumped to new highs during the early 2000s. By 2003, the city's Latinos were three times more likely than whites and African-Americans to report that street crime, burglary and auto theft were big problems in their community.

B. Growing Confidence in the Police

Does confidence in the police—and changing levels of confidence—affect fear of crime? It is important to consider this proposition because during the period described here, policing in Chicago was also in flux. The surveys were conducted to help evaluate the implementation and impact of a community policing programme. If police are thought to be becoming more effective at dealing with neighbourhood crime and disorder, responding more effectively to the particular problems that are of most concern, or just more visible while making their daily rounds, people may feel more secure. Many correlational studies have found that visible police presence on the streets is associated with lower levels of fear. In a quasi-experimental study of foot patrols in Newark, New Jersey, Pate (1986) found that foot patrols reduce levels of fear. Bennett (1989) drew the same conclusion from a quasi-experiment in Britain. Zhao, Scheider and Thurman (2002) provide a wide-ranging review of this literature, concluding that the weight of the evidence is that visible police presence reduces fear.

On the other hand, not everyone perceives their local policeman in favourable terms, and more contact and familiarity with them may not be seen to be an unalloyed good. More intensive and visible policing may be seen as intrusive, oppressive, and perhaps unfairly targeting residents. Skogan (1994) found that, in general, British Crime Survey respondents who recalled having seen police patrolling on foot in their neighbourhood felt substantially more positive about them—with the important exception of Afro-Caribbeans, for whom police visibility had no discernible favourable effects.

And it is also possible that the causal relationship between confidence in the police and fear runs in the other direction, and that improving conditions and declining levels of fear increase satisfaction with the police, rather than the other way around. A recent study by Xu, Fiedler and Flaming (2005) built the reverse assumption into a complex causal model that included measures of awareness of community policing, perceptions of neighbourhood conditions, quality of life, and fear of crime, and they found that the data fitted a model specifying that fear affected confidence in the police. However, the many intervention studies that have examined this link—including the foot patrol experiments noted above—generally support the policing-affects-fear specification. My own best evidence concerning the causal link between policing and fear comes from 1993–94. During that period, Chicago police experimented with their new programme in five police districts, while their approach proceeded as usual in the remaining 20 districts. Before-and-after evaluation surveys conducted in the experimental areas and in matched comparison districts (see Skogan and Hartnett (1997) for the details) found that these changes had an effect. Residents of most of the prototype districts noted positive changes in policing during the experimental period. There were increases in the visibility of foot officers in the experimental areas, more police were visibly driving around on patrol in the neighbourhoods, and there were more informal police contacts with citizens. Residents of the experimental districts were reassured when they saw police doing community-oriented patrols. Controlling for many factors, enhanced police visibility in the experimental areas was linked to positive changes in people's views of the quality of police service, and—especially for African-Americans and people who rented rather than owned their home—reduced fear of crime. Statistically, the effect of increased police visibility on fear was of about the same magnitude as the effects of age and gender, two important factors in the fear of crime equation.

Here, the effect of confidence in the police is captured by responses to 10 questions assessing residents' satisfaction with the demeanour, responsiveness and effectiveness of police working in their community. Respondents were asked how polite, helpful, concerned and fair the police were when dealing with residents of their neighbourhood. Other questions probed how responsive police were to neighbourhood concerns, and how good a job police were thought to be doing dealing with the problems that concern residents. Finally, Chicagoans were asked about the effectiveness

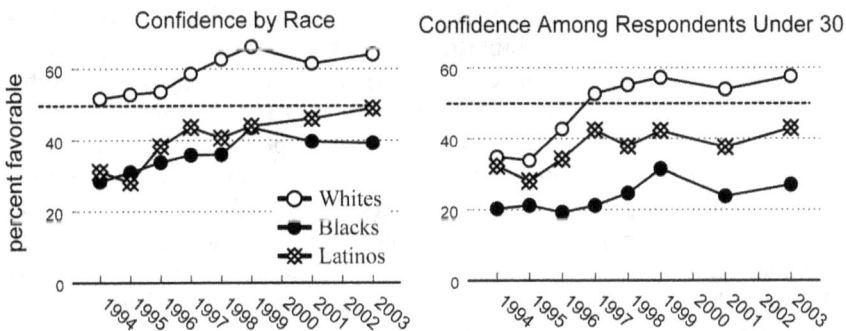

Figure 5.4: Trends in confidence in the police

with which police prevented crime and disorder, and how good a job they were doing in helping crime victims. In the 1995 survey (a typical year), responses to these 10 questions were correlated an average of +.57 and when combined they formed an overall index of opinion with a reliability (Cronbach's alpha) of .93. In these data, Chicagoans who feel that the police are doing a good job are less fearful than those who are sceptical about their effectiveness.

In addition we will examine the impact of Chicagoans' awareness that a community policing programme was in place. In a nationwide Internet-based survey, Weitzer and Tuch (2004) found that awareness of community policing was related to increased confidence, in their case measured by perceptions of the extent of police misconduct. Awareness is measured here by responses to the question: 'Now I have a few questions about a community policing program sponsored by the Chicago Police Department. It calls for more cooperation between police and the residents of Chicago. Have you heard about this policing program?' A later question gauged whether respondents had heard of the city's beat meetings. These gatherings of residents and police who work in their area are held monthly throughout the city, and they are one of the most distinctive features of the city's community policing programme (see Skogan and Steiner 2004a).

Figure 5.4 illustrates trends in confidence in police by charting the percentages of respondents each year who on average rated the police as doing a 'good job' or a 'very good job'. Confidence generally rose during the 1990s, and then levelled off at near its highwater mark in the 2000s. Confidence—and changes in confidence—also differed substantially by race and age, the two strongest correlates of views of the police. In general, only whites averaged in the favourable range throughout the entire period—this is highlighted by the dotted line delineating the 50 per cent mark in both panels of Figure 5.4. However, Latinos *gained* the most confidence, with the favourable faction growing from 31 per cent in 1994 to 49 per cent by 2003. Support among African-Americans grew between 1993 and 1999, before dropping a bit, and in 2003 almost 40 per cent of the city's blacks were in the positive range. Among those under age 30—traditionally a very sceptical group—favourable ratings of the police went up over time among all racial groups. However, it rose the most among white youths, and the least among young African-Americans. In 1994, young whites and Latinos shared a relatively jaundiced view of the police, but the growth in confidence reported by young whites over time was not mirrored by young Latinos, and they had fallen noticeably behind by 2003. Not illustrated in Figure 5.4 is that confidence in the police rose for other groups as well. Confidence went up among both renters and home-owners, and among higher- and lower-income people. To the extent to which confidence in the police affects fear, generally improving confidence in the police may help explain changes in fear over time.

C. Impact of Neighbourhood Conditions and Confidence in Police

Table 5.1 presents a multi-level analysis of fear of crime. It probes the joint effect of individual and contextual factors that may help explain the decline in fear in Chicago during the 1994–2003 period. The table examines the opinions of 16,878 respondents interviewed between 1994 and 2003.[1] The individual factors that are included were significant predictors of fear when they were examined separately. They are a mix of demographic factors and perceptual assessments, so the two were entered in separate blocks. The beat-year contextual factors include crime, which is represented by the log of personal crime and residential burglary per 10,000 residents of each beat. There are also measures of the racial composition of each beat, and demographic factors that help separate out the unique effects of crime as opposed to other features of these areas. The beat-year context data are organised so that the police beat in which each respondent lives is described by crime and (interpolated or projected) census data for the year in which they were interviewed. For example, respondents interviewed in 1993 are linked to 1993 crime rates and estimates of 1993 census characteristics for their beat, while those interviewed in 2003 are linked to crime data and census estimates for that year. In total, respondents are situated in 2,043 distinct year-beat contexts. Technically, this is a 'fixed effects' model for estimating the joint impact of individual and context-level measures on fear of crime.

Column I of Table 5.1 includes just the personal characteristics of our respondents. All of them are by dichotomies, so their coefficients can be compared in magnitude. The coefficients represent the difference in fear, net of other factors in the model, associated with being on one side of a demographic category rather than the other. The analytic variables representing race identify all but white respondents; as the 'omitted category' in this analysis, the other measures contrast the fear scores of their group's members with others and in comparison to white Chicagoans. Whites were the safest group, and even controlling for the other individual factors presented in Column I of Table 5.1, everyone else was still significantly more fearful. Across the entire period, the strongest individual correlates of fear were being female and a Spanish-speaker, followed by being older (over age 65) and African-American. Less strongly, more affluent respondents reported being less fearful (this is indexed by education, home ownership, and income, along with being in employment). Younger respondents were reluctant to express much fear. These patterns are in line with past research

---

[1] This analysis excludes respondents who failed to answer the questions itemised in Table 5.1, plus those for whom we could not identify a beat of residence. Together, these criteria excluded about 18 per cent of the 20,363 individuals who were originally interviewed between 1994 and 2003.

Table 5.1: Personal factors, neighbourhood conditions, confidence in police and fear of crime, 1994–2003

	I Individual Factors		II Neighbourhood Assessments		III Neighbourhood Context	
	Coefficient	Significance	Coefficient	Significance	Coefficient	Significance
Intercept	2.14	.00	2.12	.00	2.23	.00
Individual Factors						
African-American	.14	.00	.02	.36	-.13	.00
Latino	.08	.00	.04	.08	-.02	.30
Spanish-speaking	.29	.00	.10	.00	.09	.00
Other or undetermined race	.06	.02	.03	.26	-.00	.87
Female	.27	.00	.27	.00	.28	.00
Age 65 and older	.14	.00	.34	.00	.34	.00
Under age 30	-.04	.01	-.07	.00	-.07	.00
In the labour force	-.11	.00	-.10	.00	-.09	.00
College graduate	-.07	.00	-.01	.30	-.01	.41
Income $40,000 or more	-.10	.00	-.06	.00	-.05	.00
Home-owner	-.05	.00	-.04	.00	-.02	.00
Neighbourhood Assessments						
Crime problems (z)			.12	.00	.13	.00
Drug and gang problems (z)			.16	.00	.13	.00
Social disorder problems (z)			.11	.00	.10	.00
Confidence in local police (z)			-.17	.00	-.16	.00
Heard about community policing			-.04	.00	-.04	.00
Heard about beat meetings			-.03	.02	-.04	.00

(continued)

Table 5.1: Continued

Beat-Year Context				
Log personal crime rate (z)				.05	.00
Log residential burglary rate (z)				.03	.00
Per cent black (z)				.12	.00
Per cent Latinc (z)				.05	.00
Log linguistic isolation (z)				.04	.00
Beat stability index (z)				-.03	.00
Variance Explained				
Within-neighbourhood	4 per cent	21 per cent	22 per cent	
Between neighbourhood	37 per cent	85 per cent	90 per cent	
Number of Cases				
Individuals Contexts	16,878	16,878	16,878	
	2,043	2,043	2,043	

Note: 'z' indicates standardised measure; all other measures are 0–1 dichotomies.

on the individual correlates of fear. Note that the coefficient for being a Spanish-speaker was more than three times as great as that for being one of the city's Latino residents—this reflects the large linguistic divide among Hispanics, illustrated in Figure 5.2. This was also the fastest-changing demographic factor on the list, and the fact that there were many more Spanish-speakers at the end of this time period than at the beginning magnified their statistical impact.

Together, the variables examined in Column I explain just 4 per cent of the variance in fear. This is lower than the R^2s typical of multiple regression models of fear; in fact, the comparable R^2 for the same set of variables was 10 per cent when calculated using OLS regression. The difference is that multilevel analysis decomposes the variance that is attributable to differences between neighbourhoods from that which is due to differences among individuals, while OLS regression attributes the effects of both to the individual variables. This makes a considerable difference, because in these data the year-beat context within which individuals are situated explains 17 per cent of the total variance in fear (this is the 'intra-class correlation'). This figure is high for criminological research in general (Oberwittler 2004), but it is almost exactly the figure reported by Robinson et al (2003) for a block-level study of fear in Baltimore. Because Chicagoans are strikingly segregated by race and class, 37 per cent of the between-context difference in fear was due to 'compositional effects' (for example, some neighbourhoods exhibited more fear because many Spanish-speakers were concentrated there), and this is reported as well in Table 5.1.

Column II of Table 5.1 adds respondent's views of neighbourhood crime conditions and the police to the mix. Unlike their personal characteristics, we have seen that these perceptions shifted over time, some quite dramatically and differentially for various population groups. Together, Chicagoan's assessments of what was happening in their neighbourhoods increased the R^2 in Column II to 21 per cent, a five-fold increase over the simple demographic model.

The three indices of the extent of crime, drug and gang, and social disorder problems were standardised, so that the coefficients presented for them in Table 5.1 are comparable; this is highlighted by the 'z' displayed in those rows. The coefficients represent differences in levels of fear associated with a one standard deviation shift (which is a very substantial change) in the level of each of those independent variables. All were strongly related to levels of fear, with perceived drug and gang problems having the largest negative impact. In addition, assessments of the quality of policing were linked to fear, with an effect equalling that of drug and gang problems. The two dichotomous measures of awareness of Chicago's community policing programme each had about the same effect, which was in the range of that of being a home-owner. Not surprisingly, in addition to increasing the individual-level R^2, adding these perceptions of neighbourhood conditions and policing explained 85 per cent of differences between the neighbour-hoods.

Interestingly, taking these factors into account also dramatically altered the relationship between fear of crime and race. Being a Spanish-speaker was the only racial or ethnic factor that was still significantly associated with fear, once the effects of these measures of crime, disorder and police-community relations were accounted for. Statistical differences in fear uniquely associated with being an African-American dropped by a factor of seven (from .14 to .02), and the fear associated with being a Latino dropped by half. Even the uniquely high level of fear associated with being a Spanish-speaker dropped by almost two-thirds, from .29 to .10, although it remained statistically significant. The influence of most other individual characteristics was not much affected, for they are less geographically concentrated and covaried less with crime, disorder, and relations with the police.

Column III of Table 5.1 adds beat-year context measures of crime and associated demographic factors to the mix. All of the measures were also standardised, so the coefficients can be directly compared in terms of their magnitude. The extent of officially recorded crime mattered for fear at this level as well. Residents were more fearful in times and places with high levels of reported personal crime and residential burglary. Because crime rates were dropping in almost all areas of the city between 1993 and 2003, the inference is that neighbourhood crime decline was one factor behind the drop in fear. In addition, fear of crime was lower in more stable areas; beat stability is represented by a factor score loading heavily on home ownership and a low level of residential turnover in the area. Fear levels were higher where there were concentrations of African-Americans and Latinos, with the former evidencing the highest covariance with individual levels of fear. But whites, who were the safest group, declined by 13 per cent between 1990 and 2000, so that certainly could not explain declining levels of fear. The final contextual level factor described in Table 5.1 is linguistic isolation. For each beat in each year, this is a measures of the percentage of households in which all members 14 years old and above routinely speak a language other than English and none of them speak English (by their own assessment) 'very well'. Linguistic isolation is closely associated with the emergence of large, poor, Spanish-speaking immigrant neighbourhoods in Chicago, and these are places in which many survey respondents who report worsening neighbourhood conditions are concentrated (Skogan and Steiner 2004b). Together, the individual-level and context-level neighbourhood factors listed in Table 5.1 explained 90 per cent of the difference between beat-year contexts in fear of crime.

Interestingly, taking more neighbourhood-level factors into account further altered the relationship between fear of crime and black Chicago. The coefficient associated with being African-American became significant and *negative*. This means that in an unlikely world in which African-Americans lived in places that were 'just average' (if this was their score on these measures of gangs, drugs, social disorder, residential stability, recorded crime, and confidence in the police), they would feel even safer than whites and Latinos. Of course, this is not the real world, for they are over-concentrated in some of the worst parts of town, but many of the trends presented in Figures 5.4 and 5.5 project that this is the direction in which things are moving, a hopeful sign for the city's blacks. On the other hand, the extra dollop of fear associated with being one of the growing number of Spanish-speakers remained significantly associated with fear.

IV. MODELLING TRENDS IN FEAR

The final question is, how accurately do these factors account for *trends* in fear over time? This is addressed in Figure 5.5, which compares yearly levels of fear with trends predicted by various components of the statistical model. Three statistical predictions are presented. The first is based on the fixed personal characteristics of respondents, and it is apparent that those demographic factors account for scarcely any of the decline in fear over time. The 'demographic prediction' of fear is virtually flat over time, and does not match the observed trend at all. This is consistent with the data presented in Figures 5.1 and 5.2, which illustrated that the decline in fear in Chicago was broad-based during the 1994–2003 period, and could not be easily explained by changes in the city's demography.

Adding respondents' assessments of neighbourhood conditions, their awareness of community policing, and their confidence in the police helped a great deal. The yearly levels of fear predicted by demography plus those factors did capture some of the trend in fear, and the further addition of area crime and demography improved the fit a bit more.

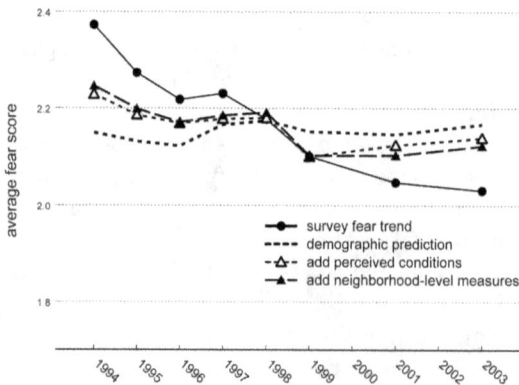

Figure 5.5: Trends in Survey and Predicted Fear

However, it is apparent in Figure 5.5 that the factors examined here can account for only part of the drop in fear witnessed in Chicago during the 1990s and 2000s. In particular, the predicted level of fear in the 2001–03 period is further from the mark than it was for the 1990s. The early 2000s was a period in which confidence in the police stopped increasing among African-Americans, and when their reports of neighbourhood gang, drug and social disorder problems ceased improving. Things also took a turn for the worse among Spanish-speaking Latinos during this period. Fear of crime continued to drop for both groups, on the other hand, suggesting that other factors *not* included in this analysis were at work during the 2000s. The large size of the individual-level coefficient associated with being a Spanish-speaker even when controlling for neighbourhood and policing factors suggests that more needs to be understood about the sources of their fear.

There are certainly many plausible causes of fear that are not examined here, because adequate measures were not included in the survey. One is a direct measure of personal victimisation, which in line with declining recorded crime rates should have declined over the course of this study. Other causes of fear include what Skogan and Maxfield (1981) dubbed 'vicarious victimisation'. People can have 'second-hand' experience of crime via a variety of channels (see also Tyler 1980, 1984). One such channel is media coverage of crime. There has also been some research on the impact of another source of second-hand information on crime—interpersonal communication—but this research is less common. As Skogan and Maxfield (1981) documented, people talk and hear about crime on a frequent basis. When they do they are more fearful, and when victims they hear about resemble themselves and come from the same neighbourhood, they are even more fearful. Given the decline in crime that Chicago experienced during the 1990s, it is plausible that talk about neighbourhood crime diminished somewhat, and data on this point might improve our understanding of trends in fear. On the other hand, I am less sanguine that media coverage of crime tracked this new reality very closely.

Also not considered here is a list of concerns about ostensibly 'non-crime' issues which research has linked to expressions of fear of crime. On this list are perceptions of growing racial diversity in the neighbourhood, the appearance of immigrants in the community (Lane and Meeker 2003), and concern about cultural diversity more generally (Merry 1981). Another study might be able to consider additional neighbourhood or contextual-level factors, including the extent of neighbourhood cohesion or solidarity, and the willingness of neighbours to intervene to protect one another. These are components of 'collective efficacy', which has been shown to deter violent crime (Sampson, Raudenbush and Earls 1997). Xu, Fiedler and Flaming (2005) document that collective efficacy is linked to fear, both directly and indirectly through its impact on neighbourhood disorder and crime. What is unknown in the present context is whether Chicagoans' 'non-crime' concerns and neighbourhood solidarity have increased enough over time, to account for declining levels of fear.

V. CONCLUSIONS

At least since the 1970s, fear of crime has been one of the barometers by which society judges its emotional condition. Mounting levels of fear provided a backdrop for highly charged political debates over crime policy and criminal justice practices. One theme of this volume is that this 'emotionalisation' of the issue threatens to dominate discussions of jurisprudence and criminology, as politicians position themselves to address the apparent emotional needs of the public. In this context, the view that trends in fear of crime have not reflected real declines in crime in the UK and elsewhere takes on real political significance.

However, it turns out that fear of crime does not inevitably ratchet up; it also can go down, and dramatically so. This chapter examined the factors lying behind this trend. Surveys conducted in Chicago between 1994 and 2004 document that fear of crime there *did* drop noticeably, as crime declined. The decline was a general one, and in addition fear went down a bit more among some of the groups that were initially most fearful, including women, African-Americans and older residents. The challenge facing the chapter was to *explain* these trends, which is an issue that has not been addressed in past research.

The analysis focused on factors that—unlike demography—can shift relatively rapidly, and could thus account for rapidly declining fear. Among them were neighbourhood conditions. These were represented by archival measures of crime and by perceptions of neighbourhood conditions gathered in the surveys. Another factor that changed during the 1994–2003 period was policing. During this period Chicago adopted a community policing programme, and the evaluation surveys indicate that awareness of the programme grew over the period, and Chicagoans became more confident in their police.

The chapter presented a statistical model incorporating these individual and neighbourhood-level factors. These factors explained a substantial fraction—but far from all—of the decline in fear that was observed over time. Among the notable findings was the importance of immigration; after women and older people, Spanish-speaking residents were the most fearful Chicagoans. This factor takes on added significance because it is the fastest-changing feature of the city's demographic landscape. The effect of confidence in the police was a strong one, and awareness of the city's community policing programme contributed to declining fear as well. Both awareness and confidence rose during the 1990s, as the programme took hold in the city. Not surprisingly, indicators of the extent of crime, gang, drug, and social disorder problems were also linked to fear, and these too declined for many residents during the 1990s and early 2000s.

REFERENCES

Bennett, T (1989) *Contact Patrols in Birmingham and London: An Evaluation of a Fear Reducing Strategy* (Cambridge, Institute of Criminology).
Cook, FL and Cook, TD (1976) 'Evaluating the Rhetoric of Crisis: A Case Study of Criminal Victimization of the Elderly' 50 *Social Service Review* 632–46.
Ditton, J, Farrall, S, Bannister, J and Gilchrist, E (2000) 'Crime Surveys and the Measurement Problem: Fear of Crime' in V Jupp, P Davies and P Francis (eds) *Doing Criminological Research* (London, Sage).
Farrall, S and Gadd, D (2004) 'The Frequency of Fear of Crime' British Journal of Criminology, 44: pp 127–132.
Fattah, E and Sacco, VF (1989) *Crime and Victimization of the Elderly* (New York, Springer-Verlag).
Finn, P (1988) *Street People* (Washington, DC, National Institute of Justice, US Department of Justice).
Gallup Organization (2005) 'U.S. Crime Problem Less Troubling to Americans', www.gallup.com/poll/.
Hart, T and Rennison, C (2003) *Reporting Crime to the Police, 1992–2000* (Washington DC, Bureau of Justice Statistics, US Department of Justice).
Innes, M (2004) 'Reinventing Tradition: Reassurance, Neighbourhood Security and Policing' 4 *Criminal Justice* 151–71.
—— and Fielding, N (2002) 'From Community To Communicative Policing: "Signal Crimes" And The Problem Of Public Reassurance' 7(2) *Sociological Research Online* www.socresonline.org.uk/7/2/innes.html.
Kelling, GL and Coles, CM (1996) *Fixing Broken Windows* (New York, Touchstone Press).
Lane, J and Meeker, JW (2003) 'Fear of Gang Crime: A Look at Three Theoretical Models' 37 *Law and Society Review* 425–56.
Leigh, A, Read, T and Tilley, N (1998) 'Brit Pop II: Problem-Oriented Policing in Practice' (London, Home Office, Police Research Series Paper 93).
Merry, SE (1981) *Urban Danger: Life in a Neighbourhood of Strangers* (Philadelphia, Temple University Press).
National Reassurance Policing Programme (2004) 'The Reassurance Gap', www .reassurancepolicing.co.uk/reassurancegap.asp.
Oberwittler, D (2004) 'A Multilevel Analysis of Neighbourhood Contextual Effects on Serious Juvenile Offending: The Role of Subcultural Values and Social Disorganization' 1 *European Journal of Criminology* 201–36.
Pate, AM (1986) 'Experimenting with Foot Patrol: The Newark Experience' in D Rosenbaum (ed), *Community Crime Prevention* (Newbury Park, Sage Publications).

Reiss, AJ Jr (1985) *Policing a City's Central District: The Oakland Story* (Washington, DC, National Institute of Justice, US Department of Justice).

Robinson, J, Lawton, B, Taylor R and Perkins, D (2003) 'Multilevel Longitudinal Impacts of Incivilities: Fear of Crime, Expected Safety, and Block Satisfaction' 19 *Journal of Quantitative Criminology* 237–74.

Sampson, RJ, Raudenbush, S and Earls, F (1997) 'Neighbourhoods and Violent Crime: A Multilevel Study of Collective Efficacy' 277 *Science* 918–24.

Skogan, WG (1990) *Disorder and Decline: Crime and the Spiral of Decay in American Cities* (New York, The Free Press).

—— (1993) 'The Various Meanings of Fear' in W Bilsky, C Pfeiffer and P Wetzels (eds) *The Fear of Crime and Criminal Victimization* (Stuttgart, Enke).

—— (1994) 'Contacts Between Police and The Public: A British Crime Survey Report' (London, HMSO, Home Office Research Study No 135).

—— (1995) 'Crime and the Racial Fears of White Americans' 539 *Annals of the American Academy of Political and Social Science* 59–71.

—— and Hartnett, SM (1997) *Community Policing, Chicago Style* (New York and London, Oxford University Press).

Skogan, WG and Maxfield, MG (1981) *Coping With Crime: Individual and Neighbourhood Reactions* (Beverly Hills, Sage).

Skogan, WG and Steiner L (2004a) *Community Policing in Chicago: Year Ten* (Chicago, Criminal Justice Information Authority).

—— (2004b) 'Crime, Disorder and Decay in Chicago's Latino Community' 2 *Journal of Ethnicity in Criminal Justice* 7–26.

Tyler, TR (1980) 'The Effect of Directly and Indirectly Experienced Events: The Origin of Crime-Related Judgements and Behaviour' 39 *Journal of Personality and Social Psychology* 13–28.

—— (1984) 'Assessing the Risk of Crime Victimization' 40 *Journal of Social Issues* 27–38.

Weitzer, R and Tuch, S (2004) 'Race and Perceptions of Police Misconduct' 51 *Social Problems* 305–25.

Xu, Y, Fiedler, ML and Flaming, KH (2005) 'Discovering the Impact of Community Policing: The Broken Windows Thesis, Collective Efficacy, and Citizens' Judgment' 42 *Journal of Research in Crime and Delinquency* 147–86.

Zhao, J, Scheider M and Thurman, Q (2002) 'The Effect of Police Presence on Public Fear Reduction and Satisfaction: A Review of the Literature' 15 *The Justice Professional* 273–99.

6

Moral Indignation in the East of England: A Youthful Twist on Ranulf's Ageing Thesis

ANNA KING* AND SHADD MARUNA

T HE ROLE OF emotions has been a badly neglected topic in criminology in general (de Haan and Loader 2002; Katz 1988), hence the importance of a collection like the present one. On the other hand, the role of emotions in the motivation to punish wrongdoers has been anything but neglected. Indeed, understanding the 'passions' of punishment or the psychosocial origins of punitive attitudes has such a long and rich history in social science that it is difficult to know where to start any review. We have Durkheim (1933) and Nietzsche (1956 [1887]), Mead (1918) and Garland (1990), Adorno et al's *Authoritarian Personality* (1956), and social constructionist classics like Cohen's *Folk Devils and Moral Panics* (1980), Stuart Hall et al's *Policing the Crisis* (1978), Geoff Pearson's *Hooligans* (1983), and Girlinget al's *Crime and Social Change in Middle England* (2000). The literature on public opinion regarding crime and justice is substantial and growing (see Roberts and Hough 2002). There are large and sophisticated bodies of research on the cognitive and psychological factors impacting punishment motives (see Carslmith, Darley and Robinson 2002; Stitka 2003; Stalans 2002), and a fascinating psychoanalytic literature on scapegoating, splitting, and the unconscious meanings of punishment (see Duncan 1996; Holloway and Jefferson 2000; Maruna, Matravers and King 2004).

Somewhat remarkably, then, considering the sheer volume of theoretical resources on punishment and the emotions, the relatively obscure work of an early twentieth-century Danish social theorist on the subject has been enjoying a minor comeback in the last few years. Some 50 years after the

* Correspondence to annaking@rutgers.edu. The authors wish to thank the editors and other participants at the Onati Conference for their helpful suggestions. This research was very generously supported by a grant from the HF Guggenheim Foundation.

author's death, Svend Ranulf's argument from *Moral Indignation and Middle Class Psychology* received prominent references in two plenary addresses (Sherman 2003; Young 2003), and has been revised and updated by JM Barbalet (2002) in *Theoretical Criminology*.

Ranulf, like Durkheim and others, sought to understand the origins of 'law and order', or what he called the 'disinterested tendency to inflict punishment'—'disinterested' because 'no direct personal advantage is achieved by the act of punishing another person who has injured a third party' (Ranulf 1938: 1). In particular, Ranulf was fascinated by societies (eg, the Nazis, Calvinists, Puritans, Jansenists) that were 'characterized by an unusually strong desire to see other people punished for their immorality' (1938: 12). He argues that such processes arise in societies with a developed class structure, and in particular an established lower middle class. Ranulf defines the lower middle class as 'a petty bourgeoisie whose lot was a kind to foster among them a certain dissatisfaction and feeling of oppression which became especially perceptible when they compared their condition with the wealth and luxury of others'.[1] Here, Ranulf was referring to merchant shopkeepers and craft workers. Barbalet (2002) argues that their equivalents in today's society would be non-manual workers in service and manufacturing industries. The important point is that the individuals see themselves as aligned to the 'powers that be', but at the same time have not enjoyed the sorts of success to which they might aspire. Barbalet writes: 'Whereas blue-collar workers are structurally subjected to anger-producing interactions, white-collar workers are structurally implicated in actions in which status envy and autonomy satisfaction are more salient' (2002: 289).

Structurally positioned between the 'haves' and 'have nots', but aligned squarely to the 'haves', the middle class suffers from envy of the rich, but channels this into a moral indignation about the vices of the poor, Ranulf argues. Members of the middle class comfort themselves with the belief that they are morally pure (or at least morally better than the poor), even if they are materially unsuccessful. He argues, for instance, that the excessive punitiveness of the Nazi regime (aggravated penalties, the creation of hundreds of new punishable acts, eliminating mitigations for crime, such as self-defence) could be understood as 'a psychological reaction of this lower middle class to the recent economic depression which in Germany also brought about a recrudescence of the bitter memories of the lost war' (1938: 9).

---

[1] Interestingly, Ranulf suggests that the United States might be the premiere example of such a society, quoting Calverton as saying: 'America is the one country whose whole tradition grew out of an unadulterated petty bourgeois psychology. It is the one country which the petty bourgeoisie was able to control from the very beginning, and shape in terms of its own destiny. In a very important sense, we can say that America is the great petty bourgeois experiment—just as Soviet Russia is the great proletarian experiment' (1938: 55).

Numerous observers have suggested that there are echoes of this sort of punitiveness in contemporary Western society, and have turned to Ranulf to help explain these emotional dynamics. For example, in the article 'American Gulag', prison reformer Jerome Miller (2004: 5) argues:

> Overall, the prevailing public mood on crime is vicious. I recently watched a video of a 'focus group' on crime conducted by a Republican pollster and consultant. In discussing a recent shooting of a teacher by a 13-year-old African-American middle-school honour student, the consultant asked the group what they would do in such a case. Their response seemed even to embarrass him. ... 'Fry him!' came the insistent shouts from the group. ... I wanted to avert my eyes from the TV. It brought to mind another mood observed by the Danish sociologist Svend Ranulf when he looked across the border into the Germany of the early 1930s to see how that country proposed dealing with criminals and crime.

In this paper we will describe an empirical study of punitive public attitudes at the University of Cambridge and selectively review some of the findings that might relate to Ranulf's thesis. We find considerable support for Ranulf's argument, with lingering themes of insecurity and resentment apparently supporting a punitive mindset. Additionally, however, we identify a possible new twist on Ranulf's argument. Individuals who harbour the most strongly punitive attitudes toward offenders seem to be those most resentful of the lives of young people. They describe the young as lazy aristocrats who seem to get everything they want without having to work for it. This barely masked envy, however, manifests itself as a passionate concern for the immoral behaviour of the young. The young today are 'out of control' and 'have no respect for anything anymore'. We conclude that Ranulf's thesis could easily be updated for today's world. That is, in a rapidly ageing society that nonetheless glorifies youth, young people are seen as posing a threat to the old in much of the same way that the rich threaten the self-esteem of the struggling middle class. Today's punitiveness may be as much a manifestation of this 'youth envy' as it is a class-based jealousy.

I. MORAL INDIGNATION AND MIDDLE CLASS PSYCHOLOGY

Although, clearly an argument about the structural impact of the class structure, Ranulf's argument also contains a theory of the psychological dynamics of punitiveness. Ranulf (1938: 1) begins his enquiry by noting that a punitive inclination was 'not equally strong in all human societies', and indeed seemed almost completely lacking in some cultures. He argued that punitiveness should be understood as a kind of 'disguised envy', where envy is understood 'not in a pejorative but in an ethically neutral sense' as a response to economic insecurities rather than increased crime.

Members of the lower middle class 'accept as legitimate the institutional framework to which they are subjected' (Barbalet 2002: 290). They also 'regard themselves as occupying the same opportunity structure as those whom they come to envy or resent' (2002: 290). As a result, they experience a deeply felt personal shame at their own failure to succeed economically: 'An experience of incomplete remunerative and career success within a distributive system the incumbent regards as legitimate is ultimately shaming' (2002: 290). In other words, if the system is perceived to be legitimate, and they have not succeeded in the way they would like, they must be personally at fault. They just did not work hard enough.

Ranulf argues that this shame is then masked and deflected, first, by a sort of 'sour grapes' system of rationalisations and denials, then second, by projecting the shame onto a scapegoat class. According to Ranulf, the petty bourgeois look upon the rich and their hedonistic ways with 'jealous eyes', and in their hearts they 'loved and longed for' this way of life. Yet, since they failed to achieve such a hedonistic lifestyle, they instead 'make a virtue of necessity' and declare that they actually disapprove of such behaviour, preferring the dignity of hard work and family values (2002: 42).

Moreover, instead of giving vent to their suppressed jealousy of the rich, the middle class channels its anger toward those below them in the social hierarchy, in particular criminal offenders. Essentially, one can improve one's own sense of self-worth and self-esteem by putting others down. Ranulf (1938: 290) writes:

> People interfere in affairs which seem to be no concern of theirs, merely for the satisfaction of giving vent to their indignation and of collaborating in the chastisement of strangers for acts which have been materially harmful only to a likewise unknown third party or perhaps nobody at all.

Here, Ranulf draws explicitly on Nietzsche (1956 [1887]): 196–97), who argued that in supporting the punishment of criminals, even the least powerful member of society is 'given a chance to bask in the glorious feeling of treating another human being as lower than himself—or, in case the actual power has passed on to a legal "authority," of seeing him despised and mistreated.' This scapegoating aspect of Ranulf's equation is underdeveloped and can be improved from the incorporation of newer research drawing on psychoanalytic themes to understand punitiveness (see Maruna, Matravers and King (2004) for a review).

Ranulf argues that the process he describes is a universal one, afflicting numerous societies and ethnic groups at different points in time, but not others (hence, he rejects notions that some ethnic groups or nationalities are somehow permanently punitive). Indeed, Ranulf argues that the characteristic of punitiveness 'tends to disappear in the middle class as soon as it has acquired a certain standard of wealth and prestige' (1938: 2). The emotions of punitiveness (or the desire to see offenders punished more severely) are structurally induced, according to Ranulf's theory. Indeed Barbalet (2002) argues that one of Ranulf's most important achievements in this work is to argue that emotions link structure and agency.

Still struggling with the agency-structure issue 70 years after Ranulf, Jock Young (2003) draws upon and develops Ranulf's thesis in his discussion of the 'sociology of vindictiveness'. Young argues that punitive attitudes can be traced to the 'precariousness of inclusion' for those struggling to remain middle class. The 'seemingly random discontinuities of career, the profligate and largely unmerited rewards in the property market and in finance, all give a sense of rewards and which are allocated by caprice rather than by the rules of merit' (2003: 399). Young argues that the lack of certainty in one's middle class status creates an ontological insecurity or identity crisis in late modern individuals. To defend against this sense of disembedded-ness, one turns to essentialisation–the dehumanisation of one's enemies as intrinsically different than oneself–resentment, and eventually popular punitiveness (see also Bottoms 1995: 785; Garland 2001).

II. THE CAMBRIDGE UNIVERSITY PUBLIC
OPINION PROJECT (CUPOP)

These aspects of the Ranulf thesis are some of the key themes we are indirectly exploring in our own research on punitive public attitudes. The Cambridge University Public Opinion Project consists of three, closely related phases mixing quantitative and qualitative methodologies, as well as experimental and quasi-experimental designs. The first phase of this research involved a postal survey measuring attitudes towards the treat-ment of offenders and some of the possible correlates to these attitudes. The surveys included a newly constructed, eight-item scale for measuring punitive attitudes (see Table 6.1). Scores on this measure were then used to identify participants for the more in-depth analysis in Phase Two. In particular, two groups of 20 participants apiece, matched case-by-case on demographic characteristics, were selected to represent individuals hold-ing 'strongly punitive' and 'strongly non-punitive' views regarding the treatment of offenders. Members of both groups participated in life story interviews in order to better understand the worldviews underlying these attitudes. Phase Three of the project will involve a series of experimental manipulations designed to test whether these scores on the punitiveness scale can be manipulated experimentally. In this following analysis, how-ever, we draw only on the second phase of the research, involving in-depth qualitative interviews with respondents to the postal survey.

A. Sample

Surveys were sent to a random sample of addresses (n = 3600) in six diverse postcode areas covering Greater London and both rural and non-rural

Table 6.1: Punitiveness measures (Alpha = .82)

Statement	% Agreeing (n = 925)
1. I'd consider volunteering my time or donating money to an organisation that supported toughening the sentencing laws in the UK.	37%
2. We should bring back the death penalty for serious crimes.	54%
3. With most offenders, we need to 'condemn more and understand less'.	35%
4. My general view towards offenders is that they should be treated harshly.	58%
5. (R) Prisoners should have access to televisions or gym facilities.[a]	58%
6. (R) If prison has to be used, it should be used sparingly and only as a last option.	47%
7. (R) I would consider volunteering my time or donating money to an organisation that supported alternatives to prison.	36%
8. (R) Probation or a community sentence (rather than prison) is appropriate for a person found guilty of burglary for the second time.	31%

Note

[a] Four items were constructed so that disagreement would indicate punitiveness. Psychometric research has shown that people are more likely to agree with positively stated items. These reverse coded items (indicated by 'R'), therefore, are included in the scale to control for such potential 'acquiescence bias' (see Hogg and Vaughan 2005). For descriptive purposes, however, percentages based on reverse scores are presented for consistency, but all items were presented to respondents with affirmative wording.

areas of the East Anglia region of England. Of those addresses identified, 940 respondents completed surveys.[2]

As with previous surveys of this kind, we found considerable diversity in views. In evaluating answers to individual items, about half could be said to hold broadly punitive attitudes. For instance, 54 per cent support the reinstatement of the death penalty in Britain. Yet, a rather smaller percentage said they would be willing to take action in support of these views. When we asked whether respondents would consider volunteering their time or donating money to an organisation that supported toughening the sentencing laws in the UK, only 36 per cent agreed. This same pattern can be found on the other side of the equation. Almost half (47 per cent) of

[2] Response rates for postal surveys are typically 20–30 per cent (Dillman, 2000), so a 26 per cent response rate was considered reasonable.

respondents agreed with the statement, 'If prison has to be used, it should be used sparingly and only as a last option.' Yet, again, only 36 per cent said they would consider volunteering for an organisation that promoted the greater use of alternatives to prison. There appears to be a 'hardcore' one-third of the respondents who could be considered 'punitive-minded' or in favour of harsher penalties for law-breakers, and a similar-sized fraction who appear to take an opposing view (see Figure 6.1).

In order to better understand these more extreme responses, the second phase of our research involved creating two, smaller samples (N = 20) of individuals with scores that are either one standard deviation above or below the sample mean on our punitiveness scale: the 'high punitive' and 'low punitive' sub-samples. These two samples were matched on a case-by-case basis as closely as possible in terms of relevant socio-demographics (see Table 6.2). Although not representative of any wider population, the 40 participants were basically 'average citizens', from a wide array of backgrounds, but with no specialised knowledge or relationship to the world of criminal justice. Included in the sample were four individuals with criminal convictions and three victims of serious domestic and childhood sexual abuse. One interviewee had experience doing maintenance in a prison and another toured the construction of a new prison with the workers. The

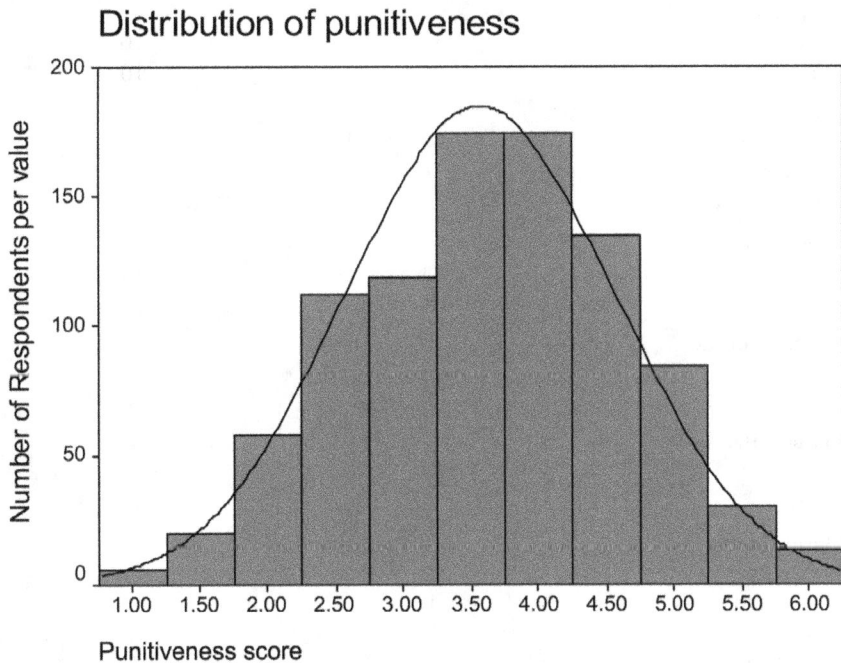

Figure 6.1: Punitiveness Scale Distribution (range 1–6, mean = 3.57, sd = 1.0)

Table 6.2: Table of matched interview samples

	Low-Punitive Group (n = 20)	Punitive Group (n = 20)
Sex		
Female	9	9
Male	11	11
Income		
Under £30,000	12	11
Over £30,000	8	8
Missing	0	1
Class upbringing		
Working	11	13
Middle	8	5
Upper	1	2
Age		
22–44	5	9
45–64	10	8
Over 64	5	3
Rural		
No	12	13
Yes	8	7
Non-deprived area		
No	11	10
Yes	9	10
Local area crime		
Low crime	4	4
Med crime	9	9
High crime	7	7
Education		
No	11	18
Yes	9	2
Victim of crime		
No	13	12
Yes	7	8
Knows offenders		
No	12	12
Yes	8	8
Marital status		
Married	12	13
Divorced	1	4
Never married	5	2
Widow(ed)	2	1

(continued)

Table 6.2: (Continued)

Children		
No	9	5
Yes	11	15
Totals	20	20

interviewees' residences ranged from country estates, to council estates in London's East End. Their ages ranged from 23 to 80, and four were foreign born. Their occupations included a company CEO, a pipe-fitter and a (semi-) professional female impersonator. Two interviewees were unemployed and seeking work, two were disabled individuals living on benefits, and eight were pensioners. Some had travelled the world, while others had stayed in one spot much of their lives. Indeed, on the surface, the only thing they seemed to have in common with one another is that they held strong views when it came to justice issues.

B. Method

Our goal in Phase 2 is to try to find out what other characteristics members of each group might share that might account for these unusually punitive (or non-punitive) views. Participants in this more in-depth phase of the research were asked to explain their survey responses in greater detail, and also to talk about their lives: their experiences with being punished, their experiences of punishing others, experiences witnessing punishment, and their general concerns and goals for the future. We used a modified version of Dan McAdams' (1995) Life Story Interview protocol, as well as additional open-ended questions about crime and justice issues. Transcripts were tape-recorded, transcribed, and inductively analysed for patterns across interviewees within both samples (punitive and low punitive).

This qualitative aspect of our research project provides a reasonable opportunity for exploring the themes of buried shame, moral indignation, projection and scapegoating intrinsic to Ranulf's theory. In these interviews, individuals were asked both to talk about their own lives and experiences in depth, but also to talk about their reasoning behind their survey responses. Their answers provide possible glimpses into the thinking underpinning punitive attitudes, especially when these themes can be compared to those respondents with parallel background characteristics in the low punitive sample.

III. ECHOES OF RANULF IN THE EAST OF ENGLAND

Most directly, echoes of Ranulf's theory could be heard in the punitive sub-sample's description of their employment histories, where disappointments and lingering frustration play a substantial role. To illustrate this consistent theme in the punitive group narratives, we draw on three individuals with very different backgrounds, but similar frustrations: Gary, Matt and Pete.

Gary, a relatively successful engineer, living in an affluent suburb of London. Gary described a time when he had had to leave work temporarily due to depression as the lowest point in his life. The depression, he said, seemed to have been brought on by his perception that at work, he needed to acquiesce to others on a regular basis, or as he put it, his tendency to try to please others constantly without thinking of himself. These constant efforts to impress made his employers happy, but left Gary deeply unfulfilled and dissatisfied with his life. Despite having earned an engineering degree (of which he was quite proud and which he saw in terms of its ability to grant him independence), Gary made a point of saying that he had never held a supervisory position in any of his jobs.

Matt, another member of the punitive group, also seemed plagued by a chronic sense that he was never quite able to attain the kind of status that he strived for. For Matt, the manager of an upscale apartment complex in Knightsbridge, however, this was a more conscious struggle than it had been for Gary. Matt resided in an area that would might make anyone hyper-aware of one's 'standing' in the world. Doormen sporting top-hats and tails, elegant coffee shops (where waiting staff speak Italian, customers—French), quiet back-street shops that display leather bags and accessories in windows (but have no need of something as ostentatious as a store sign), women in silk scarves, and men in suits, lounging languidly at tables outside, sipping wine on a weekday afternoon—this was the world outside Matt's door—a door, and a flat that came with the job. While Matt filled his flat with beautiful pieces of art, paintings and sketches and sculptures, the adornments seemed strangely like props, and less like the natural accompaniments to the life of their owner.

From one point of view, the luxury accommodations and the valuable artwork surrounding Matt could be seen as protections against the kind of resentment towards the 'haves' that Ranulf describes. However, in the context of Matt's own ambitious expectations for himself, and in the context of the population of diplomats and CEOs occupying the flats around him, Matt's relative 'position' seemed for him to be pushed 'down the ladder'. The degree to which Matt had tried to 'keep up' was evidenced when he, like Gary, described being willing to sacrifice his health in order to fight against feelings of failure at work. He had experienced physically debilitating symptoms brought on by work stress: 'It got to me. You know, my stomach was bad. Since then I've had an ulcer.' When asked what kept him at such stressful jobs, he responded:

> The golden handcuffs I suppose, the money. I've been here a long time. If I stay in the job I get a severance thing. They've dropped my retirement age from 65 to 60 because I'm in management and they retire at 60. Which is two years' time.

Matt was 'born and bred' in London's East End, and had worked his way up through many lower-status occupations (waiter, painter, porter and airport serviceman) to his current job which afforded him a relatively affluent lifestyle. However, rather than insulating him from feelings of envy and resentment, his current position seemed, ironically, to instigate feelings of inferiority.

Ranulf's argument that resentment about one's lack of material success can be channelled into a more acceptable resentment toward offenders may be especially poignant in Pete's story. Pete is a driving instructor who has, like Matt, worked in various low-status occupations (eg factory work, construction) before going on to his current occupation. Maintaining a hard line against criminals for Pete seemed directly linked to a sense of himself as respectable, as those who were seen to disagree with his stance on crime were constructed as manipulative, self-serving, and too lazy to do what is 'right'. These dissenters often included those who were more successful than Pete (eg politicians, 'do-gooders' who had time to work for charities because they didn't need to work for their own money, and others with important jobs). Ironically (or perhaps not), Pete took great pride in his own almost 'politician-like' status amongst the locals. He was quite social and friendly, and 'clued in' to local and current events. Pete also placed much emphasis on owning his own business. However, in describing his driving school business, there seemed to be a sense that he was trying perhaps too hard to convince himself that this was satisfying the needs for status and power that he had started his life with:

> [I teach] a wide range of people how to drive; the youngest student is 17 [and the] oldest is 66 years old—both male and female. [They are] learning basic skills, [I] show [them how] to control a vehicle, teach hazard perception skills, and hopefully, I make them safe drivers for the rest of their lives.

Pete also seemed, like Matt, to have expectations for himself that were never quite met. While many interviewees described falling short of their goals, Pete seemed to be particularly uncomfortable with his failure to attain a certain status. He described, for instance, not finishing a university degree. What seemed to make this event significant for him is that it was so at odds with the much larger picture he painted of himself. Perhaps Pete was acutely aware on some level that he was not living up to the image he had once held of himself:

> I started a two-year university degree but that got knocked on the head when I started this [the driving instructor job]. I basically just didn't have enough time. So, I done the foundation course and then I started the second year course, which was electronic engineering. I was originally planning just to take a year out but, a year became two years, became three years, became etc etc. Because I work for myself now, I employ people as well; it's just a full-time business trying to keep a business running so...

AK: How many employees do you have?

Two at the moment.

Finally, additional support for the idea that Pete's punitive views acted as a form of status anxiety projection can be found in his response to a question about 'personal punishment episodes' in his life story. We asked all of our interviewees to talk to us about an incident in which they had had to punish someone else and how they felt about this. In response, Pete detailed a story in which he had punished his 12-year-old daughter for apparently asking someone in town for a bus fare. The incident was reported to him via his brother, a brother who was mentioned in other parts of the interview as living in a nicer section of town and with whom there were apparent tensions over who had 'made it' and who had not. Therefore, this particular transgression on the part of his daughter seemed to trigger an instantaneous and explosive reaction on Pete's part:

> I was straight on the phone ranting and raving that she shouldn't be doing this and really having a go at her. I said 'Right, I give you pocket money, no more pocket money. I am going to speak to your mother, you're not allowed up town for two months' and everything like this. She was crying on the phone. In fact, I think she put the phone down and I spoke to her mother then and her mother was quite angry that she had done this as well. That is how I disciplined her, and then I found out it wasn't true.

Later, he found out, through the brother's wife, that there had been a misunderstanding, and his daughter had not been asking others for money. Still, it is clear that this narrative contained an element of status shame that was thought (erroneously) to have been exposed by his daughter, triggering some of the punitive response. The fact that this was the most salient example of punishing others for this participant provides some support for the suggestion that there may be an element of financial or status insecurity behind punitiveness.

IV. A YOUTHFUL TWIST ON RANULF'S THEME

An additional, important theme emerged in descriptions of moral indignation that is not mentioned in Ranulf's original theoretical discussion but seems to fit nicely within his overall framework. Punitive group members appeared particularly indignant about the behaviours of teenagers and young people. Moreover, it was this group, the young, which seemed to generate the most buried envy and outward jealousy.

In discussing their views of the younger generation, interviewees in the punitive group provided the usual laundry list of behaviours deemed to be offensive or threatening (the use of foul language and gathering in large groups on the street at night top the list). Predictably, too, respondents expressed a sense of seeming nostalgia about their own childhood experiences, protesting a bit too much that today's youth behave in ways never before seen. For instance, a 'Baby Boomer' generation (born circa 1945–59) respondent gave the following account:

> In general young people, in the main, have no respect now for their elders *whatsoever*. It's been a process that has been slowly going on for the last, well since when I was a boy. I mean when we was children *we had total and utter respect for our elders*. You *never* swore in front of your elders. But now the way of the world is that children swear, domineer, dominate their elders. They have no respect for age whatsoever. ... Children seem to be wanting to dominate their parents as opposed to the parents dominate the children–or, um, dominate, um, parents *dominating* their children is a bit harsh. I would say parents guiding the children whereas the children don't want this guidance. (Male, 58 years old; emphasis added.)

As revealed by the above slip-up about the need to 'dominate' children, the disrespectfulness of young people leads quite naturally in these narratives to the need for increased punitiveness for offenders:

> I mean we was in [town] yesterday and the policemen spoke to a gang of children for firing pea-shooters, told them to simmer down. And he's on his wireless saying, 'Yeah, they've simmered down now.' And while he's saying that they're all firing the pea-shooters at the policeman. So you think to yourself, where do you go from here?
>
> AK: When you say that, 'Where do you go from here?', how do you mean exactly?
>
> Well, criminals have got to be punished. These children are—a good deal of them—are going to be criminals, aren't they, because they've got no respect now. So the penal system has got to reflect this, in my mind has got to reflect that. And has got to be, not these softer prisons, but they've got to be harder. They've got to know that they've been in prison. They've got to know that, 'Oh dear I don't want to go to prison again.' But unfortunately they say, 'Oh dear, I'm in prison again. Never mind, I'll soon be out. Get my lovely Christmas dinner and choice of menu, etcetera, etcetera.' I just feel that they're pampered. They shouldn't get a choice of menu. I'm not saying that you give them hard tack and water. But basic grub, give them that, that's it. Make them wash up their own things. Make them grow their own stuff. Everything grows out there, they should be self-sufficient. And as regards the question you've not asked: murderers should be hung. (Male, 61.)

Additionally, all of the interviewees were asked to discuss their own lay hypotheses for why today's youth have so little 'respect for anything'. Two major themes emerged. First, in explaining their answers, almost all of the punitive scorers referred to the inability of parents and other authority figures to 'do anything to' the young today, for fear of law suits or perhaps reprisals from parents or children's advocates.

> When you're brought up in a period, a time, where if you done 'wrong' you expected to get chastised off [by] your parents or the courts or police. You fully expected it; it was a way of life. Things changed in the 70s. You had all these left-wing 'do-gooders' saying it was wrong to smack kids. Parents can't chastise their kids. Teachers can't chastise the kids. Police can't chastise them. That is one of the main reasons we've got such a 'yobbish' society. (Male, 48.)

As in the above passage, this state of affairs is almost always compared to another time—usually the speaker's youth—when things 'were different' and the speakers were very much 'chastised', or lived in fear of it:

> And they know they can get away with things. Like kids can say, you know, 'Oh he done this', and, say to his father, 'Oh the headmaster, he tapped me on the head today.' And [the father] can go up to the board and get the headmaster dismissed and everything else. ... [Kids] know headmasters can't tell you off, teachers can't touch you. When we was kids, you used to go to school. And when kids had been naughty they would get the slipper. And they'd get the slipper in front of everybody in assembly. And that's like humiliation I thought. Not that I wanted, you know, I wouldn't ever do anything because I didn't want to get hit. It weren't that, but the humiliation. I wouldn't stand up there and get whacked with a slipper and start crying in front of everyone. I just couldn't do it. I think now, you know, you hear children, you hear them swearing at the children. They do what they want, because you just can't do nothing. (Female, 34.)

Although the speaker is not clear on what is being advocated in the above passage, taken literally the argument is in favour of the projection of 'humiliation' (or one's fear of potential humiliation) on to others. The surface argument is that if today's young people experienced the fears that the speaker had felt in her youth, then they would be better off. Yet, it may be just as possible that the speaker would be also be better off if these fears were projected in this way.

The desire for strict discipline for youth is of course not unexpected, considering these interviewees were chosen because of their support for harsh disciplinary interventions for offenders. This theme in their explanations might be nothing more than a reflection of a consistent set of principles and beliefs. Perhaps more surprising, however, and more relevant to Ranulf's theory, is that a majority of punitive interviewees (12 of the 20) also spontaneously discussed the theme of consumer culture and materialism when discussing the problems with today's youth:

> ... I don't know, I think children have an easy ride and that isn't very good. Like if they want something, their parents feel like they have to go and get them. If not [the parents] are bullied. And the kids know that, so the kids get what they want. ... It's just, like my nephew, you know, he's got a mobile phone, he's got a CD player, he's got a telly, video in his bedroom. He's only like 11. But has all these things given to him, like a lot of children don't they? Like clothes: 'I can't wear them trainers. I need these trainers. I have got to have Nike.' ... You know, even

at four, my daughter knows what she wants and what she don't want. They do, they just, you know, I think, they're just given it so easy. (Female, 32.)

Interestingly, though, this is not always just the familiar lament of 'Back in my day, we had it hard.' Note, for instance, in the next quote, the speaker is clear that his own generation has been just as spoilt as his children's:

> I think mainly today everything's so easy. Life is a lot easier now than what it was, well I won't say my time, because we had a, you know, well our parents, you know, because that was the war, they had to struggle for whatever they needed. To have a car was a luxury, to go on a holiday was a luxury ... people get all that stuff now before they even get married. It's, 'I want the world' now. 'I want a car before I get married; I want a house before I get married; I want a video; I want a stereo and a CD player', ...The way technology's gone at the moment. I've got a digital camera. I don't know how to work the bloody thing. (Male, 53)

It is the speaker's parents' generation (the WWII cohort) who faced an epic struggle. The respondent's major struggle at the moment is learning to operate his digital camera and all of the other gadgets that he, perhaps guiltily, now enjoys. Also, the status that once came with being able to acquire certain 'creature comforts' such as the various forms of home entertainment he mentions (eg films on video) is lost. These goods no longer represent the attainment of an elevated or established social status (eg marriage) in the way they used to. Likewise, perhaps when the speaker in the next quotation says that adolescents are 'more like adults now', she may be mourning the loss of meaning (albeit perhaps shallow) that once came with material items, while at the same time projecting guilt about the materialism of her own age group at the same time that she is critiquing the young:

> And children are growing up too quickly as well I think. I mean they can do what they want. Teenagers are more like adults now aren't they? They have mobile phones, they have a lot of money in their pockets. You know, they can have whatever they want basically. (Female, 34.)

It is not difficult to hear in these responses something like the envy that Ranulf spoke of in *Moral Indignation and Middle Class Psychology*. What is interesting in this case is that the envy appears to be directed more toward young people as a 'class', rather than the affluent. One might expect that adult anxiety about young people might stem from many of the unconscious associations we have of youth—their sexuality, their energy, their ignorance of the world, and their freedoms. Yet, clearly these adults also associate an enviable lifestyle of materialism, freedom and leisure with the young. Indeed, the teenagers in this narrative sound a great deal like the aristocrats of old. They do not have to work, they go and do what they like, and all the while they get whatever they want at the click of their fingers. It is no wonder that they are resented, and it is interesting in particular that what these spoilt layabouts need most is a bit of rough treatment—bringing back the slap. In an ageing society that nonetheless glorifies youth and youthfulness, this sort of resentment makes perfect sense.

V. DISCUSSION

What is most interesting in many of the discussions with the punitive sub-sample is that the 'spoilt layabouts' they so resent frequently appear to be rather painful reflections of the wider society in decline. That is, these bums who need a good slap may be a lot like 'us' as a society. That is, the things that the young are being criticised for (most obviously 'acting like adults', but also valuing material goods, being selfish, and so forth) are behaviours that are not at all uncommon among the adults being interviewed.

As such, 'the young' might usefully be understood as screens for the projection of the anxieties and guilt of the old. Again, this is hardly a new phenomenon. The 'young' are often the symbolic targets in 'moral panics' that actually have less to do with teenage kicks than they do with wider, societal changes. Jock Young (2005: 102) recently argued:

> If one takes these three 'classic' accounts of moral panics—Stan Cohen's (1972) study of mods and rockers situated in 1964-6, my own study of cannabis and hippies in *The Drugtakers* (Young, 1971) situated in 1968 and Stuart Hall and his team's study of the mugging panic *Policing the Crisis* (Hall et al., 1978) situated in 1972—they all seem to represent major structural and value changes in industrial society as *refracted through the prism of youth*. (Emphasis added.)

In particular, our data suggest that perceptions of 'yob rule' and young people 'out of control' may actually be manifestations of the feeling that consumerism and materialistic values are 'out of control' (see also Vaughan 2002).

In a twist on the well-known Freudian idea that some criminals offend 'from a sense of guilt'—that is, they commit crimes because unconsciously they want to be punished for something—Garland (1990; 2001) has recently developed the notion of punishing 'from a sense of guilt'. This is the idea that some punitiveness among the public is motivated more by a sense of self-cleansing, than social control:

> The most vehement punishments are reserved for those guilty of child abuse, illegal drug use, or sexual violence—precisely those areas in which mainstream social and cultural norms have undergone greatest change and where middle class ambivalence and guilt are at their most intense. (2001: 195-96)

In the subtext, Garland offers an even more provocative possibility:

> Could it be that the extraordinary public fears and hostilities in respect of certain crimes against children stem from the residual guilt and ambivalence that families feel about their choices and the vulnerabilities that they seem to cause? If so, the pedophile and the drug dealer are screens upon which we project our guilt as well as our anxieties. (2001: 263-64 fn 64)

Although our findings suggest that, as Ranulf suggests, feelings of economic insecurity may play a role in this, the punitive worldview is hardly exclusive to the petty bourgeoisie. Our qualitative findings suggest a far more complicated portrait of punitiveness than Ranulf's rather deterministic, class-based argument. In particular, future qualitative research is needed that can explore the processes of personal shame, scapegoating and projection that Ranulf alludes to but does not develop in his argument.

REFERENCES

Adorno, TW, Frenkel-Brunswick, E, Levinson, DJ and Sanford, RN (1956) *The Authoritarian Personality* (New York, Harper).

Allen, R (2002) 'What do the public really feel about non-custodial penalties? Rethinking crime and punishment' (Esmee Fairbairn Foundation).

Altemeyer, D (1988) *Enemies of Freedom: Understanding right-wing authoritarianism* (San Francisco and London, Jossey-Bass Publishers).

Barbalet, JM (2002) 'Moral indignation, class inequality and justice: An exploration and revision of Ranulf' 6(3) *Theoretical Criminology* 279–97.

Bottoms, A (1995) 'The politics of sentencing reform' in C Clarkson and R Morgan (eds), *The Philosophy and Politics of Punishment and Sentencing* (Oxford, Oxford University Press).

Calverton, VF (1932) *The Liberation of American Literature* (New York, Scribner's and Sons).

Carlsmith, KM, Darley, JM and Robinson, P (2002) 'Why do we punish? Deterrence and Just Deserts as Motives for Punishment' 83 *Journal of Personality and Social Psychology* 284–99.

Cohen, S (1980) *Folk Devils and Moral Panics: The Creation of the Mods and Rockers* (New York, St Martins Press).

Cullen, FT, Clark, GA, Cullen, JB and Mathers, RA (1985) 'Attribution, salience, and attitudes toward criminal sanctioning' 12(3) *Criminal Justice and Behaviour* 305–31.

de Haan, W and Loader, I (2002) 'On the emotions of crime, punishment and social control' 67(6) *Theoretical Criminology* 243–53.

Dillman, DA (2000) *Mail and Internet Surveys: the tailored design method* (New York, Wiley and Sons).

Duncan, MG (1996) *Romantic Outlaws, Beloved Prisons: The Unconscious Meanings of Crime and Punishment* (New York, New York University Press).

Durkheim, E (1933) *The Division of Labour in Society* (New York, Macmillan).

Ellsworth, PC and Gross, SR (1994) 'Hardening of the attitudes: Americans' views on the death penalty' 50(2) *Journal of Social Issues* 19–52.

Farrall, S, Bannister, J, Ditton, J and Gilchrist, E (1997) 'Questioning the Measurement of the Fear of Crime: Findings From a Major Methodological Study' 37(4) *British Journal of Criminology* 657–78.

Florian, V and Mikulincer, M (1997) 'Fear of death and the judgment of social transgressions: A multidimensional test of terror management theory' 73 *Journal of Personality and Social Psychology* 369–80.

Garland, D (1990) *Punishment and Modern Society: A Study in Social Theory* (Chicago, University of Chicago Press).

—— (2001) *The Culture of Control: Crime and Social Order in Contemporary Society* (Oxford, Oxford University Press).

Gaubatz, KT (1995) *Crime in the Public Mind* (Ann Arbor, University of Michigan Press).

Gault, BA and Sabini, J (2000) 'The roles of empathy, anger, and gender in predicting attitudes toward punitive, reparative, and preventative public policies' 14(4) *Cognition and Emotion* 495–520.

Gilligan, J (1996) *Violence: Our Deadly Epidemic and its Causes* (New York, GP Putnam's Sons).

Girling, E, Loader, I et al (2000) *Crime and Social Change in Middle England* (Routledge, London).

Greenberg, J, Simon, L, Pyszczynski, T, Solomon, S and Chatel, D (1992) 'Terror management and tolerance: Does mortality salience always intensify negative reactions to others who threaten one's worldview?' 63 *Journal of Personality and Social Psychology* 212–20.

Hall, S, Critcher, C, Jefferson, T, Clarke, J and Roberts, B (1978) *Policing the Crisis: Mugging, the State, and Law and Order* (London, Macmillan Education).

Hogg, MA and Vaughan, GM (2005) *Social Psychology. 4th edition.* (Wessex, England, Pearson).

Holloway, W and Jefferson, T (2000) *Doing Qualitative Research Differently: free association, narrative and the interview method* (London, Sage).

Hough, M and Roberts, JV (2002) *Changing Public Views of Punishment—Lessons from Around the Globe* (Cullompton, Willan Publishing).

Katz, J (1988) *Seductions of Crime: Moral and Sensual Attractions in Doing Evil* (New York, Basic Books).

Kemper, TD (1978) *A Social Interactional Theory of Emotions* (New York, John Wiley).

Martin, JL (2001) 'The Authoritarian personality, 50 years later: What lessons are there for political psychology?' 22(1) *Political Psychology* 1–26.

Maruna, S and King, A (2004) 'Public Opinion and community sanctions' in AE Bottoms, SA Rex, and G Robinson (eds) *Alternatives to Prison* (Cullompton, Willan Publishing).

—— (2005) 'Instrumenal and expressive explanations for punitiveness'. Unpublished paper.

Maruna, S, Matravers A and King, A (2004) 'Disowning our shadow: a psychoanalytic approach to understanding punitive public attitudes' 25 *Deviant Behaviour* 277–99.

Mayhew, P and Van Kesteren, J (2002) 'Cross-national attitudes to punishment' in JV Roberts and M Hough, *Changing Attitudes to Punishment: Public Opinion, Crime and Justice* (Cullompton, Willan Publishing) ch 4.

McAdams, D (1995) *Life Story Interview* (Foley Center for the Study of Lives, Northwestern University, school of education and social policy): www.sesp.northwestern.edu/foley/.

Mead, GH (1918) 'The psychology of punitive justice' 23 *American Journal of Sociology* 577–602.

Miller, JG (2004) 'American Gulag: Why does the "home of the free" lock up 2 million men, women, boys, and girls-most of them people of color?' Retrieved 1 December 2010, from YES! Magazine Web site: http://www.yesmagazine.org/issues/is-it-time-to-close-the-prisons/american-gulag.

Nietzsche, F (1956 [1887]) *The Birth of Tragedy and the Genealogy of Morals* (New York, Doubleday).

Pearson, G (1983) *Hooligan: a History of Respectable Fears* (London, Macmillan Education).

Ranulf, S (1938) *Moral Indignation and Middle Class Psychology* (New York, Schocken Books).

Roberts, J and Hough, M (2002) *Changing Attitudes to Punishment: Public opinion, crime and justice* (Cullompton, Willan Publishing).

Rosenblatt, A, Greenberg, J, Solomon, S, Pyszczynski, T and Lyon, D (1989) 'Evidence for terror management theory I: The effects of mortality salience on reactions to those who violate or uphold cultural values' 57 *Journal of Personality and Social Psychology* 681–90.

Sasson, T (1995) *Crime Talk: How Citizens Construct a Social Problem* (New York, Aldine De Gruyter).

Sherman, LW (2003) 'Reason for emotion: Reinventing justice with theories, innovations, and research. The American Society of Criminology 2002 Presidential Address' 41(1) *Criminology* 1–37.

Stalans, L ((2002) 'Measuring attitudes to sentencing' in Roberts, J and M Hough (eds) *Changing Attitudes to Punishment: Public opinion, crime and justice* (Cullompton, Willan Publishing) ch 2.

Stinchcombe, AL (1980) Crime and Punishment Changing Attitudes in America (San Francisco, Jossey-Bass Publishers).

Stitka, LJ (2003) 'Of different minds: an accessible identity model of justice reasoning' 7(4) *Personality and Social Psychology Review* 286–97.

Tyler, TR and Boeckmann, RJ (1997) 'Three strikes and you are out, but why? The psychology of public support for punishing rule breakers' 31(2) *Law and Society Review* 237–65.

Tyler, TR and Weber, R (1982) 'Support for the death penalty; instrumental response to crime, or symbolic attitude?' 17(1) *Law and Society Review* 21–45.

Useem, B, Liedka, RV and Piehl, AM (2003) 'Popular support for the prison build-up' 5 *Punishment and Society* 5–32.

Vaughan, B (2002) 'The punitive consequences of consumer culture' 4(2) *Punishment and Society* 195–211.

Warr, M (1995a) 'Book reviews: Crime in the public mind' 59(4) *Public Opinion Quarterly* 635–36.

—— (1995b) 'Public opinion on crime and punishment' 59 *Public Opinion Quarterly* 296–310.

Young, J (2003) 'Merton with energy, Katz with structure: the sociology of vindictiveness and the criminology of transgression' 7(3) *Theoretical Criminology* 389–414.

—— (2005) 'Moral panics, Margate and Mary Poppins: Mysterious happenings in south coast seaside towns' 1 *Crime Media Culture* 100–05.

Part II

Emotional Experiences of Justice

7

Empathy for the Devil: The Nature and Nurture of Revenge

LAWRENCE W SHERMAN AND HEATHER STRANG[1]

THE PRIMARY TASK of justice is to manage emotions (Sherman 2003). The primary emotion for justice to manage is the desire for revenge. Whether justice can manage, or even 'cure' that desire depends on whether we see vengefulness as a product of nature, nurture, or both. The view that vengefulness is an emotional response 'hard-wired' into all human beings suggests the hypothesis that justice can only reflect that emotion, rather than trying to cure it. The view that vengefulness, like all emotions, is highly dependent on social context suggests that justice could indeed cure vengefulness through emotionally intelligent responses to crime.

Whether we think vengefulness is 'natural' (Diamond 2008) therefore matters greatly for the ways in which justice treats revenge. The idea that revenge is an innate, cross-cultural constant can provide moral and social support for its excesses, even by justice itself. At worst, torture of suspected terrorists, mandatory prison for minor crimes, long prison sentences for possessing small amounts of drugs: these and other forms of social vengeance are often described by their advocates as 'inevitable' or 'inescapable'. At best, defining vengefulness as an 'instinct' may suggest that attempts to manage it are 'impossible' (Goldschmidt 2008). The consequence of this intellectual position may be defeatism and abandonment of investments in finding better means of peacekeeping. It may also discourage further testing of its own hypothesis.

The idea that revenge is highly subject to 'nurture', or life experience and social context, in contrast, suggests a potentially fruitful line of empirically testing innovations that might reduce the harm of revenge. Our own version

---

[1] This paper is a product of the Regulatory Institutions Network (RegNet) of the Research School of Pacific and Asian Studies, Australian National University, and its affiliation with the Jerry Lee Programme of Randomised Controlled Trials in Restorative Justice, Universities of Cambridge and Pennsylvania.

of that hypothesis is that vengefulness can be dissipated by justice rituals that foster a victim's empathy for the 'devil': the easily demonised person or persons who caused a victim to suffer harm.

This chapter explores our hypothesis and its intellectual context. It begins with a brief review of the status of vengefulness as an emotion. It then considers recent work in anthropology and neuroscience suggesting that vengefulness is a biologically inevitable emotion; we find these claims excessive and unsupported by a systematic treatment of the evidence. The core of the paper presents results from our own experiments showing transformations of that emotion among victims of serious crime, making it anything but inevitable. Our evidence suggests that justice can transform revenge into empathy, and often sympathy, for the very 'devils' who have harmed us. This transformation can produce enormous benefits for victims, criminals and society. Our conclusion is that emotionally intelligent justice would devote far more effort to the nurturance of 'antidotes' to revenge than common law justice does at present.

I. WHETHER VENGEFULNESS IS AN EMOTION: DOES IT MATTER?

The empirical core of any definition is comprised of a list of phenomena that the definition includes. The definition of 'emotion' is especially linked to lists of the phenomena it includes, since the word covers such a gamut. Equally wide is the range of scholarly frameworks for the content and structure of various lists on offer over the past 3000 years. Several lists distinguish between primary and secondary emotions, while at least one version invokes three levels (Parrot 2001). Thus it seems necessary to begin this paper by asking whether the desire for revenge is a distinct emotion, and whether it matters to the debate about its causes and control.

At least since Aristotle, scholars have described revenge not as an emotion, but as an act prompted by other emotions. Just as lust is an emotion leading to an act (of sexual intercourse), Aristotle saw anger as the emotion underlying revenge. Revenge was the act of harming; anger was the emotion that proximately caused the harm. The question then becomes whether the *desire* to commit an act of revenge—what we may distinguish from anger in general by calling it the distinct emotion of 'vengefulness'—may be seen as a unique kind of emotional state, one distinct from anger. Increasingly, that state is seen as an emotion distinct from anger.

The anthropologist Jared Diamond (2008) recently put the case this way:

> We regularly ignore the fact that the thirst for vengeance is among the strongest of human emotions. It ranks with love, anger, grief, and fear, about which we talk incessantly. Modern state societies permit and encourage us to express our love, anger, grief, and fear, but not our thirst for vengeance. We grow up being taught that such feelings are primitive, something to be ashamed of and to transcend.

One way to read this view is that revenge has been intentionally left off the list of emotions as part of a socially constructed effort to make unacceptable the 'thirst for vengeance', or vengefulness. Another way to read it is that there are vital distinctions between vengefulness and other types of emotions that require us to study vengefulness as a separate phenomenon. We agree. As we suggest here, those distinctions may include a focus on specific events, low visibility, and a longer time-frame.

A. Focus on Specific Events

While vengefulness may be prompted by, or correlated with, a variety of emotions, it is arguably an extremely specific subset of one or more of those emotions. Anger, for example, or even rage can be quite general in its causes and focus. But the emotion of vengefulness is typically caused by and focused on a specific act or pattern of acts that has 'done wrong' to the person who feels vengeful. Thus a father who wants to kill the murderer of his daughter is not just angry or enraged; he is focused on a specific act by a specific person for which he desires to inflict retaliation. A Palestinian suicide bomber is not just angry about the condition of Palestinians; she is focused specifically on a pattern of acts by the nation of Israel for which she wants to seek revenge. The war veteran husband of an apparent lover of Dylan Thomas who shoots at Thomas' house is not just 'shell-shocked,' but vengeful: focused on Thomas taking both love and money from him (BBC Films 2008).

B. Low Visibility

People do not always make visible an emotional state of vengefulness. They may not feel or display anger in any other aspects of their lives, such as traffic jams or domestic quarrels. On most days, they may not even feel angry for a minute. An 'anger management' class might therefore be completely irrelevant to the emotion they feel. Yet their emotion of vengefulness may lie beneath the surface, like an underground river, flowing steadily over time until some future point where it may break out in plain view. Suicide bombers may plan for years until they have their chance to wreak revenge for a terrible wrong done to their family, appearing normal and well-controlled throughout that time (Pape 2005).

C. Long Time Frame

Low visibility of vengefulness about specific events enables vengefulness to last over a long time frame. In contrast to the immediate flash of anger in a bar-room brawl, which could have dissipated by the next day, vengefulness may last a lifetime. Writers of memoirs may use their books to 'get back' at their enemies decades after the harm was done. These characteristics of vengefulness differentiate it from most definitions of emotions that stress the moment-by-moment character of most feelings. Vengefulness can apparently survive this normally situational and transitory nature of other emotions. It may fall into a larger class of 'long-term' emotions, such as parental and marital love, that cannot be measured by facial expressions (Ekman 2007) or existing biological measurements, at least until a critical moment in which an act representing that emotion erupts. Diamond (2008) quotes his octogenarian father-in-law as saying about the murder of his own mother a half-century earlier, during World War II: 'Every day, still, before going to sleep, I think of my mother's death.'

There is also anthropological evidence that the long-term emotion of vengefulness can be culturally induced and maintained by teaching or exemplary action. Feeling vengeful about the acts of enemies of your in-group that occurred well before you were born may be a subset of the broader emotion of hate (see Scheff, in this volume). But because such feelings can focus on specific acts and relationships (eg, 'You killed my father's brother: prepare to die'), there is every reason to think of it as an emotion sui generis that differs from more generalised, or short-term and situational, forms of hatred.

D. Why It Matters—But Not Too Much

How we define our terms matters for the study of emotions more broadly, and the study of justice in particular. Our aim is not to split hairs in the classification of emotions, but to advance the emotional insights, or empathy, of people who impose justice on behalf of the state: police, prosecutors, judges, and correctional officials (Sherman 2003). The development of emotional intelligence arguably begins by recognising one's own emotions (Goleman 1995), using them to build 'empathy'. Empathy is defined not as an emotion but as a capacity for insight and understanding of the emotions of others. Pinpointing the thirst for revenge as an 'emotion' is therefore a short cut for helping millions of officials to understand the core idea of emotionally intelligent justice: that a rule of law works best when it sees justice as a peacekeeping mediator of emotion-driven conflicts among citizens, rather than as the morally driven expression of the emotions (including vengefulness) of the state on behalf of society.

That said, it may not matter much whether officials see revenge as an emotion, an attitude, a 'risk' or a 'risk factor'. Our goal is to show the fundamental nature of revenge as an *issue* in justice, one that justice officials must consider in any rational attempt to reduce harm. Calling it an emotion is simply a heuristic device to help assess the consequences of justice decisions—and innovations in justice processes.

It may matter more if defining revenge as an emotion means that the state accepts uncritically its duty to inflict it, or that the state must 'inevitably' assume the duty to exact revenge that individuals desire but have yielded to the state under a social contract. If individuals can find ways to respond to crime without vengeance, so can the state, regardless of individual or social sentiments in favour of vengeance. As we argue in the next section, describing revenge as an emotion does not require that we accept it as an incurable human malady.

II. WHETHER RESEARCH CAN 'PROVE' REVENGE IS HARD-WIRED

Rapid advances in biology have fostered intrusions into academic turf long dominated by social scientists. Yet it is anthropologists who have most baldly stated the case for nature over nurture in the causation and malleability of vengeful behaviour. Their work converges with the neuroscience of locating various emotion centres in the brain, suggesting that victims may find revenge is reinforced by a feeling of pleasure. Neither work is informed by field data from the criminology of justice processes. Neither body of work can sustain the burden of 'proof' that they imply, at least not within the framework of modern science.

A. Revenge An Instinct: An Anthropological View

The Pulitzer Prize-winning polymath Jared Diamond, author of *Guns, Germs and Steel*, has done extensive fieldwork in New Guinea for decades. Based in part on that work, he recently wrote that there is a

> terrible personal price that law-abiding citizens pay for leaving vengeance to the state … In order to induce us to do so, state societies and their associated religions and moral codes teach us that seeking revenge is bad. But, while acting on vengeful feelings clearly needs to be discouraged, acknowledging them should be not merely permitted but encouraged. To a close relative or friend of someone who has been killed or seriously wronged, and to the victims of harm themselves, those feelings are natural and powerful. (Diamond 2008).

These comments followed a case study of how one of his informants found great satisfaction in organising revenge for the killing of his uncle in an inter-tribal battle. His description shows that the informant drew great satisfaction from the crippling of his uncle's killer. Diamond then contrasts this satisfaction with the lifelong pain of his father-in-law, who decided not to kill the killer of his own mother at the end of World War II in Poland, despite the chance to do so without legal consequences. His conclusion is that vengeance is [universally] satisfying. His implication is that it is a basic human need that must be addressed, by such means as allowing survivors to watch killers be executed.

His report attracted comment from many colleagues, including anthropologist Walter Goldschmidt (2008), who characterised vengefulness as a 'basic human instinct'. While Goldschmidt notes a long history of systems in various cultures for controlling that instinct through tribute, he concludes that any attempt at curbing vengeance at the nation-state level is 'impossible'. One could even draw that conclusion about intra-state crime, such as gang killings, from Diamond's subtitle: 'What can tribal societies tell us about our need to get even?' Diamond, moreover, gives no consideration to the idea of reconciliation, nor even Hannah Arendt's (1958) rationalist argument for forgiveness: that it relieves the victim of a lifelong burden of vengefulness. Instead of considering any of the anthropology of peacemaking and apology, he signs up to the retributivist agenda of 'victims' rights' to tell courts what they have suffered, but not to have victims talk directly to offenders.

The take-away message from a compelling article like Diamond's is that because we are all hard-wired for revenge, we should not expect to succeed in tampering with that biological destiny. We may socially restrain vengefulness by brute force, but there is no way we can escape the emotions themselves. They are as essential as breathing. Neither tribesmen in New Guinea nor Europeans at war can avoid this powerful instinct, so realism requires that we simply channel its expression—not change it.

B. Can't Get No Satisfaction?: A Neuroscience of Revenge

The implication that revenge is inevitable has also been drawn from several laboratory experiments in neuroscience. These experiments have been published in the leading scientific journals in the world, presumably because of their 'significance' in revealing a fundamental feature of human biology: our satisfaction at achieving revenge against rule-breakers, even at great cost to ourselves (Knutson 2004). The idea of 'altruism' in punishment is prominent in the discussions of these experiments, showing how individuals sacrifice their own interests for the good of the group in making sure that group members obey rules (de Quervain et al 2004). Testing the hypotheses in a laboratory setting, often with positron emission topography (PET) scans or functional magnetic resonance imaging (fMRI) of the brains of people who are making decisions, means the evidence is seen as more compelling, because of the pioneering precision with which the hypotheses can be tested.

In a typical experiment, a small sample (15) of Swiss male students (mean age 25) were asked to interact anonymously in seven trials each of a game with an experimenter. In each game, the subject and the experimenter were given 'money units' to invest in ways that would advantage both of them if they cooperated, or neither of them if they did not cooperate, but which would allow one of them to derive more advantage by breaking a rule after cooperation began. The trials systematically assigned violations of trust, and all but one of the 15 subjects trusted the experimenter at least one time. When the trust was violated, the subjects retaliated in the next move. Around this time the brain region called the 'caudate nucleus' was shown to heat up (a sign of greater activity), the same region which heats up when the prospect of a sweet dessert appears. The researchers concluded the following:

> Thus, high caudate activation seems to be responsible for a high willingness to punish, which suggests that caudate activation reflects the anticipated satisfaction from punishing defectors. (de Quervain et al 2004:1258)

Thus we might say that a correlation exists between revenge and pleasure: 'revenge is sweet'. What we cannot say, of course, is how long-lasting or satisfying that pleasure may be, or whether even greater pleasure could have been derived from some other alternative. Most of all, we cannot say from correlational evidence alone that the brain is hard-wired to seek vengeance. Similar limitations would apply to most of the recent work in the neuroscience of revenge.

C. Science, Proof and Popper

The larger conceptual problem with demonstrating the causes and immutability of vengefulness is that it is a 'black swan' problem. Each case cited from anthropology or neuroscience may show that, so far, 'all swans are white', as Karl Popper (1959) famously pointed out. Yet this cannot constitute 'proof' that all swans are white, because we have no way to observe all possible swans. All we can say from any accumulation of studies with the same result is that the available evidence fails—at least so far—to disprove the hypothesis of a universal characteristic. So, too, with the 'vengeance is hard-wired' hypothesis: the hypothesis that people always experience vengefulness when they perceive that they have been treated wrongfully can be supported by repeated accounts. Yet contrary evidence that under some circumstances exceptions exist, like black swans, can enrich our understanding that what appears to be universal is in fact only conditional. If we can show that the 'natural' or even universal predisposition to vengefulness can be blocked by socially nurturant interventions, our understanding of vengefulness may become more accurate—as well as more hopeful.

If we were to set out to find conditions under which nurture counteracted nature in the emotional experience of vengefulness, we might not look first in a laboratory, as neuroeconomists have done. Nor might we even look in anthropological literature, although the Yale University's Human Relations Area Files are indeed full of evidence falsifying Diamond's conclusion.[2] Perhaps the best evidence would come from field experiments, dealing with real-life emotions about real-life harm. For whenever we seek research to support externally valid conclusions about modern societies—as both anthropologists and neuroscientists have recently done—it can be argued that field evidence generated in such societies would be more compelling than less direct evidence from laboratories or pre-modern societies.

III. FROM REVENGE TO EMPATHY: EVIDENCE OF TRANSFORMATION

Whether or not victims of crime have a neurologically located 'instinct' for revenge, there is growing evidence that vengefulness itself can be ameliorated. We discovered this phenomenon in our own work almost by accident, when Heather Strang designed the questionnaire for her interviews with victims of crime in our initial face-to-face restorative justice (RJ) experiments in Canberra—and then found large RJ effects in reducing victims' desire for violent revenge (Strang 2002). In our subsequent work, we measured the amelioration of revenge more systematically, and also (Angel 2005) in relation to other victim reactions such as post-traumatic stress symptoms. In eight out of eight tests of the hypothesis, we have found substantially fewer victims expressing a desire for physically violent revenge in the experimental group than in the control group (Sherman et al 2005).

Unlike the neuroscience of revenge to date, our evidence does not come from laboratory experiments with students and games. Rather, the qualitative and quantitative findings summarised below come entirely from randomised controlled trials in field settings with criminal justice agencies and real crime victims. While we did not employ the fMRI tools that some take as the hallmark of real science, we did employ consistent methods of experimentation and outcome measurement. Moreover, we would welcome the addition of fMRI evidence to such tests both to enhance, and be enhanced by, the field experimental designs we have used to study the transformation of vengefulness into other powerful emotions.

These designs have been informed by an explicit attempt to compare an emotionally intelligent justice to what may be called an emotionally neutral form of justice. In every case, the control group of victims was assigned to a conventional form of justice in which victims are not even present at the justice proceeding, let alone allowed to express their emotions. In every case, victims in the experimental group were invited to meet with their

---

[2] See www.yale.edu/hraf/ for over 100 examples of societies that use alternatives to vengeance.

offenders face-to-face, to express their own emotions, and to see first-hand how the offenders responded to what may be a 'contagion' of emotions among all those present in a room, including family and friends of both victims and offenders (see Rossner, in this volume) .

This section begins by briefly summarising the key features of the four experiments with large subgroups of male and female victims, comprising the eight tests in which we found RJ to transform revenge (Sherman et al 2005). It then presents extensive qualitative evidence on how victims reacted to both the experimental and control conditions. The section concludes with a brief summary and interpretation of the prospective meta-analysis we conducted on the evidence from eight tests of the hypothesis that the thirst for vengeance is transformable, rather than inevitable. While victim forgiveness was by no means the universal result, what we show is that victims developed substantial empathy for their offenders. That insight, in turn, allowed them to replace vengefulness with other emotions that may be far less damaging to victims' health. Finally, as a recent independent evaluation of seven of our experiments concludes (Shapland et al 2008), this highly emotional process also resulted in 27 per cent fewer reconvictions for new crimes by the offenders in the RJ group than found among control group offenders, over a two-year follow-up period.

A. Experiments in Restorative Justice

Since 1995, we have completed a series of 12 controlled field trials comparing face-to-face restorative justice conferences to conventional criminal justice processes. This section summarises the relevant results of four of those experiments, those in which we were able to seek (although not obtain) detailed interviews with all of the crime victims. Two of these experiments came from our first series of four in Australia in 1995–2000; two came from the second series carried out in three regions of England in 2002–2005, with both of the experiments reported here conducted in London.

Our first series of experiments was carried out in Canberra, the Australian capital. One of the four tests that we include here dealt with property crime committed solely by juvenile offenders (under 18). The second one reported here dealt with violent crimes committed by offenders under the age of 30. All cases were of sufficient seriousness that they would normally have been dealt with in court; in all cases the offender had admitted responsibility for the crime and said they would be willing to accept the experimental treatment if offered (victims were invited to attend but the conference went ahead anyway in the few cases where they did not wish to attend).

In the Australian experiments, arresting police officers referred cases meeting these eligibility criteria to the research team (24 hours a day) for random assignment instructions to one of two treatments. Cases would either be prosecuted in court in the usual way, or would be diverted away from court to a face-to-face restorative justice conference. The latter route entailed offenders, their victims and the families and friends of each meeting in the presence of a trained police facilitator to discuss what had happened and what needed to be done to repair the harm caused (Strang 2002).

The second series of randomised experiments included two carried out in London for much more serious offences than the earlier tests in Canberra: robbery and burglary prosecuted in the Crown Courts. Unlike the crimes in Canberra, most of the cases in London resulted in prison sentences. The offenders were all aged over 18. Most had extensive criminal histories. All had pleaded guilty to the offence that had brought them into our study. Because of the seriousness of the offence, they were *all* dealt with in court in the usual way. In addition, *half* of the eligible, consenting group were randomly assigned to attend a restorative justice conference as well. Eligibility in these tests was based on both offender and victim consent—in that order—as well as certain other factors (see Shapland et al 2004, 2006, 2007). These restorative justice events took place while each case had been adjourned, between plea and sentence. The format of the events was very much on the model of the Canberra conferences: both offenders and their victims were invited to attend with their families and friends and to discuss the offence and its consequences, and what the offender could do to make up for the harm endured by the victim.

The four experiments are highly comparable, in the sense that the same Australian trainers conducted the training with all the police officers leading the RJ conferences, in both Canberra and London. The subtle nuances of technique and responsiveness to the emotional progression of the discussion were conveyed in a one-day training session in Canberra, and by a five-day training session in England. Our own observations of about 100 of the RJ conferences on both continents confirm that they were conducted in substantially similar ways, although by no means identically.

These results should therefore be seen as the outcome of socially constructed interaction rituals (Collins 2004) with a range of variable properties inside a highly consistent format. Even when facilitators were consistent in technique, the composition of the persons present, their personalities, and the behaviour in each RJ conference group meant that the RJ conferences varied widely in their capacity to deliver key elements of what Collins (2004 and this volume) describes as 'interaction ritual chains'. As Rossner (2008 and this volume) has shown, these variations are even linked to the future offending behaviour of the criminals in the two Canberra tests: the better the interaction ritual, the less recidivism. And while restorative justice (RJ) conferences were far more emotional—and hence variable—than conventional justice rituals, they were clearly far more emotionally intense and intelligent.

B. Qualitative Evidence: The Stages of Transformation

This section presents a brief 'experimental ethnography' (Sherman and Strang 2004) of how victims reacted to the two randomly assigned justice processes in our experiments. It uses participants' statements and interviews to document the processes and structure we discerned in the transformation of victim vengefulness over time. It is 'experimental' ethnography, in the sense that it attempts to draw qualitative contrasts between the ways in which victims experience two different processes. We use qualitative evidence (derived from a structured interview designed for quantitative purposes) about the emotional states of similar victims who experienced different kinds of justice. Our purpose is to strengthen and inform inferences of causation about the effects of the kind of justice victims experience on their stated desire for vengeance.

The emotional foundation for this analysis is that victims of crime vary in their emotional reactions to the same kinds of crime. Some of that variability led some victims to refuse to consent to restorative justice altogether, excluding themselves from our experimental samples. For these 'refusing' victims, we can say nothing about the differences with which they might have responded to two different justice processes. Within the samples of consenting victims, however, some interesting differences emerge. Of particular importance is the large difference between Canberra and London victims in their base rates of desire for violent revenge. With a very high victim take-up rate in Canberra (around 90 per cent, for somewhat less serious crimes than our London victims experienced) the base rate for revenge was nearly 40 per cent for violent crime victims in the control group. With a much lower victim take-up rate in London (about 45 per cent, with more serious crimes and criminals than in Canberra), the base rate of vengefulness was only 10 per cent in the control group.

However far these results may be generalised, it is clear that victims vary widely in the attitudes they express in their initial interview with the facilitator who would lead the experiments if they consented. A few victims grant consent and then change their minds, often because family members pressure them not to participate. Yet the desire for revenge can have two-sided effects on victim decisions to accept or refuse restorative justice. Some UK victims (where all offenders were convicted and about to be sentenced) may have been so vengeful that they refused to attend, out of fear their presence might have somehow 'helped' the offender escape properly severe punishment. Others agreed to attend only if promised there would be no formal benefit to the offender.

Yet for most crime victims in both countries, the desire for revenge on their part was often a reason they agreed to confront their offenders in a restorative justice meeting. When offered a chance to meet their offenders, victims often said they would welcome a chance to 'let the bastard have a piece of my mind'. Even when victims hesitated to consent, they often explained their hesitation by saying: 'But I couldn't trust myself to be in the same room as him', or: 'I'm too angry to talk about it to her', or: 'If I saw him I wouldn't be able to control myself.' Skilled RJ practitioners then treated these emotions as a reason for, not against, victims meeting their offenders. They encouraged victims to take part in RJ by pointing out to them that the process provides precisely the opportunity they long for to 'tell the offender exactly what you think of her' or 'to explain why you feel so upset and angry'.

Many victims assumed that these powerful emotions must be forever contained because there is no safe or civilised way in which they can be expressed. They were astonished to hear that in RJ meetings shouting and tears are commonplace, and can occur within the boundaries set by the conference facilitator. Victims often feared the strength of their own emotions, and even the chance to release them. Thus the RJ facilitators needed to convince victims of the legitimacy of the prospective meeting, of the legitimacy of their emotions and of the chance that they may openly vent them. Victims had to accept the trustworthiness of the agency and the individual convening the RJ—usually the facilitator who met with them prior to their agreeing to attend. With this preparation, victims almost always managed the venting of the emotions powering the desire for revenge in a way that defused that desire.

Stepping back from the details of the process, what we see appears to be a transformation of vengefulness into empathy. Victims apparently enter an RJ event focused on their own feelings, and leave focused on the state the offender is in—which often strikes them as far more pathetic and tragic then anything they themselves have suffered. Victims start by venting their stories of pain and suffering from the crime. But then they listen as offenders (or offenders' supporters) tell their own stories of life-long misfortunes. The offenders' descriptions of child abuse, victimisation, feckless or drug-addicted parents and other traumas allow victims to peer inside their lives. What they see gives them *empathy*: the capacity to put themselves in the offenders' shoes and to experience the offenders' emotions. That, in turn, may make the emotions of the victim less vengeful, allowing the empathy to create positive emotions of *sympathy* or *pity*, or at least an emotionally neutral state of *acceptance* of events.

The following cases illustrate and unpack the stages in the symbolic interactions by which RJ transforms victims' vengeful emotions into the empathy that fosters a more positive emotional state. The stages include: 1) the *initial discussion* with offenders in the RJ conference, 2) the victim's *explosion of anger* that is often—but not always—vented in the RJ conference, 3) the *offender's shock realisation*, often for the first time, of the consequences of their crime in the face of the victim's moral outrage, and

4) the transformation of vengefulness to *victim's empathy* engendered by the offender's emotional collapse during the conference, as the first step in the final transformation of anger into pity for the offender.

This final viewpoint of empathy by both parties may include lengthy discussions of the offender's life history, tragedies and traumas. It may include constructive discussions of how the offender can rebuild his life to stop offending. It may even include offers by the victim to assist the offender. No matter what shape it takes, the victims who develop empathy are far more likely to adopt pity or sympathy as their primary emotion about the crime. Once they do that, they do not seem to slip back into anger or a desire for revenge.

RJ Case 1: A London Burglary

Will Riley 'met' Peter Woolf when he discovered Peter burgling his house, in a wealthy suburb of London. The confrontation led to a brutal assault by Peter, with Will putting up a desperate fight. Will's need to defend his property and his family gave him strength he didn't know he possessed to withstand Peter's attack and to ensure his arrest. Will was triumphant in the battle, but he suffered in the aftermath. He soon found that Peter's breach of his home and his sense of security had serious consequences for his mental wellbeing and for his relationship with his wife and daughter. The anger and vengeful emotions he felt were translated into deep depression. It was in this state of mind that he agreed to attend an RJ conference with Peter. He was still depressed the day he sat down in a room at a London prison at the time of their restorative justice conference. As Will describes this encounter:

> The criminal walked in, looking sheepish. However, he soon started talking social-work bollocks, parrot fashion. [*Initial discussion*]. I was thinking: 'This is getting nowhere.' Then he looked at me and said: 'When we met ....' And I lost it. [*Victim explosion*] I said: 'We didn't meet at some cocktail party. You broke into my house and hit me on the head.' And it all came out, everything I was feeling—about how terrible it was not to be able to protect my family. Stuff I hadn't even told my wife. I hadn't really known how I felt until it just came out, like water from a fire hydrant. Afterwards, I was exhausted...[3]

But it was the effect of his words and those of another of Peter's victims that had the greatest benefit for Peter, as Will says:

> Hearing this hit Peter like a bombshell [*Offender's shock*]. We could see that. He was gutted. You don't leave somebody who's in that kind of state, not unless you're a shit, so we spent about 10 minutes talking about how to help him. We

---

[3] *The Sunday Times*, 11 May 2008: www.timesonline.co.uk/tol/news/uk/crime/article3907255.ece.

said we wanted him to write to us every six months and tell us what he was doing. And I told him that if he went back to his old life, he'd be shitting on our goodwill.

He adds:

> People think restorative justice sounds easy, but it's not. It's very hard to confront somebody. But I believe you should meet and talk to criminals because that re-empowers you [*Victim empathy*]. And you realise that the crime wasn't personal ... I was so impressed that I got involved in a number of events, talking at seminars and conferences and think-tanks. I often do them with Peter—he's a great guy. People tell us we're being soft on crime. So we've turned our approach on its head: we're saying that this isn't a soft option for criminals—it's good for victims.

Will's journey from anger and depression to empathy and resolution are clear to see in his recollection of events. He had not expected very much from the restorative justice meeting—mere curiosity about his offender had brought him along—and the initial discussion he found pedestrian and predictable. It was his own furious reaction to the opportunity the conference presented to confront Peter with the reality of the crime and its consequences that was the 'engine' for Peter's emotional collapse. In the face of Will's moral outrage, Peter realised the full import of his actions. By his own testimony, the pain for Peter was terrible (Woolf 2008), similar in description to the symptoms of post-traumatic stress (Angel 2005). Will recognised that pain and felt immediate empathy, allowing the two to draw together in a common understanding of events and emotions. Six years later, both Will and Peter say they have benefited enormously from the transformation of their emotions in that intensive interaction ritual.

RJ Case 2: A London Robbery[4]

Anthony, his partner Kristy and their young baby were in dire straits financially. They were almost penniless in London, owing to Anthony's work injury and some bad financial choices they had made. On the spur of the moment, Anthony attempted to grab Anne's purse as she walked down the street. He was arrested almost immediately and expressed his remorse right away. Although there was no way at that moment to assess the sincerity of Anthony's feelings, he certainly begged the police to give him the chance to apologise directly to Anne in a restorative justice meeting, even though he

---

[4] This case was videotaped in its entirety, and is available for RJ training purposes from the Restorative Justice Consortium in London. The judge who sentenced Anthony said that he decided not to give Anthony a prison term, only because he understood the offence in a completely different way from seeing the conference on tape than from hearing the evidence in court.

knew it would make no difference to his going to court to face the charge of robbery.

When the RJ conference began, Anthony immediately expressed regret for his actions. He could only repeat saying how sorry he was [*Initial discussion*]. Anne was indifferent to his apologies. Her husband, Terry, became increasingly angry. Terry listened impatiently to Anthony's explanations and excuses for his actions, then *exploded*, telling Anthony that he was a liar who would say anything to escape the consequences of his behaviour. Anthony was *shocked* by Terry's angry words but had no reply. It was Kristy who spoke up at that point. She expressed many of the same emotions as the victims felt, feeling victimised also by her partner's crime and having previously been the victim of a robbery herself (as had Anthony). She described her own anger and agreed with them that there was no possible excuse for his actions. She spoke eloquently for 20 minutes about the state of their relationship, about their child, and about their future if Anthony received a prison sentence for his crime.

As Kristy spoke, Anne and Terry became convinced of the genuineness of Anthony's apology and of the strength of the bond between him and his partner—a bond they recognised as being one of rare strength, that needed to be preserved if this little family was to survive. The opportunity to air all the emotions connected to the crime engendered *victim's empathy* for the offender in the victim and her husband. At this point all the anger and moral outrage that they had felt evaporated. The remainder of the conference was devoted to a discussion of how best the case could be presented in court, and how the family could best cope with whatever happened next. By the end of the conference no trace remained of the anger and vengefulness that Terry had expressed at the outset.

RJ Case 3: A Canberra Assault

Jamie, an eight-year-old Canberra schoolboy, was accosted by a 14-year-old on his way home from school, and knocked unconscious. The reasons for the assault were unclear but it appeared that the offender, Scott, was acting on behalf of another boy who was a renowned bully. Jamie's parents were very upset and completely outraged by the incident, which required an ambulance and hospital treatment. They were all the more outraged when the police suggested that it could be dealt with by a restorative justice conference. They wanted Scott to be punished severely and they could not imagine that sitting down to discuss anything with Scott or his parents would give them the least satisfaction. The conference facilitator suggested that the conference would in fact give them a chance to tell Scott exactly what they thought of him—something that they would certainly be denied if the case went to court. They reluctantly agreed and did not hide their anger when the conference got underway.

Scott was embarrassed to have his parents hear about what happened, and explained that he too felt bullied. In addition he felt ashamed when he realised how young and vulnerable Jamie was and offered an apology to both Jamie and his parents. Jamie's parents realised the genuineness of Scott's remorse and accepted Scott's offer to come to their house and help in their garden. Later, Jamie's mother described the friendship that had developed between the two boys, with Jamie feeling that Scott was his protector against the boy they both feared. She also said how pleased she was the the case had been dealt with this way, because it allowed Jamie to see that Scott had had to face the consequences of his actions, and that had made him feel much better about the incident. She added: 'He would never have known that Scott had to pay for what he did if it had gone to court.'

Control Case 1: A Canberra Neighbourhood Feud

What happens to vengefulness when it is processed by conventional criminal justice? Not much good, it appears, at least from our evidence. This Canberra control group case provides some insight. Police were resentful at their time being wasted when they were called to a suburban house to investigate the theft of a child's pet rabbit. The child's parents insisted on their charging their neighbour's 12-year-old daughter, who admitted the offence, so the case was duly dealt with and referred to the RJ experiment. It was randomly assigned to court, where the young offender was given a 'good behaviour bond', a sentence that did nothing except creating a criminal record for a 12-year-old. It was only when the victim and her mother were interviewed later that we learned this case was a mere blip in a long history of tit-for-tat revenge. The parents and extended families of both children had been involved in a neighbourhood feud over many years, the origins of which were unclear. All parties were abusive at every opportunity and made life as unpleasant as possible for each other. Every new incident pro voked a renewed desire to 'get back' at the other party. This cycle affected the children of the two families directly, and the parents encouraged them to continue the feud in any way they could. The theft of the rabbit was the daughter's contribution, and she was proud of it. When the victim was asked about the aftermath of the court case she said, 'Amanda keeps saying that she'll steal the rabbit again and bash me up as well, and her parents say it too.' The court process had done nothing to break the cycle.

We cannot know what an RJ conference might have achieved. But we do know that if they had gone to an RJ conference, the parties would have had to confront their actions in a way not required in the courtroom. They would have had to appreciate the harm they were doing to their children, listening to each other and trying to comprehend the other's point of view. The airing of emotions in a safe and neutral environment may well have engendered each side's empathy for the other, and reduced the likelihood of future aggression based on the continuing and unresolved desire for revenge.

Control Case 2: A Canberra Assault without RJ

Jodie and Melanie had been friends since beginning high school together. They found a flat big enough for them to share with Melanie's baby, and became very close. Melanie then started seeing Jodie's male cousin, who sometimes babysat so that the girls could go out together. One night when Melanie became drunk and disorderly, Jodie became exasperated at her behaviour and threatened to tell her male cousin something bad about Melanie. Melanie became angry and assaulted Jodie quite seriously. Melanie felt badly about her behaviour afterwards and made full admissions of responsibiliy to the police. But when Melanie sought legal advice she was told that she should plead not guilty in court, on the grounds of self-defence. Jodie was furious about this: she felt betrayed first by Melanie's behaviour and now by her justification for the behaviour. The prosecution dropped the case. Afterwards, Melanie attempted to contact Jodie through a mutual friend. Jodie refused to have anything more to do with her saying 'the trust has been broken'.

This case demonstrates how ineffectually formal prosecution deals with the complex emotions of interpersonal conflict. Jodie felt justifiably aggrieved at her friend's behaviour, but she never had a suitable opportunity to express these emotions. At her interview two months after the case was formally dismissed, Jodie remained as angry as ever. She did not care what the law said about Melanie's actions, she only knew that Melanie had harmed her and betrayed their friendship. In all likelihood that is how Melanie saw the events as well, as evidenced by her attempt to make contact. But the formal processing of this case allowed no way to reach reconciliation. Instead, Jodie expressed an ongoing desire to hurt her former friend.

Control Case 3: A Canberra Burglary Without RJ

Sharon got home from work one afternoon to find that her flat had been broken into and ransacked. She was especially angry to find that her roller blades had been stolen: she didn't earn much money and she had saved long to buy them. She didn't think she would ever be able to afford another pair. The pointless damage that the offender had done to her home made her even more upset. She wanted badly to tell the offender what she thought of him but, as she told the interviewer two months after the incident had been dealt with in court, 'Mostly I wanted an apology for all the mess.'

Sharon had not been told anything about what happened in the court case. Her offender pleaded guilty and she was not needed as a witness, so she wasn't there when the offender told the court that he knew what he had done was wrong and that he wanted to apologise for what he had done. It was no agency's or individual's responsibility to convey to Sharon that her offender was remorseful, so she never knew what he said. She did know that he had been dealt with in court, but this did nothing to reduce her stated desire for revenge.

RJ Case 4: Success without Pity in a Canberra Rape and Near-Murder

Restorative justice may also work in more subtle and indirect ways to defuse the desire for vengeance. In Canberra, a man was brutally assaulted and almost killed by an acquaintance he knew through their mutual drug dealer. The assailant had recently been released from prison, where he had been told that his girlfriend had been raped by the assault victim. The assault had been a pure act of revenge for the alleged rape. At the RJ meeting neither party was inclined to compromise or to forgive. The assault victim (and alleged rapist) maintained that the ex-inmate's girlfriend had consented to sexual relations and that he needed financial compensation for his injuries. His assailant maintained that the assault was justified, and that in any case he had no money for compensation.

At the same time, each was aware of the strong possibility of the feud between them continuing. They were very likely to encounter each other in the course of their routine activities, and each was fearful of the eventual outcome. With the help of a clergyman who worked with heroin addicts, the two parties reached an agreement in the RJ conference that was acceptable to both of them. They agreed that each would stay physically distant from the other when going about the area. This agreement addressed their fears of further revenge. At the same time, it gave each of them a face-saving and respectable way to avoid more vengeance.

Five years later, neither party had acquired any subsequent criminal record. This agreement may or may not have reduced the initial visceral desire for revenge, but it did allow the emotional heat to go out of the conflict.

Interpretation: Power, Morality and Hierarchy

One way to interpret the transformational process is by reference to the change in status rankings RJ accomplishes between victims and offenders. A sensitivity to inequality, which may also have some hard-wiring among primates (Brosnan and de Waal 2003), may drive the vengefulness of victims in the aftermath of crime. In a symbolic sense, offenders have demonstrated their power over victims by the completion of the crime. The crime then becomes the symbol of the offender's ability to dominate the victim. This hierarchy remains a symbol of submission until the victim can overcome it in some way. One way could be to have the offender suffer the pains of imprisonment, but even that may be unsatisfactory if the offender remains defiant and contemptuous of the justice system.

Another way to relieve the victim from a perceived status inferiority relative to the offender may be even more effective than prison. That way is what RJ often (if not always) accomplishes: an apology by the offender, who thus publicly admits the moral inferiority and blameworthiness of the crime against the victim. It is indeed a symbolic form of what some television news reporters described in 2001 as 'forcing offenders to grovel on their knees to ask the victim for forgiveness'. While no one was forced to grovel in these experiments—or forced to attend RJ conferences at all—most offenders in RJ voluntarily apologised, and most victims said the offenders' apologies were sincere (Sherman et al 2005). This effect was found regardless of any material reparation that may be agreed upon in the RJ conference, which Strang (2002) reports was in any event of lesser interest to most victims in Canberra. Among victims who had experienced RJ, most said that the experience greatly increased their sympathy for the offender, greatly reduced their fear of the offender, and generally made them less fearful of crime in everyday life (Strang et al 2006). All of this may be linked to the transfer of power from the once-dominant offender back into the now-victim, who emerges as the 'top dog' (or at least higher dog) in the relationship of the parties concerned.

Thus the key to transforming powerful emotions of vengefulness into sympathy or pity appears to be the phenomenon of apology and requests for forgiveness. Retzinger and Scheff (1996: 317) have placed this process within a theoretical framework that they call 'symbolic reparation'. They believe that without apologies 'the path towards settlement is strewn with impediments, whatever settlement is reached does not decrease the tension level in the room, and leaves the participants with a feeling of arbitrariness and dissatisfaction.' It appears that only apologies perceived by the victim as sincere and heartfelt can allow them to relinquish the desire for revenge.

C. Quantitative Evidence

As we have reported elsewhere, this qualitative evidence is not merely anecdotal. It illustrates a remarkably consistent replication of the original findings in eight out of all eight tests with comparable victim data. This statistically significant pattern of findings shows that RJ reduces victim desire for revenge among both male and female victims (Sherman et al 2005: 390). While small sample sizes meant that only one of the effects was statistically significant on its own, the overall sample of 445 victims (219 RJ and 226 controls) shows that those randomly assigned to RJ were on average

75 per cent less likely to report that they desired physical revenge than those randomly assigned to the control group. The test results of the individual experiments ranged from a minimum of RJ-randomised victims being 16 per cent less likely to report vengefulness (among female victims of juvenile property crime in Canberra) than the control group, to a high of 90 per cent less likely (among male victims of violence in Canberra).

The evidence for a theory of transformation of vengefulness into at least a more neutral state extends beyond victim desire to harm offenders. Victims assigned to RJ were, on average, 26 times more likely than controls to receive an apology from their offender, across all eight tests. They were 23 times more likely to say that they had received a sincere apology. Finally, they were almost three times more likely to forgive their offenders than victims assigned to control status. These results are even more impressive when we consider that they are drawn from an 'intention-to-treat' analysis (Pocock 1983), in which the victims assigned to RJ did not always receive an RJ conference because of administrative and other reasons beyond their control. The purpose of this kind of analysis is to ensure that the benefits of random assignment are preserved, and that the influence of selection bias is eliminated. Given how angry a small number of Canberra victims were about their not having received an RJ conference as promised (Strang 2002), it is crucial to recall that even those frustrated victims were analysed as if they had actually received such a conference. Including such victims is a far higher standard to meet than victim surveys of 'completers only', which are far more common in RJ evaluations, and tend to produce even higher levels of victim satisfaction (see Shapland, et al 2007, for examples of both completers only and intention-to-treat analysis).

More recently, an independent evaluation of our London experiments showed that the offenders in those RJ conferences caused substantially less harm than consenting offenders who were randomly assigned to a control group (Shapland et al 2008: 64). While the samples for those two experiments were not powerful enough to show statistically significant differences between RJ and control offenders in the volume of crime they committed, there was a statistically significant difference in the cost of the crime they committed. That difference, in 'value-for-money' terms, was a ratio of 14 to 1: for every £1 invested in restorative justice, the cost of crimes committed by the offenders receiving restorative justice was £14 less than for the offenders in the control group. This means, for example, that people committing burglary may have downshifted to shoplifting, or people committing serious assaults may have committed fewer of them, or some combination of frequency and cost of crime to victims and criminal justice. This may be taken, in the context of this paper, as some evidence that offenders did not become more vengeful themselves as a result of the 'shock' trauma of the RJ conference, or of having their power or rank reduced vis-à-vis the victim. Rather, it may be seen as further evidence of what Strang (2002) has called the 'win-win' character of RJ as a response to crime—in contrast to the win-lose character of retributive responses to crime.

IV. CONCLUSION: JUSTICE AND HOPE

The view that vengefulness is heavily shaped by nature is not implausible. But neither is it hopeful. Stressing the biological basis for this emotion may tend to give that basis too much weight, in an empirical sense. Anthropology and neuroscience have made valuable contributions to our understanding of this emotion, but they have been too immodest. Rather than limiting their claims by noting the socially contextual influences on the experience of this emotion, they have tended to ignore the evidence for those factors in order to stress the interesting, though limited, discoveries using the tools of their own disciplines. They have, in particular overlooked the impact of justice as an institution, in its many and diverse forms.

Our evidence on the malleability of vengefulness by restorative justice suggests the need for a far more balanced approach than 'its all nature', or even 'all nurture'. Rather than saying that vengefulness has certain biological bases—full stop—we suggest that all such research be cast in the light of the enormous limitations to biology suggested by contrary evidence. Our evidence is not the only empirical support for the proposition that vengefulness can be cured. One historian of homicide, for example, has noted that while Southern (US) gentlemen leave no insult unavenged, Northern gentlemen have been taught to let no insult even be acknowledged (Butterfield 1995). This hypothesis has even been shown to have biological correlates, as measured by testosterone and cortisol levels in saliva before and after an unprovoked insult—almost no increase in Northern men, compared to large increases in Southern men, all attending the University of Michigan in the late twentieth century (Nisbett and Cohen 1996).

Our concern is that ideas have consequences, and that the conclusion that 'vengeance is biological' may reduce the level of hope a society can maintain for its efforts to achieve justice. The emphasis on nature does not encourage hope; nothing in Diamond's (2008) discussion can be read as offering any hope for a better world. Like Hobbes, Diamond offers a bleak vision of human potential. Yet even in his work on the collapse of civilisations (Diamond 2005), the counterfactual of so many non-collapsed civilisations stands out. Surely the same must be true for vengefulness. That is a fact that should give us all hope for improving the human condition.

Criminologists can foster the social emotion of hope by encouraging a more evidence-based view of the emotion of vengefulness. The causal forces for that emotion, both biological and social, are obviously massive. But that fact alone does not mean they must remain unchallenged. Criminologists are not required to accept either the prevailing doctrines of retributive justice, nor the persistence of violence motivated by vengefulness. We are free to hope, to experiment, and to demonstrate alternatives. Whether law professors, newspapers, or politicians will pay any attention in the short run is irrelevant. With hope, all contributions to knowledge may always have a chance to succeed in the long run. This claim is probabilistically true, even if the chemist Max Perutz was not entirely right when he said: 'In science, truth always wins.'

REFERENCES

Angel, C (2005) 'Crime Victims Meet Their Offenders: Testing the Impact of Restorative Justice Conferences on Victims' Post-Traumatic Stress Symptoms' (PhD Dissertation, University of Pennsylvania).

Arendt, H (1958) *The Human Condition* (Chicago, University of Chicago Press).

BBC Films (2008) *The Edge of Love*.

Brosnan, SF, DeWaal, F (2003) 'Monkeys reject unequal pay' 425 *Nature* 297–99.

Butterfield, F (1995) *All God's Children* (New York, Alfred A Knopf).

Collins, R (2004) *Interaction Ritual Chains* (Princeton, Princeton University Press).

de Quervain, DJ-F, Fischbacher, U, Treyer, V, Schellhammer, M, Schnyder, U, Buck, A and Fehr, E (2004) 'The Neural Basis of Altruistic Punishment' 305(5688) *Science* 1254–58.

Diamond, J (2005) *Collapse: How Societies Choose to Fail or Succeed* (New York, Viking).

—— (2008) 'Annals of Anthropology. Vengeance is Ours: What Can Tribal Societies Tell Us About Our Need To Get Even?' *The New Yorker*, 21 April .

Ekman, P (2007). *Emotions Revealed, Second Edition: Recognizing Faces and Feelings to Improve Communication and Emotional Life* (New York, Holt).

Goldschmidt, W (2008) 'An Eye for an Eye' *The New Yorker*, 19 May p 7.

Goleman, D (1995) *Emotional Intelligence* (London, Bantam).

Knutson, B (2004) 'Sweet Revenge?' 305(5688) *Science* 1246–47.

McCullough, ME, Worthington, E Jr, Rachal, K (1997) 'Interpersonal forgiving in close relationships' 73(2) *Journal of Personality and Social Psychology* 321–36.

McCullough, ME, Bellah, CG, Kilpatrick, SD and Johnson, JL (2001) 'Vengefulness: relationships with forgiveness, rumination, well-being, and the Big Five' 27(5) *Personality and Social Psychology Bulletin* 601–10.

Newberg, AB, d'Aquili, EG, Newberg, SK and de Marici V (2000) 'The neuropsychological correlates of forgiveness' In ME McCullough, KI Pargament and CE Thoresen (eds) (2000) *Forgiveness: Theory, Research, and Practice* (New York, Doubleday).

Nisbett, RE and Cohen, D (1996) *Culture of Honor: The Psychology of Violence in the South* (Denver, Westview).

Pape, RA (2005) *Dying to Win: The Strategic Logic of Suicide Terrorism* (London, Random House).

Parrott, W (2001) *Emotions in Social Psychology* (Philadelphia, Psychology Press).

Pocock, S (1983) *Clinical Trials: A Practical Approach* (New York, Wiley).

Popper, K (1959) *The Logic of Scientific Discovery* (London, Hutchinson Education) (reprinted 2000, Oxford, Routledge).

Retzinger, S and Scheff, T (1996) 'Strategy for Community Conferences: Emotions and Social Bonds' in B Galway and J Hudson (eds), *Restorative Justice: International Perspectives* (New York, Criminal Justice Press).

Rossner, M (2008) 'Why Emotions Work: Restorative Justice, Interaction Ritual and the Micro-Potential for Emotional Transformation' (PhD dissertation, University of Pennsylvania).

Shapland, J, Atkinson, A, Colledge, E, Dignan, J, Howes, M, Johnstone, J, Pennant, R, Robinson, G and Sorsby, A (2004) *Implementing Restorative Justice Schemes (Crime Reduction Programme): A Report on the First Year* Home Office Online Report 32/04 (London, Home Office) www.homeoffice.gov.uk/rds/pdfs04/rdsoir3204.pdf.

Shapland, J, Atkinson, A, Atkinson, H, Chapman, B, Colledge, E, Dignan, J, Howes, M, Johnstone, J, Robinson, G and Sorsby, A (2006) *Restorative Justice in Practice: The Second Report from the Evaluation of Three Schemes* (Sheffield, Centre for Criminological Research, University of Sheffield).

Shapland, J, Atkinson, A, Atkinson, H, Chapman, B, Colledge, E, Dignan, J, Howes, M, Johnstone, J, Robinson, G and Sorsby, A (2007) *Restorative Justice: the views of victims and offenders—the third report from the evaluation of three schemes* (London, Ministry of Justice) www.justice.gov.uk/docs/Restorative-Justice.pdf.

Shapland, J, Atkinson, A, Atkinson, Dignan, J, Edwards, L, Hibbert, J, Howes, M, Johnstone, J, Robinson, G and Sorsby, A (2008) *Does Restorative Justice Affect Reconviction? The Fourth Report from the Evaluation of Three Schemes* (London, Ministry of Justice) www.justice.gov.uk/restorative-justice.htm.

Sherman, LW (2003) 'Reason for Emotion: Reinventing Justice with Theories, Innovations and Research. The 2002 ASC Presidential Address' 41 *Criminology* 1–38.

—— and Strang, H (2004) 'Experimental Ethnography: The Marriage of Qualitative and Quantitative Research' 595 *Annals of the American Academy of Political and Social Science* 204–22.

Sherman, LW, Strang, H, Angel, CM, Woods, D, Barnes, GC, Bennett, SB, Inkpen, N and Rossner, M (2005) 'Effects of face-to-face restorative justice on victims of crime in four randomized, controlled trials' 1 *Journal of Experimental Criminology* 367–95.

Strang, H (2002) *Repair or Revenge: Victims and Restorative Justice* (Oxford, Oxford University Press).

——, Sherman, L, Angel, C, Woods, D, Bennett, S, Newbury-Birch, D and Inkpen, N (2006) 'Victim Evaluations of Face-to-Face Restorative Justice Experiences: A Quasi-Experimental Analysis' *Journal of Social Issues* 62(2) 281–306.

Woolf, P (2008) *The Damage Done* (London, Bantam).

8

Reintegrative Ritual: Restorative Justice and Micro-Sociology

MEREDITH ROSSNER

I. INTRODUCTION: SHAME AND RESTORATIVE JUSTICE

WORLDWIDE SUPPORT OF restorative justice as an alternative or complement to the criminal justice system has been increasing. Though Braithwaite's theory of reintegrative shaming (1989) sparked a renewed interest in restorative justice, the practice is a centuries-old way of dealing with conflict, practised by Maori, Celtic, and Native American cultures (Braithwaite 2002). The general aim of restorative justice is to repair harm due to an offence in a way respectful to both the victim and the offender. A popular form of this is a restorative justice conference. Here, offenders, victims, friends and family meet with a specially trained facilitator to talk about what happened, how everybody was affected, and positive steps the offender can take to repair the harm to both the victim and the community. The conference is then concluded with a tea break, where everyone is able to communicate on a less formal level. The format and language vary across the world but the common aim is a forum where families and communities have a direct role in creating justice.

Reintegrative shaming theory (Braithwaite 1989) seemed the perfect theoretical backing to the movement, which was gaining popularity in New Zealand and Australia in the 1980s and 1990s. At the same time, restorative justice activists across North America and in the United Kingdom were influencing local policies and developing programmes to deal collectively with crime (Braithwaite 2002). Currently, New Zealand and Australia send many of their young offenders to restorative justice conferences instead of court. The Youth Justice Board of England and Wales has also made restorative principles an explicit aspect of their youth crime policy (Home Office 2003). The restorative justice movement is gaining public and legislative support throughout the world, and hopes to make these practices an important facet of the criminal justice system.

Empirical research provides us with conflicting data on the efficacy of restorative justice. The process has been perceived as more procedurally just, with positive psychological outcomes for both offenders and victims (Angel 2005; Poulson 2003; Strang 2002). We see the potential for reduced recidivism with juvenile violent crimes (Sherman et al 2000), but an increase in offending with property crimes (Sherman et al 2000). Other research (Nugent et al 2003) shows a decaying effect of restorative justice, with recidivism increasing to levels near the control group as time goes on. Importantly, Sherman et al (2004) show differential effects of restorative justice by race, with a conference actually increasing offending for Aboriginal offenders, and reducing offending for whites. We must conclude that restorative justice decreases offending in some cases (though perhaps with a decaying power), increases it in others, and sometimes has no effect at all. Although the body of empirical research is still growing, we still do not know who the process will work for, or when. To examine this, we need to develop theory that breaks into the 'black box' of a conference. Traditional theorists tend to focus on the importance of reintegrative shaming and procedural justice as the key ingredient to a successful conference, but there has been no in-depth analysis of the dynamics of specific conferences, or of the role that shame and other emotions actually play in restorative justice, nor have there been suggestions to increase both its short- and long-term efficacy.

I argue that restorative justice theory can be strengthened and the practice improved by examining conferences as an interaction ritual (Collins 2004). Furthermore, practitioners can learn from interaction ritual theory, improving their practice and encouraging long-term offender integration. Research in restorative justice has shown the potential for a positive impact on both victims and offenders. However, research has become stagnant in the field, with little more than comparisons of court versus conferencing currently being conducted. Braithwaite (2002) suggests that we need to go beyond these measures and develop a theory of restorative justice that can be used to improve and expand the practice. Here, I suggest this is possible by using interaction ritual theory to explore the micro-dynamics of a conference.

II. THEORETICAL BACKGROUND OF RESTORATIVE JUSTICE

A. Shame Theories

John Braithwaite's now classic book *Crime, Shame, and Reintegration* (1989) sets out a theory based on the reintegrative shaming of a wrongdoer. Braithwaite's main thesis is quite simple: shaming an offence while still allowing the offender to be seen as a good person will provide that person with strong bonds to society. Braithwaite defines shaming as 'all social processes of expressing disapproval which have the intention or effect of evoking remorse in the person being shamed and/or condemnation by others who become aware of the shaming' (1989: 100). He identifies two types of shaming practice, stigmatic and reintegrative. Stigmatic shaming draws from labelling and strain theories and condemns a person's character, not just the act he has committed. Reintegrative shaming is a respectful process where disapproval of the criminal act is expressed, but the offender is given a chance to repent and is then welcomed back into the community. Braithwaite suggests that this type of shaming maintains or even increases social bonds leading to increased informal social control and lower crime rates. Reintegrative shaming allows individuals to develop a 'learned conscience' (Wilson and Hernstein 1985) through interaction with a group of non-offenders. This learned conscience is the mechanism through which reintegrative shaming is translated into future compliance with the law (Braithwaite 1989: 37).

Braithwaite goes on to present evidence that societies with cultures built around processes of reintegrative shaming (Japan and Switzerland) have lower crime rates than countries with more stigmatic methods (the United States and Great Britain). In later work, he systematically shows that nursing home inspectors who use reintegrative shaming principles produce more compliance with federal law than inspectors with a more stigmatic attitude (Makkai and Braithwaite 1994). While he presents convincing evidence that reintegrative shaming is more effective at crime control and offender integration than the more traditional stigmatic shame, he does not explain why or how reintegrative shame can lead to successful integration (Van Stokkom 2002).

Scheff and Retzinger (1991) also examine the connection between shame and crime (or violence). They argue that shame is the 'master emotion of everyday life' and is a clear signal of alienation or broken social bonds. Pride, on the other hand, is a sign of high solidarity. They claim that in Western societies, shame has become repressed over time, and individuals are encouraged to hide their feelings of shame (they are 'ashamed of being ashamed'). Repressed shame has the potential to turn into a violent cycle of rage, shame, violence, and perhaps crime. In a restorative justice context, Retzinger and Scheff (1996) argue that a conference can redirect aggressive emotions and bring shame to the surface in a way that leads to empathy and pride. However, like Braithwaite, their work involving shame and social bonds does not explain the mechanism that allows expressed shame to turn into a reintegrating experience, nor has it been empirically tested.

Although Braithwaite never explicitly mentions restorative justice in this book, it launched the movement into the international academic scene, and the process has been linked to the concept of shame ever since. In most of the restorative justice literature, shame or shaming practices are a fundamental component, though recently empathy has been added (Van Stokkom 2002).

However, more recent theories have also suggested that other processes in addition to shame are at work. Specifically Tyler's procedural justice theory (1990) and Sherman's defiance theory (1993) indicates that the trust created through the restorative justice process encourages people to comply with the law.

B. Trust Theories

Procedural justice theory (Tyler 1990; Tyler and Huo 2001) emphasises trust in the law. Tyler and Huo argue that the key to compliance with the law is through the building of trust and legitimacy into the legal process. A restorative justice conference and the democratic deliberation inherent in the process may add some much needed legitimacy to the criminal justice system. Strang's (2002) work shows much higher levels of perceived fairness of restorative justice among victims participating in a conference. Results from interviews with offenders also show that they were more likely to understand what was going on in a conference (Sherman and Barnes 1997). Tyler et al (2007) have also examined the connection between procedural justice, reintegrative shaming, and legitimacy, finding some evidence that both reintegrative shaming and feelings of legitimacy can reduce offending.

Defiance theory (Sherman 1993) has many of the same underlying assumptions as procedural justice, though also includes reintegrative and unacknowledged shame in the theory of why people do or do not commit crime. The key claim of this theory is that similar criminal sanctions have opposite or different effects, depending on the social situation and the offender. When an offender views a sanction as illegitimate, has weak bonds to the sanctioning agent, or denies their shame in the offence, defiance of the law occurs, resulting in offending. Deterrence results when sanctions are seen as legitimate, offenders have strong bonds to mainstream society, and offenders are able to express shame. Sherman suggests that a restorative conference is more likely to promote deterrence, while a courtroom appearance may produce defiance. However he and his co-authors (2004) suggest that a defiant reaction to authority is driving the increased offending among aboriginal people who have a restorative justice conference. While these theories support the movement toward restorative justice, and provide initial evidence of how the process works, they are still missing a theoretical step between the structure of a conference and social bonds, trust, and offending.

III. INTERACTION RITUAL AND RESTORATIVE JUSTICE THEORY

Micro-sociology, and in particular, interaction ritual theory, may provide an alternative explanation of how a restorative justice conference works to integrate an offender. Collins (2004; this volume), following in the traditions of Durkheim (1912) and Goffman (1967), describes how individuals interact through a series of rituals that produce emotional energy. Durkheim showed how important repeated rituals are to social solidarity. Goffman extended this thesis to show that solidarity-creating rituals occur not only in formal rituals (such as religious ceremonies), but in all facets of everyday life. He defines an interaction ritual as an instance of 'mutually focused emotion and attention producing a momentarily shared reality, which thereby generates solidarity and symbols of group membership'. Collins adds to this that interaction rituals can be linked together to produce long-term social bonding and emotional energy.

Collins lists four main ingredients for a successful ritual: group assembly, a barrier to outsiders, mutual focus, and a shared mood. These factors combined lead a group to develop a rhythmic coordination and synchronisation to their conversation. Participants get 'caught up in the rhythm and mood of the talk' (Collins 2004: 48). Once this happens, the collective effervescence that Durkheim predicted in formal religious ceremonies can occur in any social interaction, formal or otherwise.

As a result of this group coordination, participants begin to exhibit signs of strong solidarity between each other. This includes a synchronisation of gestures and movements at the micro level, including head-nodding, smiling, eye contact, and other gestures (Collins 2004: 75).The result is a shared feeling of group membership. For that moment, participants in the interaction feel like they belong. Generally, this solidarity takes on a symbolic meaning of some form. People or things turn into symbols of the social bond. While solidarity is a short-term, 'in the moment' feeling, these symbols remind participants of the event, calling forth renewed feelings of group membership and belonging. In this way, solidarity is turned into a long-term feeling that Collins terms 'emotional energy'. Emotional energy is a long-term combination of positive feelings such as confidence, enthusiasm, and pride that sustains a person between interactions. In addition, people with high levels of emotional energy are more disposed to trust others (2004: 121). The acquisition of emotional energy is a central motivating force for individuals, and encourages them to maintain the social order (Fine 2005).

In short, interaction ritual theory suggests that in certain interactions, a rhythmic coordination is developed over time, resulting in high solidarity contact. Symbols of this solidarity are generated by members, reminding them of the positive feelings felt at that time. These positive feelings represent the emotional energy gained from this particular interaction.

Placing restorative justice in an interaction ritual framework implies that it is successful ritual that builds bonds and reintegrates an offender, not shame. Note that according to Collins' model, what the participants are saying is not as important as the proper rhythm characterised by turn-taking and emotional attunement. I suggest there is a misplaced emphasis on shame as the causal mechanism of desistance. Reintegrative shaming (or acknowledged shame) is not doing the work here, but interaction ritual is. Restorative justice conferences are solidarity-creating events. Participants leave their conference with new feelings of group membership and social bonds, and with high levels of emotional energy. This energy may be externalised in a commitment to stop offending, and increased trust both in the criminal justice system, and in its representatives, the police. I suggest that procedural justice theory is relevant to restorative justice and interaction rituals, as it may be that the trust developed during the interaction is what keeps an offender from re-offending.

IV. THE EMPIRICAL STUDY

I examine how restorative justice conferences were solidarity-building interaction rituals for four serious offenders. Although they all claim that the conference was a positive experience, the long-term effect varied. These men all took part in different conferences while on remand in a London prison, awaiting sentence after guilty pleas for burglary or robbery. Examining their conferences as an interaction ritual, once can see how the structure of a conference works to create solidarity and, over the long term, emotional energy.

I conducted in-depth interviews with four men between two and three years after their restorative justice conference. Due to the serious nature of their offences, all four had received substantial custodial sentences of between two and four years. Their identities are anonymous, but I will give a brief introduction to these men.

Paul was released from prison after serving one year of a two-year sentence for burglary. He successful completed the rest of his sentence on parole, and is no longer under court supervision. At 40 years old, he is a self-professed reformed heroin addict, who is currently employed full-time and in a stable relationship, about to be married. His restorative justice conference consisted of him, a drug counsellor, his burglary victim and wife, and another burglary victim living in the same neighbourhood.

Similarly, David served one year of a two-year burglary sentence, and successfully completed parole. In his late 30s, he admits to past use of alcohol, but no drug use. He says that he does not drink anymore, and spend his days working full-time, and helping his girlfriend take care of their daughter and disabled son. His conference was with a man from his own neighbourhood whom he had burgled. Both Paul and David have had similar trajectories after their conference, and seem to be doing well.

At 30 years old, Greg is still serving a four-year sentence for burglary. He has been released on parole, but a few weeks out of prison, he went on a two-week 'binge' and breached the conditions of his parole. He admitted to me that going back to prison was a relief, as the temptation of drugs was too much for him. He did not seem optimistic about his release, suggesting that he was 'uncomfortable' outside the prison walls. His conference was with the victim of the burglary, her two friends, his mother, and his girl-friend at the time (they have since broken up).

Gareth, 22 years old, is still serving his original three-year sentence for burglary. He has been denied parole at least once. Due to behaviour prob-lems in prison, all his privileges have been revoked. He tells me that he is currently in rehab to deal with his crack and heroin problems, and that his burglary offence was drug-related. At his conference were the two victims of burglary, their partners, his parents, his two older brothers, and his younger sister.

To summarise, at the time of their interviews, two men had been released and had not re-offended. One had been released and reincarcerated due to drug offences and violation of parole, and one was still serving his original sentence, unable to qualify for parole due to significant behavioural prob-lem in prison.

The interview consisted of an in-depth analysis of their actual confer-ence, as well as a discussion of their experiences while serving their prison sentence, and what had happened to them since their release, if appropri-ate. This research is able to problematise and bring some perspective to the ritual dynamics of these conferences, and to investigate whether these men see the conference having any long-term effect on their lives. The next section uses these men's narratives to detail how a restorative justice conference may parallel the interaction ritual ingredients and outcomes sug-gested by Collins (2004). Then, I will examine how the degree of success in generating emotional energy through the interaction ritual may explain patterns of desistance.

V. RITUAL INGREDIENTS

Restorative justice conferences are unique as they are formal rituals that try to force emotional energy and successful interaction from parties that generally would be adverse to it, namely an offender and his victim. First, there is *group assembly*, at which a facilitator arranges a face-to-face meet-ing of an offender, the victim, family, friends, or anyone else involved in the criminal incident or with a stake in repairing the harm. Conferences can be as small as three people, the victim, offender, and facilitator, or can include extended family, friends, witnesses, and in some cases probation officers, prison officers, police officers, and lawyers.

Barriers to outsiders are built into the design of a conference. They are held in a special room specifically set up for a conference, with chairs arranged in a circle in the centre of the room. Only conference participants are allowed in the room. The men I spoke to all had their conferences in prison, in a private room in the education or legal visits wing. They were given adequate time and privacy and were not interrupted by anyone.

The *mutual focus of attention and shared mood* is also apparent. A good facilitator spends significant time preparing everyone in the group for what is about to take place. They all know that they are there to discuss the crime. The shared mood generally increases as the conference progresses. At the beginning, the victim and his family may be feeling anger or fear of the offender. The offender may also be feeling fear, but for the victim, as well as anger maybe for being caught, and perhaps some sense of guilt or shame. The meeting is initially disjointed, with everyone reluctant to talk and many long silences with disrupted rhythm. However, the facilitator guides the group through the three main phases of the conference. First, the offender provides a description of exactly what happened on the day of the incident: The events leading up to it, exactly how it was carried out, and all that happened until he was caught. Then the victim relates how he was affected by the crime and the results of that for him and his family. The victim and offender supporters also have a chance to tell how they have all been affected by the crime. As everyone tells their story, the rhythm of the conference solidifies. Often the facilitator goes for long periods without saying anything, as the participants take over the conversation and communicate their shared feelings. During the conference, offenders and victims finally see each other's point of view. This leads to the final stage of the conference, where they discuss positive steps that the offender can take to repair the harm. Reparations can be material, as in paying back the money that was stolen, or symbolic, such as agreeing to do volunteer work for a charity of the victim's choice, or even a heartfelt apology followed by forgiveness.

My data support this description of conferences developing a rhythmic focus over time. The shared mood generally increases as the conference progresses. The men told me that there were quite nervous going into the conference, and considered cancelling at the last minute. For some, this pre-conference anxiety translated into an inability to communicate one's feelings and thoughts at the beginning of the conference. Gareth talks of his inability to say what was on his mind when I asked him how he felt at the start of the conference. He tells me, 'I felt a bit nervous, coming in, some people told me about these kind of things, but it wasn't called restorative programme, where they meet victims. And uh, I knew that they could be angry and all that stuff. That's why I wasn't even looking at them.' When I asked him to describe for me what went on in the conference, he replies:

> At first they [the victims] didn't understand because I wasn't talking. So they kinda got a bit angry. Not angry, but didn't know why they were bothering, I just

sat there. I wanted to have words, but I just couldn't say anything. And at the end, they were all, 'We understand.'

Interviewer: So you think they were angry at you toward the beginning?

Yeah, 'cus it was like I wasn't paying attention, or even caring. Then my brother had to stand up and say something ... but at the end of it I told them what I was really thinking. It was good.

This conference continued in a disjointed manner, with Gareth not speaking and the victims becoming increasingly frustrated, until Gareth's brother stood up in the conference and confronted him, asking why he wasn't speaking. This transitional moment allowed Gareth to begin to take part in the dialogue, resulting in what he judged as a successful conference. As the conference progressed, the anxiety slowly dissipated and the rhythm solidified, allowing victim, offender, and family to have a productive conference.

Another conference participant, David, explicitly notes how the conference settles into a rhythm where victim and offender focus together on communicating their shared feeling and addressing the aftermath of the offence:

As the conversation starts flowing, the nervousness tends to start to go away a little bit, doesn't it? Start getting to know each other, in that sense, right? And, he was putting questions to me, I was putting questions to him, and um, it went as it should of, in that way. You know, there was no abusing, or anything like that, you know?

Although conferences are often at first lacking continuity, with long pauses and unnatural silences due to the nerves of both parties, over time, participants develop a mutual focus of attention, with the rhythm of the conversation generating intense feelings among the group. In fact, facilitators are trained to use these unnatural silences to motivate people to speak. I've observed numerous conferences where after initial disruptions, the facilitator barely speaks, instead allowing the participants to feed off each other's energy. This is apparent when David told me that his facilitator 'wasn't really involved in it too much. He obviously made the introductions and all that, and then he didn't do much of the talking. Until the end where he spoke again.'

The large part of the success of a conference depends on the ability of the facilitator to encourage rhythmic participation. It is a facilitator's job to guide participants through their emotions, and to manufacture solidarity. One way this is done is by assuring all participants that they are on an egalitarian footing. Facilitators must ensure that everyone in the group is treated as an equal, and follows the rules of turn-taking. People are discouraged from interrupting each other and the facilitator makes sure that no one person dominates the conversation. This practice of symmetrical deference (Goffman 1981) adds to the mutual focus and shared mood of participants.

These techniques guarantee the presence of the necessary ritual ingredients for solidarity.

Facilitators recognise that there will be disruptions to the rhythm in the early stages of conference. They are not anxious about the frequent frame breaks in the beginning, when victim and offender are reluctant to start talking to each other (the silences could be upwards of 10–20 seconds: deafening, in an ordinary conversation). Instead, the facilitator takes advantage of the silence to encourage speech. Others in the room are probably equally uncomfortable with the length of silence and will begin to talk to each other just to fill up space, thus creating the interaction that will eventually lead to the emotional energy.

Another technique commonly used by facilitators they refer to as the 'click and drag' approach. This forces the offender and victim to make eye contact. Usually at the start of conferences, participants are nervous and afraid and do not want to look at each other. They see the facilitator as a 'safe' person and tend to focus their eyes on them or at the ground. If this were to continue, the meeting would be a series of separate conversations between the facilitator and the different members of the group. To encourage eye contact between the offender and victim, the facilitator will lock eyes with the offender and then change their direction of gaze to the victim (who may also be looking at the offender). The offender, without even being aware, follows the facilitator's gaze to the victim, and soon the two are looking at each other (perhaps unwillingly at first), and no longer at the facilitator. This too encourages rhythm and emotional attunement.

VI. RITUAL OUTCOMES

A. Solidarity

The ritual outcomes of a successful restorative justice interaction are clear from observing a conference. Solidarity is externalised towards the end of the conference by the coordinated attunement of the participants, such as crying together, laughing together, hugging, and shaking hands. Offenders who at the beginning of the conference were slouched in their seats (literally drained of energy) are now sitting upright and smiling. The experience is much as Durkheim describes a successful religious ritual: 'it seems to him [the offender] that he has become a new being ... and because his companions feel transformed in the same way at the same moment ... it is as if he was in reality transported into a special world entirely different from the one in which he ordinarily lives' (Durkheim 1912). The moment has become a sacred transforming experience.

Van Stokkom (2002) suggests that the important emotion here is shared empathy. During the conference, offenders and victims finally see each other's points of view, in Mead's terms 'taking the role of the other' (1934). Mead argues that only through juxtaposition of the self and other can an individual become self-aware. Paul makes it clear that empathy is important:

> Until you accept that you were doing wrong, until you accept that you hurt whoever by the action your doing, you aren't gonna change anything. You have to accept these things, you have to feel the other person's pain. You have to experience the darkness to appreciate the light.

Paul is emphasising that change cannot occur until you can see yourself from the victim's point of view. Acknowledging the pain caused is a necessary step. This puts offenders and victims on level playing field. They both agree on the harm caused, and both are motivated to repair that harm. This is an instance of group solidarity as discussed by Collins. It is important to note that this empathy is not one-sided. The offenders also perceive that the victims 'understand where they are coming from'.

> Paul: The victims of my crime were very understanding and a lot of empathy, towards me, as well as wanting to see the right thing done for themselves. You know, they are clued-up people. There was a sort of awareness about them.
>
> Interviewer: What do you mean by that?
>
> Paul: I think he [the victim]'s got a better understanding, he's got more knowledge, he's become if anything, more open-minded about things. I mean he's not a fool, by any stretch of the imagination. I didn't know him previously, but I think he may have become a little more kinder. Not so harsh in his judgements.

It is clear from these examples that developing empathy and a shared morality is necessary to successful outcomes. David tells me of a significant point in his conference when he realised the victim was disabled. His son also suffers from a crippling disability, so he fully understood the hardship and frustration that goes along with it. This made him even more remorseful for the harm that he had caused. Later on in the conference, David and victim, who lived in the same neighbourhood but had never met before, realised that they both frequented the same local pub. This new connection brought them even closer, with David volunteering to buy the victim a drink if they ever ran into each other again. These revelations that the offender and victim are not so socially and emotionally distant from each other allowed them to develop a closer bond.

An important postscript to the conference that further cements the group solidarity is the final tea-break. Here, participants leave the circle and continue their discussion over refreshments. It is at this point that offender and victim often find things they have in common, such as that they frequent the same bars, or are fans of the same sports team, or even that the victim knows someone who may be able to give the offender a job (I have witnessed all of these things in a conference). This allows for another spontaneous interaction ritual that works to further increase emotional energy. In fact, in observations of conferences in New Zealand, Retzinger and Scheff (1996) note that true symbolic reparation was made after the formal end of the conference, when the participants were waiting for the agreements to be copied and passed out, or on the walk to the car, in one poignant instance when a victim pats an offender on the shoulder after a tearful apology.

B. Symbols and Shared Morality

Conference participants also formulate and sign an outcome agreement that lists things an offender is willing to do to repair the harm. The outcome agreement also notes whether an apology was made and accepted. This piece of paper is copied and given to everyone to take home. The outcome agreement becomes a symbol of the special interaction that just took place. It also highlights a new standard of morality that all group members share. They all understand each other's perspective and share a feeling of how to right the wrong.

What is surprising to most offenders is the victim's apparent disinterest in material reparation or punitiveness; rather they focus on steps the offender can take to improve himself. As in the creation of solidarity, empathy seems key to symbolic reparation. Through the outcome agreements, victims all expressed a desire that the offenders 'better themselves'—through addressing drug problems, employment opportunities, or mental health issues. The offenders in my interviews all interpreted this as the victims expressing empathy, and were pleased at the outcome. From this, I suggest that in order for a restorative justice conferment to act as a successful interaction ritual, empathy seems to be a key emotion that activates solidarity, shared morality, and symbolic reparation. Greg, who is finishing his burglary sentence, makes this clear when we discuss his outcome agreement:

Interviewer: Do you remember what she [the victim] recommended?

Greg: Um, just basically that I should get help. 'Cus my head was quite messed up.

Interviewer: So, how did you feel about those things?

Greg: I was okay, I was okay. In my eyes she could of said a lot different. And, I mean she coulda said, 'Well I hope this man goes away for a long time'. And she never did. She said that I should get counselling. The second one was to get rehabilitation whilst in prison. Another one, I was trying to do my NVQ fitness instructor. I think that just made me feel even worse. 'Cus she seemed like such a nice person. And her house had been burgled.

For Greg, discussion around the outcome agreement symbolises the victim's respect for him, and her willingness to see him as a good person.

It seems that the actual piece of paper that is the outcome agreement is not really a strong symbol to these offenders. Rather, it is the exchange of words that took place in getting to the outcome agreement that is symbolic of the group solidarity and the offender's reintegration. Paul has a similar experience when he tells me:

> I was quite amazed at the outcome, the outcome of the conference blew me away ... there was no malice, no malice there ... they just wanted me to get on with my life, you know, they just wanted what's best with me, which is quite unbelievable ... and they said to me, 'You know, why don't you get some formal education, why don't you address your drug problem?'

By focusing on things that he can do to better himself, the outcome agreement represents the shared empathy of victim and offender and the new standard of morality that Paul is willing to accept, by addressing his drug problem and finding employment.

VII. IS EMOTIONAL ENERGY SUSTAINABLE? PAUL'S STORY

Emotional energy is the final, and perhaps most important, ritual outcome. In Collins' model, emotional energy is the long-term result of a specific interaction, where interactions build on each other to supply positive energy. It is like a physical high that an individual gets out of a positive interaction that he carries with him into his next series of interactions, keeping him bonded to society.

The problem with emotional energy is that without further positive interaction rituals it is likely to decay. Symbols act as memories that remind us of the ritual, which in turn reminds us of membership to the group. However, if the ritual is not performed periodically, then the symbol will begin to fade away and the emotional energy generated during the ritual will be drained. A fundamental flaw of many restorative justice programmes is that the ritual is only performed once. There may be a lot of emotional energy and group solidarity created, and the outcome agreement may act as a symbol of that membership, but it can't last for ever. Collins suggests that in the absence of repeated ritual, emotional energy may fade as soon as a few days after the ritual (2004: 140). In the restorative justice conference, this is theoretically easy to believe. Many conferences are held in prisons or with offenders who are about to go to prison. If not in prison, many come from extremely disadvantaged neighbourhoods with little opportunity for advancement. Worse still, many are serious drug addicts. All of these obstacles can easily and quickly drain one of any emotional energy (and subsequent desire to desist from crime) gained from a two-hour-long meeting with a victim. This presents a serious problem to the efficacy of the process.

However, it is clear that some are able to use the emotional energy created in a conference to work towards desistance. To examine this in depth,

I use the narrative of Paul. I will show how his conference mediated certain negative interactions he experienced in prison and during re-entry back into the community. He uses his restorative justice experience to make future interactions positive, by creating a narrative of change with restorative justice at the centre.

It is important to note that not all stories are like Paul's. While all the offenders I spoke to were glad they took part in a conference and describe positive outcomes, some were not able to maintain the high emotional energy from their conference, moving back into drugs and crime. However, Paul's story is useful material, allowing us to examine the potential of inter-action ritual theory.

First, we can see that Paul can identify particular moments during his conference where he gained emotional energy. Specifically, he attributes the conference to increases in confidence, enthusiasm, pride, and trust, as predicted by Collins. He explains how interaction with the two highly educated victims of his burglaries enabled him to gain some much-needed self-esteem:

> There I was, sitting in the room. A fellow like me who's spent his life on the streets, no formal education, with a very low self-worth, total lack of belief in himself, and I suddenly realised, that these people told me that I was quite an intelligent person yeah? Which, I suppose I'd always known, but maybe to have a little bit of affirmation. And I thought to myself, well there I was, with two university-educated people, you know a surgeon, and a financial manager, having a nice conversation, even after what I done to them. And suddenly, I had a voice, and I started speaking and they listened.

The victims taking an interest allowed him to acknowledge himself as an intelligent person. He notes that in his past, he never thought it worthwhile to say anything. This is an interaction that Goffman would consider as having symmetrical deference, where the social status of the two parties is ignored, and they treat each other as equals. It may also be a type of interac-tion that is less likely to produce a defiant reaction to authority.

A further externalisation of Paul's emotional energy is the pride he feels from his participation in a conference. He describes what it was like to tell his mother, whom he acknowledges he has a long-standing troubled relation-ship with, about the conference. She said to him, 'So now you want to be on Jerry Springer [day-time TV talk show host] next?' His mother understood his conference to be more drama and show than anything. He said know-ingly to me: 'She didn't understand, how could she understand?' He sees his conference as a sacred experience, which outsiders can't comprehend.

He also explains how the outcome agreement encouraged him to actually address his problems:

> Paul: Oh yeah. You know, not just because it's on an outcome agreement. That set the board, you know probably, that got it all in motion. But it was something

I wanted to do for years anyway. But never had the courage to do it. Or the know-how. Or whatever, just didn't have the courage really. They enabled me. It brings it out for me. And they listened to me.

Interviewer: What sort of things did you do?

Paul: You know I addressed my drug problem, alcohol problem. And I done some courses. All of a sudden, now I found myself graduating from RAPT [an intensive prison-based drug rehabilitation programme].

In addition, he has specific memories of the conference that gives him new-found initiative. While reading the newspaper one day in prison, he sees an advertisement for a distance learning course in counselling. Paul decides that he actually wants to be a counsellor, helping people like himself. However, this is a daunting task for someone with no education and still serving a prison sentence. He begins a series of back and forth letters with the university, first explaining his situation and asking for admission, then requesting funding, finding references, etc. At times he felt discouraged by his lack of progress, but he explains:

Paul: At the time I'm doing this, I remember particularly [victim]. I particularly remember him saying you're a clever guy, you can do this sort of thing. I keep hearing that, I keep seeing that conference ... eventually, they write me massive amounts of money, they just let me do it. Yeah and I wind up doing a distance learning course for nothing.

Interviewer: And this was all while you were still serving you sentence?

Paul: Yeah, all while I'm still serving my sentence.

Finally, Paul describes how his conference gave him the ability to trust the police. He developed a close relationship with his conference facilitator, Karl, and describes how this transformed his thinking:

Paul: Oh I love him. A lovely man, Karl 's a good man. He's got a wealth of experience. If it wasn't for Karl, I probably wouldn't be sitting here today.

Interviewer: What was it like when you first met him? Did you two hit it off right away?

Paul: When I first met Karl, my barriers [were] up. Because Karl's a policeman. And I've never had a mate who's a policeman, they've always been the enemy. And, don't trust a policeman, they'll fit you up or beat you up, one of the two. But as I've come to know Karl, well he's gonna be my best man for God's sake, you know? So that says it all, doesn't it, that says it all.

Although he (like many offenders) had an inherent distrust of the police, he was able to look past the uniform and see the facilitator as a warm and caring person who he feels comfortable confiding in. He now comes to see both the police, and restorative justice, which is run by the police, as a legitimate institution.

In addition describing instances of emotional energy generated from his conference, we can see that Paul is able to articulate a specific change in his own character and identity, using his emotional energy as a tool of desistance. This is similar to Maruna's (2001) notion of the development of a narrative of change. Maruna shows how individuals develop redemption scripts that lead to cognitive change and renewed commitment to abstain from crime and drugs. One can generate a story that separates the self from the acts they have done, empowers them with an optimistic perception of the future, and fills them with a desire to 'give something back'. This final aspect of the redemption script is important. Throughout his interviews, Maruna repeatedly comes across the theme of the 'professional ex's' (Brown 1996), offenders who were either working full- or part-time as counsellors or social workers, or were doing volunteer work in this sector hoping for full-time employment. From an interaction ritual perspective, these people can be seen as emotional energy-seekers. They want to help others, and counselling other offenders can also allow ex-offenders to repeatedly participate in an interaction ritual where they can tell their story of desistance and empowerment. This can reinforce symbols or generate new symbols of desistance that one needs to 'make good'. As one of Maruna's ex-offender puts it, 'Working here [at a reintegration programme], I meet people every day who are still stealing, still using drugs, and I look at them, and it's a real reminder of how far I've come ... So, I use these reminders to keep me honest, keep me from being depressed' (2001: 124–25). Through repeatedly interacting with others and telling their story of redemption, ex-offenders can maintain the high level of emotional energy needed for the daunting task of staying straight against the many obstacles facing convicted criminals.

It is important to note that Paul faces serious obstacles on his road to desistance. He has numerous negative interactions, with prison guards, the local government, doctors, and employers. For instance, while taking his distance learning course in prison, he received almost no support from prison officials:

> I received very little support from the prison education system. I even asked them for some paper, 'cus I'd run out of paper. And I was doing the distance learning course. And they said no we can't give you any but you can have some scrap paper from the bin if you want. To put me assignments on. Computer, I needed access to the computer. Oh, you can have access to a computer only if you do some sort of course. But I didn't need to do that. 'Cus I didn't want to do spread-sheets and database. All I wanted to do is type up my assignments.

However, Paul mediates these negative experiences with other, more positive interactions that he uses to form his new identity. Paul is able to use his new-found emotional energy to participate in numerous future interaction rituals that create chains of positive experiences. For instance, he takes on the gratifying role of the 'professional ex', as discussed by Maruna. Upon release from prison, he begins work as a plumber, spending a lot of time in different houses, meeting different people. At one job, he meets a woman who reminds him of his old self:

> Paul: I found myself counselling someone the other week. Yeah, an alcoholic lady, she asked me to go and get her a bottle and all this, and eventually I walked her up the shop because she can't, I've got her on my arm, and … And I walk her up the shop and I explained to her that you don't have to be this way, and I tell her a little bit about myself, and blah blah blah, and I give her the AA helpline number. And about a month later, six weeks later, we get called back to the next door property, I thought, I wonder what happened to this woman? And out she comes, she looked a million dollars. She went, 'I just thought I'd let you know, I've been going to meetings.' Great, great.
>
> Interviewer: Oh wow, yeah. How'd that make you feel?
>
> Paul: Ahhh, beautiful, beautiful. Made me feel, just made me feel like I'd done the right thing.

He is able to remind himself of his change in identity while at the same time gaining emotional energy by helping someone in a similar position to his 'old self'. Not only does he have a desire to help others, he makes a significant distinction between criminal and non-criminal identity. This is best shown in a story he related about a friend who recently relapsed back into drugs, and how his experience of restorative justice changed the way he viewed the situation:

> [Restorative justice] played a big big major part in my life, a big major part . To the point where we have another friend, and he recently relapsed, he started using drugs again. And when he first started, we brought him over to stay at ours, to try and help him. And he went out and went missing, and we found him at the pub. But in between that period, he was missing for a couple of hours, I was worried that he was gonna commit a crime, and I was gonna have to tell him that if I found out he committed a crime, that I would have to tell the police. That was coming from me. Yeah, there was me who's been a crook all his life, but I would have to tell the police, because that is the right thing to do.

This is a remarkable statement, as he articulates a distinct change in his identity, and also shows a new feeling of trust for traditional agents of social control, something that his old self would never have acknowledged. All throughout his interview, Paul distinguished between his old self and his new self. At one point, in talking about prisoners, he refers to the collective group as 'we'. He quickly corrects himself, switching to 'them', saying 'Why am I saying "we"? I'm not one of them.'

He can also articulate his new identity. He sees himself as a normal person, completely able to separate his past identity from his present self. He revels in describing the everyday aspects of his life, how he is just like any other, law-abiding citizen. This is clear when I ask him what he does in his free time with his girlfriend.

Interviewer: Do the two of you go out socially at all?

Paul: Well, we don't drink. So we don't go to the pub anymore, clubbing or anything. We do a lot of family things, cycling too.

Interviewer: Cycling?

Paul: Yeah, I started. I went in the time trials [laughing].

Interviewer: How'd you do?

Paul: Dead last [laughing ... extended] well it was my weight you see. Everyone goes on about my weight. Since I've been home I've put on a couple of pounds [laughing]. Couple a stone, and uh, people buy me presents like bicycles and scales. Keeps going on about the Atkins diet, I eat everything. You know what? I love saying it, I'm just a normal fella. That's all it is. I'm just a normal fella, who goes to work, comes home to his old woman, she don't like me calling her that, but [laughing] it's a term of endearment, my fiancé [laughing]. And I play with the kids and just do things that people do. 'Cus that's what I am, I'm a human being. And it's like being a born again human being for me, I just love my life. And I ain't got no worries. I ain't gotta worry about if anyone's gonna kick my door in, 6 o'clock in the morning and come and arrest me. I don't do nothing wrong.

He also has future goals of helping others, through 'spreading the gospel' of restorative justice, as he puts it. We see how he participates in further interaction rituals that help to solidify his new self. For instance, he was recently invited to speak at an academic conference about his restorative justice experience. He and his victim got up on stage together and answered questions from the audience about this. Telling me this story, Paul and his girlfriend, who was at the event with him, recall how good he felt afterwards:

Paul: We had a great time, I had a great time. [Afterwards] when we were walking in the street, and people kept coming up and shaking me hand.

Girlfriend: It was an amazing, amazing experience.

Paul: It drove me mad.

Girlfriend: Even in the local coffee shop, people started coming up ... And you were, absolutely amazed at it. At how they were experiencing it, feeling it. And you were honest, telling them how it is.

Paul: See I couldn't work it all out. I was like 'What's this all about, keep coming up and shaking my hand?' I said I'm only me. [Laughing]. God, help me.

Girlfriend: You loved it.

Paul: Yeah I loved it, it was my 15 minutes of fame, lasted three days, and I revelled in it.

Paul uses these experiences as emotional energy-building interaction rituals. He seeks the good feelings that he felt when he first met his victims, and is able to recreate that emotional energy in his subsequent interactions. He also hopes to continue in his role of a 'professional ex', engaging in a series of interaction rituals that continually reinforce his identity as a 'normal person.'

> But one day, I'd just like to give something back, that's all I want to do. I just want to sit down and talk to somebody, and say look, I'm giving something back. 'Cus that's what it's all about. This particular restorative justice gave me something, gave me a gift, and anything I can do to, it's a strong belief, a strong belief. I love it, I love it. The greatest thing. I think the added advantages I could bring is that I talk the same languages as the perpetrator. Don't take no prisoners [laugh].

Paul sums us his cognitive transformation at the end of our interview, when he says: 'That's about it really, I can't think of anything else I can say. That's me. How it was to how it is.' He clearly sees a transformation from his old self to his new self. He is a prime example of someone who uses his emotional energy to engage in a series of interactions that fill him up with more positive energy, encouraging him to form a script of redemption.

VIII. STRATEGIES FOR SUCCESSFUL RESTORATIVE JUSTICE

We have seen how interaction ritual plays an important role in the success of the restorative justice process. However, the process can be improved by developing ways to renew emotional energy and group solidarity regularly. Reconvening periodic conferences with all the same participants would be ideal. Understandably, this would be quite hard to do, though not impossible. Another idea would be to form support groups for offenders and victims who have gone through the restorative justice process. This can allow participants to relive the moments of their own particular conference with others who have undergone similar experiences. This may be especially helpful for offenders in prison or those who are re-entering the community after a prison sentence. In both of these environments there are many forces working to create negative emotional energy. Regular meetings may provide group membership with others of a common morality as well as continually creating and re-creating important symbols of both membership and their collective efforts at desistance. This strategy may enable people to develop identities as professional ex's, easing the transition back into the law abiding community.

Symbols are very important to the process. Durkheim stresses the importance of symbols for the maintenance of emotional energy:

> Those feelings are very strong so long as men are assembled mutually influencing one another, but when the gathering is over, they survive only in the form of memories that gradually dim and fade away if left to themselves ... But if the movements by which these feelings have been expressed eventually become

> inscribed on things that are durable, then they too become durable. The things keep bringing the feelings to individual minds and keep them perpetually aroused, just as would happen if the cause that first called them forth was still acting. (Durkheim 1912: 232)

Current symbols of restorative justice interactions include the outcome agreement signed by all participants. Perhaps more emphasis can be placed on these agreements. Also, a formal celebration of successful desistance may provide an ex-offender further symbols of membership of a law-abiding group, and in 'drug courts' that hold a graduation ceremony for juveniles who successfully stay off drugs (Burns and Peytrot 2003).

An example of a restorative justice programme that satisfies all the criteria for successful interaction ritual is the North Minneapolis African American Circles (Braithwaite 2002: 103), run by a local community organisation. The main difference between this practice and other restorative justice practices is that a series of circles are held for each offender. First, the facilitator holds separate meetings with the offender and his family and the victim and his family to fully understand the circumstances of the event and to assess eligibility. The offender and his family then have a series of conferences, one with different volunteers from the community, who ascertain the offender's interests, talents and weaknesses in order to personalise the reparation for the offender to agree to, followed by a series of meetings with the victim and their supporters, where they hold an in-depth discussion of how everyone was harmed by the crime, and reasonable steps he can take to make reparations (often with the aid of community volunteers). The facilitator then makes ongoing contact with the offender, to ensure compliance with the outcome agreement. Upon completion, all parties (offender and family, victim and family, and community volunteers) reconvene for a celebration of the success of the individual.

This model theoretically seems the most effective for promoting interaction rituals and sustained emotional energy. The offender is given the chance to participate in a number of emotional energy-building interaction rituals. Unfortunately, unlike other less comprehensive restorative justice programmes (Sherman et al 2000), this particular example has never been systematically evaluated in terms of offender recidivism and victim trauma. However, from the success of other, less inclusive restorative justice methods, one can reasonably suppose that the benefits to the offender, victim, and community are substantial. Compared to lifelong therapy and support such as Alcoholics Anonymous (Valverde and White-Mair 1999), however, even this model falls short, as the repetition is not ongoing. More research into sustained interaction in a restorative justice setting needs to be done, but it is clear we need to include the micro-process of human interaction in developing ways to improve justice for offenders, victims, and communities.

IX. EVALUATING INTERACTION RITUALS:
HOW TO KNOW WHAT WORKS

In order to understand if solidarity and emotional energy are the key outcomes of a conference, we need to develop a way of isolating and measuring these variables. A scale of these constructs needs to be developed that can be used by observers of a restorative justice conference. Collins emphasises that emotional energy can be seen as an empirical variable and suggests some ways this can be measured (2004: 134–39): 'in high solidarity moments, bodies touch, eyes are aligned in the same direction, movements are rhythmically synchronized' (2004: 135). He emphasises that emotional energy is a long-term feeling, and in a specific interaction ritual, observers are viewing the emotional entrainment that creates emotional energy. There can be both subjective and objective measurements of these emotions. One can use self-reported data to ask conference participants about their feelings of confidence, enthusiasm and trust (all indicators of emotional energy; Collins 2004: 121). An observer can also look for externalisations of these feelings in a conference. This may include laughing, crying, eye contact, voice rhythms, bodily postures, shaking hands, hugging, or any sort of touching. Facilitators may also be further trained to encourage this type of behaviour. For example, at the end of the conference a facilitator might suggest that all participants shake hands. While this can be deemed a forced move, it may spontaneously create some of the other feelings indicative of solidarity, such as eye contact, or even hugging.

One can also conduct randomised experiments of different way to maximise the long-term effectiveness of emotional energy in reducing recidivism. One research design consists of a control group, a second group receiving one conference, and a third experimental group who participated in a certain number of follow-up conferences. One can also experiment with the timing of a conference.

Perhaps holding a conference right before the offender goes to prison is not the most effective way of promoting emotional energy, considering all the negative emotions he is likely to experience once incarcerated. Tests are currently underway in the United Kingdom, with groups having confer ences both at the pre-sentence stage and prior to release from prison, as well as with offenders in the community (Sherman et al 2002). A further experiment can be conducted with facilitators' techniques. Conferences can be randomly assigned where the facilitator suggests that victim and offender (and supporters) shake hands. This way one can test the possibility of forced interaction ritual.

Other experiments could include testing different kinds of support groups as a more cost-effective alternative to repeated conferences. Support groups could be run in prison, by prisoners who have participated in a conference. They can also take place in the community either upon release from prison, or for those who are serving a community sentence. A further idea would be to include victims in the support circles. Any offender and any victim (and any supporter) who went through the process would be eligible to attend these meetings.

If interaction ritual is more important than shame in this context, than theoretically this interaction can take place without the victim. Although there are clear benefits for victims who do participate, many offenders do not get a chance to have a conference, as their victims refuse to meet with them. In these cases, a solidarity-creating conference may still be successful between an offender, his supporters, and perhaps volunteer community members (as in North Minneapolis). A further idea would be to have an initial conference with offender and victim present, but only offender and supporters need to be there for follow-up conferences. All of these propositions can be tested using random experiments. The results of these experiments may further the ideas of Durkheim, Goffman, and Collins, showing that the social glue that holds our society together (or at least reduces crime) can be manufactured by the police and other criminal justice agencies, in the form of a successful restorative justice conference.

REFERENCES

Angel, C (2004) 'Crime Victims Meet Their Offenders: Testing the Impact of Restorative Justice Conferences on Victims' Post-traumatic Stress Symptoms' (PhD Dissertation, University of Pennsylvania).

Braithwaite, J (1989) *Crime, Shame, and Reintegration* (Cambridge, Cambridge University Press).

—— (2002) *Restorative Justice and Responsive Regulation* (Oxford, Oxford University Press).

Brown, DJ (1996) 'The Professional Ex-: An Alternative for exiting the Deviant Career' in E Rubington and M Weinberg (eds), *Deviance: The Interactionist Perspective* (Needham Heights, Allyn and Bacon).

Burns, SL and Peytrot, M (2003) 'Tough Love: Nurturing and Coercing Responsibility and Recovery in California Drug Courts' 50(3) *Social Problems* 416–38.

Collins, R (2004) *Interaction Ritual Chains* (Princeton, Princeton University Press).

Durkheim, E (1912) *Elementary Forms of Religious Life* ([1995] New York, The Free Press).

Fine, GA (2005) Review of Randall Collins, 'Interaction Ritual Chains' 83(3) *Social Forces* 1287–88.

Goffman, E (1967) *Interaction Ritual* (New York, Doubleday).

—— (1981) *Forms of Talk* (Philadelphia, University of Pennsylvania Press).

Home Office (2003) *Restorative Justice: The Government's Strategy* (London, The Home Office).

Makkai, T and Braithwaite, J (1994) 'Reintegrative Shaming and Compliance with Regulatory standards' 32(3) *Criminology* 361–83.

Maruna, S (2001) *Making Good: How Ex-Convicts Reform and Rebuild Their Lives* (Washington, American Psychological Association).

Mead, GH (1934) *Mind, Self and Society* (Chicago, University of Chicago Press).

Nugent, W, Williams, M and Umbreit, M (2003) 'Participation in Victim-Offender Mediation and the Prevalence and Severity of Subsequent Delinquent Behaviour' *Utah Law Review* 137–66.

Poulson, B (2003) 'A Third Voice: A Review of Empirical Research on the Psychological Outcomes of Restorative Justice' *Utah Law Review* 167–203.

Retzinger, S and Scheff, T (1996) 'Strategies for Community Conferences: Emotions and Social Bonds' in Galaway, B, and Hudson, J (eds) *Restorative Justice: International Perspectives* (New York, Criminal Justice Press).

Scheff, T and Retzinger, S (1991) *Emotions and Violence* (Lexington, Lexington Books).

Sherman, L (1993) 'Defiance, Deterrence, and Irrelevance: A Theory of the Criminal Sanction' 30(4) *Journal of Research in Crime and Delinquency* 445–74.

—— (2001) 'Reasons for emotion: Reinventing Justice with Theories, Innovation, and Research' 41(1) *Criminology* 1–37.

—— and Barnes, G (1997) *Restorative Justice and Offender's Respect for the Law.* RISE Working Paper 3 (Law Programme, Australian National University, Canberra).

Sherman, L, Strang, H and Woods, D (2000) *Recidivism Patterns in the Canberra Reintegrative Shaming Experiments (RISE)* (Canberra, Centre for Restorative Justice, Australian National University).

Sherman, L Strang, H, Woods, D and Barnes, G (2004) 'Restorative Justice Effects on Repeat Offending After Violent and Property Crimes: Differential Effects in Two Randomized Trials', Paper presented at the American Society of Criminology, Nashville.

Sherman, L Strang, H, Inkpen, N, Newbury-Birch, D and Bennett, S (2002) *Developing and Testing Restorative Justice in English Sentencing: Probation and Prisons. Sixth quarterly Report* (Philadelphia, University of Pennsylvania).

Strang, H (2002) *Repair or Revenge: Victims Participation in Restorative Justice* (Oxford, Oxford University Press).

Tyler, T (1990) *Why People Obey the Law* (New Haven, Yale University Press).

—— and Huo, Y (2001) *Trust in the Law: Encouraging Public Cooperation with the Police and Courts* (New York, Russell Sage Foundation).

Tyler, T and Sherman, L, Strang, H, Barnes, G and Woods, D (2007) 'Reintegrative Shaming, Procedural Justice, and Recidivism: The Engagement of Offenders' Psychological Mechanisms in the Canberra RISE Drinking-and-Driving' 41(3) *Law and Society Review* 553–86.

Valverde, M and White-Mair, K (1999) '"One Day at a Time" and other slogans for everyday life: the ethical practices of Alcoholics Anonymous' 33(2) *Sociology* 393–410.

Van Stokkom, B (2002) 'Moral Emotions in restorative justice conferences: managing shame, designing empathy' 3(3) *Theoretical Criminology* 339–60.

Wilson, JQ and Hernstein, R (1985) *Crime and Human Nature* (New York, Simon and Schuster).

9

Shame, Ethical Identity and Conformity: Lessons from Research on the Psychology of Social Influence

NATHAN HARRIS*

U NDERSTANDING EMOTIONS IS essential to developing an account of why people commit crime and how they react when caught. Research across a number of disciplines suggests that shame, which is the focus of this chapter, plays a significant role in how societies achieve conformity (Barbalet 1998; Benedict 1946; Braithwaite 1989; Scheff 1988). This literature highlights the role that shame plays in preventing individuals from committing criminal offences (Grasmick and Bursik 1990; Svensson 2004; Tittle, Bratton and Gertz 2003; Wikström 2004), as well as its impact on how individuals respond to criminal justice interventions (Ahmed et al 2001; Braithwaite 1989; Retzinger and Scheff 1996). While this breadth of inquiry suggests that shame is an important topic for criminologists, this chapter will draw on social psychological research to argue that current theoretical conceptions do not provide an adequate explanation of the role that shame plays in conformity or deviance. An alternative explanation based on the premise that shame reflects threat to an individual's ethical identity will be forwarded.

The first task in addressing this question is to explore the way in which shame has already been cast as an emotion that is central to explaining social conformity. Despite being described by many as an inherently social emotion, it will be argued that limited attention has been given to understanding the social factors that lead to feelings of shame. We will then turn to some findings from research on social influence. These suggest that shame is unlikely to be an emotion that only reflects fear of disapproval by

* Regulatory Institutions Network (RegNet), Australian National University.

others. It is argued that the emotion should instead be conceptualised as a response to the perception of having violated an ethical norm, and that this involves threat to the individual's ethical identity. This conception of shame, or shame-guilt,[1] which was developed as a consequence of an earlier research project (Harris 2001), is then used to explain the way in which individuals respond to criminal justice interventions. Research that suggests individuals manage shame-related emotions in different ways is reviewed and it is argued that the reactions of others are critical in explaining how an individual responds to the threat shame poses to their identity. Finally, some implications for why individuals engage in crime are explored. It is proposed that commitments to moral norms, and conformity to social expectations, are dependent upon having an integrated ethical identity.

I. SHAME AND CONFORMITY

Emotions such as shame, guilt and embarrassment occur when an individual perceives that they have violated a norm, as judged by themself or by others. So a central characteristic of these shame-related emotions is that they are concerned with judgements about what is wrong or undesirable. It is this perception that results in an emotional response that might include feelings of awkwardness, rejection by others, personal failure, a sense of having done wrong, etc. At the micro level these emotions occur as a result of how individuals define their own values (Braithwaite 1982) or norms in relation to the values or expectations of those around them. However, these expectations also reflect broader social norms, and so these emotions are also important for understanding how social groups or societies seek to maintain conformity with particular values.

This is not a new or revolutionary claim, as there are strong theoretical traditions that have conceived of the shame-related emotions in this way. This is particularly evident in the work of anthropologists like Mead (1937) and Benedict (1946), who sought to distinguish between forms of social control by examining the differences between shame cultures and guilt cultures. Shame in this context is the emotion most obviously related to conformity, because shame cultures are described as those that rely primarily on social disapproval to maintain conformity. Guilt cultures are described as those that rely on individuals internalising social values and regulating their own behaviour.

---

[1] Conceptualising shame in this way suggests a convergence between shame and guilt that is in contrast to some conceptualisations of these emotions (see discussion below). For an in-depth discussion of this issue, see Harris (2003) and Harris, Walgrave and Braithwaite (2004).

This distinction between shame and guilt provides the basis for one of the dominant conceptions of shame, the *social threat conception*, which conceives of the emotion as a response to the fear of rejection. An implication of Benedict and Mead's analysis is that shame results from fear of disapproval or rejection by others. This idea is elaborated on by a number of scholars who have argued that shame is a response to the perception that one's social bonds with others are threatened (Leary 2000; Scheff and Retzinger 1991), the perception of having transgressed others' values (Gibbons 1990), or the perception of having lower social status (Gilbert 1997). It will be argued in the next section that the cause of shame is more complex than this implies because shame is related to the normative judgements that individuals make, rather than simply the acceptance of others' judgements. To adequately account for shame we need to examine the process by which individuals come to believe that something is wrong or undesirable.

The other dominant conception of shame, the *personal failure conception*, explains the emotion as a primarily intra-psychic response to negative self-evaluation. This idea stems from psychoanalytic perspectives (Piers and Singer 1953; Lewis 1971; Wurmser 1981), which argue that shame is a consequence of tension that arises from a discrepancy between the individual's perceived self (ego) and their perception of who they would like to be (ego-ideal). The individual perceives that they are a failure, because they haven't lived up to their own standards. An alternative explanation based on attribution theory, but with a similar emphasis, is that shame results from the individual's attribution that the whole self is a failure (Lewis 1992; Tangney 1991). These perspectives emphasise the significance of the individual's interpretation of events but provide little explanation as to the social circumstances in which this occurs.

II. IMPLICATIONS FROM RESEARCH ON INFLUENCE

A. Shame as a Product of Social Influence

The only explanation of conformity that can be taken from these conceptions of shame, given that one of them says little about the social context in which the emotion occurs, is that individuals conform so as to avoid being disapproved of or looked down upon by others. Conformity to social expectations, from this perspective, occurs because the consequence of non-conformity is an unpleasant emotion that we feel as a direct result of the perceived disapproval of others. This depiction of shame is remarkably consistent with what social psychology has termed normative influence, which is understood as having occurred when the individual alters their attitude or behaviour in a public context so as to avoid appearing different from the majority (Deutsch and Gerard 1955; Cialdini and Trost 1998). While normative influence leads to changes in the attitudes or behaviours that are publically expressed by an individual, which allows them to comply with group norms and avoid disapproval, it does not represent a change in the individual's private attitudes. Of course, like the description of shame in shame cultures, the concept of normative influence is primarily concerned with why individuals act to avoid social censure, rather than the consequences of social censure itself. Nevertheless, it is reasonable to conclude that the social threat conception of shame and theories of normative influence share the same underlying explanation of conformity (Scheff 1988).

However, research into social influence suggests that this understanding of shame is simplistic for the simple reason that the opinions of others often affect our beliefs about the world (Festinger 1950). While initial research suggested that this is particularly significant in contexts where the truth is ambiguous (Sherif 1936) research has since shown that the importance of social validation is more pervasive. This is particularly evident in research based on Asch's (1956) influential conformity studies. These studies show that individuals are influenced to make incorrect judgements about fairly easy perceptual tasks when the task is performed among a group who unanimously give an incorrect answer. While, on its own this effect looks like evidence of normative influence (Scheff 1988), subsequent research has shown that some influence still occurs, though less, when people are allowed to make their judgements in private (Deutsch and Gerard 1955), and that the amount of influence is dependent upon other factors such as consistency amongst the group (Asch 1956), external verification of the group's response (Crutchfield 1955), and the identity of the other participants (Abrams et al 1990). These additional findings suggest that a reasonable proportion of the conformity that occurs is explained by perceptions that the group is actually right. This shows that even on a fairly simple task, individuals accept others' judgements as a valid source of information, and as a result are influenced (Hogg and Turner 1987).

Moscovici (1976) has argued that uncertainty about one's beliefs, and subsequently influence, occurs when we disagree with people who we would expect to agree with. Thus, social validation is seen as underlying a broad range of beliefs that we hold, and that individuals are much more dependent upon others for confirmation of their perceptions about the world than is often recognised.

> It is true, of course, that technical instruments permit an individual to make decisions about the environment by himself; but even these instruments conceal a consensus, since the mode of action of a tool or the appropriateness of a measuring device must be agreed upon by all if the result of such operations is to carry any information. (Moscovici 1976: 70)

Hogg and Turner (1987; Turner 1991) have built upon the concept of informational influence in forwarding a theory of referent informational influence. This theory argues that others' opinions are accepted as providing accurate information about reality, but only when those people are seen as having the same social identity (Tajfel 1972; Tajfel and Turner 1979). Having the same social identity is critical, because the perception that the other person as similar to oneself on relevant dimensions is necessary to accept that they are a valid reference point for one's own beliefs. This claim is supported by a number of studies which show that when others are perceived as having the same identity, they exert greater influence (Abrams et al 1990).

Psychological research which shows that individuals are responsive to others' interpretations of what is right, is consistent with Williams's (1993) philosophical characterisation of shame and moral decision-making. He criticises the Kantian notion that individuals are morally autonomous and argues that without social support for a particular view, it is hard to tell whether an individual is 'a solitary bearer of true justice or a deluded crank' (1993: 99). Shame, according to Williams, should be understood as a response to the perception that what one has done violates values that are important to one's identity, but this is based upon a shared conception of morality. As research in social influence suggests, disapproval is likely to result in feeling shame not just because disapproval communicates what is negatively judged, but because it expresses a judgement which the individual perceives as legitimate: the individual accepts the interpretation that what they have done is shameful. Significantly, this also suggests that shame is an emotion that is centrally concerned with the question of what individuals think is right or wrong. Others' opinions are important because, as research on neutralisation theory (Maruna and Copes 2005; Sykes and Matza 1957) shows, decisions about the morality of behaviour and possible justifications for actions often occur in contexts that are perceived as ambiguous. Shame, then, might be understood as the painful recognition that one's behaviour is inconsistent with social values that oneself, and other people like oneself, ascribe to.

Some evidence that shame is dependent upon acceptance of others' opinions, rather than fear of rejection, was found in interviews with drink-driving offenders in the Reintegrative Shaming Experiments (Harris 2001). An important predictor of feeling shame-guilt in these cases was that other people disapproved, but only when the people present at the case were both very disapproving and highly respected by the offender. This finding suggests that disapproval is only significant when it comes from people whom the individual respects. Analyses also showed that shame-guilt was negatively related to stigmatisation (but positively related to reintegration). This also seems contrary to the hypothesis that shame is a response to normative pressure, because it suggests that social rejection results in less shame.

B. Shame, Beliefs and Identity

Research on influence may also help explain the observation by numerous scholars that shame is intimately tied to notions of identity (Lewis 1971; Lindsay-Hartz 1984; Lynd 1958; Sabini and Silver 1997; Williams 1993; Wurmser 1981). Indeed, a defining characteristic of the emotion according to a number of conceptions is that shame is the emotion that is evoked when the individual feels that their 'whole self' is deficient in some way (Lewis 1971; Lewis 1992; Tangney 1991). As discussed above, social identity theory argues that the individual's identity is central to understanding how they react to disapproval from others. Genuine influence will only occur, according to the theory, where individuals perceive others as sharing a relevant identity (Hogg and Turner 1987). This is because someone who is similar to oneself is seen as having opinions that are valid to oneself. Identity in this framework is logically tied to normative beliefs: individuals have particular normative values because they are consistent with their identity. Identity is seen as providing the individual with a framework with which to understand the world as well as their place in it.

What is interesting about this understanding of influence is the implication that an individual's identity is also dependent upon them having values that are consistent with their identity. Someone is unlikely to hold a particular identity if they are aware that they have inconsistent beliefs. So the relationship between values and identity is reciprocal, and having certain values is essential to having a particular identity.

> If shared social identity is the basis of mutual influence between people (Turner, 1991), it is also a central object of influence: the construction and validation of people's definition of who they are (and are not) are basic to the task of developing shared norms, values and goals... (Turner and Onorato 1999: 27)

If an individual's identity is dependent upon their having particular values, then the violation of these values also has important implications for their sense of who they are. In effect, the individual is presented with evidence that is inconsistent with who they thought they were. Thus, shame would seem to involve a threat to identity that involves an inconsistency between beliefs about who one is, and evidence to the contrary (Harris 2001).

While this suggests that shame is a response to the violation of internalised beliefs and has consequences for an individual's sense of identity, there are some important differences between this ethical-identity conception of shame and the proposition that shame is principally defined by negative self-evaluation (Lewis 1992; Tangney 1991; Tangney et al 1992). The latter implies that shame is an almost dysfunctional response, which is damaging to the individual and impedes their ability to respond appropriately to the situation. In characterising the emotion in this way, Tangney and Dearing (2002) describe it as 'an extremely painful and ugly feeling that has a negative impact on interpersonal behaviour' (2002: 3).

The ethical-identity conception suggests that shame has a more complex relationship with sense of identity than simply diminished esteem. The proposition that a defining characteristic of shame is a threat to identity highlights the individual's capacity to respond in various ways to the inconsistency between behaviour and identity. While an individual may resolve feelings of shame by seeing themself as defective (accepting the group's norms, but internalising one's low status), they might alternatively respond by emphasising a different identity (perceiving themself as having an alternative identity, which is consistent with their behaviour) or by diminishing the significance of their behaviour in some way (neutralising the behaviour to avoid acknowledging that it is shameful, or repairing and apologising, which allows the behaviour to be integrated into a positive identity). It is hypothesised that which of these responses occurs will depend upon the degree to which the individual accepts that what they have done is wrong. In turn, this will be influenced by their social relationships with others and the type of social validation they receive.

To summarise, if the research on social influence discussed is applied to shame then it has a number of implications for how we understand the emotion. The first of these is that a precondition for feeling shame is the perception of having violated a social norm, and that this perception is often based upon social validation. The relationship between values and identity suggests that violation of an important norm will undermine the individual's identity because it provides evidence that they don't subscribe to values that define that identity.

III. IMPLICATIONS FOR UNDERSTANDING THE ROLE OF SHAME IN CRIMINAL JUSTICE

This analysis of shame has a number of implications for understanding the significance of the emotions in criminological contexts. One of these is that criminal justice interventions represent a context in which shame is very likely to be felt, even if it is sometimes hidden, as is suggested by Scheff and Retzinger (1991). Censure through a court appearance for many people will represent a failure to live up to an accepted value (eg not breaking the law) that is important enough for its transgression to represent some kind of threat to their moral identity (eg as a good member of society). This will be even more so in cases where the offence is perceived as serious, where the institution is perceived as having greater legitimacy and where the individual's actions are disapproved of by significant others. Thus, it is important to acknowledge that shame is present or at least threatening in many criminal justice interventions (Harris, Walgrave and Braithwaite 2004).

A second implication is that the way in which individuals manage feelings of shame may determine the effect that criminal justice interventions have on them (Ahmed et al 2001). There is growing evidence that individuals manage or respond to shame in a variety of ways. Lewis (1971), Scheff (1990), Retzinger (1991) and Scheff and Retzinger (1991) have distinguished between acknowledged and unacknowledged forms of shame. While acknowledged shame involves the overt acceptance of the emotion, unacknowledged shame involves either the mislabelling of the emotion (overt undifferentiated shame) or an attempt to suppress the emotion entirely (bypassed shame). They argue that acknowledgement of shame is important, because failure to do so is associated with ongoing psychological problems, including feelings of anger and hostility towards others. This is consistent with research which shows that individuals who experienced a response similar to unacknowledged shame (unresolved shame) were more likely to feel hostility towards others, following a criminal justice intervention, than other participants (Harris 2003). In contrast, overt feelings of shame-guilt were associated with empathy for victims and lower feelings of hostility. Important differences between types of shame have also been found by Ahmed and her colleagues (Ahmed 2001; Ahmed and Braithwaite, this volume; Ahmed and Braithwaite, 2006) in samples of school children and adult workers in Australia and Bangladesh. The types of shame reported by participants in these studies were significant predictors of whether children or adults had bullied others or had been the victims of bullying. This and other research (Nathanson 1997; Retzinger 1991; Tangney 1991) seems to confirm that differences in the emotional responses of people to shameful situations is important in understanding their behaviour.

Understanding the emotion of shame is particularly relevant to reintegrative shaming theory (Braithwaite 1989; Braithwaite and Braithwaite 2001), which predicts that reintegrative shaming will reduce offending but that stigmatising shaming will increase offending. The relationship between identity and influence that is proposed above suggests that the important difference between stigmatisation and reintegration is their effect on the way in which individuals manage shame. Acknowledgement of shame depends upon the individual's acceptance of an interpretation of their behaviour as shameful. Stigmatisation acts in two ways to make this less likely. Firstly, it diminishes the ability of those who are disapproving to provide social validation, because an obvious function of stigmatisation is to differentiate between the identities of the shamers and the shamed. Secondly, stigmatisation also makes reacceptance into that group, and hence acknowledgement of shame, less attractive to the individual. Stigmatisation might be particularly destructive in cases where it undermines important identities, because the individual is left with the choice of maintaining the same social identities but with lower status or attempting to define a new identity. Reintegration, on the other hand, maintains the disapprover's status as a source of social validation by emphasising similarity in identity and maintains that social identity as attractive for the individual.

IV. IMPLICATIONS FOR UNDERSTANDING WHY PEOPLE COMMIT CRIME

The relationship between shame and identity that is proposed here may also have implications for understanding why it is that people do or don't commit crime. The significance of shame for explaining the propensity to engage in crime has already been explored within a number of theoretical frameworks. One of these, which is implicit in the anthropological approaches discussed earlier, is as a deterrent. This perspective has been explored by a number of studies that have compared the deterrent qualities of the shame-related emotions, as perceived by participants, with perceptions of official sanctions (Grasmick and Bursik 1990; Paternoster and Iovanni 1986; Tibbetts 1997). In general, these studies have shown that expectations of feeling shame are associated with lower self-reported projections of offending, and in some cases that the effect is comparable with, or greater than, official sanctions.

While these studies suggest that shame may be a significant deterrent, it has been argued in this chapter that of greater significance is the emotion's relationship to ethical values. This is also the basis of the alternative premise that the propensity to feel shame is related to lower offending because it is a reflection of the individual's moral values (Braithwaite 1989; Svensson 2004; Wikström 2004). Reintegrative shaming theory (Braithwaite 1989; Braithwaite and Braithwaite 2001) suggests that the primary reason why individuals do not commit crime is because disapproval of these behaviours is internalised, in the form of conscience. From this perspective, individuals do not desist from crime just because they are deterred by negative consequences, but because they perceive the behaviour as the wrong thing to do. Braithwaite argues that one advantage of reintegrative shaming is that it appeals to the individual's moral sensibilities, and in doing so reinforces their commitment to those values. Wikström (2004), who places a similar emphasis on shame's moral qualities, argues that the emotion is a protective factor in preventing offending. Shame in this framework represents a response to the individual's commitment to do the right thing, which in turn influences their perception of the choices available in a given context. Studies by both Wikström (2002) and Svensson (2004) show that juveniles who report that they would feel shame in front of others (eg friends) if they committed a crime also reported lower levels of delinquency.

The emphasis that is placed by these theories on the significance of having a commitment to pro-social norms reflects the importance placed on commitment to the law by criminological theory, particularly control theory, and empirical findings that it is a significant factor in predicting delinquency (eg Grasmick and Green 1980; Hirschi 1969; Siegel, Rathus and Ruppert 1973). Shame is seen as a significant emotion because it reflects the individual's commitment to norms. However, the relationship between identity and moral values, that was discussed earlier, suggests that the individual's sense of self may play an important mediating role in this relationship.

A key prediction of social identity theory (Tajfel 1972) is that individuals have many social identities and that different identities will be salient, depending upon the social context. Furthermore, each identity will emphasise different personal characteristics. So the identity of daughter implies very different characteristics to the identity of heavy metal rocker, yet both might belong to the same person. This is significant because if identities and values are interdependent, then it also predicts that an individual's commitment to pro-social values will vary across identities. For example, the value of being a careful driver (especially in relation to drink-driving) that someone might hold as a good family man, may not be as relevant on a Thursday night after football training, when being a member of the team is more salient. This suggests that the interaction between an individual's identities is important in determining their commitment to particular values.

An important tension exists between this idea that individuals have multiple identities and research on the self, which suggests that having a consistent or integrated self is psychologically healthy (Baumeister 1998; Swann 1987). The social identity perspective takes this into account by arguing that the identities an individual will adopt are limited by the individual's previous beliefs about who they are (Turner et al 1987). This is supported by a study (Reicher and Hopkins 1996), which suggests that individuals engage in a process of negotiating shared identities based upon the underlying values inherent in that identity. It would seem that individuals play an active role in determining how they see themselves, and that they tend to adopt identities that are consistent in the underlying values they espouse. Prior commitments to particular identities mean that others cannot be taken on as easily, and so it would follow that most people have commitments across identities to the same ethical values.

The implication of this research is that weak commitment to social norms may be the result of a weakly integrated self, which is characterised by inconsistent identities. This proposition is supported by the research on social validation that was discussed earlier, which shows how influential the opinions of others are in forming our own beliefs. If sharing an identity provides a means of validating the opinions of others, as Hogg and Turner (1987) argue, then it is unsurprising that individuals without coherent social identities are less sure of the moral decisions that they make, or whose judgements they should believe. One context in which having multiple, and sometimes conflicting, identities may explain a low commitment to social norms is adolescence. It is conceivable that the age at which one's social identities are least integrated is during adolescence when the individual starts to form new social relationships that potentially have different value structures. This is exactly what was found by Emler and Reicher (1995). In their research on 12- to 16-year-olds in the United Kingdom, they found that young people often held representations of themselves that were mutually incompatible. They concluded that this was possible because the peers and families of these young people had very limited contact with each other, and that that this was even more pronounced for those youths who reported the greatest levels of delinquency. It might be speculated that a characteristic of many delinquents is that they struggle to manage identities that are defined by different values.

This framework for understanding commitment to ethical norms, and moral decision-making, suggests that a central issue for at least some offenders may be developing a coherent and stable sense of self. This conclusion is similar to the one reached by Maruna (2001), that what distinguished the long-term criminals who had reformed in his sample, from those who persisted in crime, is the narrative the individual has about their own identity. Those who reformed, developed narratives in which offending was not part of their 'real self'. The self that was associated in the past with crime had been the product of bad luck or bad circumstances, but was now less relevant to their ongoing sense of self. In contrast, their 'real self' was presented as having the ambition and capability to 'make good'. These findings might be interpreted as showing that the ability to act according to one's social values, and perhaps acknowledge feeling shame for violating them, is a result of having a coherent sense of self.

V. SHAME AND INTEGRITY

Conceptualising the value of having an integrated self might be helped by the notion of integrity that can be found in moral philosophy. A number of philosophers, such as Frankfurt (1971), Taylor (1985), Williams (1973) and Calhoun (1995) have espoused the virtue of having integrity. It is argued that to have integrity, the person must make decisions about what they want or value, rather than simply acting on every desire, as well as being able to behave in accordance with these higher-order goals. Threats to integrity include self-deception about one's desires, weakness of will to act in accordance with one's values, and conflict between competing values

(Frankfurt 1971). An important characteristic of integrity is the notion of wholeness: that the individual's values cohere and that this is reflected in their actions. A second important characteristic, which follows from this, is that individuals must identify with these values. This is important, because having integrity means that one's actions are determined by who the person is and what they believe in (Williams 1973).

This sense of integrity does not mean behaving in accordance with a predetermined set of moral values. It is better understood as having a coherent set of values that the individual feels able to live up to. Shame, as it is described in this chapter, is central to this because it represents a threat to having this coherent set of values (an ethical-identity). The emotion occurs when one's ethical-identity is threatened by a particular act. However, it might also be suggested that for individuals who have low integrity (weak ethical-identities), the threat of shame is always present. Disparate social identities mean that that the individual must fight a continual battle to live up to contradictory normative expectations, and often fail. This suggests that integrity is not just a virtue for ethical reasons, but that psychological integrity is a virtue because it underlies the individual's ability to develop coherent values that they feel able to live up to. These skills are necessary for developing social relationships, for having a sense of self-respect (Taylor 1985), and behaving in ways that are accepted by one's community.

VI. CONCLUSION

This chapter has developed, on the basis of research on social influence, an account of the social context in which shame occurs. Rather than being a simple response to the fear of rejection, it is argued that shame occurs as a result of the individual's perception that what they have done is wrong. An important characteristic of the emotion is that it emerges in a context in which individuals often perceive that there is ambiguity about what is right. The connections between an individual's beliefs, identity and social relationships suggest that the emotion and its resolution have important implications for how the individual sees their self and their relationships with others.

It has been argued that understanding the significance of social context and identity, and their relationship to shame, is important for criminology because it may have significant implications for understanding why it is that some individuals engage in crime and why they stop. Findings that offenders have a weaker commitment to particular values, and that they are less likely to acknowledge feeling shame for committing offences, may reflect weakly integrated identities. If this is so, then its significance is that the interaction between the individual and the social context will be of central importance

(Wikström 2004). Individuals with lower integrity between their possible identities may have weaker commitment to particular values in some social contexts, than they might in others, because of how they understand themself and others in that context. Measuring an individual's commitment to pro-social values in a way that does not consider context may be a fairly blunt way of understanding the relationship between values and offending. It also ignores the possibility that the individual may not hold strong commitments to any values, rather than just pro-social ones, which would have a different significance for understanding the behaviour.

If ethical-identity is important, then this also suggests that attempts to reform or rehabilitate need to include opportunities for the offender to build a more integrated sense of self. Whether such opportunities can be provided through counselling, or even within prison contexts, remains to be seen. Research suggests that of primary significance is the way in which relationships to others, and particularly significant others, are understood, which suggests that change often occurs through what are perceived as profound social interactions (Maruna 2001). One context in which such interactions might begin are family group conferences, where the offender is asked to account for, or make sense of, their behaviour in a social context that often includes actors from various quarters of their life: partners, children, extended family, work colleagues, friends, and victims. Developing a coherent narrative in such a context and receiving social validation from a range of significant others may be the kind of event that is capable of instigating change.

Significantly, these changes in identity and in relationships seem to be inextricably linked to emotion. Acknowledgement of shame occurs with the offender's willingness to accept the negative judgement of others. Expression of, and resolution of, the emotion would seem to be necessary for the individual to repair social bonds with others and to put past behaviour behind them. Negative emotions of unacknowledged shame and anger are equally important indicators that the individual remains alienated (Ahmed 2001; Scheff and Retzinger 1991). Furthermore, if a number of psychologists (eg Tomkins 1962; Brehm 1999) are right, it is emotions that provide individuals with the motivation that is necessary to translate their beliefs into behaviour, and thus they need to be central to the concerns of criminologists.

REFERENCES

Abrams, D, Wetherell, M, Cochrane, S, Hogg, MA and Turner, JC (1990) 'Knowing what to think by knowing who you are: Self-categorization and the nature of norm formation, conformity and group polarization' 29(2) *British Journal of Social Psychology* 97–119.

Ahmed, E (2001) 'Part III Shame Management: Regulating Bullying' In E Ahmed, N Harris, J Braithwaite and V Braithwaite (eds) *Shame Management through Reintegration* (Cambridge, Cambridge University Press) 209–311.
—— and Braithwaite, V (2006) 'Forgiveness, reconciliation and shame management: Three key variables in reducing school bullying' 62(2) *Journal of Social Issues* 347–70.
Ahmed, E, Harris, N, Braithwaite, J and Braithwaite, V (2001) *Shame Management through Reintegration* (Cambridge, Cambridge University Press).
Asch, SE (1956) 'Studies of independence and conformity: A minority of one against a unanimous majority' 70(9) *Psychological Monographs* 70–102
Barbalet, JM (1998) *Emotion, Social Theory, and Social Structure: A Macrosociological Approach* (Cambridge, Cambridge University Press). Baumeister, RF (1998) 'The Self' in DT Gilbert, ST Fiske and G Lindzey (eds), *The Handbook of Social Psychology* (Boston, McGraw-Hill) vol 1 680–740.
Benedict, R (1946) *The Chrysanthemum and The Sword; Patterns of Japanese Culture* (Boston, Houghton Mifflin).
Braithwaite, J (1989) *Crime, Shame and Reintegration* (Cambridge, Cambridge University Press).
—— and Braithwaite, V (2001) 'Part I Shame, Shame Management and Regulation' in Ahmed, E, Harris, N, Braithwaite, J and Braithwaite, V (eds), *Shame Management through Reintegration* (Cambridge, Cambridge University Press) 1–69.
Braithwaite, V (1982) 'The structure of social values: Validation of Rokeach's two-value model' 21 *British Journal of Social Psychology* 203–11.
Brehm, JW (1999) 'The intensity of emotion' 3(1) *Personality and Social Psychology Review* 2–22.
Calhoun, C (1995) 'Standing for something' 92(5) *The Journal of Philosophy* 235–60.
Cialdini, RB and Trost, MR (1998) 'Social influence: Social norms, conformity and compliance' in DT Gilbert, ST Fiske and G Lindzey (eds), *The Handbook of Social Psychology* (Boston, Mcgraw-Hill) vol 2, 151–92.
Crutchfield, RS (1955) 'Conformity and character' 10 *American Psychologist* 191–98.
Deutsch, M and Gerard, HB (1955) 'A study of normative and informational social influences upon individual judgement' 51 *Journal of Abnormal and Social Psychology* 629–36.
Emler, N and Reicher, S (1995) *Adolescence and Delinquency* (Oxford, Blackwell Publishers).
Festinger, L (1950) 'Informal social communication' 57 *Psychological Review* 271–82.
Frankfurt, HG (1971) 'Freedom of the will and the concept of a person' 68(1) *The Journal of Philosophy* 5–20.
Gibbons, FX (1990) 'The impact of focus of attention and affect on social behaviour' in WR Crozier (ed), *Shyness and Embarrassment: Perspectives from Social Psychology* (Cambridge, Cambridge University Press) 119–43.
Gilbert, P (1997) 'The evolution of social attractiveness and its role in shame, humiliation, guilt and therapy' 70 *British Journal of Medical Psychology* 113–47.

Grasmick, HG and Bursik, RJ (1990) 'Conscience, significant others, and rational choice: Extending the deterrence model' 24(3) *Law and Society Review* 837–61.
—— and Green, DE (1980) 'Legal punishment, social disapproval and internalization as inhibitors of illegal behaviour' 71(3) *The Journal of Criminal Law and Criminology* 325–35.
Harris, N (2001) 'Part II Shaming and shame: regulating drink driving' in E Ahmed, N Harris, J Braithwaite and V Braithwaite (eds), *Shame Management through Reintegration* (Cambridge, Cambridge University Press) 71–207.
—— (2003) 'Reassessing the dimensionality of the moral emotions' 94(4) *British Journal of Psychology* 457–73.
—— Walgrave, L and Braithwaite, J (2004) 'Emotional dynamics in restorative conferences' 8(2) *Theoretical Criminology* 191–210.
Hirschi, T (1969) *Causes of Delinquency* (Berkeley, University of California Press).
Hogg, MA and Turner, JC (1987) 'Social identity and conformity: A theory of referent information influence' in W Doise, S Moscovici and et al (eds), *Current Issues in European Social Psychology* (Cambridge, Cambridge University Press) vol 2, 139–82.
Leary, MR (2000) 'Affect, cognition, and the social emotions: A theory of relational devaluation' in JP Forgas (ed), *Feeling and Thinking: The Role of Affect in Social Cognition* (Cambridge, Cambridge University Press).
Lewis, HB (1971) *Shame and guilt in neurosis* (New York, International Universities Press,).
Lewis, M (1992) *Shame: The exposed self* (New York, Free Press).
Lindsay-Hartz, J (1984) 'Contrasting experiences of shame and guilt' 27 *American Behavioural Scientist* 689–704.
Lynd, HM (1958) *On Shame and the Search for Identity* (New York, Harcourt, Brace, and World).
Maruna, S (2001) *Making Good: how ex-convicts reform and rebuild their lives* (Washington, American Psychological Association).
—— and Copes, H (2005) 'What Have We Learned in Five Decades of Neutralization Research?' 32 *Crime and Justice: A Review of Research* 221–320.
Mead, M (1937) *Cooperation and competition among primitive peoples*, (New York, McGraw-Hill).
Moscovici, S (1976) *Social Influence and Social Change* (London, Academic Press).
Nathanson, DL (1997) 'Affect theory and the compass of shame' in MR Lansky (ed), *The Widening Scope of Shame* (Hillsdale, The Analytic Press) 339–54.
Paternoster, R and Iovanni, L (1986) 'The deterrent effect of perceived severity: A reexamination' 64(3) *Social Forces* 751–77.
Piers, G and Singer, MB (1953) *Shame and Guilt: A Psychoanalytic and a Cultural Study* (New York, Norton).
Reicher, S and Hopkins, N (1996) 'Seeking influence through characterizing self-categories: An analysis of anti-abortionist rhetoric' 35(2) *British Journal of Social Psychology* 297–311.
Retzinger, SM (1991) *Violent Emotions: Shame and Rage in Marital Quarrels* (Newbury Park, Sage Publications).

——— and Scheff, TJ (1996) 'Strategy for Community Conferences: Emotions and Social Bonds' In B Galaway and J Hudson (eds), *Restorative Justice: International Perspectives* (Monsey New York, Criminal Justice Press) 315–36.

Sabini, J and Silver, M (1997) 'In defense of shame: Shame in the context of guilt and embarrassment' 27(1) *Journal for the Theory of Social Behaviour* 1–15.

Scheff, TJ (1988) 'Shame and conformity: The deference-emotion system' 53(3) *American Sociological Review* 395–406.

——— (1990) *Microsociology: Discourse, Emotion, and Social Structure* (Chicago, University of Chicago Press).

——— and Retzinger, SM (1991) *Emotions and violence: Shame and rage in destructive conflicts* (Lexington, Lexington Books/DC Heath).

Sherif, M (1936) *The psychology of social norms* (New York, Harper).

Siegel, LJ, Rathus, SA and Ruppert, CA (1973) 'Values and delinquent youth: An empirical re-examination of theories of delinquency' 13 *British Journal of Criminology* 237–44.

Svensson, R (2004) *Social control and socialisation: The role of morality as a social mechanism in adolescent deviant behaviour* (Stockholm, Almqvist and Wiksell International).

Swann, WB (1987) 'Identity negotiation: Where two roads meet' 53 *Journal of Personality and Social Psychology* 1038–51.

Sykes, G and Matza, D (1957) 'Techniques of neutralization: A theory of delinquency' 22 *American Sociological Review* 664–73.

Tajfel, H (1972) 'La categorisation sociale' in S Moscovichi (ed), *Introduction a la psychologie sociale* (Paris, Larousse) 272–302.

——— and Turner, JC (1979) 'An integrative theory of intergroup conflict' in WG Austin and S Worchel (eds), *The social psychology of intergroup relations* (Monterey, Brooks/Cole).

Tangney, JP (1991) 'Moral affect: The good, the bad, and the ugly' 61(4) *Journal of Personality and Social Psychology* 598–607.

——— and Dearing, RL (2002) *Shame and Guilt* (New York, The Guilford Press).

Tangney, JP, Wagner, P, Fletcher, C and Gramzow, R (1992) 'Shamed into anger? The relation of shame and guilt to anger and self-reported aggression' 62(4) *Journal of Personality and Social Psychology* 669–75.

Taylor, G (1985) *Pride, shame and guilt: Emotions of self-assessment* (Oxford, Oxford University Press).

Tibbetts, SG (1997) 'Shame and rational choice in offending decisions' 24(2) *Criminal Justice and Behaviour* 234–55.

Tittle, CR, Bratton, J and Gertz, MG (2003) 'A test of a micro-level application of shaming theory' 50(4) *Social Problems* 592–617.

Tomkins, SS (1962) *Affect, imagery, consciousness: Vol I The positive affects* (New York, Springer).

Turner, JC (1991) *Social influence* (Pacific Grove, Brooks/Cole Publishing Co).

———, Hogg, MA, Oakes, PJ, Reicher, SD and Wetherell, MS (1987) *Rediscovering the social group: A self-categorization theory* (New York, Basil Blackwell).

Turner, JC, Hogg, MA, Oakes, PJ, Reicher, SD, Wetherell, MS and Onorato, RS (1999) 'Social identity, personality, and the self-concept: A self-categorizing perspective' in TR Tyler (ed), *The psychology of the social self Applied social research* (Mahwah, Lawrence Erlbaum Associates) 11–46.

Wikström, P-O (2002) *Adolescent crime in context* (Cambridge, University of Cambridge, Institute of Criminology).

—— (2004) 'Crime as alternative: Towards a cross-level situational action theory of crime causation' in J McCord (ed), *Beyond Empiricism* (New Brunswick, Transaction Publishers).

Williams, B (1973) 'A critique of utilitarianism' in JJC Smart and B Williams (eds), *Utilitarianism: For and Against* (Cambridge, Cambridge University Press).

—— (1993) *Shame and Necessity* (Berkeley, University of California Press).

Wurmser, L (1981) *The Mask of Shame* (Baltimore, Johns Hopkins University Press).

10

Procedural Justice, Emotions and Resistance to Authority

KRISTINA MURPHY*

I. INTRODUCTION

R ULES MAKE UP a part of any civilised society. When well designed, they reflect the social norms of the society in which they are developed and they are used as a way to ensure that citizens do not unfairly disadvantage others. For those who develop and police these laws, it is hoped that compliance can be elicited voluntarily. If not, then there are most often procedures that can be used to coerce people back into compliance. Compliance research has shown, however, that harsh sanctions and punishments, and the way in which they can sometimes be administered, can sometimes lead to overt opposition or defiance to laws in the future; a situation that can be extremely costly to a regulator (see Murphy 2004).

Research into procedural justice has shown that if authorities treat people with trust, fairness, respect and neutrality during an enforcement encounter, people will not only be more willing to cooperate with authorities, but they will also be more likely to comply with authority decisions and directives in the future (Tyler 1990). Advocates of procedural justice have therefore argued that to encourage people to comply voluntarily with decisions and rules, authorities should attempt to nurture compliance through strategies that are seen to be procedurally fair.

An interesting issue that has only just begun to receive attention in the procedural justice literature is the degree to which emotions play a role in people's decision to ultimately defy or comply with an authority. A handful of studies have found that perceptions of procedural justice (or injustice) can lead people to experience discrete emotions such as happiness, joy,

* Kristina Murphy PhD, Associate Professor, School of Criminology and Criminal Justice, Griffith University, Australia. The data reported in this chapter was collected when Kristina Murphy was employed at RegNet, Australian National University. At the time of writing this article, Kristina was employed at RegNet.

pride, guilt, disappointment, anger, frustration, and anxiety. Other research has also shown that people's emotional state at the time of making procedural justice judgements can determine whether or not they perceive an encounter with an authority to be procedurally fair or not.

This research, however, has failed to examine the impact these emotions might have on subsequent compliance behaviour. In addition, few studies examined the real-life emotions felt by people experiencing serious regulatory enforcement action, and the role that these emotions have in determining their subsequent behaviour towards an authority. What I intend to do in this chapter is present survey data collected from taxpayers who were engaged in a long-standing dispute with the Australian Taxation Office (ATO) over their involvement in controversial tax avoidance schemes. I intend to show how emotions played an important role in taxpayers' formulation of procedural justice judgements about how the ATO handled their case, and how these emotions, in conjunction with views about procedural injustice, went on to impact upon their subsequent resistant behaviour. Before doing so, however, I want first to review the procedural justice and emotion literature, before then laying out the theoretical question of interest in more detail.

II. PROCEDURAL JUSTICE AND RESISTANCE TO DECISIONS

Many citizen contacts with legal institutions are involuntary, and even those that are initiated voluntarily often involve the imposition of involuntary decisions and rulings (Lind and Tyler 1988). In this context it is not surprising that legal authorities are concerned about the risk of hostility on the part of those who come into contact with the law. Lind and Tyler suggest that one way to minimise such hostility is to use procedural justice.

Procedural justice concerns the perceived fairness of the procedures involved in decision-making and the perceived treatment one receives from a decision-maker. More specifically, the normative perspective on procedural justice suggests that people are not only concerned with the outcomes they receive, but that they are also concerned about their experience. Normative aspects of experience include neutrality, lack of bias, honesty, efforts to be fair, politeness and respect for citizens' rights (Tyler 1990). Tyler and Lind (1992) argue that procedural justice is important to people because the treatment one receives from an authority provides information about how much they are valued as a group member. Fair procedures communicate respect and value, while unfair procedures communicate disrespect, marginality, or even exclusion from a valued group.

So what has the procedural justice literature generally found? In the law enforcement context, it has generally been found that procedural justice enhances citizens' willingness to comply with law enforcement officials.

For example, Tyler (1987, cited in Lind and Tyler 1988: 65–83) interviewed a random sample of citizens living in Chicago about their encounters with police and the courts. Of the 652 citizens who had had encounters with these authorities, Tyler found that the procedural justice features of their encounter had substantial effects on their evaluations of the authorities involved and their views about the legitimacy of the authorities involved. It was found that these variables in turn went on to affect citizens' acceptance with decisions and their compliance with laws (see also Tyler and Huo 2002; Tyler 2004). Similarly, in a study that examined how litigants' evaluations of the outcome and process of lawsuits affected their judgements about the fairness of procedures and their acceptance of outcomes, Lind et al (1993) found that decision acceptance was strongly correlated with judgements of procedural justice.

In other contexts, similar findings have also been revealed. For example, Lind et al (2000) found that wrongful termination claims were more likely to be filed by laid-off employees when workers felt they had been treated in a procedurally unfair manner by their place of employment. Kim and Mauborgne (1993) found that managers from multinational corporations were more likely to comply with corporate strategic decisions if they felt head office had used procedural justice, and research conducted in the Australian taxation context has shown that perceptions of procedural injustice can in fact lead to disputes between authorities and those they regulate. Murphy (2004) found that taxpayers who had been fined by the Australian Taxation Office (ATO) over their involvement in controversial tax avoidance schemes were more likely to resist ATO directives if they viewed the handling of their case to be procedurally unfair.

While the studies discussed above have shown that perceptions of procedural injustice can affect people's future willingness to accept decisions and comply with directives in a multitude of different areas, the psychological mechanisms underlying why this occurs are not so clear. For example, why is it the case that some people are more likely to have perceptions of procedural injustice than others? Why is it that some people respond in a more negative way to procedural injustice than do others? And why is it that some people go on to defy authority while others in the same situation do not? Such questions cannot be answered by theories of procedural justice alone, because procedural justice theory fails to explain the emotional reactions behind defiance and resistance to authority (see also Sherman 1993, 2003).

III. EMOTIONS AND PROCEDURAL JUSTICE

The discourse on emotions in the criminal justice system has recently started to engage psychologists, criminologists and socio-legal scholars in a vibrant debate (Karstedt 2002; Sherman 2003). For example, Karstedt (2002) argues that legal institutions are institutions that deal with some of the most intense emotions and emotional conflicts, both at an individual and at the collective level. Offenders, victims and witnesses bring their emotions to the courtroom, court decisions sometimes spark public outrage and anger, and victims often express feelings of vengeance towards those who have inflicted harm. Karstedt argues that these emotions therefore need to be considered by those working in the justice context. Sherman (2003) also argues that justice officials need to be made more aware of the emotional impact of their words on citizens if they wish to develop a more effective criminal justice system. Finally, in the field of regulation, Lange (2002) notes that regulating is not just about formal law, but also involves the generation, expression, and management of emotions.

While the arguments presented above suggest that practitioners and scholars are beginning to recognise the role that emotions play in the justice system at a theoretical level, there is not yet much *empirical* evidence to show how emotions play a role in people's perceptions of justice (but see Mikula et al 1998; Montada 1994; Montada and Schneider 1989). In particular, empirical research has been extremely limited with regard to procedural justice, with only a few studies being published in this area.

The majority of work in this area has shown that procedural justice can go on to affect discrete emotions (Krehbiel and Cropanzano 2000; Weiss et al 1999). For example, in an experimental study, Cropanzano and Folger (1989) found that when unfair outcomes were paired with unfair processes, then this went on to produce negative emotions among participants. Similar findings were also obtained by Weiss et al (1999). Assigning 122 students to conditions crossing either positive or negative outcomes with a procedure which was fair, biased in the participant's favour, or biased in favour of another, Weiss et al found that the emotion of happiness was overwhelmingly a function of outcome, with procedural fairness playing little role. Anger was highest when the outcome was unfavourable and the procedure was biased against the participant. Guilt was highest when the outcome was favourable and the procedure was biased in favour of the participant, and pride seemed highest whenever the outcome was favourable (for similar findings see Hegtvedt and Killian 1999; Krehbiel and Cropanzano 2000).

Another line of research has been interested in the subjective quality of social justice. For example, van den Bos (2003) argued that it is not uncommon for people forming justice judgements to rely on how they feel about the events they have encountered. In an experimental study, he found that students who had been put into a positive mood prior to making procedural justice judgements were significantly more likely to judge the way in which they had been treated by the experimenter to be procedurally fair. Those in negative moods were in turn consistently more likely to judge their treatment by the experimenter to be procedurally unfair. In a follow-up study, van den Bos et al (2003) also argued that a person's emotional state at the time of having to make procedural justice judgements can influence how positively or negatively they see their treatment.

A small number of real life studies have also reported similar findings to the experimental research discussed above. For example, in a study conducted in the health care context, Murphy-Berman et al (1999) assessed the relationship between individuals' appraisals of procedural justice following health care treatment decisions. It was found that respondents who felt they had been treated fairly by their health care provider were more likely to experience increased levels of pride and pleasure, as well as lower levels of anger as a result of their treatment. In another study, Chebat and Slusarczyk (2005) surveyed consumers who had previously made a complaint against a major Canadian bank. They were interested in testing whether emotions mediated the effect of justice concerns on their loyalty versus exit behaviour from the bank, and it was found that they did. Those who felt they had been treated in a procedurally unfair manner by the bank were more likely to display negative emotions, and those who displayed negative emotions were subsequently less likely to remain loyal to that particular bank (see also Van Yperen et al 2000; Ball et al 1994). Hence, taken together, the findings of the studies presented above suggest that emotions may have an important role to play in procedural justice research.

IV. WHY STUDY EMOTIONS?

So why is it so important to study the relationship between emotions and procedural justice? The answer is simple. At a practical level, for regulatory institutions to be effective, they need to better understand how to read defiance and respond to it appropriately. By having a better understanding of how procedures may impact upon people's emotions and subsequent behaviour, authorities can more effectively respond to and manage resistance and defiance in the future. We know, for example, that many justice scholars have found that if decisions and actions are deemed unfair or unjust, then those affected experience feelings of anger, outrage and resentment (eg, Skarlicki and Folger 1997). It has also been shown that unfair treatment can elicit a desire for retribution, whereby the affected person experiences a need to punish those blamed for the problem (Sheppard et al 1992). Being better able to predict when these types of sentiments are likely to be felt, and what outcome they result in, can tell authorities a lot about what they need to do to prevent resistance and retribution being taken against them.

At a theoretical level, emotions matter in the context of procedural justice because they help people to deal with the potential threat that poor treatment poses to their identity or group membership. As noted earlier, Tyler and Lind argue that procedural justice is important to people, because the treatment one receives from group authorities provides information about how much one is valued as a group member. Unfair procedures communicate disrespect, marginality, or even exclusion from a valued group. Based on some of this previous research, I propose that a person's emotions will lead them to choose a type of behaviour which will allow them to regain their sense of self-worth and self-identity. A person who feels angry in response to poor treatment may be motivated to resist an authority, for example, as a way of reassuring to themselves that they are an important member of the regulatory community and that they have a right to make their views known. In other words, such an emotion can help them to restore the status quo. By studying the role that emotions play in encounters with authority it will allow scholars to better understand the psychological mechanisms involved in resistance to authority. It is for these reasons that the study of emotion in the context of procedural justice research is so important.

V. EMOTIONS, PROCEDURAL JUSTICE AND REAL-LIFE REACTIONS

While the issue of emotional responses to injustice has been present on a theoretical level for a few years now, empirical studies in this area are few and far between. I want in this chapter to extend the empirical research that has explored the relationship between emotions and procedural justice. In an earlier study, I examined the possible reasons behind why a large group of Australian taxpayers actively protested a decision made by the Australian Taxation Office (ATO). I found that perceptions of procedural injustice significantly predicted taxpayers' level of resistance against the ATO; those who were more resistant were more likely to have judged the ATO's handling of their case to be procedurally unfair (see Murphy 2004). Using the same group of taxpayers, I want now to explore whether a taxpayer's emotional state prior to forming procedural justice judgements about the tax authority may have an impact on their justice sentiments. For example, following van den Bos's (2003) line of argument, are taxpayers who view past punishment in a more emotional manner more likely to make negative procedural justice judgements about the ATO than taxpayers who are less emotional? And do these emotions, in combination with perceptions of procedural injustice, predict the level of resistance exhibited by these taxpayers?

Before proceeding to answer these questions, however, it is important at the outset to first recognise a limitation of my study. The data I use are cross-sectional in nature. It is therefore very difficult to prove causal relationships between the variables of interest. If at any stage I hint at a causal relationship between variables, further research will need to be conducted to demonstrate the causal validity of the relationships presented.

VI. METHOD

A. Participants and Procedure

The data used in this chapter came from surveys completed by 2292 taxpayers. All taxpayers selected to participate had been involved in a taxation dispute with the ATO over their involvement in controversial tax avoidance schemes.

The names and addresses of 32,493 taxpayers were available for selection from the ATO's case files. In January 2002—four years after the ATO had initially sought to recover tax owing from scheme investors—a 27-page survey (Murphy 2002) was sent to a random sample of 6000 of these investors. The sample was stratified by Australian State/Territory jurisdiction (eg 42 per cent of all investors resided in the state of Western Australia, so 2549 West Australian investors were sampled). Non-respondents were followed up over time using a procedure based on the Dillman Total Design Method (Dillman 1978), and follow-up was accomplished using an identification number attached to each questionnaire, which was in turn linked to the sample name at the ATO. In order to protect investors' privacy, the ATO was responsible for all mailings of the survey and reminder letters. Scheme investors who agreed to participate were asked to return their completed questionnaires in a reply-paid envelope to the Australian National University (ANU) for analysis. This procedure ensured that researchers at the ANU did not have access to the names or addresses of sampled investors. It also ensured that the ATO did not have access to any individual taxpayers' survey responses.

A total of six mailings were made and by the end of July 2002, a total of 2292 usable surveys had been received. When adjusted for out-of-scope taxpayers who had died or moved address (N = 677), a response rate of 43 per cent was obtained.[1] The respondents in the final sample were between 24 and 81 years of age, and 82 per cent were male. For detailed information on the survey's methodology see Murphy and Byng (2002a).

B. The Questionnaire

The survey of tax scheme investors contained a total of 270 questions designed to test respondents' attitudes towards the Australian tax system, the ATO and the paying of tax. A number of questions were also designed with the aim of assessing investors' self-reported tax compliance behaviour

---

[1] This response rate compares very well with experiences from other recent tax surveys conducted in Australia (eg Mearns and Braithwaite 2001).

(for an overview of the survey's findings see Murphy and Byng 2002b).[2] For the purposes of this chapter, however, only those questions relevant to five categories of variables were used: emotion variables, procedural justice variables, an outcome favourability variable, a measure of taxpayer resistance, and demographic control variables. Those interested in the items used to construct the scales used in this chapter are referred to the Appendix.

VII. RESULTS

A. Predicting Procedural Justice Judgements

In order to test van den Bos's (2003) theory that procedural justice judgements may be strongly influenced by the emotional state one is in prior to making judgements, a hierarchical regression analysis was performed using the 'demographic', 'outcome favourability' and six 'emotion' measures as predictors of perceived 'procedural justice'.[3]

As can be seen in Table 10.1, the regression analysis failed to explain a significant portion of the variance in Step 1, indicating that the demographic variables did not have any effect on procedural justice judgements. 'Outcome favourability' was entered into the regression analysis at Step 2 before the emotion measures to test whether emotions affected justice judgements more so than financial self-interest concerns. If emotions are more important to justice judgements than outcome favourability, then we would expect the R^2 change value to be greater between Steps 2 and 3 of the model than between Steps 1 and 2. While we can see that Steps 2 and 3 both explained significant portions of the variance, the emotion variables as a group contributed more unique variation to the dependent measure than did the outcome favourability measure (22 per cent versus 3 per cent respectively).

When considering all variables together, it can be seen that four of the six emotion variables were found to have a negative effect on taxpayers' justice sentiments. For example, the emotion of 'anger' had a negative effect on taxpayers' general perceptions of procedural justice ($\beta = -0.17$, p<0.001), indicating that taxpayers who expressed more anger towards the ATO were more likely to believe that the ATO generally treats taxpayers in a procedurally unfair manner. Likewise, those who were more 'embarrassed'

---

[2] Many of the questions contained in the survey had previously been tested on a sample of Australian taxpayers from the general population, and that survey yielded reliable results (see Mearns and Braithwaite 2001).

[3] Before proceeding with the regression analyses, a factor analysis was performed to test for the assumed conceptual differentiation between all attitudinal variables used. As anticipated, all items that were used to produce scales loaded clearly onto their respective factors.

Table 10.1: Hierarchical regression analysis showing predictors of procedural justice

Predictor	Step		
	1	2	3
Age	0.04	0.05*	0.03
Sex	0.01	−0.00	0.01
Education level	0.04	0.04	−0.02
Family income	−0.02	0.02	−0.02
Outcome favourability		−0.16***	−0.08***
Embarrassment			−0.09***
Regret			0.12***
Anxiety			−0.16***
Blame			−0.26***
Anger			−0.17***
Shame			−0.02
R^2	0.00	0.03	0.24
Adjusted R^2	0.00	0.03	0.24
R^2 change	0.00	0.03	0.22
F change	1.68	48.43***	88.48***
Df	4, 1874	1, 1873	1, 1867

Note: Predictor entries are standardised regression coefficients (β). *p<0.05; **p<0.01; ***p<0.001.

(β = −0.09, p<0.001), those who placed more 'blame' at the feet of the ATO (β = −0.26, p<0.001), and those who had higher levels of 'anxiety' as a result of their punishment (β = −0.16, p<0.001) were also more likely to have formed negative procedural justice judgements about the ATO.[4] The emotion of 'regret' had a positive effect on perceptions of procedural justice (β = 0.12, p<0.001), indicating that those who felt more regret over their scheme involvement were significantly more likely to view the ATO's decisions or treatment of taxpayers to be procedurally fair. The emotion of 'shame' had no effect on general procedural justice judgements.

When it came to the self-interest variable 'outcome favourability', it was found that this item also had a significant negative effect on taxpayers' perceptions of procedural justice (β = −0.08, p<0.001). This finding indicates that those who had more to lose financially as a result of their scheme

[4] Note that lower scores on the procedural justice measure indicate perceptions of procedural unfairness.

involvement were also more likely to make negative procedural justice judgements.

So while the findings do not deny that financial self-interest plays a role in taxpayers' construction of procedural justice judgements, the R^2 change values indicate that perceptions of unfair treatment by the ATO were more likely to be a result of taxpayers' negative emotional state at the time of making their justice judgements.

B. Predicting Taxpayer Resistance

In the analysis performed earlier, I found that scheme investors' perceptions of procedural justice could be predicted by both the level of debt they had incurred as a result of their scheme involvement (ie their outcome favourability) and by the emotional state they were in at the time of making their justice judgements. However, I found that emotions contributed more to the variation in procedural justice judgements than did the self-interest variable. Of interest to the second analysis is whether taxpayers' emotions, in combination with their general perceptions of procedural injustice, can predict the level of resistance they exhibit towards the ATO.

Once again, a number of variables were entered into a hierarchical regression analysis with the intention of ascertaining which variables explained most of the variation in taxpayers' level of resistance towards the ATO. Table 10.2 presents the results for this analysis.

First of all, it can be seen from Table 10.2 that 42 per cent of the variation in taxpayers' resistance could be explained by all of the variables in the model. Further, all four steps of the analysis explained significant portions of the variance (1 per cent for demographic variables, 2 per cent for the outcome favourability variable, 16 per cent for the emotion measures, and 24 per cent for the procedural justice measure, respectively). Analysis of the regression results will therefore focus on the most complete fourth step.

When all the variables were in the model together, only 'age', 'education level', 'blame', 'anger', and 'procedural justice' were found to significantly predict level of taxpayer resistance. Specifically, it was found that 'age' had a significant positive effect on taxpayer resistance ($\beta = 0.05$, $p<0.01$), and 'education level' had a significant negative effect on taxpayer resistance ($\beta = -0.04$, $p<0.05$), suggesting that those who were older and those who were less educated were more likely to be resistant towards the ATO. Both 'blame' ($\beta = 0.05$, $p<0.01$), and 'anger' ($\beta = 0.13$, $p<0.001$) had positive effects on taxpayer resistance. In other words, those who were angrier and those who placed more blame on the ATO for their circumstances were also more likely to be resistant towards the ATO. Finally, the 'procedural justice' measure had a strong and significant negative effect on taxpayer resistance ($\beta = -0.56$, $p<0.001$). This finding indicates that those who made more

Table 10.2: Hierarchical regression analysis showing predictors of taxpayer 'resistance'

Predictor	Step			
	1	2	3	4
Age	0.01	0.01	0.03	0.05**
Sex	–0.02	–0.02	–0.02	–0.02
Education level	–0.09***	–0.08***	–0.03	–0.04*
Family income	–0.01	–0.04	–0.01	–0.02
Outcome favourability		0.13***	–0.05**	–0.01
Embarrassment			0.08*	0.03
Regret			–0.06*	0.01
Anxiety			0.11***	0.02
Blame			0.20***	0.05**
Anger			0.23***	0.13***
Shame			0.04	0.03
Procedural justice				–0.56***
R^2	0.01	0.02	0.19	0.42
Adjusted R^2	0.01	0.02	0.18	0.42
R^2 change	0.01	0.02	0.16	0.24
F change	4.14**	28.99***	62.76***	760.59***
Df	4, 1873	1, 1872	6, 1866	1, 1865

Note: Predictor entries are standardised regression coefficients (β). *$p<0.05$; **$p<0.01$; ***$p<0.001$.

negative procedural justice judgements about the ATO's decision processes and treatment of taxpayers were also more likely to be resistant towards the ATO. 'Outcome favourability' had no significant effect on taxpayer resistance.

Overall, these findings taken together suggest that perceptions of procedural injustice, along with the emotions one feels surrounding an event, are much more likely to explain taxpayer resistance levels than either demographic factors or financial self-interest concerns.

VIII. DISCUSSION

To date, there have been a limited number of empirical studies conducted that have explored either the role of people's emotions in their formation of procedural justice judgements or on people's emotional reactions to procedural injustice. This is despite the fact that there have been numerous calls for research to be conducted in this area (eg Adams and Freedman 1976; Cook and Hegtvedt 1983; Greenberg 1984). I was therefore interested in exploring whether a person's emotional state prior to being asked to make general procedural justice judgements about an authority might have had an impact on the type of judgements they made. More specifically, I was interested in whether a taxpayer's emotional state prior to being asked to make general procedural justice judgements about a tax authority which had punished them in the past may have had an impact on their justice sentiments. As a reminder, all of the taxpayers who completed surveys in my study had been reprimanded and penalised by the ATO about four years earlier for engaging in tax avoidance.

To summarise, I found that taxpayers who were in a more negative emotional state at the time of completing a survey, were more likely to judge ATO decisions and treatment of taxpayers in general to be procedurally unfair. Those who were less emotional were less likely to make negative procedural justice judgements. Further, I found that a taxpayer's emotions, in combination with their perceptions of procedural injustice, predicted the level of resistance they exhibited towards the ATO. Specifically, those with more negative emotions (ie those with higher levels of anger and blame) and those with more negative procedural justice sentiments were more likely to be resistant towards the ATO. Financial self-interest concerns were found to play little role in either taxpayers' procedural justice judgements or in the level of resistance they exhibited towards the ATO.

If we relate these findings back to previous research, we can see that they support the findings and claims that have been raised in some of the earlier procedural justice research into emotions. Van den Bos (2003), for example, suggested that when people form justice judgements, they can be influenced by the affective state they were in beforehand (see also van den Bos et al 2003). Using an experimental technique whereby he placed participants into either a positive or negative mood prior to making justice judgements, van den Bos found that those who were placed into negative moods beforehand were subsequently more likely to make negative procedural justice judgements about the experimenter. Those who were placed into positive moods were significantly more likely to make positive procedural justice judgements. In my study, those taxpayers who reported having more negative emotions as a result of prior punishment were significantly more likely to make negative procedural justice judgements about the ATO's general treatment of taxpayers than those who reported more positive emotions. I believe this finding is important, because it extends the work of van den Bos (2003) by showing that in a real life setting, emotions can and do play a role in influencing people's procedural justice judgements. But what implications do these findings have for procedural justice research in general?

A. Implications for Procedural Justice Research

My findings have a number of such implications. First of all, they have implications for procedural justice research into defiance. The regression analysis presented in Table 10.2 showed that people's emotions, in combination with their perceptions of procedural injustice, predicted the level of resistance they exhibited towards the ATO. The implication of such a finding is that if authorities hope to prevent widespread resistance to their decisions they should ensure, as far as possible, that their dealings with citizens are handled in such a way as to prevent either eliciting negative emotions or perceptions of injustice (suggested strategies for how this might be done are discussed in more detail later). The other implication of this specific finding is that procedural justice researchers might need to consider people's emotional state of mind when trying to explain their defiance towards authority decisions and rulings. As I discussed in the introduction to this chapter, emotions may be used to motivate some people to restore their standing within a group. For those who feel their standing within a valued group has been threatened by disrespectful treatment, anger may motivate them to defy or resist an authority as a way of combating this sense of threat.

My findings also highlight the subjective nature of procedural justice judgements. Specifically, perceptions of procedural justice might be in the eye of the beholder. For example, the ATO generally uses an automated lettering system to communicate and gain compliance from non-compliant taxpayers. These letters are generally produced using a letter template and are constructed in such a way that the messages contained within them are kept consistent across all taxpayers who receive them. In the case of the schemes situation, all taxpayers involved would have received similarly worded letters informing them that their deductions had been disallowed under Part IVA of the Income Tax Assessment Act 1936, and that they were required to repay their tax with interest and penalties within two weeks of the date of notice (hence, it can be assumed that the type of treatment taxpayers received over their scheme involvement was kept relatively constant). Yet my findings showed that some of these taxpayers made negative procedural justice judgements about the ATO, while others made neutral or positive judgements. The results I presented in Table 10.1 suggest that the differences in procedural justice judgements might be partly explained by the emotional state taxpayers were in prior to making their judgements. These findings are important because they suggest that when trying to explain subjective differences in procedural justice judgements, researchers might benefit by further considering the emotional states people are in prior to making their judgements.

The broader implication of such a finding is that regardless of how regulators go about making decisions or enforcing laws, there will always be some people who regard the features of their experience to be procedurally unfair. In particular, those who are affected in a more emotional way by their experience are more likely to judge their treatment to be unfair. In fact, Makkai and Braithwaite (1994) have also found evidence to suggest that managers of nursing homes who scored high on a measure of emotionality were subsequently more likely to judge deterrent threats by nursing home inspectors to be procedurally unfair.

This does not mean that regulators should not try to improve or develop strategies that are less likely to spark negative emotional reactions among those they regulate. If we look at the tax schemes situation, for example, it can be seen that the use of a deterrence-based strategy did not appear to be as effective as desired in bringing about compliance with the ATO's decisions. Instead of complying, the majority of tax scheme investors actively resisted the ATO's attempts to recover taxes. My findings showed that for many of the taxpayers involved, the ATO's enforcement action had a negative effect on their emotions. Such findings suggest that regulators might benefit by moving beyond enforcement strategies linked purely to deterrence.

B. Moving Beyond Deterrence

In an earlier study, I made the suggestion that an enforcement strategy that initially places trust in the foreground of a regulatory encounter might be more effective in gaining voluntary compliance among taxpayers than one based solely on legal coercion (Murphy 2004; see also Ayres and Braithwaite 1992; Cherney 1997). I suggested that such a strategy is likely to be particularly effective because it will be seen to be procedurally fair, and those being regulated are likely to feel that their past good faith efforts at compliance have been acknowledged. It is also probable that such a strategy will be less likely to spark negative emotions among those being regulated.

Another option for regulators trying to identify effective enforcement strategies that reduce the chance of eliciting negative emotions would be to use an evidence-based approach. An evidence-based approach usually entails methods of evaluation research to test the effectiveness of treatments or programmes by systematic observation (Wenzel and Taylor 2003). Usually, randomised controlled experiments are used where participants are randomly assigned to various treatments—potentially including an untreated control group—in order to measure and compare the effects of each treatment uncontaminated by any other potential influence (Boruch 1997). The advantage of using such an approach is that decisions on how to best gain voluntary compliance among those being regulated would be based on empirical evidence and intelligence, not on myths or untested preconceptions.

Findings suggesting that such an evidence-based approach might be effective in the regulatory context come from other research conducted on taxpayers in Australia. Wenzel (2003) studied the effects of procedural justice on tax compliance behaviour. His field study tested the effectiveness of different letter styles on business owners' tendency to file their business activity statements with the ATO. The study tested whether reminder-to-file letters that were based on principles of procedural fairness would yield more positive reactions from taxpayers and yield greater rates of compliance compared to the standard letter used by the ATO (ie that made penalties salient). Although the effects were weak, it was found that the procedural justice letters yielded greater subsequent filing compliance compared to the standard letter.

Coupled with the findings of my study, Wenzel's results suggest that regulators should acknowledge the specific importance of procedural justice in their dealings with non-compliers, and that they should make a commitment to implement and nurture the principles of justice and fairness in their compliance strategies. It might be interesting to follow up Wenzel's study by measuring the emotional reaction taxpayers might have on receiving different letters. If different letters are found to lower the negative emotional reactions that taxpayers experience, then it would be interesting to see whether these effects go on to affect compliance rates.

IX. CONCLUSION

The findings I have presented in this chapter—along with some other procedural justice research (eg Krehbiel and Cropanzano 2000; van den Bos 2003)—have told us something about the way people may feel in response to past punishment. What I have been able to show above and beyond much of the previous research is that emotions are involved in perceptions of procedural injustice, and that these two factors together can predict the level of resistance exhibited by people being regulated. Future research will need to be conducted, however, to replicate these findings in other fields and to further explore the causal links among the variables of interest.

X. APPENDIX

Contained in this Appendix is a complete list of the measures used in the analyses in this chapter. The Appendix also details the original scale formats, the recoding of data if applicable, reliability coefficients of each scale, the mean score and standard deviation obtained on each scale.

A. Emotion Variables

A number of different measures were used to assess scheme investors' emotional reactions to being previously punished by the ATO. They included shame, anger, embarrassment, regret, anxiety, and degree of blame apportioned to the ATO. A description of how each of these measures was constructed is described below.

i. Shame

Scheme investors' shame reaction in response to prior punishment was assessed via a scale originally designed by Ahmed (2001). Ahmed designed her shame scale for use in the context of school bullying. However, it was adapted here for use in the taxation context. Respondents were asked five questions about how they felt about having to pay a substantial fine for claiming an illegitimate tax deduction. Responses to these questions were combined to form the shame scale (Chronbach's $\alpha = 0.88$; $M = 2.76$; $SD = 0.91$). These questions assessed whether the respondents felt ashamed and humiliated after being punished, and whether they felt that they had let down their families. Measured on a 1 'not likely' to 4 'almost certain' scale.

— Felt you had let down your family.
— Felt ashamed of yourself.
— Felt angry with yourself for what you did.
— Felt humiliated.
— Felt guilty.

ii. Anger

Taxpayers were asked to indicate whether they felt angry in response to having to pay a substantial tax fine. Responses to three questions were combined to form an anger scale (Chronbach's $\alpha = 0.80$; $M = 2.38$; $SD = 0.90$), whereby taxpayers' feelings of anger and vengeance towards the ATO was of interest. Measured on a 1 'not likely' to 4 'almost certain' scale.

— Felt angry with the Tax Office.
— Felt bothered by thoughts I was being unfairly treated.
— Felt I wanted to get even with the Tax Office.

iii. Regret

In order to measure the emotion of regret respondents were asked to reflect on how they were feeling in relation to the ATO's enforcement action against them. Regret was assessed via a four-item scale developed by the author (Chronbach's $\alpha = 0.71$; $M = 2.80$; $SD = 1.00$). Measured on a 1 'strongly disagree' to 5 'strongly agree' scale.

— I regret the mistakes I made that led to the amendment of my tax return.
— Getting involved in the issues surrounding my amended tax return went against my moral standards.

— I can't believe I got involved in the issues surrounding my amended tax return.

— I would never get involved again in the kind of thing that resulted in the amendment of my tax return.

iv. Embarrassment

Taxpayer embarrassment over their involvement in tax schemes was measured using two items developed by the author (Chronbach's α = 0.89; M = 3.29; SD = 1.19). Measured on a 1 'strongly disagree' to 5 'strongly agree' scale.

— The situation surrounding my amended tax return has caused me a lot of embarrassment among my family.

— The situation surrounding my amended tax return has caused me a lot of embarrassment among my friends and acquaintances.

v. Anxiety

Taxpayers' level of anxiety was assessed via one question, which asked respondents to rate how much anxiety the ATO's enforcement action against them had caused them (M = 4.19; SD = 0.88). Measured on a 1 'no anxiety' to 5 'extreme anxiety' scale.

— How much anxiety has it caused you to received the amended tax return?

vi. Blame

Finally, the amount of blame taxpayers apportioned to the ATO for their circumstance was measured using one question developed by the author (M = 3.42; SD = 0.73). Measured on a 1 'none' to 4 'completely to blame' scale.

— How much blame do you place on the Tax Office for the situation surrounding your amended tax return?

B. Procedural Justice Variables

The procedural justice variables used in my study were designed to assess taxpayers' general perceptions about the way they think the ATO *generally* makes its decisions and treats taxpayers. It should be noted that the items did not measure taxpayers' perceptions of the ATO's handling of the schemes situation.

The procedural justice variables were taken from previous research conducted by Tyler (1997). They were adapted for use in the taxation context and were designed to test Tyler's sub-concepts of trustworthiness, neutrality, and respect. The trustworthiness scale was designed to test whether the ATO can be seen to be treating taxpayers in a fair way when it makes its decisions. The measure of neutrality included assessments of the ATO's honesty, impartiality, and the use of fact, not personal opinions, in decision-making. Finally, the respect scale assessed whether the ATO is seen to have genuine respect for taxpayers' rights. Two additional scales adapted from Braithwaite and Makkai (1994) were also used to measure two sub-concepts of procedural justice: trustworthy treatment and consultation. The measure of trustworthy treatment assessed whether taxpayers believe the ATO treats them as trustworthy citizens, and the consultation measure assessed whether the ATO can be seen to give taxpayers a say in decision processes. An overall procedural justice scale (Chronbach's α = 0.90; M = 2.28; SD = 0.68) was constructed by combining responses to all five individual scales. Measured on a 1 'strongly disagree' to 5 'strongly agree' scale.

— The Tax Office respects the individual's rights as a citizen (respect).
— The Tax Office is concerned about protecting the average citizen's rights (respect).
— The Tax Office considers the concerns of average citizens when making decisions (trustworthiness).
— The Tax Office tries to be fair when making their decisions (trustworthiness).
— The Tax Office cares about the position of taxpayers (trustworthiness).
— The Tax Office gets the kind of information it needs to make informed decisions (neutrality).
— The Tax Office gives equal consideration to the views of all Australians (neutrality).
— The Tax Office is generally honest in the way it deals with people (neutrality).
— The Tax Office treats people as if they can be trusted to do the right thing (trustworthy treatment).
— The Tax Office treats people as if they will only do the right thing when forced to (trustworthy treatment; reverse coded).
— The Tax Office consults widely about how they might change things to make it easier for taxpayers to meet their obligations (consultation).
— The Tax Office goes to great lengths to consult with the community over changes to their system (consultation).

C. Outcome Favourability

An objective measure of outcome favourability was used for the purposes of my study. Taxpayers were presented with one question in the survey that required them to disclose how much money they owed the ATO as a result of their tax scheme involvement. Hence, this question's inclusion was designed to measure financial self-interest concerns (M = $48,727; SD = $70,691).

— What is your best guess of how much your tax situation has cost you and will cost you in tax, interest and penalties?

D. Resistance

To measure taxpayers' level of resistance toward the ATO at the time of conducting the study, respondents were presented with six statements asking them to rate how they viewed the ATO. These statements were taken and adapted from Braithwaite's (1995) research of motivational postures in the nursing home industry. The six statements were combined to form a taxpayer resistance scale (Chronbach's α = 0.67; M = 3.73; SD = 0.57). In the taxation context, resistance reflects doubts about the intentions of the ATO to behave cooperatively and benignly towards those it dominates and provides a rhetoric for calling on taxpayers to be watchful, to fight for their rights, and to curb Tax Office power (Braithwaite 2003). Measured on a 1 'strongly disagree' to 5 'strongly agree' scale.

— It's impossible to satisfy the requirements of the Tax Office completely.
— The Tax Office is more interested in catching you for doing the wrong thing, than helping you do the right thing.
— It's important not to let the Tax Office push you around.
— If you don't cooperate with the Tax Office, they will get tough with you.
— Once the Tax Office has you branded as a non-compliant taxpayer, they will never change their mind.
— As a society we need more people willing to take a stand against the Tax Office.

E. Demographic Variables

Survey respondents were asked to indicate their age (M = 45.73; SD = 8.99), sex (0 = male; 1 = female), family income (on a scale from 0 to 250+ thousand dollars; M = $94,170; SD = $54,928), and education level (on a scale from 1 'not much formal schooling' to 8 'post-graduate degree'; M = 5.85; SD = 1.63).

REFERENCES

Adams, JS and Freedman, S (1976) 'Equity theory revisited: Comments and annotated bibliography' in L Berkowitz and E Walster (eds), *Advances in experimental social psychology* Vol 9 (New York, Academic Press).

Ahmed, E (2001) 'Shame Management: Regulating Bullying' in E Ahmed, N Harris, J Braithwaite and V Braithwaite (eds), *Shame Management through Reintegration* (Cambridge, Cambridge University Press).

Ayres, I and Braithwaite, J (1992) *Responsive Regulation: Transcending the De-regulation debate* (Oxford, Oxford University Press).

Ball, GA, Klebe Trevino, L and Sims, HP (1994) 'Just and unjust punishment: Influences on subordinate performance and citizenship' 37 *Academy of Management Journal* 299–322.

Boruch, RF (1997) *Randomized experiments for planning and evaluation: A practical guide* (Thousand Oaks, Sage).

Braithwaite, J and Makkai, T (1994) 'Trust and compliance' 4 *Policing and Society* 1–12.

Braithwaite, V (1995) 'Games of engagement: Postures within the regulatory community' 17 *Law and Policy* 225–55.

—— (2003) 'Dancing with tax authorities: Motivational postures and non-compliant actions' in V Braithwaite (ed), *Taxing Democracy: Understanding Tax Avoidance and Evasion* (Aldershot, Ashgate Publishing).

Chebat, JC and Slusarczyk, W (2005) 'How emotions mediate the effect of perceived justice on loyalty in service recovery situations: An empirical study' 58 *Journal of Business Research* 664–73.

Cherney, A (1997) 'Trust as a regulatory strategy: A theoretical review' 9 *Current Issues in Criminal Justice* 71–84.

Cook, KS and Hegtvedt, K (1983) 'Distributive justice, equity and equality' 9 *Annual Review of Sociology* 217–41.

Cropanzano, R and Folger, R (1989) 'Referent cognitions and task decision autonomy: Beyond equity theory' 74 *Journal of Applied Psychology* 293–99.

Dillman, DA (1978) *Mail and telephone surveys: The total design method* (New York, John Wiley).

Greenberg, J (1984) 'On the apocryphal nature of inequity distress' in R Folger (ed), *The sense of injustice* (New York, Plenum Press).

Hegtvedt, KA and Killian, C (1999) 'Fairness and emotions: Reactions to the process and outcomes of negotiations' 78 *Social Forces* 269–303.

Karstedt, S (2002) 'Emotions and criminal justice' 6 *Theoretical Criminology* 299–317.

Kim, W and Mauborgne, R (1993) 'Procedural justice, attitudes and subsidiary top management compliance with multinationals' corporate strategic decisions' 36 *Academy of Management Journal* 502–26.

Krehbiel, PJ and Cropanzano, R (2000) 'Procedural justice, outcome favourability and emotion' 13 *Social Justice Research* 339–60.

Lange, B (2002) 'The emotional dimension of legal regulation' 29 *Journal of Law and Society* 197–225.

Lind, EA and Tyler, TR (1988) *The social psychology of procedural justice* (New York, Plenum Press).

Lind, EA, Greenberg, J, Scott, KS and Welchans, TD (2000) 'The winding road from employee to complainant: Situational and psychological determinants of wrongful termination claims' 45 *Administrative Science Quarterly* 557–90.

Lind, EA, Kulik, CT, Ambrose, M and de Vera Park, M (1993) 'Individual and corporate dispute resolution: Using procedural fairness as a decision heuristic' 38 *Administrative Science Quarterly* 224–51.

Makkai, T and Braithwaite, J (1994) 'The dialectics of corporate deterrence' 31 *Journal of Research in Crime and Delinquency* 347–73.

Mearns, M and Braithwaite, V (2001) 'The Community Hopes, Fears and Actions Survey: Survey method, sample representativeness and data quality' Centre for Tax System Integrity Working Paper No 4 (Canberra, The Australian National University).

Mikula, G, Scherer, KR and Athenstaedt, U (1998) 'The role of injustice in the elicitation of differential emotional reactions' 24 *Personality and Social Psychology Bulletin* 769–83.

Montada, L (1994) 'Injustice in harm and loss' 7 *Social Justice Research* 5–28.

—— and Schneider, A (1989) 'Justice and emotional reactions to the disadvantaged' 3 *Social Justice Research* 313–44.

Murphy, K (2002) *The Australian Tax System Survey of Tax Scheme Investors* (Canberra. The Centre for Tax System Integrity, Research School of Social Sciences, The Australian National University).

—— (2004) 'The role of trust in nurturing compliance: A study of accused tax avoiders' 28 *Law and Human Behaviour* 187–209.

Murphy, K and Byng, K (2002a) 'A User's Guide to the Australian Tax System Survey of tax scheme investors' Centre for Tax System Integrity Working Paper No 39 (Canberra, The Australian National University).

—— (2002b) 'Preliminary findings from the Australian Tax System Survey of Tax Scheme Investors' Centre for Tax System Integrity Working Paper No 40 (Canberra, The Australian National University).

Murphy-Berman, V, Cross, T and Fondacaro, M (1999) 'Fairness and health care decision making: Testing the group value model of procedural justice' 12 *Social Justice Research* 117–29.

Sheppard, BH, Lewicki, RJ and Minton, JW (1992) *Organizational Justice: The Search for Fairness in the Workplace* (New York, Lexington Books).

Sherman, LW (1993) 'Defiance, deterrence, and irrelevance: A theory of the criminal sanction' 30 *Journal of Research in Crime and Delinquency* 445–73.

—— (2003) 'Reason for Emotion: Reinventing Justice with Theories, Innovations, and Research—The American Society of Criminology 2002 Presidential Address' 41 *Criminology* 1–37.

Skarlicki, DP and Folger, R (1997) 'Retaliation in the workplace: The roles of distributive, procedural, and interactional justice' 82 *Journal of Applied Psychology* 434–43.

Tyler, TR (1987) 'Why citizens follow the law: Procedural justice, legitimacy and compliance' Unpublished manuscript, Northwestern University.

—— (1990) *Why people obey the law* (New Haven, Yale University).

—— (1997) 'The psychology of legitimacy: A relational perspective on voluntary deference to authorities' 1 *Personality and Social Psychology Review* 23–45.

—— (2004) 'Legitimacy and cooperation: Why do people help the police fight crime in their communities?' Paper presented to the International Institute of

Sociology of Law's Conference on Emotions, Crime and Justice, Onati, Spain, 13–14 September.

—— and Huo, YJ (2002) *Trust in the Law: Encouraging Public Cooperation With the Police and Courts* (New York, Russell Sage).

Tyler, TR and Lind, EA (1992) 'A relational model of authority in groups' 25 *Advances in Experimental Social Psychology* 115–91.

van den Bos, K (2003) 'On the subjective quality of social justice: The role of affect as information in the psychology of justice judgments' 85 *Journal of Personality and Social Psychology* 482–98.

——, Maas, M, Waldring, IE and Semin, GR (2003) 'Toward understanding the psychology of reactions to perceived fairness: the role of affect intensity' 16 *Social Justice Research* 151–68.

Van Yperen, NW, Hagedoorn, M, Zweers, M and Postma, S (2000) 'Injustice and employees' destructive responses: The mediating role of state negative affect' 13 *Social Justice Research* 291–312.

Weiss, HM, Suckow, K and Cropanzano, R (1999) 'Effects of justice conditions on discrete emotions' 84 *Journal of Applied Psychology* 786–94.

Wenzel, M (2003) 'Principles of procedural fairness in reminder letters: A field-experiment' Centre for Tax System Integrity Working Paper No 42. (Canberra, The Australian National University).

—— and Taylor, N (2003) 'Towards evidence-based tax administration' 38 *Australian Journal of Social Issues* 409–30.

Part III

'Emotion Work' in Criminal Justice Institutions

11

Dealing with Defiant Citizens: Building Emotional Intelligence into Police Work

BAS VAN STOKKOM

I. INTRODUCTION

S INCE 1998, AMSTERDAM'S police force has practised what is called 'Streetwise'—a policy that entails fining citizens for minor breaches of the law such as urinating in public and cycling on footpaths. The force aims to break with the soft and tolerant attitudes that characterised Dutch policing for a long time. Police officers are obliged to generate more fines and call citizens to account. This repressive policy has had great consequences for police–public interaction: more involuntary contacts with citizens evoke more conflict situations, and citizens who are forcibly stopped and fined for breaking minor rules are motivated to contest or complain about the officers' decision. Many Amsterdam citizens were, moreover, taken by surprise. They were accustomed to quasi-anarchical habits in traffic and nightlife. Many citizens, including the apparently decent ones, experience proactive stopping and fining as unacceptable attempts to curtail freedom. They thus tend to resist what they see an unwarranted police interference.

In the Netherlands, incivilities such as ignoring red lights, jumping the queue and drinking beer in parks are viewed as outcomes of increasingly assertive attitudes amongst its metropolitan citizens (Van den Brink 2001; WRR 2003: Van Stokkom 2010). Nowadays these incivilities are met with more opposition. A large part of the population is no longer prepared to tolerate loutish behaviour and is in favour of re-establishing order and tough policing. Others continue to cherish the 'do what you want' freedom.[1]

But has public–police interaction become more unruly? Why are many citizens so eager to defy officers' decisions? In this study police–citizen encounters are interpreted as a charged ritual in which both parties deploy

---

[1] For a wider discussion of Dutch repressive security policies, see Van Swaaningen (2005).

emotions to preserve and restore their status. In the first part, I delve more deeply into 'Streetwise' and discuss some research findings about police–public encounters in Amsterdam. I discuss the motives of citizens who were arrested for insulting police officers, as well as unprofessional police performances. It turns out that what I term 'mirroring' and 'forcing' police styles are highly problematic. 'Mirroring' leads to emotional contagion; 'forcing' to a cool and detached stance, not being accessible. The verbal aggression which attends these styles is illustrated with quotes taken from the research material.

The second part of the chapter focuses on some micro-sociological and moral-psychological issues. First I explore why exercising authority and receiving respect is so complicated nowadays. Here two tendencies are discussed: the difficulties police officers have in securing cooperation, and assertive citizens whose status expectations bring them into conflict with officers. Second, the encounter between police officer and citizen is interpreted as a 'moral contest' in which both parties seek to defend their self-worth and status. The various emotions that surface during this 'classification ritual' are briefly sketched. In the final section, I argue that better understanding of emotion management and argumentation styles may enhance professional police performance.

II. 'STREETWISE' IN AMSTERDAM

The Amsterdam 'Streetwise' policy is an explicit form of 'broken windows' policing in the Netherlands. 'Streetwise' aims to combat minor offences and annoying behaviour that irritate the public and corrode feelings of security. This entails more intensive control and maintenance of law and order: making more proactive stops in the street and addressing citizens in an active way. Many local acts have been introduced (a ban on the use of alcohol in streets and parks, and on dogs running free, for example), and traffic rules have been tightened. The police have also sought to enhance their authority. Insulting police officers is rigorously counteracted and prosecuted.

Although police managers regularly point to the achievements of New York's zero tolerance policing, the Amsterdam police does not aim to introduce unscrupulous and aggressive strategies. Streetwise does however have its repressive aspect. All officers are obliged to issue more tickets and to issue fines at least two times a day (to reach a quota of 300 fines a year). Since 1999 the police have issued more than 400,000 extra bookings each year. More than 250,000 of these bookings go hand in hand with conversations in which citizens are called to account (so that citizens are not taken by surprise when the payment request arrives). In 1998—the first 'Streetwise' year—only 55,000 citizens were fined in this way. Achieving this ambitious target could only be carried out by mobilising more manpower.[2] In short, the police have distanced themselves from former relaxed routines and now take the lead in upholding law and order and shoring up public morality. At one time, Amsterdam's police were not really eager to book citizens; now the force leaders proudly declare that there is not a police force in Europe that issues more tickets.

Police data indicate that 'Streetwise' is a success. Most cyclists drive with lights, fewer cars are 'jumping' red lights, traffic-accidents are reduced, and urinating in public has disappeared. The public seems to approve of Streetwise, because loutish behaviour is counteracted. Street scenes are more predictable and citizens feel safer. The enforcement of 'minor norms' appears to reduce feelings of insecurity.[3]

But 'Streetwise' has its dark side. The increased number of involuntary contacts with citizens generates many potential conflict situations and moments of resistance. In many respects, police–public interaction has become more unruly, and fuelled with verbal aggression. Many Dutch research findings (Kop et al 1997; Timmer 1999) suggest that repressive performances go hand in hand with coercive and threatening attitudes that prompt citizen defiance and aggression. In the period 1994–2002 the number of citizen complaints against the Amsterdam police doubled.[4] Complaints of 'unseemly treatment' and 'disproportionate behaviour' increased most. Another problem is that the local prosecution counsel is overloaded with thousands of minor cases.[5] Streetwise transforms annoying behaviour, like pollution and verbal threats, into illegal behaviour. Some types of behaviour that involve no explicit norm transgression, such as drinking beer in public parks and playing music on the street, have also been targeted. This generates defiance and much contention. The same is true regarding certain minor traffic offences, such as 'giving signals other than allowed' and 'standing still in bicycle lanes'. When these often unintentional behaviours result in fines, citizens typically protest and dispute the officer's decision.

Of course the public has to become accustomed to a more repressive policy. When a formerly customer-friendly police switches to strict enforcement, the public becomes frustrated and irritated. Citizen expectations

---

[2] Since 1995 more than 1000 extra officers were assigned. The number of police officers in the Amsterdam-Amstelland district in 2004 was 5800. The district contains 900,000 inhabitants.

[3] These trends seem to validate the 'broken windows' policing paradigm (Kelling and Coles 1996; Roché 2002; Van Stokkom 2008). For critical notes on zero tolerance policing, see Harcourt (2001).

[4] The Amsterdam police force has its own complaints service. In 2002, citizens filed 633 complaints against officers.

[5] In 2002 more than 15,000 criminal cases resulted from violations of local ordinances (not including the huge amounts of traffic and public transport violations).

are thwarted. The same goes for tourists and other strangers who are not familiar with Streetwise's new moral order.

III. VERBAL AGGRESSION: SOME RESEARCH FINDINGS

But in what respects has police–public interaction become more unruly? To answer this question I analysed interrogation reports of citizens who were arrested for insulting officers in May and June 2003, and complaint letters about unseemly police treatment sent to the complaints department of the Amsterdam force in 2002.[6] The incidents selected were those which took place in public space and stemmed from proactive stops and/or fines, or direct and spontaneous encounters.[7] In addition, 15 police officers were interviewed, including officers who had attracted several complaints in one year and those who were nominated for the force-award for issuing the most Streetwise fines in one year (the 'prolific writers'). I will first go briefly into the motives of citizens who were arrested for insulting police officers, and then discuss the coercive behaviour of officers that can be inferred from complaint letters and interviews.

A. Citizens' Motives to Insult

The arrested citizens are predominantly male and younger than 40. Moroccan and Surinamese men are over-represented. Nearly half of the arrested persons had previous contact with the police (so the group is not representative of the whole population). The rebellious behaviour of many young persons can be attributed to street customs and street language and the accompanying inclination to provoke, impress and outdo. Many look down on the status of police officers. On the streets they are in charge and someone special. Police officers challenge and puncture these subcultural codes.

The interrogation reports reveal the following motives. First, it turns out that being controlled or forced to stop is experienced as unwarranted and 'bothersome' interference. This runs counter to the feeling of self-esteem or is viewed as an improper infringement of private life. For example:

A barkeeper consumes a glass of beer on the street, in front of the pub where he works. He is addressed by two female officers who cross the street. The man says: 'I won't put up! I live here! Just fuck off!' The case escalated as the man spat in the face of one of the female officers. The man was arrested and during the

---

[6] The research was conducted in 2003 and published in 2005 (Van Stokkom 2005).
[7] From the 229 police reports and 178 complaint files, ultimately 106 and 77 cases were studied.

interrogation he said: 'I tried to discuss with the officers. But I didn't succeed. The fact that those officers addressed me was terrible. Because I didn't annoy anyone. That's why I got fed up.'

Secondly, the arrested persons believe that using abusive language is expressing an opinion. They think they have the right to swear and express their irritation. Entering a discussion entails the utterance of profane words (which in many ways belongs to Amsterdam folklore). Some examples:

> A defendant says during the interrogation: 'That officer said I had to stay out. I said he was an oaf. He said that I was arrested for insulting an officer. I said it was my opinion and that I may utter that safely.' Another identical case: 'I said that the officer was a bastard. That's just giving my opinion, it's not insulting.'

A third pattern is that answering the officer back is normal, even thought of as one's duty. The arrested person wants to be treated as an equal, and rejects the roles of super- and sub-ordination.

The arrested person wishes, in other words, to speak without restrictions. This is not only typical of the arrested rebellious young man, but also of the average, 'reasonable', more law-abiding, complainant. The complaint letters show that many citizens are offended when police officers force them to stop. They object to the fact that police officers are allowed to give warnings, reprimands and commands 'just like that'. They launch a counterattack, ignore the remarks of the officer, or refuse to cooperate. These reactions are understandable when citizens want to counteract a loss of face. But the complaint letters reveal that police utterances which do not contain denigrating intentions, like refuting an assertion, are nevertheless experienced as irritating or threatening. In the same way unforced forms of communication, like requests for explanations (which are different from commands or reproaches), are experienced as intrusive.

B. Coercive Officer Behaviour

Let's turn now to police performances. The complaint letters reveal that trivial cases often escalate, for instance because officers talk down to citizens or refuse requests for reasons. Coercive and non-respectful treatment often leads to verbal aggression and resistance, especially when arrests are made and handcuffs put on. In 28 of the cases of unseemly behaviour studied (n = 77), the complainants were arrested and most were accompanied with physical resistance. In a way, issuing fines for minor offences seems to be escalating in itself, especially if citizens do not consider them as offences. Many cases have trivial causes or appear 'out of nothing'.

Fines seem to have a particular capacity to generate conflict. For instance, a citizen throws the ticket that he received just a minute ago out of the window of his car, or ostentatiously tears up that ticket. The police officer cannot accept such behaviour and the citizen is subsequently arrested. Another example: a market vendor who was requested to move his car from the square addressed the officer in comical, assertive Amsterdam language using words such as 'oliebol' (pudding head). The result was dozens of officers and stallholders confronting each other and two arrests being made.

Being transported to a police station with handcuffs on evokes agitation and anger. Many complainants criticise that practice. Police requests for assistance are another complicating factor. When the reinforcement arrives there is no way back. Citizens who accidentally pass such a disorderly scene, are treated harshly without exception.

In sum, strictly upholding one's authority has a high price: it evokes serious conflicts and incidents. The question is in what respects police officers—by cracking down on minor misbehaviour and looking for confrontations—are bringing insults upon themselves. What is a 'laconic game' for Moroccan boys, provoking police officers without much understanding of the consequences, officers take rather seriously. So within the scope of 'Streetwise' many 'elicited' or 'fabricated' offences occur. 'Get even' strategies—such as making citizens wait for longer than is necessary—also play a dominant role. The interviews indicate that many officers cannot resist the temptation to do the 'bastards' a bad turn. Many cops evince a 'tit-for-tat' outlook that reveals their incomprehension of the behaviour of citizens, in particular juveniles and members of ethnic minorities.

In many ways officers behave unprofessionally: a lack of correct manners, giving unsatisfactory reasons for making arrests, conducting unnecessary body searches and use of handcuffs, intimidating those they have stopped, expressing value judgements too hastily, informing individuals in a pitying tone that a ticket cannot be undone and protest is futile. Based on the complaint letters and interviews, two types of unprofessional treatment can be reconstructed: displays of power, and bad-mannered behaviour. The first can be traced to a 'forcing' style, the second to a 'mirroring' style.

C. Forcing Styles

The display of power (showing dominance, imposing one's will, being rigid and dogmatic) is often accompanied with a forcing attitude that invites disproportional responses. Often officers hide behind the rules, refrain from answering questions and giving information. These responses indicate that the police are 'above' and the citizen 'beneath'. Forcing can also entail rushing through a fine, failing to notice how citizens react and displaying a 'frozen' front. In such situations, citizens are left in a state of frustration or rage. Although forcing may be professional in some circumstances, in most cases forcing needlessly generates a hostile atmosphere. An officer reports a case in which a bus driver did not obey his orders in the heart of the city:

> I said: 'Move on, carry on with that bus.'. But contrary to my orders the driver started to load passengers. Again I commanded him to drive. One of the men interrupted me which I found extremely irritating. I said: 'Shut your face.' Meanwhile the traffic got jammed. I said to the driver he's got five seconds to move away, and if not he would be arrested for not following my commands. Indeed, I counted from five to zero but the driver did not move. I arrested him.

'Prolific writers' are a special case. Typically they do not hesitate to fine a citizen for all the offences they have committed. Many act in a rigid way without much concern for the specific context of 'offence' and 'offender'. In one case a woman threw a number on the ground that she had just before taken when she was not being served fast enough at a post office. A policewoman that passed by, coincidentally one of the force 'leaders' when it came to fining (about 1600 a year), ordered her to pick up the piece of paper. In the end the woman and her mother were arrested and at the police station the case completely escalated as both women lost their cool. During the interview the police woman said:

> Yes, that case completely kicked off. Because of something trivial. Yes. But they have to do what I say. Otherwise I am just a nobody. It's not in my character to say 'Leave it'. ... Next time she would use that. ... If she had said 'Sorry', maybe ... No, if I had given her more scope, she would have enjoyed that in abundance.

Some prolific writers—including this policewoman (who got eight complaints in one year)—are forced to stop by their superiors and requested to work in a more measured way.

D. Mirroring Styles

Mirroring involves officers assuming the role of the other. Police officers get carried away with the emotions of citizens. If forcing is characterised by a cool and unbending stance, mirroring implies a form of 'emotional contagion'. These officers lose their temper and poise, and run themselves down. There are all kinds of examples, ranging from childish behaviour ('Yes, I am going to enjoy giving you this fine'), to putting down ('If you call me a bastard, I'll call you asshole?'). An example from the interviews:

> Someone is spitting right in front of your feet. What do you do? I am spitting back. Because I know, when I take that lad to the office, nothing happens. Because he says: 'Just prove that that one was directed at me!' Yeh, yeh. That's contempt. Migrants do that. They pass by and spit. Then I turn round and spit back. The lad says: 'What are you doing?' I said: 'Well, I do what you do. Obviously we are greeting each other in this way.'

In these situations officers are not able or willing to control their irritation or anger, or to keep their dignity. The interviews suggest that mirroring is endemic (and all too human, one might add) and is even practised by officers who at first sight are keen not to lapse into that mistake. Often mirroring involves demonstrating streetwise attitudes: countering in assertive ways, out-bluffing and trumping the opponent.

In many ways, forcing and mirroring are the antithesis of each other—depersonalisation (suppressing emotions) versus emotional contagion (letting emotions off the leash)—but in both cases professionalism and trust are eroded. Whereas forcing seems to be a structural problem in the psychological make-up of a relative small subgroup of police officers, all officers are (now and then) prone to mirroring. Mirroring can be overcome because it is normally 'only' the result of situationally specific loss of control. There are signs that many young policemen adopt rival behaviour and swear words in a structural way. But they deal with it playfully and are not burdened with the stress, discomfort and cynical worldviews that are typical of forcing officers.

The research findings suggest that officers who use forcing and coercive styles encounter more resistance (see also Mastrofski et al 1996 2002). However, many prolific writers do not encounter defiance. This suggests that police style and resistance are highly related: officers who prefer cooperative and problem-solving approaches meet less resistance. For this reason, receiving many complaints ought not to be ascribed so much to high productivity, but to the ways citizens are addressed and treated (see Terrill and McCluskey 2002). Thus it might be rewarding for officers to develop their communicating skills.

IV. DEALING WITH ASSERTIVE CITIZENS: COMPLICATING FACTORS

Before addressing this theme, I want to discuss in more detail some factors that complicate the interactions between officer and citizen. Why is it that exercising authority and conferring respect cause so much trouble these days? The answer, at least in part, lies in some long-term changes in Dutch society.

Policing on the streets seems to be more demanding than it was some decades ago. Citizens are more assertive and stick up for themselves. Assertiveness means saying directly and spontaneously what you think and want, without considering whether the 'opponent' is offended, and without feeling guilty or responsible (Van den Brink 2001; Van Stokkom 2010; also Wilson and Gallois 1993). As mentioned, 'respectable citizens' also tend to view being addressed in public as annoying or meddlesome. There seems to be a natural tendency to resist the interference of police officers (and probably other professionals). The norms of the private sphere—the domain that safeguards against troublesome behaviour, without the need to justify oneself—seems to penetrate public morality and public spaces. Citizens are keen to denounce incorrect treatment, and are skilled in interpreting misfortune and trouble as hindrance.[8]

We should not overstate the case of defiance among 'respectable citizens'.[9] Most citizens agree with requests for control and accept being fined. Two-thirds of Dutch citizens who come into involuntary contact with the police (and receive warnings, tickets etc) report being 'content' or 'very content' about these contacts (Politiemonitor Bevolking 2004).

A. Contentious Authority

Citizens nevertheless judge police activities differently from their predecessors of half a century ago: proactive police stops that involve questioning and controls are now considered more disrespectful. In democratic contexts, authority is granted on other grounds and takes on other forms (Warren 1996).[10] First, formal types of authority seem to give way to discursive and personal types of authority. Formal and legalistic acting is less acceptable because it means citizens being withheld the respect they count on. Within informal communication contexts, assigning authority is more and more based on trustworthiness. Public professionals do not set themselves up only as representatives of the state, but develop personal forms of persuasion which indicate integrity and build confidence (Wouters 1986).

Secondly, authority is not accepted blindly. Acting as a superior is only accepted conditionally. Citizens only accept their role of controlled or supervised person when is explained why these 'interventions' are necessary. It seems that cooperation is considered as a reward for police officers. That reward is withheld when officers give no reason for interrogation, or when these reasons do not convince (see also Tedeschi and Felson 1994; Wilson and Braithwaite 1993). For that reason authority has taken on a contingent and uncertain character, and needs to be proved and renewed again and again. Authority can thus be easily forfeited, for instance by acting in brutal ways or, conversely, in hesitant and vague ways.

---

[8] Compare sociological findings on 'incivilities' and over-sensitive public behaviour (Katz 1999; Miller 2001; Kowalski 2002; Phillips and Smith 2003).

[9] The situation for the many subgroups that 'have nothing to lose', like long-term jobless people, is of course completely different (see Sherman 1993).

[10] The sociologists Scheepers and Te Grotenhuis (1999) concluded that the Dutch accept authority less and less. The anti-authoritarian disposition of the Dutch increased to a large extent: from 30 per cent in 1970 to 52 per cent in 1996. That might incorrectly suggest that the anti-authoritarian Dutch reject any request from authorities and define the rules themselves. It seems more accurate to say that authority is defined as the ability to persuade people in a respectable way.

Thirdly, citizens seem to be more and more oriented towards fairness and procedural correctness. They expect equal treatment. Perceived unfairness ('Why me and not others?') creates considerable scope for potential conflicts.[11] Such fixation about being neglected or passed over might be attributed to higher social expectations and norms, or over-sensitive narcissistic reactions (Van den Brink 2001; Kowalski 2002).

These long-term changes have several implications. Exercising authority in a metropolitan milieu of short-tempered citizens has become more demanding and more vulnerable: obtaining cooperation and securing citizen compliance is 'hard work'.

B. The Shadow of Status Hierarchies

In principle the relation between police officer and citizen is asymmetrical. The citizen is assumed to show more respect than the police officer. But this disparity—including the formal and detached attitude of the officer—is now less accepted than in former days. Police officers today are expected to be more responsive and to give reasons for their actions. Citizens do not feel obliged to cooperate in every situation. But there are other factors that complicate the 'natural' dominance of police officers. Their performances are embodied in status hierarchies that contain not only formal positions but also ethnicity, gender, age and social class. These divergent forms of status disrupt a regular and smooth encounter between officer and citizen (Sykes and Clark 1975).

Ethnic minorities no longer behave submissively. In a time of multicultural emancipation, subordination and special forms of deference are condemned, while proud and militant behaviour is accorded greater weight, even celebrated. For that reason, officer dominance is considered problematic because it manifests a lack of respect for ethnic dignity. The behaviour of a fair-minded officer who expects civility from a Moroccan boy is interpreted by that boy as exhibiting ethnic superiority. The police officer interprets the attitude of the boy as a refusal to show respect for his lawful status. Both tend to reject the other, by virtue of mutually discordant expectations and appraisals of status differences. Thus it is not surprising that police officers and members of ethnic minorities rather avoid each other and restrict social contacts, because an encounter is shot through with conflicting expectations and constraints.

Persons with high social standing expect to be treated with respect by police officers. Citizens with low social status expect to be treated less

---

[11] See Tyler and Huo (2001). In his study on defiance Lawrence Sherman (1993) endorses this interpretation and suggests that citizens feel unfairly treated when they meet a lack of respect, notwithstanding the fact that the sanction is considered deserved.

respectfully. The lower classes have less 'status resources' at their disposal, to behave decently and with self-control (Sykes and Clark 1975). For that reason police officers take their verbal aggression less seriously. They have far more trouble in accepting the loud mouth of a well-to-do citizen. This person is supposed to have more 'status resources' at his or her disposal, but deliberately chooses not to use them. Many respondents in the research were indignant about this:

> Fining somebody in an expensive car, always evokes protest. Lower classes are more compliant. Respectable people are much more whiney and complaining. An expensive Mercedes: they are allowed to do anything.

The complaint letters from Amsterdam citizens suggest that assertive citizens have 'emancipated' themselves from these status resources, conceived as high standing or good manners. It is not respectable to be modest, because that would reveal a vulnerable and weak-minded self. Assertive behaviour has become the order of the day, signalling power and decisiveness.

In sum, the uncertainties of exchanging respect between police officers and many members of ethnic minorities, and the 'new' public morality of assertiveness, has disrupted the 'normal' interaction between 'dominant' officers and 'obedient' citizens.

V. THE 'MORAL CONTEST'

Many citizens are unwilling role players who quickly feel embarrassed and attacked. This has of course to do with the unusual character of proactive stopping or police interference. Citizens feel themselves made ridiculous and the public staging of 'being accosted' reveals that foolishness. How can we explain this defiance in social-emotional terms?

When it comes to this question, the 'loss of face' theory seems very fruitful (Brown and Levinson 1987; Tedeschi and Felson 1994; Cupach and Metts 1994). Citizens are strikingly concerned about their self-worth. A threat to their status evokes resistance, sometimes so much that they seem to be blind to the consequences of their defensive actions. They defend themselves in ways which vary from criticism of the behaviour of the police officer, to launching a counter-attack. The resistant stance confirms that they have the right to make a choice. Agreeing with the officer would accentuate their weakness and confirm their subservience. Police officers, for their part, can ill afford loss of face: they act upon a public platform where they must uphold the reputation of lawful enforcer. Condoning an insult would have a devastating effect. Officers must reply and teach resisting citizens a lesson.

A contest arises in which power, prestige and respect are at stake. It is a moral contest not only because the resilience (the morale) of the opponent is tested, but also because the combatants aim to garner a special type of respect (Van Maanen 1978). After all, respect has many (sub)cultural meanings, ranging from uncompromising attitudes (honour) to decency (class distinction). The verbal controversy can also be described as a 'classification ritual', in which the hierarchy of respect is established (Gabriel 1998). Swear words and insults seek to establish a reversed status hierarchy. When the citizen stresses the incompetence or insignificance of the opponent, the balance of 'above' and 'beneath' is suddenly switched. In fact insults are tests to determine the pecking order and produce coalitions in the presence of bystanders and other police officers. Everyone's humour, venom and courage can be displayed and tested and the public gets the opportunity to take sides (Gabriel 1998).

Not only insults but also publicly expressed complaints and accusations may endanger the status of police officers. If bystanders witness these incidents, police officers have to protect their reputation. Moreover, to be criticised in public reduces the opportunities for effective reply, so the accused gets involved in a delicate situation. An aggressive reply discredits the public image of calmness; a defensive reply may elicit negative judgements such as 'weak' or 'lacking authority'.

Often juveniles have fun trying to draw a policeofficer out, for instance by looking amusing or laughing benignly. If they successfully elicit publicly uncontrolled emotions, they have practically won the battle. An officer who yells loses his balance and dignity. Juveniles are masters at manipulating the emotions of superior persons, exactly because they are accustomed to subservient positions. They initiate a contest because they have little to lose. Even if they come off worst eventually, they have shown courage and may gain reputation within their group. This may explain the irrational forms of defiance that are typical of many young Moroccan men in Amsterdam: insulting officers to the bitter end gains honour and standing, although they know that they cannot alter the power balance.

Police officers have their own repertoire to put down citizens. Often their responses have the elements of a degradation ceremony (Van Maanen 1978). The most frequent one in Amsterdam is to make citizens wait for nothing. However, most replies of police officers are of a more subtle nature. Many reactions occur in part unconsciously. Accusing looks, a hostile stance and an irritated voice can be taken as mild forms of rejection—just as many forms of citizen defiance and irritation are expressed indirectly. They resort to 'off-record markers', remarks that undermine normal conversation such as insinuations, sarcasm, understatements and rhetorical questions.

A. Emotions and Status Conferral

The moral contest is characterised by negative emotions such as annoyance, anger, rage, dislike, aversion and contempt. These unpleasant emotions function as instruments to regain status, particularly because they deter and arouse fear and shame. Anger and pride are explicitly associated with higher status (Tiedens 2001). Both express dominance, transmit a latent aggressive message and function to position oneself as deserving dignity. By contrast, contempt indicates that the other is not a worthy opponent. For that reason, contempt is rather accompanied by rejecting, ignoring or avoiding rivals (Tiedens 2001; Jones 2002).[12] While anger can be used to address someone, contempt blocks communication.

Anger communicates competence and the ability to exert power. As mentioned, this only applies for anger that is controlled and well timed. Acting wildly often gives the impression that you are harmed or confused. It damages one's reputation. By contrast, a calm and imperturbable stance contributes in itself to a higher status.

Most police officers in Amsterdam know very well that such a stance upholds authority, and that convincing messages need 'controlled anger'. But it is very difficult to suppress bursts of anger: internally felt anger easily 'leaks out', especially when insults enter the person behind the uniform. Some quotes from the interviews:

> That bad-ass says: 'I am going to smash your face in, boy.' 'Just try it, and I'll make you mad.' Very simple. At that moment you downgrade yourself to his level.

> I said: 'I hope you got three cells in your brain to remember what I said.' That's not making any sense. Later on you know that she won.

These officers confirm that a 'mirroring' style damages their status. Other officers don't mind, and simply want to be superior:

> Cynicism that's the first thing I learned myself. You need it when people are smart. ... Well, I start and it goes continually to a higher degree, and I hope for them that they do not go along with me.

Many 'forcing' officers resort to violence. One of them received six complaints within three months and was plainly burned out. His frustration was also directed at his colleagues and the management. He showed mainly contempt:

> It just happens. If you have the bad luck to meet six of those bumpkins than I am spoiled ... They just want to screw me. If I taste that, then I'm finished with them. Totally ... They don't make a fool of me. Not at all.

Embracing cynicism, these officers want to win the battle by all possible means, and do not sense that they in fact debase their public status.

---

[12] According to emotion-sociologist Theodore Kemper (1990), the majority of emotions stem from realistic, anticipated, recollected or imagined outcomes of power and status relations.

For respectable citizens the dominant emotion is usually embarrassment, a transient unease related to specific circumstances (in contrast with shame, which is usually focused on profound moral values and generally does not arise during minor incidents). They become aware that they are the centre of attention and are being judged. However, this discomfort easily evokes impulsive anger, especially when assertiveness 'orders' one to protest. By contrast, the sense of pride in lower-status subgroups simply demands that police officers are defied. Many Moroccan and Antillean boys show that they are 'independent' and ready for action. Their contest-behaviour is couched in what William Ian Miller has termed a 'moral economy of honour', focused on strict reciprocal norms that must prevent disgrace and cowardice (Miller 1993).

In sum, proactive stopping and fining brings forth a moral contest which forces both parties to defend their status. Both are tempted to retaliate when an attempt to degrade reveals itself. For that reason it is hardly possible to think away 'mirroring' from police work in the streets. How to prepare police officers properly for these contests without sacrificing integrity and respect? I will argue that developing emotional intelligence and affirming argumentative styles are of utmost importance.

VI. BUILDING EMOTIONAL INTELLIGENCE INTO POLICE WORK

Arlie Hochschild (1983) has pointed out that members of specific occupational groups show emotions that meet occupational demands. Shopworkers smile and show friendliness, nurses care and show comforting feelings. Those 'display-rules' will often be at odds with the personal feelings that these workers have in the face of a customer who annoyingly criticises all the commodities you offer, or a patient who complains continuously. The shop worker and the nurse are not expected to reveal these feelings.

In the same way, police officers are expected to suppress their personal feelings. They are supposed to act properly and correctly, and look earnest, confident and in control. The public expects a self-confident and calm attitude. This 'feigned' attitude keeps private feelings of fear, revulsion or, occasionally, attraction at bay, feelings that could disrupt their professionalism. Surface feelings meet display-rules, the rules that ought to be presented during work time. Internal feelings, related to what officers 'really' feel, must be suppressed. Police officers on the beat ought to radiate attentive signs even when bored by the grind of daily work. They also must be able to sympathise with complaining victims. When they impose a fine, they must show a resolute stance. They must convey the message that any citizen would have received that fine! All unfairness and arbitrariness that might possibly attend the issue of the fine must be prevented.

Were police officers unable to control their private emotions, their authority would be compromised. The expression of too harsh or too soft emotions (infuriated or grieved) points to professional weakness (Martin 1999; Rafaeli and Sutton 1991; Sutton 1991). Hence police officers are expected to manage their irritation, dislike and amusement. At the same time they ought to manage and control the feelings of others. Police officers are, one might say, engaged in 'double-faced emotion management' (Tracy and Tracy 1998). This is for instance the case when officers give advice to agitated residents: they try to calm them down, and at the same time they reduce their own feelings of powerlessness or embarrassment. This double emotion management occurs especially in situations of high urgency or stress.

Professional police work on the streets involves adequate social-emotional competence: being in control in stressful situations, being resolute, raising oneself above conflicts and squabbles, and beaming out a relaxed stance. One might define police professionalism as a mix of sober-minded and recognisable acting (Denkers 1983). This means reacting in a more detached style than most citizens, while at the same time showing authentic and sincere feelings to build up trust. This second aspect requires 'expression in office': showing commitment and that you really mean what you say. Here, primary impulses and emotions must be suppressed, while feelings of citizens must be responded to in such a way that a sense of urgency is conveyed and the concerned parties are stimulated to take their responsibility. In the case of fining, it is a real art to perform within the confines of behaving soberly (keeping a distance) and yet being involved (point with some passion at the responsibility of booked citizens). The other way round, when police officers ignore, keep off or play down the feelings of citizens, they give the impression that nothing is at stake. But in reality trust is harmed and the interaction ends with a disturbed relation.

The second aspect of this social-emotional competence is not very well developed. Many police officers only learn to stay under control and to keep their distance. This 'stoic pose' may bring to the fore many problems. Suppressing real feelings may generate stress and become a psychic burden, particularly when distressing incidents are not coped with. That might give rise to 'emotional dissonance': officers are not capable of adapting their own feelings to public display rules and the expectations within the force. This imbalance also affects the quality of interaction with citizens (Rafaeli and Sutton 1991; Ashforth and Humphrey 1993). The forcing styles of many police officers in the context of Streetwise policing in Amsterdam reveal just such a lack of responsiveness.[13]

---

[13] Dutch research findings indicate that stressed and depersonalised police officers operate less responsively and more insensitively (Kop 1999).

In police organisations, the importance of understanding and expressing emotions is not very well-recognised. Discussing emotions is usually discouraged. The need to close ranks is of more importance (Martin 1999; Kop 1999). The education and training of police officers could be more attuned to emotion management: to understanding how emotions like anger and contempt are aroused, and how they can be avoided or channelled. Four principles of emotional intelligence are of major interest here (Saarni 1999; Jones 2002):

— *Emotional awareness*: the ability to detect emotional states in self and others (decoding skills).
— *Emotional perspective-taking* (or empathy): the ability to recognise and understand emotional experience from others' point of view, particularly in victims and offenders.
— *Cultural understanding*: the ability to appropriately follow display rules that prescribe emotional expression and understand that different (sub)cultures operate with different display rules, particularly minority cultures wherein respect is experienced and expressed differently.
— *Strategic expression*: the ability to regulate one's impulses and emotional experiences, particularly in conflicts and other emotion-eliciting events; the ability to respond convincingly to conflicts, calm down emotions and inspire confidence.

Next to emotional intelligence, developing argumentative skills is important. Not being able to respond adequately or offer proper arguments when you are challenged undermines the authority of police officers. The chance that they then react aggressively is increased. After all, a person who lacks argumentative abilities is tempted to attack not the position that someone takes up in a discussion, but the personality of the opponent. Thus good communication is an important pre-condition for preventing verbal aggression (Infante and Rancer 1996). Besides, it turns out that people who are able to communicate well are perceived as more sincere and trustful: they reveal aspects of themselves and invite others to cooperate.

Authority thrives on credible acting. Infante (1988) points out that credibility is an image that people have of someone in terms of three factors: expertise (possessing valuable knowledge), trustworthiness (the audience believes the person in question is reliable and feels 'safe') and dynamism (the impression that you are a forceful person with an appealing personality). This last factor seems to be the most important one: 'the more you are seen as dynamic, the more you tend to be viewed as expert and trustworthy' (1988: 126). Being perceived as dynamic means being seen as having energy, strength and vitality, which gives the impression that you are an approachable person and that you seem to know what you are talking about.

To prevent verbal aggression, it is important that rejecting messages (like cautioning or fining) are accompanied with relaxed, attentive and sincere vocal responses and facial expressions. An affirming communicative style is viewed as less threatening: it supports rather than attacks the citizen's self-identity and focuses the perception of citizens on the case itself (Infante et al 1996). Affirming styles prevent citizens feeling inferior. If they are addressed as subordinates, they adopt defensive attitudes and tend quickly to interpret 'normal' arguments as personal attacks. Thus police officers should not display explicitly superior behaviour, although they should guide the conversation with citizens. For that reason they cannot evade displaying signs of non-verbal behaviour that suggests a higher status: nodding one's head only now and then when the citizen is talking, adopting a relaxed posture and gestures, looking the citizen in the eye and not turning away (Infante 1988).

VII. CONCLUSION

'Streetwise' produces more brutal and unseemly officer behaviour. In some ways it seems to delegitimise police work. What is gained at the front door (the benefits of 'broken window' policing: more familiar and ordered street scenes, reassessment of informal social control) may be lost at the back door (loss of trust in the police; opposition and non-cooperation, especially by minorities). Repressive routines evoke many furious reactions from the public. Citizen-defiance often puts the police in an awkward position and elicits disproportionate reactions and unnecessary use of force. The relevant questions are: when stopping a citizen, how to prevent insults? How to deal with a first insult (and shift its emotional momentum)? In case of giving fines or making arrests, what space can the citizen be granted to vent his emotions? When are aggressive words supposed to be counteracted (risking escalation)?

Occupational training may draw attention to these problems and dilemmas. Next to that, officers need more knowledge of subtle and subconscious ways of 'saving face'. More insight is needed in communicative strategies to settle questions, using affirmative styles and being aware that forms of personal authority determine credibility. These recommendations are not without pertinence. Many research findings (Kop et al 1997; Wilson and Braithwaite 1993; Infante and Rancer 1996) indicate that a lack of social and communicate skills augments verbal aggression.

The pitfalls of forcing and mirroring deserve special attention. 'Mirroring' officers, who adopt the emotions of their 'adversaries', fail to keep distance (self-control) and to act responsibly, the double core of police professionalism. 'Forcing' officers generally keep a distance but fail to express a trustful and dynamic attitude. They do not supply reasons, and are not well prepared to meet verbal attacks. Forcing points to deficient argumentative and personal forms of authority.

Reverting to formal authority does not convince in Dutch society. More and more, citizens cooperate conditionally. Conferring authority has become dependent on recognisable and sincere acting that reveals trustworthiness. Police officers have to develop more personal forms of respect capable of building citizen compliance.

REFERENCES

Ashforth, BE and Humphrey, RH (1993) 'Emotional Labour in Service Roles: the Influence of Identity' 18 (1) *Academy of Management Review* 88–115.

Brown, P and Levinson, SC (1987) *Politeness* (New York, Cambridge University Press).

Cupach, WR and Metts, S (1994) *Facework* (Thousand Oaks, Sage).

Denkers, F (1983) *'Daar pakken ze je op' Emoties tussen rechtstaat en politie* (Lelystad, Vermande).

Engel, RS (2003) 'Explaining suspects' resistance and disrespect toward police' 31 *Journal of Criminal Justice* 475–92.

Gabriel, Y (1998) 'An Introduction to the Social Psychology of Insults in Organizations' 51(11) *Human Relations* 1329–54.

Harcourt, BE (2001) *Illusion of Order: The False Promise of Broken Windows Policing* (Boston, Harvard University Press).

Hochschild, AR (1983) *The Managed Heart* (Chicago, University of Chicago Press).

Infante, DA (1988) *Arguing Constructively* (Prospect Heights, Waveland Press).

—— and Rancer, AS (1996) 'Argumentativeness and Verbal Aggressiveness: A review of Recent Theory and Research' in BR Burleson (ed) *Communication Yearbook 19* (Thousand Oaks, Sage).

Infante, DA et al (1996) 'Affirming and Nonaffirming Style, Dyad Sex, and the Perception of Argumentation and Verbal Aggression in an Interpersonal Dispute' 22(3) *Human Communication Research* 315–34.

Jones, TS (2002) 'Pride and Prejudice: Considering the Role of Contempt in Community and Conflict' (unpublished manuscript).

Katz, J (1999) *How Emotions Work* (Chicago, University of Chicago Press).

Kelling, G and Coles, C (1996) *Fixing Broken Windows: Restoring Order and Reducing Crime in American Cities* (New York, Free Press).

Kemper, TD (1990) 'Social Relations and Emotions: A Structural Approach', in Th Kemper (ed), *Research Agendas in the Sociology of Emotions* (Albany, State University of New York Press).

Kop, N (1999) *Blauw licht in het donker Een onderzoek naar burn-out van en conflictbehandeling door politieagenten* (Amsterdam, Thesis).

—— et al (1997) *Politie en publiek Een onderzoek naar de interactie politie-publiek tijdens de surveillancedienst* (Arnhem, Gouda Quint).

Kowalski, RM (2002) *Complaining, Teasing, and other Annoying Behaviours* (New Haven and London, Yale University Press).

Martin, SE (1999) 'Police Force or Police Service? Gender and Emotional Labour' 561(January) *The Annals of the American Academy.*

Mastrofski, SD et al (1996) 'Compliance on Demand: The Public's Response to Specific Police Requests' *Journal of Research in Crime and Delinquency* 33(3) 269–305.

—— (2002) 'Police Disrespect toward the Public: An Encounter-Based Analysis' 40(3) *Criminology* 519–51.

Miller, RS (2001) 'Breaches of propriety', in RM Kowalski (ed), *Behaving Badly. Aversive Behaviors in Interpersonal Relationships* (Washington, American Psychological Association).

Miller, WI (1993) *Humiliation and Other Essays on Honor, Social Discomfort and Violence* (Ithaca, Cornell University Press).

Phillips, T and Smith, P (2003) 'Everyday Incivility: Towards a Benchmark' 51(1) *The Sociological Review* 85–108.

Rafaeli, A and Sutton, RI (1991) 'Emotional Contrast Strategies as Means of Social Influence: Lessons from Criminal Interrogators and Bill Collectors' 34(4) *Academy of Management Journal* 775.

Roché, S (2002) *Tolérance Zéro? Incivilités et insécurité* (Paris, Odile Jacob).

Saarni, C (1999) *The Development of Emotional Competence* (New York, Guilford Press).

Scheepers, P and TE Grotenhuis, M (2000) 'Tanend gezag van autoriteiten in een individualiserende samenleving' in L Gunther Moor and K van der Vijver (eds) *Het gezag van de politie* (Dordrecht, SMVP).

Sherman, LW (1993) 'Defiance, Deterrence and Irrelevance: A Study of the Criminal Sanction' *Journal of Research in crime and Delinquency* 30 445–73.

Sutton, RI (1991) 'Maintaining Norms about Expressed Emotions: The Case of Bill Collectors' 36 *Administrative Science Quarterly* 245–68.

Sykes, RE and Clark, JP (1975) 'A Theory of Deference Exchange in Police-Civilian Encounters' 81 *American Journal of Sociology* 584–600.

Tedeschi, JT and Felson, RB (1994) *Violence, Aggression, and Coercive Actions* (Washington, American Psychological Association).

Terrill, W and McCluskey, J (2002) 'Citizen complaints and problem officers Examining officer behavior' 30 *Journal of Criminal Justice* 143–55

Tiedens, LZ (2001) 'Anger and Advancement Versus Sadness and Subjugation: The Effect of Negative Emotion Expressions on Social Status Conferral' 80(1) *Journal of Personality and Social Psychology* 86–94.

Timmer, J (1999) *Politiewerk in gevaarsituaties Omgaan met agressie en geweld van burgers in het basispolitiewerk* (Amsterdam, VU).

Tracy, SJ and Tracy, K (1998) 'Emotion Labor at 911: A Case Study and Theoretical Critique' 26 *Journal of Applied Communication Research* 390–411.

Tyler, T and Huo, YJ (2001) *Trust and the Rule of Law: A Law Abidingness Model of Social Control* (New York, Russel Sage).

Van den Brink, G (2001) *Geweld als uitdaging De betekenis van agressief gedrag bij Jongeren* (Utrecht, NIZW).

Van Maanen, J (1978) 'The asshole' in PK Manning and J van Maanen (eds) *Policing; A View from the Street* (New York, Random House).

Van Stokkom, B (2005) *Beledigd in Amsterdam; verbaal geweld tussen politie en publiek* (Alphen a/d Rijn: Kluwer).

Van Stokkom, B (2008) *Disorder Policing and Community Need* 'Revising' Broken Windows Theory, in M Easton et al (eds) *Reflections on reassurance policing in the Low Countries* (The Hague, Boom Juridische Uitgevers) 53–72.

Van Stokkom, B (2010) *Wat een hufter! Ergernis, lichtgeraaktheid en maatschappelijke verruwing* (Amsterdam, Boom).

Van Swaaningen, R (2005) 'Public Safety and the management of fear' 9 (August) *Theoretical Criminology* 289–305.

Warren, M (1996) 'Deliberative democracy and authority' 90(1) *American Political Science Review* 46–60.

Wilson, C and Braithwaite, H (1993) 'Police Patroling, Resistance, and Conflict Resolution' in N Brewer and C Wilson (eds) *Psychology and Policing* (LEA).

Wilson, K and Gallois, C (1993) *Assertion and Its Social Context* (Oxford, Pergamon Press).

WRR (Dutch Scientific Council) (2003) *Waarden, normen en de last van het gedrag* (Amsterdam, Amsterdam University Press).

Wouters, C (1986) 'Formalization and Informalization: Changing Tension Balances in Civilizing Processes' 3(2) *Theory, Culture and Society*.

12

Managing Prisoners, Managing Emotion: The Dynamics of Age, Culture and Identity

ELAINE CRAWLEY*

I. INTRODUCTION

I WANT IN this chapter to reflect on, and to integrate, aspects of two distinctly different pieces of research in which I have recently been engaged. The first project, completed in 1999, was an ethnographic study of the working lives of prison officers (Crawley 2004a). The second project, begun in 2002, was an ethnographic study of the impacts of imprisonment on older men (see Crawley and Sparks 2005a, 2005b, 2006; Crawley 2004b)[1]. In certain important—but perhaps somewhat obvious—respects, the two projects had very different aims. My work on the occupational lives of prison officers focused specifically on the meanings of prison work for those who do it. My aim was to understand how ordinary people become prison officers, and what being a prison officer inevitably involves—not merely in terms of the carrying out of specific practices and tasks, but also in terms of the psychological and emotional impacts of the job itself. In contrast, my work on elderly prisoners with Richard Sparks aimed to understand the psychological, emotional and social impacts of imprisonment on those incarcerated in later life.[2] Put simply, the first

---

* I would like to thank Peter Crawley for his insightful thoughts and comments during the writing of this chapter, and Ian Loader and Heather Strang for their constructive responses to an earlier draft.

[1] This project focused solely on the prison experiences of older men. The main reason for this is that in the UK the numbers of older female prisoners are very small, at least relative to the numbers of incarcerated older men. According to data provided by the Research, Development and Statistics Directorate of the UK Home Office, there were 16 women prisoners over 60 years in 2002. We decided that with limited resources, and since these 16 women were geographically spread, we should not attempt to include them in our sample.

[2] In the international literature there is a general lack of agreement on what age is to be defined as the starting point for defining the 'older' or 'elderly' offender. In Europe and the

project attempted to demonstrate the emotional and psychological impacts of prison work on prison officers, while the second attempted to demonstrate the emotional and psychological impacts of imprisonment on elderly men.

This chapter is set out as follows. First, I will discuss the emotional character of prison work, the cultural norms and 'rules' that underpin 'appropriate' emotional expression and the strategies that prison officers use to manage emotion in specific circumstances and settings. I have discussed these issues at length elsewhere (see Crawley 2004a and b) but it is necessary for me to re-state them here, albeit rather more briefly, in order to 'set the scene' for what follows. I then discuss how working with elderly prisoners—or more specifically, elderly men—requires the management of emotions that are very different from those experienced whilst working with younger adult prisoners. This is largely because younger men in prison are more active and energetic, more likely to be confrontational with staff, more volatile, more impulsive, more aware of their prison rights and less compliant than their older counterparts. As a group, elderly prisoners do not represent a physical threat to prison officers and they pose relatively little threat to the security of the prison. In terms of the maintenance of order and control, therefore, younger prisoners present a greater challenge to prison officers than do elderly men. As we shall see, however, other, distinctly different challenges present themselves to staff working with the elderly—challenges for which most prison officers (in the UK at any rate) are untrained and ill-prepared.

Our research with elderly men in prison was a response to a 'gap' in the prisons literature, in this case a gap in our understanding of the psychological impacts of imprisonment on the elderly. Although the notions of 'coping with', or 'adapting to' imprisonment had been important concerns of prison sociology during its 'classic', mid-century phase (Clemmer 1940; Sykes 1958) not since the work of Cohen and Taylor (1972) had the experiential, ontological and conceptual challenges of extreme (and sometimes literally lifelong) confinement received sustained analysis. Moreover, even Cohen and Taylor's work focused on the anxieties and fears of prisoners sentenced well before middle age, and, since most of them could expect to be released at some point, on their anticipations about life *after* prison.

United States of America, the base age used by researchers of older persons and crime has been as low as 25 years (Strauss and Sherwin 1975) and as high as 82 years (Aday and Webster 1979), with a variety of ages in between. In our own research (Crawley and Sparks 2005b, 2006) the definitions of 'older' and 'elderly' are reserved for those prisoners aged 65 years and above. Our rationale was that, in the UK at any rate, 65 is the age used for social purposes to determine the point of retirement from employment, and to establish eligibility of older persons for various entitlements. Our definition was also based on our findings that prisoners who are in their fifties do not tend to define themselves as 'older', and certainly not as part of an 'elderly' prisoner group.

In contrast, little was known about the experiences and survival strategies of men who *entered* the prison in later life, and whose lives were likely to end in prison.

We wanted to understand the social, psychological and emotional impacts of imprisonment on elderly men and the coping and survival strategies they adopt in coming to terms with custody and with the cultures, architecture, routines, rules and practices of the prison. We were also concerned to understand how prison officers working with these prisoners perceive their own role, given that this prisoner group—by virtue of their age—have markedly different attitudes, needs, problems and experiences from the general prisoner population, and, as such, make very different demands on uniformed staff. In an attempt to draw some conclusions about the management of elderly prisoners in jurisdictions other than the UK, we also gathered a limited amount of empirical data from staff and elderly prisoners I spoke to in Germany and in British Columbia, Canada.[3]

Each of these projects generated 'up-close' understandings of the needs of, and challenges for, two distinctly different prison-based groups. When we consider the interplay of the needs, expectations, experiences and problems of these two groups, however, and the challenges each group faces as it interacts with the other, it is possible to generate further, more nuanced evidence of the relation between emotion and criminal justice. It is this interplay, and the emotions subsequently produced and managed, that is the focus of this chapter. First, of all, though, I want to say a little about the expression of emotion itself.

II. A NOTE ON EMOTION

Explanations of what, exactly, emotions *are* vary across academic disciplines; they range from the strictly biological, in-the-body explanations offered by experimental psychologists, to anthropological, sociological and social-psychological explanations which argue that emotions simply cannot be understood outside the context of their embodied enactment. I do not propose, here, to debate the merits and demerits of these competing explanations; however it will become clear to the reader that I favour a constructionist approach. Readers who wish to explore different definitions and explanations may like to read the work of Darwin for a useful starting point (Darwin 1998 [1872]) before turning to the growing specialist literature

[3] In 2002, Ruth Jamieson and I conducted (with financial assistance from the Canadian High Commission's Institutional Research Programme) a small-scale comparative study of the experiences of older prisoners in Mission and Mountain Institutions, British Columbia (see Jamieson et al 2002). In 2005, I made a research visit to a prison for older men in Singen, Germany, at the kind invitation of the Justizvollzugsanstalt Konstanz (see Crawley and Sparks 2006).

in the sociology of emotions (see especially Hochschild 1983, 1998; Barbalet 1998). The latter texts are extremely helpful in demonstrating the centrality of emotions to routine operations of social interaction.

When I use the term 'emotion' in this chapter, I use it as most of us use it in everyday life—ie to refer to how we are *feeling* 'inside'. However, it is important to understand that the expression of emotions is a form of *language* (see Crawley 2004b). This language of the emotions is *learned* in a way that is analogous to the learning of verbal language, and it conforms to a powerful set of conventions attaching to 'proper' exhibition and expression. Like verbal and other 'languages' (eg the more familiar 'body language' which we all express and interpret in our interactions with others), the language of emotions is a means by which human beings communicate and convey meaning(s). However, as the influential Russian psychologist Vygotsky asserted (Vygotsky 1986, 1987) human beings do not communicate just for the sake of it; communication always has a *purpose*. Vygotsky's crucial point about language is that it is primarily a tool of social interaction, and like all tools, we use it to act more effectively in the world—for example, we can use it to get people to do what we want them to. Since emotional expression is also a language, it follows that the language of the emotions allows us to act more effectively in the world too. Like the verbal language we all acquire during childhood, the language of the emotions must be learnt and practised during childhood, and is then perfected over time. Getting any language 'right'—including the language of the emotions—is a lengthy business at which humans have to work hard.

Mastery of emotional language develops over time and with practice. Full competency is difficult to achieve and maintain, but we know that emotional interchanges are more likely, more meaningful and more fluent in contexts in which there are high levels of intimacy, shared knowledge of context and a never-ending but intermittent 'dialogue'. The emotional interchanges of family life are the most obvious and best example of this, but there are striking similarities between the nature and structure of relationships in prisons and those in the familial setting of the home (Crawley 2004a, 2004b). This is largely because of the highly domestic character of the prison and, subsequently, of much prison work.

III. DOING PRISON WORK

Until very recently criminologists had, in their efforts to understand the impacts of the prison on its prisoners, failed to ask how the prison might impact on those for whom it is a place of work. While we have known for some decades that the prison is an emotionally painful place for prisoners (see Sykes 1958; Serge 1977 Cohen and Taylor 1972; Boyle 1984) and that sudden immersion into the prison environment invariably represents—especially for the 'first-timer'—a psychological and cultural shock, we had not considered the emotional demands that the prison places on prison officers. In other words, as both sociologists and criminologists, we had failed to consider the emotional and psychological adjustments which ordinary men and women have to make in order to *become* and to *be* prison officers. My research attempts to fill that 'gap' in our understanding of criminal justice processes.

A. Emotion and Performance

In the sociology of the prison, the ways in which prison officers manage and perform emotion at work has been poorly understood—largely because as an occupational group they were (surprisingly, given their pivotal role in the running of prisons) of little interest to academic researchers. When things very publicly 'go wrong' in prisons, however (ie when a prison disturbance occurs), the emotional life of prisons becomes a topic of academic, policy and media discussion. On such occasions there is typically much debate about the (largely negative) emotions experienced by all those involved, including the anger of prisoners regarding their conditions of confinement, the disgust of prison officers at the apparently wanton destruction of the prison fabric, and the degree of confusion and fear experienced during the disturbance itself (see Fitzgerald 1977; Woolf 1991; Adams 1992). In contrast, the emotional life of prisons on a day-to-day basis—on the days when prisons are not beset by trouble and when nothing (much) goes wrong—has attracted less research interest. Drawing on key ideas in the sociology of emotions and the sociology of occupations, I have tried in recent work to demonstrate that everyday life in prisons is suffused with emotion, and that emotions are *routinely* performed and managed by both prison officers and prisoners—albeit for very different reasons.

B. The Prison as an Emotional Arena

In *Doing Prison Work* (Crawley 2004a) I employ Hochschild's (1983) concept of 'emotional labour' to explain the emotional performances, strategies for emotion management and performance failures that I encountered during my study of the working lives of uniformed prison staff. 'Emotional labour' (also known more recently as 'emotion-work') refers to the management of feelings at work, in order to create a publicly observable facial and bodily display that is appropriate to, or consistent with a situation, role or an expected job function, and with socially accepted norms. Here, I have space only to give the reader a sense of prison officers' understandings of the work they do, including their efforts to manage the emotions of prisoners, to perform emotion according to the occupational norms of the prison, and to manage their own emotional responses to what they have to see and do. In terms of the latter, it is necessary for prison officers to perform emotional labour in order to perform their job in the 'appropriate' manner (I will return to the question of what is deemed appropriate in a moment). I do not use the word 'performance' lightly; on the contrary, prison officers are acutely aware that they must play parts and stage-manage their actions if they are to control the impressions they convey to prisoners and, just as importantly, to fellow staff.

Prisons are emotionally charged places, largely because they are places in which large numbers of people are held captive against their will. Pioneering studies by sociologists (such as Sykes 1958; Serge 1977; Cohen and Taylor 1972) have shown us that the prison is an emotionally painful place for prisoners. Here, feelings of anxiety, fear, sadness, hopelessness, frustration, regret, anger, resentment and depression are commonplace—joy, hope, satisfaction and happiness much less so. Prisoners are also forced into close proximity to others—others they may fear, hate, feel disgusted by and resent—often for extended periods of time. Prisoner–prisoner and officer–prisoner relationships are emotionally charged. Emotional interchanges cannot be avoided because the degree of *intimacy* involved in working with prisoners is great. Unlike others working in the criminal justice system (eg police officers, magistrates) whose relationships with offenders are relatively fleeting, prison officers spend sustained periods of time with the same prisoners, many of whom will have suffered a variety of personal traumas, difficulties and disappointments, both inside and outside the prison.

The emotions generated by prison work are—irrespective of the specific demands of prisoners—many and varied. For example, many officers feel i) jealous that some colleagues are able to do 'quality work' (ie help to run 'treatment' courses) while they pound the landings; ii) disappointed that 'their' prison has 'gone downhill'; iii) frustrated at the apparent lack of interest in them among prison managers widely perceived as unsympathetic to the needs of uniformed staff and ignorant of the day-to-day realities of life at the 'sharp end', and iv) bewildered and disgusted that some of their fellow officers choose to work with sex offenders. Others complained that they were bored working on a wing that was 'more like an old folks' home than a prison' because it was inhabited by elderly prisoners.

On a day-to-day basis, prison officers' emotions cannot be freely expressed. Rather, officers try to ensure that when they perform emotion, they do so in the 'right' circumstances and settings. Consequently, prison work requires an often significant engagement in emotion management and, relatedly, the employment of specific emotion-work strategies. At the level of the individual officer, emotion-management has two dimensions. First, s/he must deal, on a day-to-day basis, with the emotions expressed by prisoners. The ability to do so varies from officer to officer; while most are confident that they can deal with prisoners' anger (officers always have the option of removing the prisoner to the segregation unit), many are ill-equipped to deal with emotions that require a tender and patient response. For such officers, the prospect of working with elderly, frail prisoners is repellent, since it entails an engagement in tasks that bear little relation to what they imagine the 'proper' role of the prison officer to be about (see Crawley 2004a; Crawley and Sparks 2005a, 2005b). Many officers are, for very similar reasons, unable to cope with juveniles and young offenders. On transferring from adult prisons, for example, officers may be dismayed by the relatively 'tame' nature of the young offender regime, and the dent that they feel their new role has made in their occupational identity (Crawley 2004a).

Secondly, the officer must manage the emotions that the prison generates within him or herself. This is an important issue. How officers *feel* about the work they do, how they feel about prisoners—and the extent to which they perform or manage such feelings—has significant implications for the routine practices of prisons, for staff–prisoner/staff–staff relationships and, ultimately, for the character and quality of imprisonment itself.

C. Managing Feelings

When prison officers express emotion, they do so in clearly structured ways. Prisons, like other organisations, have their own 'feeling rules' about the kinds of emotions it is appropriate for officers to express (and to indeed feel) at work, and it is imperative that prison officers learn them. Such 'rules' are the subtle product of working arrangements and the social history of each workplace; unspoken and largely invisible, they regulate myriad impression-management behaviours, as well as the open expression of feelings. Those who transgress the feeling rules of an organisation risk presenting themselves as unreliable, untrustworthy or simply unsuitable employees (Mangham and Overington 1987; Bendelow and Williams 1998). Certainly most officers understand the need to manage emotion at work, since there are risks associated with the expression of emotions deemed inappropriate to the prison officer role. Not only will the officer (and indeed his colleagues) feel embarrassed if (s)he expresses the 'wrong' emotions (as Goffman (1959) notes, the anticipation of embarrassment is at the heart of social interaction), the acquisition of a 'spoiled identity' (Goffman 1963) may be the price paid for ineffective impression/emotion-management.

Because—despite dramatic changes to working conditions and to recruitment policies and processes—the occupational culture of prison officers continues to stress the importance of 'machismo' for successful job performance, male officers often tend to be particularly careful, in their interactions with prisoners (and indeed fellow officers) not to show qualities traditionally regarded as female, eg sensitivity, sympathy and compassion.

Female officers, in contrast, may deliberately—and legitimately—employ these qualities with prisoners in order to prevent and manage conflictual situations (for a fuller discussion of this, see Crawley 2004a). Although I would not wish to generalise, it may be that in the context of elderly prisoners, female officers—particularly those with elderly parents—may be more competent than their male colleagues, since it is generally women who take the most responsibility for infirm parents, ie collecting shopping, doing housework, providing advice and support on financial matters. As we shall see, the proper management of elderly prisoners necessarily entails tasks where patience and compassion—or at least sensitivity—are foregrounded, and machismo and bravado entirely inappropriate. Many officers, however, given their lengthy socialisation to the occupational norms and cultures of more mainstream prison regimes, find it impossibly frustrating to work with infirm, needy and compliant old men.

D. 'Getting the Job Done': Strategies of Emotion Management

Generally speaking, working at close quarters with prisoners entails 'face-work' and a variety of coping strategies.[4] Like others whose work involves intimate interactions with distressed individuals and the carrying out of intimate, sometimes unpleasant, sometimes frightening tasks (I have compared prison officers' work to that of medical staff, ambulance crews and fire-fighters), prison officers employ humour, strategies of de-personalisation (prisoners are merely 'bodies' to be counted) and a rhetoric of detachment to get through the working day. An important distinction between prison and medical staff should perhaps be made here. Prisons are concerned primarily with the delivery of custody, while medical and rescue services are concerned primarily with the delivery of care. Consequently the 'emotion-work' that medical staff and rescue workers engage in is primarily carried out in the context of alleviating the distress of worthy individuals, ie individuals who, as blameless patients, are seen as worthy of sympathy and compassion.[5] Prison officers' 'emotion-work', on the other hand, is likely to be more problematic, since it emerges in interactions with

---

[4] In contemporary communication theories (see especially the work of Erving Goffman), the term 'face' refers to the positive social value we effectively claim for ourselves, and an image which others may share. The term 'face work' refers to the actions we take to make whatever we are doing consistent with face. These actions become habitualised and standard; each person, occupational group and society has its own characteristic repertoire of face-saving practices.

[5] Of course, some medical staff may also think of certain patients as 'unworthy' of treatment eg heavy smokers with chronic lung problems, and those requesting treatment in accident and emergency units after a night of heavy drinking.

individuals who are often perceived as unworthy of such emotions (this applies to elderly sex offenders in particular). Even officers who strive to work positively with such prisoners often find it difficult to manage feelings of anger and disgust; similarly they may feel guilty when feelings of sympathy and compassion do emerge (these conflicting feelings are not ameliorated by the 'nonce-bashing' attitudes of some fellow staff). There is evidence (see Crawley 2002 2004a) that prison officers often feel stigmatised by their work; this is rarely—if ever—the case with medical staff, who are generally held in high social esteem.

As a strategy for conveying, disguising and expressing emotion, humour plays a significant (if somewhat unexpected) role in the working lives of prison officers. The type of humour prison officers appreciate is what they themselves call 'sick', 'black', 'toilet' or 'gallows' humour, which finds its expression in day-to-day banter and joshing, pranks and practical jokes. Humour is also employed in tragic and shocking situations, such as when a prisoner has committed suicide or 'cut up'. It is here that its form and function most resembles the humour employed by those in the medical profession. Like the nurses interviewed by Lawler (1994 and the medical students interviewed by Lella and Pawluch (1988), prison officers use humour during certain hands-on, dirty, messy tasks, particularly where there is blood, excreta or vomit to be cleared away. Just as many nurses tell 'dead body stories' (Lawler 1994: 190) and make 'dead body jokes' when confronted by dead patients, prison officers often joke during, and after, dealing with dead or seriously injured prisoners, since humour neutralises, and thus makes bearable, the fear of death (Mercier 1926). Resorting to humour in such circumstances may strike one as unprofessional and callous; indeed, when prison officers do so, 'outsiders' may assume that they are simply performing true to the stereotype of the heartless, insensitive guard. However, it is not so easy to resort to stereotypes when nurses joke about death and dying, since nurses are generally thought of as compassionate and caring individuals. Importantly, acts of apparent callousness and their accompanying 'gallows humour' go against the publicly held stereotype of nurses, whereas they are seen (by the general public) to fit perfectly with the stereo type of the 'prison guard'. A more general defence mechanism for coping with the demands of emotionally charged work is to simply 'switch off' or 'go robot'. Traditionally, an occupational characteristic of a 'good' nurse was the ability to hide emotional reactions and to cultivate an air of detachment—to develop a professional distance from the work. Formal nursing training dictates that staff displays of emotion are inappropriate to the hospital setting; they demonstrate that the nurse is 'not made of the right stuff' to be a competent nurse.

An occupational ethos in which de-personalisation and emotional detachment are distinctive features is also present in most prisons (Crawley

2004a and b).[6] Officers speak routinely about the number of 'bodies' that must be fed, brought from reception, got ready for court and so on; arguably this language of 'emotional distancing' enables officers to deal with large numbers of prisoners without emotional involvement. Prison officers, like nurses, are expected to remain emotionally detached; they are warned, during basic training, not to get too friendly nor too relaxed with prisoners, on the grounds that this may lead to 'conditioning' and hence to compromises of security (see Home Office 1994). 'Detachment' is a strategy commonly employed by prison officers to avoid being manipulated by prisoners. Indeed, the fear of being seen as a 'soft touch' colours all aspects of officers' interactions with prisoners.

Detachment, however, does not remove all the stressors of prison work. In particular, it does not alter officers' awareness that their job is *unpredictable*; indeed, this is what creates the most stress and anxiety at work. According to this officer working in a prison holding in excess of 400 young men:

> There's an underlying stress the minute you walk through the gate. That's mainly because of the layout and the unpredictability of the job. To me, just being aware of something all the time (ie the possibility that a prisoner may suddenly cause trouble) is stress itself. Officers know that at any time they can get a smack in the face opening a cell door.

As we shall see, keeping elderly men in custody presents a very different set of challenges for prison staff.

IV. ELDERLY PRISONER POPULATIONS

At the time of writing there are more than 4000 men aged over 50 in prison in England and Wales (roughly five per cent of the total prison population). This number has more than doubled in the last decade. The rate of growth is even higher for those over 60 years of age. In 2002 there were 1129 men aged between 60 and 69 years under sentence in England and Wales. This represents a more than three-fold increase since 1994. In 2002 the age group 70 to 79 years comprised a total of 225 men, while there were 17 men aged 80 years and above.

Since the elderly population increase exceeds the rate of growth for the prison population as a whole, it is necessary to find an explanation. I can do no more here, however, than to note some of the key dynamics. We have previously argued (see Crawley and Sparks 2005a, 2005b) that one important factor is the very much greater readiness (and technical

---

[6] Therapeutic communities, which place particular emphasis on the development of positive, relationships between prisoners and staff, are an obvious exception.

capacity) of police and prosecutors to pursue and secure convictions against sex offenders, including in cases of 'historic' offences. This shift in societal and judicial responses to sex offending has been well discussed elsewhere (see Thomas 2005). In 2000 one-third of adults aged 60 years or over received into prison under immediate sentence in England and Wales had been convicted of a sexual offence (compared with about three per cent for the prison population as a whole). About half of older male prisoners under sentence are sex offenders (Fazel et al 2002), which partly explains the disproportionate number of elderly sex offenders in the studies conducted by ourselves (see Crawley and Sparks 2005a, 2005b, 2006).

The courts have clearly concluded that, although age is 'a factor' to be taken into consideration when making confinement decisions, it is of less consequence than either retributive proportionality or risk. Elderly men convicted of sexual offences are to this extent 'captured' by both the punitive and the risk-management narratives of contemporary penality, a conjunction nicely condensed by Simon (1998) as 'managing the monstrous'. Various other prospects follow; for example, in terms of their offences, many elderly prisoners will be considered sufficiently dangerous to merit being kept in fairly secure or very secure conditions. This has a significant material bearing on many aspects of these prisoners' lives, including their experiences of programmes, facilities and regimes.

Perceptions of risk also impact, of course, on release and resettlement practices; indeed the combination of presumed gravity with risk, together with evident difficulties in finding safe and appropriate resettlement opportunities (Crawley and Sparks 2006) tends to extend the length of time actually served, especially for life sentence prisoners. Whilst only a handful of elderly men receive 'natural life' sentences, a substantial minority have entered advanced old age in prison, and some will die before the end of their sentences. Despite the growing numbers of imprisoned elderly, and repeated calls for concerted action from a variety of reform groups (see Prison Reform Trust 2003) and a former Chief Inspector of Prisons (HMCIP 2001), there is still no national strategy in England and Wales for the proper management of elderly prisoners.

Elderly prisoners are not a homogeneous group. They come from a variety of socio-economic backgrounds and have distinctly different histories. Data on the social and criminal histories of older prisoners indicate that diversity is a hallmark of the long-term prisoner group. Within the older prisoner population as a whole it is possible to identify a number of prisoner 'sub-groups' (Barnes 1999; Aday 2003; Crawley and Sparks 2005a, 2005b). Some have grown old in prison as a result of lengthy sentences, while others are repeat offenders with prior prison experience. Many more have received their sentences late in life and have no prior experience of prison. Sentences range from a few months to life imprisonment for a variety of offences, including fraud, manslaughter, murder, war crimes and the sexual abuse of minors. It is notable, as I indicated above, that many of the latter are 'historic' crimes ie offences allegedly carried out two, three or four decades ago.

Elderly prisoners are much more likely than younger prisoners to experience a strong sense of identity loss, especially if they have come into prison late in life. Such prisoners—the vast majority of whom will never have seen the inside of a prison before except perhaps on the television—are likely to be in a state of trauma, particularly if convicted of 'historic' crimes for which they did not anticipate imprisonment. For these men, a sentence of imprisonment is truly a catastrophe (Crawley and Sparks 2005b). When one considers that the deprivations of prison life are likely to be accompanied by the emotional pain of leaving behind an aged and lifelong spouse, and a way of life and identity that have taken decades to establish, the trauma of receiving a prison sentence in old age is intense. As this 69-year-old man put it:

> It upsets me. We'd never been apart before this. Sometimes I wish I could die. It [the sentence] broke our lives. It's the last part of our life and she's out there and I'm in here.

V. MANAGING DISGUST: PRISON OFFICERS AND THE ELDERLY SEX OFFENDER

The tendency to ignore age-related needs can be compounded by the fact that many elderly prisoners have been convicted of sexual offences. Although these prisoners characteristically require the same services and provisions as elderly people outside prison, they are open to being seen as a less eligible group because of what they have done. For example, when one very elderly man with two sticks hobbled past me during one of my visits to a prison, the officer who was with me said that he called him 'Mr Broken Wing', and that he was:

> A perfect example of somebody that's just trying it on to get sympathy. As soon as he gets past us he'll be walking perfectly.

The use of humour with prisoners—ie joshing, joking and general banter—is much less evident amongst officers working with the elderly than amongst those working with younger adult men. This is largely because the values and social norms of the elderly are very different—both in prisons and in the 'free' community—from those held by young people. As a result, there is little shared experience—and hence no identification and no ongoing dialogue of competent language use—between 'prison officer' and 'old man'. Unlike with male prison officers and young adult prisoners, there is no recognition that there is only a 'thin line between a blue and white shirt and a white shirt' (see Crawley 2004a). This is especially true if the elderly prisoner was imprisoned for a sexual offence.[7]

There is often, then, conflict between the needs of an elderly prisoner (his claim on legitimate expectations as an elderly or infirm individual) and officers' perceptions of him as a 'dirty old man'. In such cases we can clearly see an erasure of needs claims. 'Institutional thoughtlessness', thus conceived, envisages a certain moral and affective flattening, without which it may be difficult to sustain institutional routines. But it also signifies here a tension between the handling of older prisoners *qua* prisoner and the recognition of need or vulnerability *qua* older person. From the prisoner's perspective, the sorts of age-inappropriate treatment involved here may do more than occasion a degree of physical discomfort. They can also be humiliating, serving to remind him of the lowly position that he occupies amongst the prison's concerns and the ease with which the goods and services on which he depends can be withheld from him.

It is also important to note that the idea of 'rehabilitation'—and the policies and practices expressly aimed at bringing 'rehabilitation' about—have no real purchase in the context of elderly prisoners, particularly the very elderly, since they see themselves, and are seen by others in the prison, as 'too old to change' their views and their habits, to benefit from education or training, or to work after release, even if they were to be offered it.

VI. EMOTIONAL SUPPORT FOR ELDERLY PRISONERS

Uniformed staff are generally unaware that elderly prisoners frequently have deep feelings of fear, guilt, loneliness, stress, anxiety or depression, and that positive intervention in the form of group discussions can ameliorate such concerns. They may not be aware, for example, that counselling groups can provide a place for prisoners to identify and express their emotions and to find support from other inmates who feel the same way (Kratcoski 2000). As Kratcoski notes, it is essential for those who work with older inmates 'to become thoroughly familiar with the process of grieving' since loss is a theme that frequently emerges when working with this prisoner group. Feelings of grief about the many losses incurred through imprisonment—loss of freedom, loss of work role, loss of intimate relations with loved ones, loss of identity and the loss of family members and marriage partners—are commonplace amongst elderly men in prison. Support groups

---

[7] During my research into the working lives of prison officers in the UK, numerous officers commented on the similarity of their socio-economic backgrounds to many prisoners. They also recognised that their own behaviour, when younger, could have easily landed them in prison; fortunately, however, they had been able either to grow out of such behaviour or to avoid getting caught. It is in this respect that officers recognise that a 'thin line' exists between the wearing of a white shirt (their own) or the striped blue and white shirt of a prisoner.

can also be helpful in alleviating the emotional pain of prisoners dealing with the death of a loved one, and who would otherwise have no opportunity for structured grief (Aday 2003).

It is also important that officers recognise the abilities and capabilities of many elderly prisoners. As Aday (2003) rightly notes, the elderly prisoner population has very diverse interests and abilities and some elderly men—albeit the more articulate and mobile—are extremely keen to get involved in social activities, even in activities normally reserved for younger men eg computing classes and physical exercise (on this see also Crawley and Sparks 2005b). Participation in such activities can increase feelings of self-esteem, reduce feelings of isolation and depression and help create a sense of purpose. Several of my Canadian interviewees commented that precisely because of their perceived patience, wisdom and ability to calm potentially volatile situations, older prisoners were often made use of by uniformed staff to reduce the level of 'trouble' from younger men on their wings. These elderly men did not, however, *want* this responsibility; as one put it:

> The CSC [Correctional Services of Canada] thinks of us older guys as stable, and that we will keep the boat stable, but we can't and we don't want to. It's too stressful for us.

There are, however, non-exploitative ways of drawing on the talents and experience of older prisoners. It has been argued that those prisoners who will remain incarcerated until they die (either because they have a natural life sentence or because they were already old and in poor health when sentenced) can be helped to cope with the monotonies and emotional challenges of prison life through engaging in special programmes and activities with others (see Aday 2003: 156). In the United States, 'one of the [most] significant phenomena in the health and mental health fields in recent years has been the development of groups in which [elderly] members provide mutual help in dealing with shared difficulties' (Aday 2003: 156).

In the UK the value of mutual support was evident in the (now defunct) Barlinnie Special Unit set up in Scotland in 1974 to manage the most 'disruptive' and 'dangerous' prisoners in the Scottish prison system. These mutual-help/support groups aimed to serve a variety of functions related to the debilitating effects of long-term deprivation. One aspect of the support group was the attempt to minimise the social isolation by the sharing of the prison experience, on the grounds that any negative experience seems less negative if shared with others. Another aspect of this approach was to provide a vehicle for more social interaction. Creative activities such as writing and story-telling can be effective in encouraging elderly prisoners to express and share their experiences, emotions and memories of happier times.

VII. EMOTIONS, EMOTIONAL LABOUR AND ELDERLY PRISONERS:
CONCLUDING REMARKS

Recognising and meeting the needs and predicaments of different groups of prisoners clearly poses a variety of distinctive challenges for prison staff. Working with younger prisoners requires the management, by prison officers, of a range of emotions, including pity, fear and exasperation. While there is evidence that working with the elderly generates a concomitant range of often equally negative emotions amongst prison officers, and that imprisonment can produce extremely painful emotions amongst those incarcerated in the last part of their lives, discussion of these issues is rare in prison sociology. Working with both categories of prisoner—young and old—not only demands that prison officers manage (ie in the sense of suppressing) negative emotions, it also demands that officers are constantly engaging emotionally with prisoners. Indeed, to do their job properly, prison officers have, on occasion, to draw on *all* their resources, intellectual, physical and emotional. Currently, there is no recognition in the job specification or in staff training that working in prison *is* emotionally demanding, and that it can be emotionally draining. Prison officers' partners and families inevitably bear the brunt of the emotional impacts of the job, something for which they themselves were not recruited and for which they are not, of course, paid. This is stressful for both officers and their partners, and it is perhaps no coincidence that amongst this occupational group, levels of domestic violence and marital breakdown are relatively high (Crawley 2002; 2004a).

Working with elderly men presents distinctive emotional challenges to prison officers, for which most are ill-prepared. Whereas they may be able, when pressed, to empathise with younger prisoners by drawing on their knowledge and understanding of their own siblings and children—or indeed memories of themselves at a similar age—their understandings of elderly people's experiences, needs, worldview and difficulties are relatively poor. I have also tried to show that the fact of imprisonment weighs differentially on the older prisoner, with imprisonment in later life often giving rise to high incidences of ill health and psychiatric morbidity, fears of dying in prison or of being released into insecurity and isolation, and a sense of being irrevocably cut off from the past.

My aim in this chapter has been to demonstrate that emotions are central to prison life, not only for the elderly prisoner who must serve out his sentence, but for the prison officer entrusted with his care. Emotions—and their management and mobilisation—are not merely an 'add on' to prison life. On the contrary, the language of the emotions is a central—and very powerful—means by which to communicate what it *means* to live and to work in a prison.

REFERENCES

Adams, R (1992) *Prison Riots in Britain and the USA* (London, Macmillan).

Aday, R and Webster, E (1979) 'Aging in Prison: The Development of a Preliminary Model' 3 (3) *Offender Rehabilitation* 271–82.

Aday, RH (1994) Golden Years Behind Bars: Special Programs and Facilities for Elderly Inmates 58 (2) *Federal Probation* 47–54.

—— (2003) *Aging Prisoners: Crisis in American Corrections* (Westport, Praeger Publications).

Barbalet, J (1998) *Emotion, Social Theory and Social Structure* (Cambridge, Cambridge University Press).

Barnes, L (1999) 'Doing Time Quietly: A Profile of Older Prisoners and their Experiences of Imprisonment in South Australia' (unpublished thesis, Faculty of law, University of Sydney, Australia).

Bendelow, G and Williams, SJ (eds) (1998) *Emotions in Social Life* (London, Routledge).

Boyle, J (1984) *The Pain of Confinement* (London, Pan Books).

Burnside, I and Schmidt, MG (1995) *Working with Older Adults* (Sudbury, Jones and Bartlett).

Clemmer, D (1940) *The Prison Community* (Boston, Christopher Publishing Company).

Cohen, S and Taylor, L (1972) *Psychological Survival* (Harmondsworth, Penguin).

Crawley, E (2002) 'Bringing it all Back Home? The Impact of Prison Officers' Work on their Families' 49(4) *Probation Journal*.

—— (2004a) *Doing Prison Work: the Public and Private Lives of Prison Officers* (Cullompton, Willan Publishing).

—— (2004b) 'Emotion and Performance: Prison Officers and the Presentation of Self in Prisons' 6(4) *Punishment and Society* 411–27.

—— (2004c) 'Release and Resettlement: Older Prisoner Perspectives' 56 *Criminal Justice Matters*.

—— (2004d) 'Prison Officers and Prison Work' December *Prison Service News*.

—— (2005) 'Life After Imprisonment? Resettlement and Elderly Men' July *Prison Service Journal*.

Crawley, E and Sparks, R (2005a) 'Hidden Injuries? Researching the Experiences of Older Men in English Prisons' 44(4) *The Howard Journal of Criminal Justice*.

—— (2005b) 'Older Men in Prison: Survival, Coping and Identity' in A Liebling and S Maruna (eds), *The Effects of Imprisonment* (Cullompton, Willan Publishing).

—— (2006) 'Is There Life after Imprisonment? How Elderly Men Talk about Imprisonment and Release' 6(1) *Journal of Criminal Justice*, Special Issue 'What Lies Beyond? Problems, Prospects and Possibilities for Life after Imprisonment'.

Darwin, C (1872) *The Expression of the Emotions in Man and Animals* (London, Murray).

Fazel, S, Hope, T, O'Donnell, I and Jacoby, R (2002) 'Psychiatric, Demographic and Personality Characteristics of Elderly Sex Offenders' 32 *Psychological Medicine* 219–26.

—— (2004) 'Unmet Treatment Needs of Older Prisoners: a Primary Care Survey, short report' *Age and Ageing*.

Fineman, S and Gabriel, Y (1996) *Experiencing Organisations* (London, Sage).

Fitzgerald, M (1977) *Prisoners in Revolt* (Harmondsworth, Penguin).

Goffman, E (1959) *The Presentation of Self in Everyday Life* (New York, Doubleday).

—— (1963) *Behaviour in Public Places* (New York, Free Press).

Hochschild, A (1983) *The Managed Heart* (Berkley, University of California Press).

—— (1998) 'The Sociology of Emotion as a Way of Seeing' in G Bendelow and SJ Williams (eds) *Emotions in Social Life* (London, Routledge).

HMCIP (2001) *HM Prison Kingston: Report of a Full Announced Inspection 12–16 February* (London, Home Office),

Home Office (1994) *Report of the Enquiry into the Escape of Six Prisoners from the Special Security Unit at Whitemoor Prison, Cambridgeshire on Friday 9th September 1994 (The Woodcock Report)* (London, HMSO).

Jamieson, R, Crawley, E, Grounds, A and Noble, B (2003) *Older Prisoners in Custody and on Release: Lessons from the Canadian Experience* Report to Canadian High Commission Institutional Research Programme.

Kratcoski, PC (2000) 'Older Inmates: Special Programming Concerns' in PC Kratcoski (ed) *Correctional Counseling and Treatment* (Prospect Heights, Waveland Press).

Lawler, J (1994) *Behind the Scenes: Nursing, Somology and the Problem of the Body* (Melbourne, Churchill Livingstone).

Lella, JW and Pawluch, D (1988) 'Medical Students and the Cadaver in Social and Cultural Context' in M Lock and DRGordon (eds) *Biomedicine Examined* (Dordrecht and Boston, Kluwer Academic Publishers).

Mangham, I and Overington, M (1987) *Organizations as Theatre* (Chichester, Wiley).

Mercier, V (1926) *The Irish Comic Tradition* (Oxford, Clarendon Press).

Prison Reform Trust (2003) *Growing Old in Prison: a Scoping Study on Older Prisoners* (London, Centre for Policy on Ageing and Prison Reform Trust).

Santos, M (1995) *Profiles from Prison: Adjusting to Life Behind Bars* (Westport, Praeger Publishing).

Serge, V (1977) *Men in Prison* (London, Writers and Readers Publishing Co-operative).

Simon, J (1998) 'Managing the Monstrous: Sex Offenders and the New Penology' 3 *Psychology, Public Policy and Law* 452–67.

Sparks, RJ, Bottoms, AE and Hay, W (1996) *Prisons and the Problem of Order* (Oxford, Oxford University Press).

Strauss, AA and Sherwin, R (1975) 'Inmate Rioters and Non-Rioters: A Comparative Analysis' 34(3 and 4) *American Journal of Corrections* 34–35, 54–58.

Sykes, G (1958) *The Society of Captives* (Princeton, Princeton University Press).

Thomas, T (2005) *Sex Crime: Sex Offending and Society* (Cullompton, Willan Publishing).

Toseland, RW (1995) *Group Work with the Elderly and Family Care-Givers* (New York, Springer).

Vygotsky, L (1986) *Thought and Language* (Cambridge, MIT Press).

—— (1987) *The Collected Works of LS Vygotsky* vol 1 'Problems of General Psychology' (New York, Plenum Press).

Woolf, Lord Justice (1991) *Prison Disturbances, April 1990* (London, HMSO).

Part IV

Violence, Reconciliation and Conflict Resolution: Dealing with Collective Emotions

13

*Alienation, Love and Hate as Causes of Collective Violence**

THOMAS J SCHEFF

I. INTRODUCTION

MOST CONTEMPORARY DISCUSSIONS of group violence are entirely descriptive (see, for example, Kressel 2002). Psychological explorations of collective 'evil' are also largely descriptive, even though they refer to the most basic component of ethnocentrism, the 'us-them' attitude. Both Baumeister (1997) and Staub (2003) have written about collective violence, but lack an explicit theory of individual and collective dynamics.

A first step into a dynamic theory of ethnocentrism is suggested by Durkheim's (1915) idea that any enduring religion requires the interplay between belief, on the one hand, and ritual, on the other. He proposed that the elemental basis for religion is the reciprocal relation of belief to ritual, and vice versa. Belief leads to ritual, and ritual to belief, in a closed loop. Organised religion can be viewed as a social system arising out of the interaction between belief and ritual, ideas and actions.

Viewing religion as a social system can further understanding of blind allegiance to one's group. But more detail will be needed. In particular, we need to understand how ethnocentrism is generated not only in the world of ideology and action, but also in the emotional/relational world. How is collective violence forged out of belief, ritual, emotion and relationships?

Benedict Anderson (1991) has suggested that a nation is an 'imagined community.' Although he doesn't develop the idea, this phrase suggests what might be seen as an anomaly. We all know many people personally: our neighbours, work associates and members of our own families and other groups. Yet we may identify with, and will lay down our lives to protect people we don't necessarily know. For reasons that will be considered

* This chapter is based in part on ch 11 in my book on Goffman (Scheff 2005). I am indebted to Bernard Phillips for his advice on both versions.

below, it may be much easier to identify with imagined people you don't know then real ones that you do. Even in smaller groups, such as families and youth gangs, much of what participants know about each other may be largely imagined.

The social theory of GH Mead (1936) and recent discussions of infatuation may be the next steps toward further understanding. Mead argued that the self is social, a response to a community that is, in great part, imagined. The core of this theory is what he called 'taking the role of the other', by which he meant viewing a situation not only from our own point of view, but also from the point of view of the other(s). His concept of 'the generalised other' makes it clear that role-taking refers not only to people that we know, but also to those that we only imagine. Although Mead didn't explicitly discuss the possibility of identifying with the imagined other, his theory implies it.

One example of an imagined point of view that one might identify with is posterity: one imagines what future generations might think of oneself, and judges oneself, from that point of view. A more common generalisation of the other would be for a white person to imagine the point of view of all other whites and all non-whites, identifying with the imagined white point of view. The only step remaining for forming an 'us and them' mentality would be to idealise the one at the expense of the other.

Imagining the point of view of the other(s) occurs not only in ethnocentrism, but is a commonplace requirement of everyday life. Since ordinary language is extremely ambiguous, one must take the point of view of the other in order to understand even fairly simple statements. A crucial part of the context of any message is the point of view of the person(s) from whom one received the message. As Cooley (1922) said, 'We live in the minds of others without knowing it'. But the 'us and them' mentality requires not only imagining points of view of two communities, but also identifying with one and rejecting the other. When I complained to one of my in-laws about our careless destruction in Iraq and the death or injury of many of its people, he said: 'Better them then us.'

One problem with Mead's scheme is that he didn't worry about the accuracy with which we imagine the point of view of the other(s). His theory seems to imply accuracy, which can't possibly be always, or even, typically, true. I will return to this issue below, in the discussion of infatuation. The other issue pursued here, more extensively than the issue of accuracy, will be the emotional aspects of role-taking. Neither Mead nor Anderson has anything to say about emotions. This paper will suggest that they play a dominant part in the kind of identification and rejection that leads to aggression.

Most discussions of ethnocentrism give little or no attention to the role of emotions. For example, it has been argued that military service simply involves the meeting of one's obligations, as in any other institution (Hinde and Watson 1994). The willingness of soldiers to die for others is simply normative. It is probably true that much of what goes on in the human world can be explained in this way: we merely follow the rules. Perhaps this kind of explanation is best for understanding the everyday world. But it is also true that every day, some rules are broken or ignored. In times of change or crisis, many key rules are ignored. Without invoking the emotional/relational world, it is difficult to understand the fervour of ethnocentrism. Untold millions of people have gratuitously laid down their lives, and taken the lives of others, in the name of their nation or other imagined communities.

Such willingness is understandable when it is quite clear that one's group is in danger because of a threat by another group. Yet current and past history suggests that most participants support killing and the threat of being killed purely 'on spec', even without plausible evidence. The war on Iraq is one instance, and WWI, which commenced without any real attempt at peacemaking, and with little immediate threat (Scheff 1994), is another.

Few people would be willing to die for their neighbourhood, county, state, trade or other group. My own professional association is the American Sociological Association. Although I have been laying down dollars every year for many years in order to belong to it, I wouldn't kill to avoid its hostile take-over by another discipline. The ASA *may* have a few such members, disciplinary patriots. For the rest of us, words, yes, but not bombs and bullets.

There is another, much smaller group that may demand blind loyalty, the immediate family. An earlier study illustrated this dynamic (Scheff 1995). In conflict-ridden families, the child will often identify with, and idealise one parent, and vilify the other. This pattern is particularly prevalent in, but not limited to families of divorced parents. Lakeoff (1996) has argued that the family of origin ideology forms the basis around which extreme ethnocentrism is built. In particular, the father's role is seen as strict and unyielding, rather than compassionate.

This paper proposes that both family dynamics and ethnocentrism can be further understood by investigation of the emotional/relational worlds in which they occur. In particular, that infatuation and shame/rage are the key elements of the social psychological dynamics shared by conflictual families, gangs, nations and ethnic groups

II. INFATUATION AND HATRED

To begin to understand the social/psychological dynamics of fervent ethnocentrism, it will be necessary to understand what is meant by 'love of country', on the one hand, and hatred of its supposed enemies, on the other.[1]

---

[1] I use the phrase 'love of country' because these exact words are often used in us-them situations, but it should be understood that the dynamics discussed here apply to any and all ingroup-outgroup conflict.

These terms in vernacular usage may not be as simple and straightforward as they seem. They can be used as mystifications that both distort and hide the nature of the emotional/relational world.

The use of ordinary words, rather than well-defined concepts, is a pressing problem in all of social science. If one uses ordinary language, rather than clearly defined concepts, one runs the risk of entrapment in the assumptive world of one's culture. For example, there have been a vast number of studies of alienation and of self-esteem that assume these words need not be defined. Although there are many, many standardised scales, there have been few attempts to decide, conceptually, what it is that these scales are supposed to be measuring.

To this day, most key concepts in social science are quite ambiguous. Some of them, such as alienation and self-esteem, may involve too many potentially orthogonal meanings (such as individual, relational, cognitive, and emotional dimensions) to be measured by a single instrument. Others, such as irrationality or context, for example, may be mere residual categories, conceptually empty boxes, because they encompass the enormously wide variety of different kinds of things that remain after their polar opposite has been explored in detail.

A. Ambiguity in the Meaning of Love

The word 'love' provides a vivid example of the first kind of ambiguity, a kind of umbrella word that encompasses many different facets. Aldous Huxley suggested 'we use the word love for the most amazing variety of relationships, ranging from what we feel for our mothers to what we feel for someone we beat up in a bordello, or its many equivalents.'

The comment about beating someone up out of love is probably not an exaggeration. A recent set of experiments suggests that subjects' condemnation of murder is softened if they are told that it was caused by jealousy (Puente and Cohen 2003). These subjects seem to entertain the idea that one can love someone so much that one kills them, loving them to death. Solomon (1981: 3–4) elaborates on the broad sweep of the word love:

> Consider ... the wealth of meticulous and fine distinctions we make in describing our feelings of hostility: hatred, loathing, scorn, anger, revulsion, resentment, envy, abhorrence, malice, aversion, vexation, irritation, annoyance, disgust, spite and contempt, or worse, 'beneath' contempt. And yet we sort out our positive affections for the most part between the two limp categories, 'liking' and 'loving.' We distinguish our friends from mere acquaintances and make a ready distinction between lovers and friends whom we love 'but not that way.' Still, one and the same word serves to describe our enthusiasm for apple strudel, respect for a distant father, the anguish of an uncertain romantic affair and nostalgic affection for an old pair of slippers ...

In modern societies this usage may defend against the painful absence of true intimacy and community. The idea seems to be that *any* kind of relationship that has positive elements in it, even if mixed with extremely negative ones, can be called love.

B. What does Love Mean?

One place to seek definitions is the dictionary. In the English language, unabridged dictionaries provide some *two dozen* meanings for love, most of them applicable to romantic or other human relationships. These are the first two meanings in the *American Heritage Dictionary* (1992):

1. A deep, tender, ineffable feeling of affection and solicitude toward a person, such as that arising from kinship, recognition of attractive qualities, or a sense of underlying oneness.
2. A feeling of intense desire and attraction toward a person with whom one is disposed to make a pair; the emotion of sex and romance.

These two definitions are of great interest, because they touch upon several complexities. The distinction between non-erotic and erotic love that the two definitions make is obviously necessary. The idea that love is ineffable (indescribable), however, is tendentious. I can sympathise, because genuine love turns out to be complex and counter-intuitive. For this and other reasons, both popular and scholarly accounts flirt with the idea that one of the crowning qualities of love is that it is mysterious and therefore indescribable.

Contradicting this idea, I propose two definitions of love, one in its romantic form, the other the non-romantic form, that might be used instead of the vernacular word. The idea that love is ineffable, it seems to me, while romantic, may be a way of defending the status quo in modern alienated societies. My definition of romantic love contains three components. Two are physical: sexual attraction and attachment. One is cognitive/emotional; I call it attunement (balanced mutual awareness between self and other). Omitting the component of sexual attraction, non-romantic love is otherwise the same: it is made up of the other two 'A's', attachment and attunement.

The attunement component is like Solomon's idea (1994: 235):

> love [is] shared identity, a redefinition of self which no amount of sex or fun or time together will add up to ... Two people in a society with an extraordinary sense of individual identity mutually fantasise, verbalise and act their way into a relationship that can no longer be understood as a mere conjunction of the two but only as a complex one.

Although Solomon doesn't use terms like 'mutual awareness' or 'intersubjectivity', they are clearly implied. In passing, he also might be implying another aspect of what I would call genuine love, that one's individual identity is held in balance with identifying with the other(s). One's own autonomous self is valued no more than the other(s), but also no less. It is this feature that differentiates between true solidarity and engulfment. The implication is that moments of unity with the other(s) are, in the long run, balanced against moments of individual autonomy.

This idea is expressed in the poem, 'To Have without Holding', by Marge Piercy (1980):

> Learning to love differently is hard...It hurts to thwart the reflexes
> of grab, of clutch; to love and let go again and again...
> as we make and unmake in passionate diastole and systole the rhythm
> of our unbound bonding, to have and not to hold, to love
> with minimized malice, hunger and anger moment by moment balanced.

The poem comes very close to making explicit the moment-by-moment dance of togetherness and separateness, unity and autonomy that characterises genuine love/solidarity.

This idea can be used to distinguish love from its look-alikes, such as infatuation and engulfment. What most participants profess to be love of their country, ethnic group or gang lacks the perquisite of balanced shared identity, but is closer to being infatuation. Similarly, what is called hatred of supposed enemies could be a gloss on a complex process of hiding feelings of inadequacy and alienation under the cover of 'pride' in one's country, as will be discussed below. The meaning of love and pride are so ambiguous in ordinary language that that they can easily be used in the service of defensive manoeuvres, such as denial and projection.

Genuine love requires detailed knowledge of the other(s). Having only an image of the other's appearance, say, or some other single quality, is not love but infatuation. In this sense, it is not possible to actually love a celebrity whom one has never met, and whose real life and character are unknown. If one were to ever get a chance to know the actual person, 'love' might receive a rude shock. The star who seemed wonderful from a distance might turn out to be, at best, a mere mortal person like the rest of us, rather than a god or goddess. Genuine love means loving warts and all, not just admiring best or imagined features from afar.

Love is distinguishable from infatuation, which is mostly about the lover, rather than the love object or the relationship, since infatuation is self-generated fantasy. Collective infatuation is not only self-generated, but also socially amplified. Groups, like fan clubs, can whip their participants into an ecstasy of adoration. Unlike fan clubs, groups also do the opposite, amplifying individual negative feelings into orgies of hatred and rage.

Both individual and collective infatuation can be an enormously arresting, intense experience. The idealisation of a mere image of the other(s), unlike genuine love, has no reality check, and therefore can spiral into infinity. The great never-ending stream of poetry of romantic infatuation bears witness to the infinitely intense experience of the 'lover':

For should I see thee a little moment,
Straight my voice is hushed;
Yea, my tongue is broken, and
Through me
'Neath the flesh, impalpable fire
Runs tingling;
Nothing sees mine eyes, and a
Voice of roaring
Waves in my ear sounds;
Sweat runs down in rivers, a
Tremor seizes
All my limbs, and paler than
Grass in autumn,
Caught by pains of menacing
Death, I falter,
Lost in the love-trance.
(Symonds 1833).

In the last line, Sappho calls her ecstasy/nightmare a 'love-trance'. But I would call it, at the risk of seeming a killjoy, an infatuation-trance. Although this particular poem was written over 2500 years ago, the same sentiments can be found in current pop song lyrics, if much less artfully represented.

Similarly intense feelings of infatuation form the dominant emotion in the propaganda of any nation preparing for or engaging in war. One clear example occurred in the patriotic novels, lyrics, and poetry of France during the period between wars with Germany (1871–1914: Scheff 1994). Most exiguous was the 'military poetry' of the right-wing extremist Paul de Roulede. His 'Songs of a Soldier' (1872) gushed passionate 'love' for the glory of France, and demanded revenge on Germany as necessary for the honour of France. It had gone through an unprecedented 83 editions by 1890, making it one of the most popular French language books ever published.

The infatuation-trance of blind patriotism is like the naked trust that small children have in their parents. For the first six years of life, at least, most children form an idealised image of their parents as authorities who can do no wrong, like gods on earth. It appears that for many adults, whether or not they retain this nursery image of the actual parent, they transfer it to the leader of their nation or other group. It is very difficult to overcome such an image, no matter the mounting evidence that it is untrue.

After 9/11, some of my colleagues were asking 'Why do they hate us?' But if I answered by pointing to the machinations of our government over the last 50 years in the Middle East and the slaughter and mayhem that had resulted, they rapidly lost interest. They didn't want to hear, with no concern even with whether what I had said was true or not.

III. COLLECTIVE HATRED AND RAGE

Collective hatred, like collective 'love', can achieve much higher levels of intensity than that of individuals, but the spiral is hidden and complex. To understand this process, it may be necessary to forgo everyday vernacular explanations. I propose that hatred is the commonly used word for overt anger-based hidden vulnerable emotions, particularly grief, fear, and shame. One elemental source of hatred may be the shame of not belonging, forming groups that reject the group(s) supposedly rejecting them. The culture of such groups generates *techniques of neutralisation* that encourage hatred and mayhem. At the level of individuals, there is rage generated by threatened or damaged bonds. There are also social and cultural spirals that give rise to collective hatred and rage.

Dictionary definitions of hatred focus on hostility as the key component:

Hatred: 1. To feel hostility or animosity toward. To detest.
2. To feel dislike or distaste for: I hate washing dishes.
Animosity: Bitter hostility or open enmity; active hatred.
American Heritage Dictionary (2000)

The inclusion of animosity in the definition is important because it emphasises the intensity that is usually involved in hatred, counteracting the scaling-down of the word in everyday, non-conflict situations, as in encounters with dirty dishes. The definition of animosity includes both bitter hostility, an attitude that may or may not be expressed, and open enmity.

The key to the intensity or bitterness of hatred seems to be an emotion that is a hidden component of rage and aggression: unacknowledged shame or humiliation. One way to deal with the feeling that one has been rejected is to reject the rejector, rather than to blame oneself as unworthy. This is the process that needs to be expressed in emotional/relational language, as well as in cognitive and behavioural terms.

Hidden, covert shame, in combination with either hidden or overt rage, may be the primary components of hatred. The first step is to discuss intense rage. An immediate problem in making this argument persuasive is the difficulty of describing in words the experience of rage and other compelling emotions. When readers are sitting the comfort of their study, feeling more or less safe and secure, it will take some effort to visualise the intensity of 'war fever', or of the feelings that lead to massive violence.

The intensity and primitiveness of humiliated fury beggars verbal description. Unless one is a great artist, how is one to convey intense feelings with mere words? A verbal description of emotions is two-dimensional and flat, like a mountain represented on a map. The twelfth-century Irish epic, *The Tain* (cited in Cahill 1995) attempted verbally to bridge the gap between word and reality:

> [Cuchulainn then] went into the middle of them and beyond, and mowed down great ramparts of his enemies' corpses.

This sentence is excerpted from a long passage that describes intense fury by exaggeration, since it is impossible that a single warrior, no matter how powerful, could wage such wholesale destruction.

Certain emotions in sequence, and the social and cultural settings that generate these emotions, could be key causes of the kind of intense hatred that leads to rage and violence. Most social science writing on violent conflict assumes a 'realist' or materialist perspective, that the real causes of human conduct always involve physical, rather than social and psychological reality. Nevertheless, eliminating emotional and relational elements as causes of violence may be a gross error. It is easy to do because of the difficulty of conveying emotional states in words, as already indicated. Those who map mountains without also viewing them can easily lose touch with their immensity.

I am not arguing that material conditions are unimportant, only that violence is caused by a combination of physical and social/psychological elements. Greed is usually an important component of the motivation of leaders, but much less so for followers. I will consider hatred first at the level of individuals, then at the collective level, showing how both hatred and violence are products of unacknowledged emotions, which are in turn generated by alienation and by cultural scripts for demonising purported enemies.

This is another example from *The Tain* (Cahill 1995) describing the outward appearance of a warrior in a fit of rage:

> The first warp-spasm seized Cuchulainn, and made him into a monstrous thing, hideous and shapeless, unheard of. His shanks and his joints, every knuckle and angle and organ from head to foot, shook like a tree in the flood or a reed in the stream.

The extraordinary intensity of enraged actions, as described in the first quotation, and of the experience of rage, as suggested in the second, leads to the belief that rage is a virtually irresistible force and that it is an elemental component of human nature. This essay will contradict both of these beliefs, first that it is an elemental, and secondly, that it is irresistible.

The ability of primitive warriors and current killers on the world scene to work themselves into a state of rage suggests that it is something that can be constructed, rather than an elemental. How is it done? We will probably never know the answer to that question. But studies of actual discourse suggest a sequence of events that seem always to occur prior to the outbreak of violent rage. At the group level, it may be that alienation and certain cultural beliefs militate toward states of hatred, rage, and violent behaviour.

A. Shame and Hate

As already indicated, rage seems to be a composite affect, a sequence of two elemental emotions, shame and anger. This idea has been advanced by other authors, notably Heinz Kohut (1971), and Helen Lewis (1971). Kohut proposed that violent anger of the kind he called 'narcissistic rage' was a shame/anger compound. Lewis suggested that shame and anger have a deep affinity, and that one can find indications of unacknowledged shame occurring just prior to any episode of intense hostility.

This sequence has been shown in many transactions during psychotherapy sessions by Lewis (1971), in four marital quarrels (Retzinger 1991), and in Hitler's writings and speeches (Scheff 1994). Retzinger demonstrated that prior to each of the 16 episodes of angry escalation in her cases, there had been first an insult by one party, indications of unacknowledged shame in the other party, and finally intense hostility in that party. This sequence can be seen as the motor of violence, since it connects the intense emotions of shame and anger to overt aggression.

Although there has been little research focused explicitly on pure, unalloyed anger, indications from the studies of discourse by Lewis (1971), Retzinger (1991) and my own work, (such as Scheff 1990) suggest that pure anger is rare and unlikely to lead to violence or even social disruption. On the contrary, anger by itself is usually brief and instructive. A person who is frustrated and unashamed of her anger is mobilised to tell succinctly what is going on, and to do and say what is needed, without making a huge scene.

In my own case, I can testify that most of my experiences of anger have involved shame/anger, either in the form of humiliated fury, or in a more passive form, what Labov and Fanshel (1977) call 'helpless anger'. Both of these variants are long-lasting and extremely unpleasant. Shame-induced anger was unpleasant while happening, and even more unpleasant when it was over, since I inevitably felt foolish and out of control.

But in the few episodes of what seems to have been, in retrospect, pure anger, the experience was entirely different. I did not raise my voice, nor did I put anyone down or any other kind of excess. I simply told my view of what was going on directly, rapidly and with no calculation or planning. I was overcome with what might be called 'machine gun mouth'. Everyone who was present to one of these communications suddenly became quite respectful. I didn't feel out of control, even though my speech was completely spontaneous; on the contrary, I was wondering why I had not had my say before. It would seem that anger without shame has only a signal function, to alert self and others to one's frustration.

When anger has its source in feelings of rejection or inadequacy, and when the latter feelings are not acknowledged, a continuous spiral of shame/anger may result, which may be experienced as hatred and rage.

Rather than expressing and discharging one's shame through laughter ('Silly me!', or 'Silly us!'), it is masked by rage and aggression. One can be angry that one is ashamed, and ashamed that one is angry, and so on, working up to a loop of unlimited duration and intensity. This loop may be the emotional basis of lengthy episodes, or even life-long hatred that seems intense beyond endurance.

Earlier essays (Scheff 2003; 2005) proposed that physical aggression or complete withdrawal are common components of hypermasculinity, which in turn has social/emotional bases, as follows: 1. No affectional attachments. 2. A single overarching obsession. 3. Complete repression of shame. Only to the extent that all three of these conditions are fully met is silence or destructive violence likely. My 2005 essay used Hitler's and William Calley's (US Army officer found guilty of murder for his role in the the My Lai Massacre on 16 March 1968) biographies to show how completely episodes from their lives illustrate all three of these conditions. Although women with this pattern would be as likely as men to commit or condone violent acts, men appear to qualify much more frequently and fully than women.

Most men are trained from early childhood to suppress all vulnerable emotions, especially fear, grief, love, and shame. Parents and male children usually confound fear with cowardice, and grief and shame with weakness. After thousands of episodes of intentional suppression, men learn to numb out these feelings automatically. In terms of the theory proposed here, the repression of shame is the core process in hypermasculinity, because it numbs out both fear and conscience. Killing or maiming other humans would be intensely painful if the automatic shame response were still in play.

In her essay, *Let Them Eat War*, Hochschild (2005) suggests a similar mechanism of defence to explain why working class men, against their economic interests, supported a cowboy ex-President. She argues that Bush covered his own fears and other vulnerable emotions by aggressive action, a pattern that these males also follow, or would like to. This analysis points to key issue in understanding how reactionary leaders generate support among their followers (as was the case with Hitler's appeal to the Germans). Their appeal is largely social and emotional, rather that economic or ideological.

Similarly, youth gangs, especially male gangs, serve as arenas for the inculcation and testing of hypermasculine toughness. Although there are also female gangs in large US cities, they are much fewer in number and produce substantially less physical violence. The penchant for multiple killings, especially at random, is virtually a male domain. Gangs serve the material interests of their members, but violence is hardly ever good business. Next to the military, youth gangs are the primary vehicle for the numbing out of the emotional/relational world, that results in hypermasculinity.

Collective hatred and violence seems to depend on the suppression of other vulnerable emotions, not just shame. Volkan (2004) has made a convincing case that the most lethal violence is caused by the humiliation of groups that have suppressed collective grief. Many groups, he notes, have what he calls 'Chosen Traumas', a historical episode of massive loss. For examples, he shows that the chosen trauma of the Serbs, their defeat at the Battle of Kosovo in 1389, has taken on such a great symbolic/emotional value that reference to it is needed to understand the tragedies in Bosnia in 1992 and Kosovo in 1999 (2004: 50).

Particularly relevant to the understanding of mass violence is Volkan's idea that chosen traumas may give rise to collective feelings of entitlement to revenge. He also makes the connection between collective and individual emotions:

> serious threats to large-group identity, such as shared helplessness and humiliation, are perceived by members of that large group as *individually* wounding and *personally* endangering: they induce a collective response of anxiety or terror. (2004: 33)

This linking of personal and collective responses makes sense to me in terms of responses to 9/11 that I have seen in persons close to me. Within my large extended family, only two persons reacted in this way. But their response exactly illustrates Volkan's point; they went into an aggressive funk, continually declaring their hatred of 'the enemy' and their love for their country. They exhibited blind trust for the Bush regime, in exactly the way that Volkan proposes.

My own initial reaction to 9/11 was also extreme, but in a different way. Rather than an aggressive funk, I went into a depressive one. After watching the assault on the Towers on TV many times, I fell into a trance-like state of disorientation and horror. This state persisted even after I finally turned off the TV. On the next day, however, a different kind of episode occurred that lifted me out of depression.

As I was driving in my car, I heard radio interviews of survivors from the WTC. I noticed that several of them mentioned that when they were running down the stairs to escape, they were quite surprised to see policemen and firemen running up the stairs. As it turned out, some of these men sacrificed their own lives trying to help others escape. After turning off the radio, as I was thinking of the courage of these men, I burst into tears. I cried for a long time, convulsively, like a baby. After the cry, I felt myself again.

What happened? My interpretation is that seeing the Towers fall had left me in a state of helpless humiliation, grief, and fear. Like most men, I was unable to manage these particular emotions, since at some level, I am still ashamed of them. So I suppressed them, leading to my funk. But I felt pride when I identified with the brave men who sacrificed their lives helping others. The pride countered my shame, leading to an episode of effective mourning. A comparison of my episode, and the failure to mourn by my two in-laws, illustrates Volkan's idea about the importance of unresolved grief and shame in collective responses to trauma.

Smith (2006) has contributed to the understanding of the role of humiliation in violence with his analysis of the social-emotional impact of globalisation. He is able to integrate the political, economic and social approaches with a social-emotional one, showing how people who have been subjected by military or economic means tend to feel intense humiliation, how this feeling can lead to terrorism and/or chains of revenge and counter-revenge.

B. Conditions for Intergroup Hatred

Another essay (Scheff 1997: ch 3) described how *bimodal alienation* generates violence at the collective level. Bimodal alienation between groups occurs when there is 'isolation' between them, but 'engulfment' within them. On the one hand, members of group A are distant from members of group B, and vice versa. But on the other, members of each group are infatuated with each other, to the point that they give up important parts of themselves, in order to be completely loyal to the group. A very wealthy and influential person in my local community said to me: 'I am a patriot. When my country wants something, I give it, no questions asked.' I said, 'Suppose you have doubts?' He said, 'Not possible. My country comes first.' Idealising the nation means suppressing one's own thoughts and feelings.

The initial motor in this theory is the need to belong. It makes sense that the German language has the most beautiful word for home, in the sense of the place that you belong: *die Heimat*. As both Elias (1995) and I (1994) have argued, historically the Germans seem to have long had an unsatisfied yearning for a place in which they belong, and have had great difficulty in managing the feeling of rejection, of not belonging and being accepted.

Members of a group who feel unaccepted both by foreigners and in their own group are in a position to surrender their individual identity in order to be accepted, giving rise in the German case to the principle of *Obrigkeitsdenken* (blind loyalty and obedience). Bimodal alienation (isolation between groups and engulfment within them) may be the fundamental condition for inter-group conflict.

Under the condition of bimodal alienation, a special culture develops within each group that encourages the acting out of unacknowledged resentment and hatred. There are various ways of characterising this culture, but for my purposes I will describe it in terms of 'techniques of neutralisation'. This idea was originally formulated in criminology (Sykes and Matza 1957) to explain how and why teenagers engage in delinquent behaviour, how a special culture develops among them that neutralises the norms in their larger culture that oppose crime. But the idea has also been carefully applied by Alverez (1997) to the behaviour of the German people in tolerating or actually engaging in genocide.

Alverez shows how each of Sykes' and Matza's five techniques of neutralisation can be used to explain the special culture that developed during the Nazi regime, a culture which neutralised the norms in the larger culture that forbid murder.

First, The Denial of Responsibility. Alverez shows that this technique in the German case usually took the form that the perpetrator was only carrying out orders from above.

Secondly, the Denial of Injury under the Nazi regime took the form of special language that hid or disguised what was actually being done, euphemisms in which killing became 'special treatment', 'cleansing' (also applied to the massacres in Bosnia), and many other similar examples.

Thirdly, the Denial of Victim asserts that the victim actually brought about their own downfall. In the German case, Hitler and his followers believed that the Jews were involved in a conspiracy to enslave the whole world, so that killing them was a matter of self-defence. Although entirely fictitious, many Germans appear to have believed this account to have been literally true.

Fourthly, Condemning the Condemners involved, in the German case, claims by the German government and media that other countries that were condemning Germany were historically guilty of even worse crimes, such as the treatment of blacks and Native Americans in the United States, and the treatment of native peoples in the French, British and Spanish empires.

Fifthly, in the Appeal to Higher Loyalties, German perpetrators of genocide thought of themselves as patriots, nobly carrying out their duty.

Finally, the Denial of Humanity is a category that Alverez himself added to those formulated by Sykes and Matza, because of its special relevance to the Holocaust. Typical Nazi propaganda portrayed Jews and other non-Aryans as subhuman, filled with bestial impulses, such as the urge for destruction, primitive desires, and unparalleled evil. Although dehumanisation often accompanies inter-group conflict, it seems in the German case that it was explicitly orchestrated by the government. There are many cognates, such as the use of the German word for 'extermination', ordinarily applied only to the killing of insects.

Any one of these six techniques can serve to encourage violence by neutralising the norms against aggression and murder. To the extent that they are all implemented together, as they apparently were under the Nazi regime, to that degree a whole society can forgo its normal moral values in order to engage in wholesale slaughter. The idea of techniques of neutralisation suggests the cultural foundation for collective violence. In the remainder of this section, I will focus on the issue of reducing the emotional bases of violence, by dealing with shame and alienation that has gone unacknowledged.

It is important to note that including emotional/relational dimensions of conflict adds new meaning to the idea of rationality, and the sources of rationality and irrationality. Volkan's (2004) idea of collective regression especially emphasises the irrationality that is generated by unacknowledged emotions. Another aspect of irrational violence is suggested by the idea that conscience and morality are basically driven by access to emotions. When emotions, especially shame, are repressed, any kinds of irrational violence are admissible. This view makes emotional repression the key to techniques of neutralisation, rather than ideology. Ideologies that are connected with collective violence are extraordinarily various, but underlying these many varieties, there seems to be a single emotional/relational dynamic.

C. Practical Applications

How can spirals of unresolved grief, unacknowledged shame and anger be avoided or slowed when they are occurring? One answer may lie in the direction of effective mass mourning and acknowledgement of shame. Acknowledgement, however, does not refer to merely verbal acknowledgement, as in the routine confessions at Alcoholics Anonymous and its spin-offs. Unfortunately, there have been very few discussions of this issue. Acknowledgment is one of those terms, like 'working through' in psychoanalysis, that play a central role in professional discourse, but are seldom defined or even illustrated through concrete examples.

This discussion points toward several paths for conciliation between belligerent groups. My theory of protracted conflict suggests that the foremost cause is mass alienation within and between the groups. Any steps that would decrease mass alienation would lessen the potential for conflict. Some examples follow.

An earlier essay on alienation (Scheff 1997: ch 4) proposed that teachers need to be retrained to be aware of the way in which they reject women, working class and minority students. I also suggest classes on family relations that would help young people form stable families. In that same essay I recommend reform for welfare programmes, to lessen rejection and shame. Young men form the bulk of combatants for inter-group and international conflict. If they could be better integrated into work or welfare, school, and family, they would be less vulnerable to pressure to fight an external, and often, what amounts to an imagined enemy.

At the level of culture, to undermine the sources of intergroup conflict, we may need to counter the techniques of neutralisation (Sykes and Matza 1957; Alverez 1997) that are used to foment hatred and violence toward purported enemies. Although there are attempts to control hatred and hatred in the mass media, they still have not been comprehensive enough to help reduce the pressure toward violence.

An obvious example is the continuing sexism and violence toward women in commercial films, not to mention fringe films. An expensive mainline film, 'Revenge', with major stars (Kevin Costner, Madeleine Stowe, Anthony Quinn) degrades women and encourages violence toward them, yet is still shown on TV and video. Although racism and xenophobia have been toned down somewhat, it still forms an undercurrent in many current films. It seems particularly flagrant in 'action' films (such as those produced by Sylvester Stallone). Needless to say, both sexism and racism are rife in most of the old films that are constantly being rerun on TV.

Learning to identify and acknowledge emotions in self and others is also a fundamental direction toward decreasing conflict. I have proposed in this essay that alienation and unacknowledged emotions are basic causes of destructive conflict, as important as material causes. Obviously material interests matter in human affairs. They are topics of quarrels. But these interests can always be negotiated, if there is no unacknowledged emotion, in a way that allows parties maximum benefit, or perhaps least destructive outcomes. Unacknowledged emotion figures large because it make rational negotiation of interest difficult or even impossible, given the non-rational, that is, the elements of insult, rejection, loss and threat, when the underlying emotions are not acknowledged by both parties.

The manipulation of fear, shame and rage in the public seems to be the key element in the irresponsible political and ethnic regimes. The George Bush regime found outside enemies that seemed plausible to the majority of the public, serving to protect reckless political and economic manoeuvres from criticism.

The framing of aggression against Iraq by the US government made ample use of techniques of neutralisation. Denial of Victim has been especially important, in that the US government made the claim, with no evidence, that Iraq posed a threat to the US and to the world at large. The war against Iraq made frequent use of the Denial of Injury. One example is the use of the phrase 'collateral damage' to obscure the killing of civilian men, women and children. Another example is the idea that the purpose of the war was to 'liberate', rather than control, Iraq, which was also an Appeal to Higher Loyalties.

IV. DISCUSSION

This essay concerns the emotional/relational components of blind infatuation and hatred, how they are generated, and how they might be overcome. I have proposed that there is always an irrational component in mass infatuation and hatred that is the product of unacknowledged emotion and alienation. Can anything be done?

Changing individuals would require long-term projects. One approach would be to introduce courses on emotional/relational issues in early schooling. In an American setting, for instance, a course on mediation and conflict resolution could be introduced in junior high schools, and at the high school level, a course on dating and family communications. I have been teaching a course on communication for many years to American university students in their first year. Most of the students have been very receptive. A large majority in every class seem to understand that their own communication practices can be improved, as well as those of the people in their life.

Even if all schools introduced such courses (itself unlikely), major changes in the management of the emotional/relational world would still be a long time coming. In the meanwhile, it might be worth the effort to try to make changes at the collective level. One impressive institution that might work is the kind of Truth and Reconciliation Committees that proved to be effective in the transformation of relationships in South Africa. A by-product of the acknowledgment of aggression by the perpetrators, and suffering by the victims and their kin, is the acknowledgment of shame and rage.

Perhaps in the future it will be necessary to institute a project to clarify the origins and emotional, political, and economic origins and consequences of the war on Iraq. A first step might be to form committees on the Gulf War, since there are many questions that need to be raised. One would be the origins of that war. Ramsey Clark (1994), the Attorney General during Carter's presidency, has claimed that the US instigated this war through Kuwait, and by deceiving Iraq. Another issue would be the treatment of the US veterans of that war, especially the claims that many were physically and psychologically sickened by the war, but have been unable to get treatment.

At a more general level, it may be necessary to pursue reforms that could make the sentiments that the majority hold for their country less like infatuation and more like love, warts and all. And the sentiments that they hold toward the enemy less like blind hatred and more like understanding or at least objectivity. Most supporters of the Iraq war don't know where it is, much less the history of US interference. Perhaps they don't want to know. But in any case, one reform that might help would be the requirement that citizens pass an examination before being allowed to vote.

Getting knowledge relevant to the major issues of the day is not easy, even for a scholar. One problem is the complexity and depth of many of the issues. Another is the poor job the mass media do. Can relevant knowledge be made available to everyone?

Knowledge for public consumption can be presented in a format that would result in easy access, yet could be a step toward understanding. A wonderful model for such a format is available online for film and book reviews on the website www.metacritric.com. For virtually all films of the last three or four years, there are a large number of reviews (20–120) for *each* film. The website is designed remarkably well, enabling a quick look at professional and lay opinions on films expressed as average rating, a crucial sentence from each review, and finally, each review in its entirety.

By seeing the wide range of critical opinion, the average reader might rapidly come to an adequate judgement of a film. Seeing how the experts agree and especially, how they disagree, gives the reader the possibility of what might be called binocular judgement (seeing an issue from many points of view, rather than just one). With this kind of material, the reader is in a position to form her/his own opinion.

A similar format for expert opinion on political and social matters could be made available in order to help citizens prepare to take their voter's examination. Such a reform, along with others mentioned above, and others, might move us back toward a democracy based on genuine love of country, rather than blind infatuation with it, and hatred of purported enemies.

Finally, one last idea. It is possible that electing/appointing women to high office, rather than men, might be a step, on the average, of slowing down the leap into war and violence. There are exceptions, of course, like Margaret Thatcher, who manipulated collective emotions more skilfully than most men. But most women, it seems to me, are at least somewhat less easy with this kind of exploitation than our present leaders, hypermasculine men. Women also would be less trigger happy then men, who have a strong tendency to fight first and ask questions later.

Each of these initiatives may be only a small step or a step that could be taken in the distant future. Having a majority of leaders be women, rather then men, for instance, seems a long way away. In *Lysistrata*, a drama from ancient Greece, women joined together to deny sex to men who fought. Perhaps modern women might take note, not only to lessen war directly, but also, indirectly, to encourage men to vote for women or at least, less arrogant leaders.

REFERENCES

Alverez, A (1997) 'Adjusting to Genocide: Techniques of Neutralization and the Holocaust' 21 *Social Science History* 139–78.

The American Heritage® Dictionary of the English Language, 3rd edn (1992) (Washington, Houghton Mifflin).

Anderson, B (1991) *Imagined Communities* (London, Verso).

Baumeister, R (1997) *Evil: Inside Human Violence and Cruelty* (New York, WH Freeman).

Cahill, T (1995) *How the Irish Saved Civilization* (New York, Doubleday).

Clark, R (1994) *The Fire This Time: U.S. war crimes in the Gulf* (Emeryville, Thunder's Mouth Press).

Cooley, CH (1922) *Human Nature and the Social Order* (New York, Charles Scribner's Sons).

Durkheim, E (1915) *Elementary Forms of the Religious Life* (Glencoe, Free Press).

Elias, N (1995) *The Germans: Power Struggles and the Development of Habitus in the Nineteenth and Twentieth Centuries* (Cambridge, Polity).

Hinde, R and Watson, H (eds) (1994) *War, a cruel necessity?: The bases of institutionalized violence* (London, IB Tauris).

Hochschild, A (2004) 'Let Them Eat War' 6(3) *European Journal of Psychotherapy, Counseling and Health* 1–10.

Kohut, H (1971) 'Thoughts on narcissism and narcissistic rage' in H Kohut (ed) *The Search for the Self* (New York, International University Press).

Kressel, N (2002) *Mass Hate* (Cambridge, Westview).

Labov, W and Fanshel, D (1977) *Therapeutic Discourse* (New York, Academic Press).

Lakeoff, G (1996) Moral Politics: *What Conservatives Know that Liberals Don't* (Chicago, University of Chicago Press).

Lewis, H (l971) *Shame and Guilt in Neurosis* (New York, International Universities Press).

Mead, GH (1936) *Mind, Self, and Society* (Chicago, University of Chicago Press).

Piercy, M (1980) *The Moon is Always Female* (New York, Random House).

Puente, S and Cohen, D (2003) 'Jealousy and the Meaning of Love' 29 *Personality and Social Psychology Bulletin* 449–60.

Phillips, B and Kinkaid, H (eds) (2002) *Beyond Babel: Reconstructing Sociology.* (New York, Aldine de Gruyter).

Retzinger, SM (1991) *Violent Emotions: Shame and Rage in Marital Quarrels* (Newbury Park, Sage).

Scheff, T (1990) *Microsociology: Discourse, Emotion and Social Structure* (Chicago, University of Chicago Press).

—— (1994) *Bloody Revenge: Emotions, Nationalism, War* (Boulder, Westview).

—— (1995) 'Conflict in Family Systems: the Role of Shame' in J Tangney and K Fischer (eds), *Self-Conscious Emotions* (New York, Guilford).

—— (1997) Emotions, the Social Bond, and Human Reality: Part/Whole Analysis (London, Cambridge University Press)

—— (2003) 'Male Emotions and Violence' 56 *Human Relations* 727–49.

—— (2005) Goffman Unbound!: Toward a New Microsocial Science (Boulder, Paradigm Publishers).

—— and Retzinger, S (l991) *Emotion and Violence: Shame/Rage Spirals in Interminable Conflicts* (Lexington, Lexington Books).

Smith, D (2006) *Globalization: the Hidden Agenda* (Cambridge, Polity).

Solomon, R (1981) *Love: emotion, myth, and metaphor* (Garden City, Anchor Press/Doubleday).

—— (1994) *About Love: Re-inventing Romance for our Times* (Lanham, Littlefield Adams).

Staub, E (2003) *The Psychology of Good and Evil* (Cambridge, Cambridge University Press).

Sykes, G and Matza, D (1957) 'Techniques of Neutralization: A Theory of Delinquency' 22 *American Sociological Review* 664–70.

JA Symonds (trans) (1833) Sappho Fragment 2. *The Ode to Anactoria*.

Volkan, V (2004) *Blind Trust: Large Groups and their Leaders in Times of Crisis and Terror* (Charlottesville, Pitchstone).

14

Dealing with Emotions in Peacemaking

JOHN D BREWER

I. INTRODUCTION

EMOTIONS ARE WHERE law and sociology meet. Sociology helps
us understand the social changes that have made emotions such an
important feature of late modernity; law their increasing impact in
legal systems. Two social changes in particular are important: the collapse
of the public–private distinction that permits the penetration of emotions
into public space; and globalisation, which spreads their reach.

The public–private distinction has been eroded as part of the transformation of modern society into what sociologists call 'reflexive modernity'
(Beck, Giddens and Lash 1994), in which self-awareness is heightened
and public displays of emotion intensified. Emotional behaviour normally
preserved for the private sphere is now part of public life (Sennett 2002),
in its appearance politics becomes almost like an extension of the domestic
(Holmes 2000), and counselling, therapy and the 'perfect relationship' provide the meaning of life (Giddens 1994). Globalisation spreads the reach
of these emotions by compressing time-space distances. Emotions are not
just locally felt and enacted, for time-space compression ensures that real
or imagined 'communities of emotion' exist across the globe. Through
diaspora networks, global media, international aid agencies and the like,
people are better able than ever before to empathise with others across ter-
ritorial boundaries, allowing generalised others to share emotional experiences at a great distance (Boltanski 1999).

The application of the sociology of emotions to law and criminal justice now constitutes a new paradigm in legal studies. This appears odd,
since law is supposed to be the most emotionless of processes, and modern
legal structures and systems are designed to eliminate emotion as best they
can from due process. Crime, however, is emotive. The emotional effects
of crime can momentarily reinforce the solidarity amongst 'communities of emotion', in which the immediate emotional response of victims is

culturally disseminated and circulated to generalised others who come to share some of the emotion, and respond in kind. Popular punitiveness (de Haan and Loader 2002: 247) dominates legal discussions, giving a censorious moral tone to public policy on crime and inflaming the moral panic about certain sorts of crimes or victims, giving debates about law and order a strong emotional tone. The *publicness* of these emotional responses to crime and punishment is what is remarkable (Karstedt 2002: 302). It is easy to see why. Emotions are social as much as personal, group as well as individual sentiments, and people's emotions take on greater import and intensity when reinforced by an audience. Emotions are, sociologically at least, performative behaviours and language scripts that are socially learned and disseminated repertoires, making them, in this sense, *public* emotions able to performed and spoken by whole groups and communities, giving them far greater reach and effect.

However, there is only a narrow range of emotions identified in the sociology of law because the pioneering idea of reintegrative shaming initiated the concern with emotions in law. The emotionalisation of law can be rendered primarily into a shame-guilt-reintegration paradigm: the 'return of emotions' is really the 'return of shame' (Karstedt 2002: 302). Shame and guilt are strong emotions, but limited in the range that people can publicly hold and display. Some criminologists are beginning to recognise this. In their depiction of possible new directions in the field, de Haan and Loader (2002: 248) suggest practitioners address what emotions are, the number of them and the relationship between them. Other people have unpacked the separate emotions involved in shame (van Stockkom 2002), which has led some progenitors of the paradigm into psychological reductionism by encouraging them to ask where bad feelings like shame and guilt come from (Harris, Walgrave and Braithwaite 2004: 193). We are now also aware of 'hidden shame' (Scheff 1997a: 8) as a mediating factor in feelings of humiliation. Moreover, the paradigm is beginning to be challenged by sociologists, as well as others who draw on the sociology of emotions, who address a broader set of sentiments, such as moral indignation (Barbalet 2002), hope (Bar-Tal 2001), rage (Scheff 1997b) and revenge (Scheff 1994). Katz (2002: 379) accordingly urged that we dethrone shame from the primacy it is routinely given.

This chapter is devoted to exploring another development of the shame-guilt-reintegration paradigm, namely its application to dealing with the emotions aroused by communal violence, which Braithwaite (2002) has called 'restorative peacemaking'. Although in its infancy, restorative peacemaking has potential to become one of the most significant approaches to conflict resolution. It will be argued however, that this case offers a serious challenge to the shame-guilt-reintegration paradigm. This is in part because communal violence provokes a broader range of emotions than is normally discussed in criminal justice, and is complicated by the emotions aroused by peace itself. In addressing post-violence adjustments, the shame-guilt-reintegration paradigm also tends to focus too narrowly on restorative conferences and other shame-guilt management structures adopted from criminal justice settings, neglecting the broader public policy framework that facilitates successful peacemaking. It will be argued that part of the reason for this is that the paradigm is heavily influenced by human rights and governance discourses that neglect a range of other policy issues.

A. Emotions and Communal Violence

Collective violence has always fascinated sociologists, and in its earlier form as 'crowd behaviour' was used to establish the very foundations of the discipline, by showing the existence of social forces separate from individual behaviour. Instances of collective killings have given this focus a new edge and there are several explanations of its causation and nature, as well as studies of particular instances of mass killing and genocide. As Tilly makes clear (2003: 4), collective violence takes many forms and requires only two perpetrators inflicting physical damage acting in co-ordination. Some instances of collective violence, such as the 9/11 and 7/7 tragedies, or the bombings in Bali and Madrid, are singular events that are capable of structural explanation but are not endemic to the societies in which they occur. It seems appropriate to refer instead to communal violence, since this kind is embedded in particular social structures as an ongoing conflict between its communities, such as that between Protestants and Catholics in Northern Ireland and conflict between South Africa's various racial formations.

This enables us to focus on the influence of particular kinds of social structure on the sorts of violence that occur, rather than on the effect of different kinds of political regime, and draws attention to the effect of social processes like 'race', structural inequality, colonialism, ethnicity and religion as sources of communal violence. This has resulted in several studies of racial and ethnic violence (Horowitz 2001), religious conflicts (Appleby 2000) and violence in which colonial expropriation is still reproduced long after the first settlement (for Northern Ireland see Ruane and Todd 1996). The social structural dynamics behind communal violence force our attention to the impact of globalisation. Communal violence is often linked to local forms of resistance to cultural hegemony, in which the survival of what Giddens (1996: 15) calls 'little traditions' reinforces violent conflicts over such cleavages as 'race', ethnicity and religious fundamentalism. Whilst most analyses of communal violence in the new post-Cold War international order portray it as new kinds of war wrought by globalisation (Kaldor 1999), some suggest it represents older conflicts appropriating new forms (Moore 2000).

Embedding communal violence in particular social structural cleavages in this way links it with the very strong emotions aroused by identity, and in particular with identities that are shaped by membership and loyalty toward the group. Groups are often transnational, describing 'imagined communities' that can reflect patterns of extensive migration and diaspora, impacting on social structures stretched across significant space distances. Identity also involves feelings of tradition and contains senses of history and memory, which mediate both how the past is understood and the future envisioned. This often means that communal violence is reified so that it helps to define what it means to be a group member. Past incidents of violence and its forms of resistance, struggle and suffering, can become represented in a tradition of principles, memories, commemorations, symbols and iconography that are shibboleths determining the nature and course of the communal violence and limiting the flexibility in managing it (on South Africa and Northern Ireland, see Brewer 2003: 69). These symbolic resources can encourage notions of 'vengeful justice' (Ray 1999), which promote genocidal nationalism as a response to some real or imagined historical slight. In as much as identity, tradition and memory generate all-encompassing passions, instances of communal violence can be very large scale in terms of the number of protagonists. There are sporadic, intermittent acts of communal violence, sometimes directed at the state, leaving much of the population unscathed once supporters of the old regime are discounted. But where the communal violence gets wrapped up with group identity, the scale and intensity of victimhood is spread widely throughout the social structure, and the memory of the scale of the killings provokes very strong feelings of hate and revenge amongst survivors (Scheff 1994). And where there are vanquished victims, there is the emotional legacy of feelings of 'defeat', 'surrender' and 'humiliation', if not also of the annihilation of the group's culture.

Perhaps with the exception of 'hate crimes', the 'ordinary' crimes processed by the criminal justice system to which the shame-guilt-reintegration paradigm is normally applied, rarely reach the range or intensity of emotions aroused by identity, memory and tradition in communal violence. While the emotions provoked by criminal law offences are public, and the moral economy of crime disseminates emotions collectively to the generalised other, perpetrators and victims rarely have a sense of 'groupness'. They have not absorbed their personhood in the group and do not suffer the thousands of cuts every time an injury to a group member is experienced as a personal one. The public's reaction to criminal law offences might render them into 'highly emotional "moral spectators" in the spectacles of distant suffering of victims and perpetrators' (Karstedt 2002: 303), but the empathy is at a distance and is not perceived to affect the person's very ontological self. When self-identity is absorbed into the group, however, members are not diffuse individual spectators, for the emotional experience becomes a collective threat. This is not to suggest that identity is inflexible and unchanging, but in rigid social structures where patterns of cleavage coalesce around one major fault line, people participate in fewer groups and group membership subsumes and envelops more of an individual's total identity. This has the effect of broadening communal violence, for group interest defines the position taken on all other issues and ensures that every issue is reduced to a simple matter of whether or not group interests are served by it. This makes for no bystanders to communal violence.

B. Restorative Peacemaking

The shame-guilt-reintegration paradigm has none the less been proffered as a way of dealing with emotions after communal violence as a viable form of peacemaking, and its potential is huge. There is admittedly only a very limited range of literature on restorative peacemaking, but there are at least five possible usages:

— Restorative justice in reintegrating belligerents.
— Restorative conferences in healing divisions between people.
— Truth commissions as a way of handling the past.
— The use of shame apologies for assigning culpability.
— Restorative diplomacy and responsive regulation.

A strong case has been made for the use of restorative justice in the reintegration of former perpetrators and combatants as an alternative to the criminal justice system (for example Braithwaite 2002; Ciabattari 2000; Dinnen, Jowitt and Newton-Cain 2003; Justice Network nd; Roche 2002; Wilmerding 2002). Victims and their relatives chiefly desire retributive justice, but most peace accords involve an amnesty for combatants, which is often deeply troubling to the victims. Braithwaite (2002: 202–4) stresses the contribution of restorative justice in dealing with problems around amnesty, epitomised by Rwanda's use of traditional *gacaca* courts. Scheff (1997a) has advocated the use of restorative conferences in Northern Ireland. Community conferences bring together on a larger scale the same dynamics as when dealing with 'ordinary' crime, with a skilful facilitator mediating between the victim (and their supporters) and the offender (and their supporters) as representatives of the communities involved. Formerly warring communities confront one another, eliciting anger, guilt and shame, and in the process become restored.

Truth commissions, or other truth recovery projects, have strong restorative justice elements (in South Africa's case, see Leman-Langlois and Shearing 2003) which are intended to achieve much the same purpose but by means of dealing with the emotions around memory of past violence (for a discussion of memory as a problem, see Ray 1999). Hamber (2001) argues that truth is healing, and knowledge of culpability a way of handling problematic memories. 'Truth' is thus thought to dissipate emotions, rather than reproduce or inflame them. It is for this reason that truth commissions proliferate (for a review of earlier examples see Hayner 1994; for later comparisons see Chapman and Ball 2001) or take different forms as judicial enquiries, recovered memory projects (in Guatemala's case see Recovery of Historical Memory Project 1999; in Northern Ireland's see Smyth 2003) or commemoration projects through the collation of people's narratives (for example Lundy and McGovern 2001). What matters however, is how the 'truth' is received. Apologies have to be heard by the former enemy to be meant and Scheff (1997a: 9) sees shame-guilt as the key to their genuineness. Both Scheff (1997a: 8) and Braithwaite (2002: 203) see 'shame apologies' as critical to the effectiveness of community conferences and truth recovery processes in managing post-violence emotions. In the former case, shame apologies help with victims' feelings of moral indignation; in the latter they soften the emotional reactions to amnesties. The failure of Ulster Protestants to hear what they consider to be an apology from Sinn Fein has been used by anti-Agreement Unionists as one of the grounds for suspending the Belfast Agreement, bearing witness to the importance of shame apologies in dealing with emotions in post-violence settings.

The final contribution of the paradigm to peacemaking is the advocation of what Braithwaite (2002: 170ff) calls restorative diplomacy (for initially negotiating the settlement) and responsive regulation (for maintaining it afterwards). Restorative diplomacy is not restricted to elites, but extends simultaneously to the grassroots in order to generate bottom-up consent to the deal (see Braithwaite 2002: 194). It involves as a first choice 'restorative peacemaking' amongst elites and masses, on the lines established above, but carrying with it the threat of escalating intervention by the international community—UN Security Council warnings, selective or comprehensive sanctions and UN peacekeeping forces—in a hierarchy of responses intended to generate reintegrative shame that brings perpetrators to the negotiating table. Encouraging shame, however, is only one part of restorative diplomacy. It also involves the international community strengthening the hand of tolerant elites and supporting, materially and symbolically, a range of grassroots peacemaking initiatives. This is tantamount to downgrading—but not dethroning—shame in a way that Scheff does not.

The augmentation of shame-guilt as peacemaking strategies is evident further in Braithwaite's account of responsive regulation. He stresses a range of regulatory measures to manage adjustment problems, including economic regulation to prevent warlords using patronage to sustain the conflict, the introduction of human rights law to regulate the use of state power, and forms of legal regulation that prioritise restorative justice to avoid retributive criminalisation. Braithwaite is silent on political regulation, but Horowitz (2000: 7–9) has complemented the argument. The regulation of governance in post-violence societies involves 'specially crafted' democratic institutions that are conciliatory in their effects; the availability of rewards and incentives for moderate elites in the form of participation in political institutions; electoral systems that recognise bloc votes but also encourage multi-group coalitions, such as, Horowitz argues (2000: 9), consociationalism; and political executives and cabinets composed of proportionately represented members of all parties, able to apply mutual group vetoes, allocate resources proportionately and keep 'own group' cultural matters off the collective agenda. These ideas are frequently advocated in the governance literature on post-violence transitions and key features are found in the Belfast Agreement (O'Leary 1999), amongst other settlements (Horowitz 1993).

C. The Success of Bougainville

The civil war in Bougainville during the 1990s was over the secession of the island from Papua New Guinea. Factional violence between secessionists became very intense towards the end of the decade, and was overlaid with violence between the rebels and the state and deep memories of division going back to the collaboration of some islanders with the Japanese in the Second World War (for details of the case see Braithwaite 2002: 176–80). Australian and military peacekeepers restored calm and the New Zealand Overseas Development Agency's PEACE Foundation in combination with the military began a process of restorative justice to deal with the emotional dynamics of the conflict. Ten thousand islanders were trained in restorative justice, 500 as facilitators and another 70 as trainers, equipping nearly 800 active-village mediation schemes. Some of the mediators are traditional chiefs, and Bougainvilleans are implementing traditional Melanesian restorative justice principles known as *wan bel* ('one belly') as a form of reconciliation. Advocates of restorative peacemaking champion the case (Braithwaite 2002: 179) and the PEACE Foundation considers it a huge success (PEACE Foundation 1999). Perpetrators were persuaded to desist from killing, warring groups came together in joint meetings, locals were able to define their own ordering of priorities in dealing with the issues that drove war, peacemakers were sufficiently supported to win local elections and the criminal justice system on the island was reformed along restorative justice principles.

It is noteworthy however, that as in Rwanda, the conflict did not destroy traditional forms of authority, which were readily adapted to deal with post-violence adjustment problems, and these traditional structures already contained deep respect for restorative justice principles that were easily reoriented to the new setting. Local senses of place remained strong in Bougainville, in part because of the strong identity fostered amongst small island peoples, which allowed local value systems to be drawn on in indigenous orderings of priorities after the violence. The military peacekeepers played a positive role and there was significant involvement by regional powers. Many instances of communal violence, however, pose a sterner test of restorative peacemaking because traditional authority is either destroyed in the atrocity or has not survived modernisation, and restorative justice is an alien idea. Involvement by regional powers and peacekeepers can either be non-existent or negative, and some conflicts involve multiple localities and value systems that lead to no agreement even on whom the indigenous are, let alone what priorities they have. However, while Bougainville and Rwanda offer good illustrations of restorative justice working in post-violence societies, they have social structures so unusual as to permit no further generalisation.

D. The Limitations of Restorative Peacemaking

Restorative peacemaking is admittedly a new venture for the paradigm, and the arguments advanced in its favour are not fully formulated. Even at this early stage, however, it is possible to identify three weaknesses:

— Naivety over what post-violence means.
— The privileging of shame-guilt as post-violence emotions.
— Narrow depictions of the post-violence regulatory framework.

Violence very rarely ends with peace processes, not even in the medium term. Most peace processes are fragile and easily collapse, go through various iterations as the killings continue, and have to manage the constant risk of renewed violence either from warlords for whom the continuance of conflict maintains their local control and patronage, or in the form of what Darby (2001) calls 'spoiler violence', deliberately intended to undermine the peace agreement. Restorative peacemaking has to operate, in other words, in a situation where the old enmities continue, where mistrust has not been assuaged and where violence can destabilise elite and grassroots initiatives by closing the space for compromise. This in itself would not be problematic except that restoration conferences, to be successful, tend to assume the communal violence to be at an end and that the emotions brought to them have to be managed but are not continually inflamed and revived by events surrounding them. Restoration conferences in criminal justice offences may not prove to be successful—the offender may be recidivist and the victim's fear undiminished—but offender and victim bring into restoration conferences an event that is over and done with, the emotional reaction toward which requires management that is not reinforced and repeated during the conference as a result of events taking place outside and for which the parties involved are taken to be representatives.

The paradigm assumes willingness to compromise, even desire to *want* to participate in restoration conferences, that cannot be guaranteed or may only exist for a very short 'honeymoon' period before renewed conflict and killing destroys it. The suggestion by Scheff (1997b: 11) that 'forums of conciliation' be established prior to community restoration conferences as a foundation setting, presupposes there is enough willingness to search for common ground; and the experience of many peace processes shows that rarely do spokespeople talk in the way Scheff says is required: 'exquisite courtesy, avoiding any kind of language or action that might occasion insult' (1997b: 11). The streets of Belfast and the corridors of Stormont, Northern Ireland's parliament building, resound to more vengeful language. Another example of naivety will suffice. Facilitators for large restoration conferences that deal with post-violence emotions need 'to have considerable skill and cunning in order to manage the intense emotions ... be trusted by both sides prior to the meeting ... and need the skill to detect unacknowledged emotions' (Scheff 1997a: 3–4). These people may exist, and they may exist in sufficient number to deal with the thousands of such conferences that will have to take place in every town, neighbourhood and locality if every incident of communal violence is to be dealt with separately, as Scheff suggests (1997a: 3), but the ongoing violence may undermine facilitators' efforts, lose them trust and never put an end to the emotions they need to manage.

The error Scheff makes is to transpose too literally the restoration conference techniques in criminal justice cases to communal violence. However, the restorative elements of truth recovery processes offer nationwide mechanisms to achieve much the same purpose. Braithwaite notably omits mention of individual conferences in restorative peacemaking, preferring to emphasise truth commissions as a way of ensuring grassroots consent, particularly mentioning South Africa's commission as 'touching the hearts' of its people (2002: 170). Less sanguine assessments of the Truth and Reconciliation Commission exist (Jeffrey 1999; Wilson 2001), despite it being in many respects the optimal case since the elite consensus represented by South Africa's agreed settlement ensured its deliberations did not occur amidst political instability or major outbreaks of communal violence. In most other settings where truth commissions are being counselled, peacemaking has to take place alongside sporadic violence and where the political agreement remains unsettled or insecure. Sometimes states or parties design them to disguise their own culpability, or partisanly expose that of their opponents. 'Truth' may merely be a bludgeon with which to beat the other side, to criticise their position as elected representatives or dispute their place in parliament, and disclosures and revelations used to continue the war not end it, inflaming not assuaging emotions. 'Truth' in these settings may lead to revenge killings rather than emotional recovery from earlier deaths and injury. Truth commissions work best, if at all, as part of a settlement that has already stopped the killing, not as a mechanism to end the violence.

Misconceptions about the nature of violence impact negatively also on the paradigm's focus on shame-guilt as the primary emotion through which restoration and reintegration is delivered. Peace processes require an envisioning of the future as much as an emotional packaging of the past. Politicians and lay people alike may lack a peace vocation, being concerned only for the killings to stop, rather than enacting an agreed future, or be dominated by short-term expectations—wanting change now and quickly—rather than being prepared for the long haul. Elster (2004) makes the point that emotions encourage impatience; the likelihood of travails during the long haul require there be a vision to sustain people and encourage patience. Hope, in other words, is as critical to restorative peacemaking as shame-guilt; a point made with regards to Israel by Bar-Tal (2001) and repeated with respect to prisoners of ordinary crime by Burnett and Maruna (2004: 395; also see Maruna 2001) who show its positive role in preventing recidivism. A thoroughgoing sociology of hope explores the impact social conditions have on structuring hope, both in the sense of hope as the *act of imagining* a future desirable state and in the sense of hope as the *emotion* aroused by the end state that is being envisioned. In this way hope is a public emotion that can be constructed for social goals, to manipulate private loyalties and to imagine a desirable future. There are various social practices or technologies for this purpose, including museums that envision the future as much as record the past, such as the Holocaust Museum or Robben Island Museum (on which see Shearing and Kempa 2004), education curricula in schools, media initiatives, citizenship education programmes, public memorials and so on.

In addition to the neglect of more positive emotions, the paradigm under-estimates the array of negative ones by its concentration on shame-guilt. This is in part because it overlooks the emotions aroused by the peace process itself. Peace as much as violence provokes emotions that need to be managed. For example, peace comes with an ontological cost (Brewer 2003: 86–89). It threatens feelings of security because it requires the overthrow of familiar ideas and ways of understanding the world, and poses what Lederach (cited in Knox and Quirk 2000: 26) calls the 'identity dilemma': people who have defined their group identity, tradition and loyalties for so long in terms of 'the enemy' suddenly find they have to reshape their sense of who they are and what groups they feel loyalty towards. These feelings are only enhanced for victims and their relatives. People can find an emotional anchor in the continuance of the old routines, behaviour, language and moral codes rather than in change, encouraging a resistance to peace, opposition to peacemakers, whom they accuse of being 'sell-outs', and a fear of compromise. The remarkable feature of emotions is their short shelf-life, as Elster puts it (2004), and our lack of anticipation that they will decay: we expect to continue to feel what our emotions tell us. Peace processes tend to keep negative emotions alive for longer for those people for whom the peace comes at a cost. These emotions need management too, and they limit the utility of shame-guilt emotions to effect restoration.

The most serious objection to the paradigm's characterisation of emotions after communal violence is that shame-guilt can be problematic, even counter-productive in this setting. There are two difficulties with shame-guilt in post-violence societies: problems around its elicitation and its appropriateness. Some of the former apply equally to criminal justice cases, as noted by many critics. The elicitation of shame from the offender and its perception as genuine by the victim is what unlocks reintegration, and one of the keys to this is its genuineness. Emotions involve performative behaviour and their display can be artful. Shame-guilt is socially constructed by institutionalised practices and language scripts that are socially learned and performed. Communal violence can in some cases destroy the social bond, abolishing the moral system in which shame-guilt could operate, or cause the collapse of the institutionalised practices and language codes through which it is expressed. Even if this is not the case, large communal restoration conferences are not conducive to picking up the subtle cues that display genuineness. It is likely to be community representatives speaking in public on behalf of the group whose genuineness is put to the test and since most of these will be political representatives they will be under considerable constraint arising from the nature of political discourse; and a politician's artfulness will condemn the whole group for whom they are taken to speak. Where violence continues, even sporadically, expressions of shame-guilt are difficult to be heard as 'true', so the whole group will be perceived as duplicitous. The failure of Sinn Fein to say the precise words Ulster Unionists want to hear, despite Sinn Fein's genuine commitment to the Belfast Agreement, shows the political constraints peacemakers are under when offering shame apologies and the temptation of opponents to impose a specific set of institutionalised practices and expressions in order to obstruct the process.

One other key to reintegration is that the elicitation of shame-guilt has to operate under what Karstedt (2002: 309) calls a 'fairness rule', in which the emotion is genuinely felt by the perpetrator but the victim's anger is channelled to preserve some self-esteem and self-respect for the offender. Shame-guilt works in criminal justice settings on the basis of benign assumptions about the willingness of both parties to listen and learn. After communal violence it is often harder to be non-judgemental, to hear the other's narratives reflexively in order to learn something about one's own group from it, and to avoid the temptation to humiliate. Communal violence may have destroyed or distorted the idea of what is fair, or made it very one-sided.

The appropriateness of shame-guilt as an emotion depends upon the nature of the communal violence. In some cases the violence may have been one-sided, victimhood thus being unambiguous, and an outright winner to the conflict has emerged able to look down from the moral high ground with world opinion on their side, the vanquished—the corrupt regime, toppled dictator—having no cultural capital or moral claims. There are instances that approximate to this, such as the collapse of Nazi Germany, the ending of apartheid and the overthrow of Latin American dictatorships, but in most cases of communal violence, victimhood is widespread across the social structure and most, if not all, groups can claim themselves victims and the others perpetrators. Victimhood is every group's experience; every group a perpetrator. If we were to ask the question that Elster (2004) poses in his account of transitional justice—who is it whose emotions count—it can in some transitional settings be everyone. Thus, people need to enter restoration conferences as both victim and offender at the same time, if they are to be successful. The difficulty is that multiple victimhood is likely to be unacknowledged, for victimhood itself can become politicised. One's own group's culpability may be denied or a hierarchy of victims imposed based on either partisan preferences for victims from one's own group or on a hierarchy of crimes in which the other groups' actions were more heinous. Self-righteous indignation and moral superiority distort victimhood (noted by Scheff 1997a: 12) so that victimhood has the effect of perpetuating rather than healing the conflict; in some instances deliberately so. Shame-guilt in these circumstances seems not to fit the emotions required for peacemaking.

It does not fit for another reason: shame-guilt is an emotion that some do not feel. Sometimes the acknowledgement of guilt could be so overwhelming ontologically as to leave it suppressed. In other cases, shame-guilt is not only unacknowledged, there is an ardent refusal to countenance it. It might be that notions of justice, equality, human rights or political cause legitimise the resort to violence, making it a 'just war'; sometimes people feel they were left with no choice. In conventional restoration conferences offenders may well use what Sykes and Matza (1957) famously called 'techniques of neutralisation' to explain to victims their recourse to 'ordinary' crime, but these hardly constitute moral justifications, even if they are claimed as such by the offender for the purposes of neutralisation. Perpetrators of communal violence, however, can under certain circumstances genuinely feel themselves morally justified. Whilst 'ordinary' crime itself offers no neutralisation—it is something that requires to be neutralised—communal violence often comes with its own morality: defending one's group from the others' violence, political oppressiveness, economic unfairness or whatever gives 'just cause' and makes shame-guilt inappropriate. The moral nature of these claims gives them a different nature than the neutralisation techniques used by 'ordinary' criminals. These moral claims are made frequently in the wake of communal violence by all sides—people can deliberately make themselves victims (say, suicide bombers) or exaggerate the emotional experiences of their victimhood in order to mount a moral challenge to their enemies—and since most such claims are disputed, shame-guilt becomes political. Of all the post-violence emotions, shame-guilt is the one most likely to be used politically, because of its moral tenor. It thus risks perpetuating the conflict. Both the elicitation of shame-guilt and its expression are political acts and thus constrained by wider political developments. In Northern Ireland, for example, neither Unionists nor Republicans believe they have anything to feel shame-guilt about, but that the other side does. Shame-guilt is not an emotion that helps to realise peace, it is permissible only after it.

A feature of Braithwaite's approach to restorative peacemaking is the extension beyond shame-guilt to focus on responsive regulation in post-violence societies (2002: 204ff). This approach fits the governance discourse that dominates the literature on post-violence transitions (for example Maley 2002; Maley, Sampford and Thakur 2003; Stedman, Rothchild and Cousens 2002). The emphasis on governance regulation has become part of international discourse, used by key research centres and funders in the United States, like the Institute for Peace, the Woodrow Wilson Center and the MacArthur Foundation, represented locally in Braithwaite's backyard by the Australian National University's Centre for Democratic Institutions.

Proper forms of governance, which include democratic political institutions, restorative justice and human rights law, are indeed critical to the success of post-violence transitions. The stability of peace accords depends in large part on people's experience of governance and law after the violence has stopped or reduced and the way resistance to the accord is managed within the new governance and human rights parameters. Good governance in part helps to assuage negative emotions and encourage positive ones in post-violence settings. However, important as governance is, it does not adequately capture the range of policy issues that communal violence leaves and which need to be managed. The paradigm's narrowness in depicting the regulatory framework that should accompany restorative peacemaking derives in part from the limited approach it takes to the emotional dynamics of post-violence societies. While much of what the paradigm writes about shame-guilt is applicable, with a wider understanding of the range of emotions that require management it is possible to identify a broader set of public policy issues for dealing with post-violence emotions. Public policy is used here to refer to political and social policy, and illuminating the policy dilemmas in post-violence societies is useful for highlighting the social and cultural setting within which such policies have to be worked out.

E. Public Policy and Emotion after Communal Violence

The emotional dynamics after communal violence translate in a number of policy issues, an outline of which is sketched here.

— The tension between 'truth' and 'reconciliation'.
— The tension between 'justice' and 'peace'.
— Victimhood.
— The problem of remembrance and commemoration.
— The social reintegration of former combatants.
— The development of 'citizenship education' for the new society.
— Extenuating the mundane over the sense of crisis.

F. The Tension between 'Truth' and 'Reconciliation'

In the transition to post-violence there is a desperate need to know the 'truth'. The idea of truth, however, is problematic; hence the universal complaint that truth commissions disclose partial truths. Analysts know that 'truth' tends to be relative, truth-from-a-perspective and is subjective, but common sense renders the idea of truth as objective, unaffected by partisan standpoints (Shapin 1994). Not unnaturally therefore, lay people often wish to know what happened and who was responsible, and tend to believe that there is but one objective course of events and decisions in the past that represent this 'true' account. They want to know whose hands are dirty and bloodstained, and believe such identification is unproblematic and non-partisan. Thus, while 'truth' is therapeutic and part of the healing process, it can re-open wounds and hinder or slow the process of reconciliation, because the 'truth' may be used from one standpoint to damn another group. In short, 'truth' can be incompatible with 'reconciliation'. The management of emotions must thus address two problems: finding the balance between the need to know what happened in the past and moving forward, and encouraging people to see the truth from someone else's standpoint. Positive emotions like hope that envision the future are as important here as negative ones that allow the packaging of the past.

G. The Tension between 'Peace' and 'Justice'

All too often, peace can be understood narrowly to mean the ending of violence and fails to address wider issues of justice. The wish for the killing to stop is natural enough. However, peace incorporates well-being and a sense of flourishing, and narrow notions of peace can ignore the range of issues around social justice, such as social redistribution, the introduction or restoration of equality and fairness in the allocation of scarce resources, and the opening up of life chance opportunities that were once closed to some groups. Part of the emotional dynamics that need to be managed therefore are feelings toward both 'peace' and justice', from which follows the requirement to persuade people to value equally non-violence and social redistribution.

H. Victimhood

Victimhood produces grieving relatives, dominated by their hurt and loss, and survivors, maimed physically or psychologically, who take their victimhood into the future as a burden of grief and pain. Managing these emotions is foundational to peacemaking. These emotions are particularly divisive when all groups can claim themselves victims. The emotions around victimhood therefore need to be managed in such a way as to permit victimhood to be recognised as an issue, and the victims honoured, while moving them and the rest of society beyond the memory. This requires as a starting point a plural approach to victimhood by recognising that all have suffered in different ways.

I. The Problem of Remembrance and Commemoration

The conflict needs to be remembered and commemorated, but in ways that permit people to move forward. Amnesia has been part of the nation-building project in many post-violence societies in the past, such as post-Franco Spain and post-war Germany. Public memories can also be recast and reconstructed by means of historical re-envisioning of the conflict (in which, for example, it might be denuded of its ethnic origins, blamed on third parties—normally colonisers—or shown to have affected all groups equally). There are even cases where memories have been publicly recovered when they pertain to a pre-conflict past or become convenient as part of the reconciliation of social divisions (as in the new public recognition of Tamil contributions to Sinhalese culture in Sri Lanka, or of Irish Catholics who served in the British armed forces in two world wars or in the colonial Royal Irish Constabulary). But when memories continue to divide people in the transition, there is a shadow that causes continual strain. Therefore ways have to be found for handling divided memories and encouraging the development of a 'social memory' (Misztal 2003) that honours all people, victims and perpetrators, combatants and civilians, in ways that release society collectively from the burden of people's personal memories.

J. The Social Reintegration of Combatants

Just as victims need to have their emotions addressed, former combatants need to be socially reintegrated. The release of prisoners and amnesties risks continued disharmony, and restorative justice procedures are essential for the management of the emotions this arouses. Social reintegration, however, is broader than restorative justice, and takes the form of economic integration through the provision of jobs and education (thus eliminating the patronage power of warlords and reducing the economic incentive to communal violence), cultural reintegration to avoid feelings of ostracism and marginality, and psychological readjustment through various support structures. However, whatever is done for ex-combatants needs simultaneously to avoid dishonouring victims if the social reintegration mechanisms are not themselves to reproduce the old conflict.

K. The Development of 'Citizenship Education' for the New Society

Violence can sometimes be all that young generations have known, and marked social cleavages can leave most people without the citizenship skills for living with their former 'enemies'. Citizenship education is about acquiring the knowledge and learning the skills for tolerance, that is, for recognising, dialoguing with and understanding 'the other' sufficiently to conduct orderly social relations. This is encapsulated prosaically in the practice of tolerance. Tolerance is both a personal and public quality. It is something that is practised in people's private lives in their perceptions of 'the other', in their ways of communicating with and about 'the other' and in the relationships they conduct with them. It is also a public virtue that can be reinforced by civil society and the state when opportunities are provided for people from all sides to come together to tell their personal narratives in a non-threatening setting by means of local networks through which groups from across the former divide meet to create a dialogue and seek understanding of each other. These networks are similar to yet broader than community conferences and do not ennoble shame-guilt as the master emotion.

L. Extenuating the Mundane over the Sense of Crisis

Perhaps with the exception of genocide, situations of communal violence involve people trying to maintain the daily routines of life as a way of managing and routinising the violence. Conventional war might not evince it, but communal violence is contradictory: violence occurs in the midst of the reproduction of social routine. Ironically this extenuation of the mundane, which helped in the normalisation of the violence as a way of managing its ontological effects, can be disrupted in the post-violence setting as disputes over the negotiation process or over the actual settlement come to dominate the public agenda, increasing people's senses of insecurity. Victimhood can attach a special price to peace, but more generally the public obsession with the inevitable lurching ebbs and flows and vicissitudes of the negotiations can unsettle the mundane and cause emotional crises to be manufactured out of dramas. Emotion management procedures should encourage people into maintaining perspective; to deal in the public domain with war and its amelioration, while extenuating in the private sphere the same mundaneness that allowed them to cope while the violence raged.

II. CONCLUSION

These dilemmas represent difficult problems. However, they better describe the emotional dynamics of post-violence societies than shame-guilt, and successfully broaden the policy challenge facing peacemakers beyond responsive regulation of governance and human rights law. Restorative peacemaking is a fertile idea, but the 'return of shame' tends to limit the ability of the shame-guilt-reintegration paradigm to understand the emotions aroused by communal violence, accordingly limiting its depiction of restorative peacemaking. This paper has not sought to impugn the principle of restorative peacemaking, but to amplify it. A broader understanding of the emotional dynamics of post-violence societies allows us to see that the policy challenge in handling post-violence emotions has some parallels with restorative justice but much more besides, so that a simple transposition of its procedures and practices only inadequately addresses the emotional dynamics of post-violence societies.

REFERENCES

Appleby, SR (2000) *The Ambivalence of the Sacred* (Lanham, Roman and Littlefields).
Barbalet, JM (2002) 'Moral indignation, class inequality and justice' 6 *Theoretical Criminology* 279–97.
Bar-Tal, D (2001) 'Why does fear override hope in societies engulfed by intractable conflict, as it does in the Israeli society?' 22 *Political Psychology* 601–27.
Beck, U, Giddens, A and Lash, S (1994) *Reflexive Modernisation* (Cambridge, Polity Press).
Boltanski, L (1999) *Distant Suffering* (Cambridge, Cambridge University Press).
Braithwaite, J (2002) *Restorative Justice and Responsive Regulation* (Oxford, Oxford University Press).
Brewer, JD (2003) C. *Wright Mills and the Ending of Violence* (London, Palgrave).

Burnet, R and Maruna, S (2004) 'So "prison works" does it?' 43 *The Howard Journal of Criminal Justice* 390–404.

Chapman, A and Ball, D (2001) 'The truth about truth commissions' 23 *Human Rights Quarterly* 1–43.

Ciabattari, J (2000) 'Rwanda gambles on renewal not revenge' *Women's E News* wwwwomensenewsorg/articlecfm/dyn/aid/301/context.

Darby, J (2001) *The Effects of Violence on Peace Processes* (Washington, United States Institute of Peace Press).

De Haan, W and Loader, I (2002) 'On the emotions of crime, punishment and social control' 6 *Theoretical Criminology* 243–53.

Dinnen, S, Jowitt, A and Newton Cain, T (2003) *A Kind of Mending: Restorative Justice in the Pacific Islands* (Canberra, Pandanus Books).

Elster, J (2004) *Closing the Books* (Cambridge, Cambridge University Press).

Giddens, A (1994) *The Transformation of Intimacy* (Cambridge, Polity Press).

—— (1996) *In Defence of Sociology* (Polity Press, London).

Hamber, B (2001) 'Does truth heal? A psychological perspective on political strategies for dealing with the legacy of political violence' in N Bigger (ed), *Burying the Past*, (Washington, Georgetown University Press).

Harris, N, Walgrave, L and Braithwaite, J (2004) 'Emotional dynamics in restorative conferences' 8 *Theoretical Criminology* 191–210.

Hayner, P (1994) 'Fifteen truth commissions' 16 *Human Rights Quarterly* 597–655.

Holmes, M (2000) 'When is the personal political?' 34 *Sociology* 305–21.

Horowitz, DL (1993) 'Democracy in divided societies' 4 *Journal of Democracy* 18–38.

—— (2000) 'Some realism about peacemaking' in *Facing Ethnic Conflicts* (Durham, Centre for Development Research, Duke University).

—— (2001) *The Deadly Ethnic Riot* (Berkeley, University of California Press).

Jeffrey, A (1999) *The Truth About the Truth Commission* (Johannesburg, South African Institute of Race Relations).

Justice Network (nd) 'Dealing with mass atrocities and ethnic violence A case study of Rwanda' wwwacjnetorg/docs/queenpdf.

Kaldor, M (1999) *New and Old Wars* (Cambridge, Polity Press).

Karstedt, S (2002) 'Emotions and criminal justice' 6 *Theoretical Criminology* 299–317.

Katz, J (2002) 'Response to commentators' 6 *Theoretical Criminology* 375–80.

Knox, C and Quirk, P (2000) *Peace Building in Northern Ireland, Israel and South Africa* (London, Macmillan).

Leman-Langlis, S and Shearing, C (2003) 'Repairing the future: the South African Truth and Reconciliation Commission at work' in G Gilligan and J Pratt (eds), *Crime, Truth and Justice* (Cullompton, Willan Publishing).

Lundy, P and McGovern, M (2001) 'The politics of memory in post-conflict Northern Ireland' 13 *Peace Review* 27–34.

Maley, W (2002) 'Twelve theses on the impact of humanitarian intervention' 33 *Security Studies* 265–78.

——, Sampford, C and Thakur, R (2003) *From Civil Strife to Civil Society* (New York, United Nations University Press).

Maruna, S (2001) *Making Good* (Washington, American Psychological Association).

Misztal, B (2003) *Theories of Social Remembering* (Maidenhead, Open University).

Moore, B (2000) *Moral Purity and Persecution in History* (Princeton, Princeton University Press).

O'Leary, B (1999) 'The nature of the agreement' 22 *Fordham Journal of International Law* 1628–67.

PEACE Foundation (1999) *Report on Bougainville for the Year 1999* (Port Moresby, PEACE Foundation Melanesia).

Ray, L (1999) 'Memory, trauma and genocidal nationalism' 42 *Sociological Research Online* wwwsocresonlineorguk/socresonline/4/2/rayhtml.

Recovery of Historical Memory Project (1999) *Guatemala: Never Again* (Maryknoll, Orbis Books).

Roche, D (2002) 'Restorative justice and the regulatory state in South African townships' 42 *British Journal of Criminology* 514–33.

Ruane, J and Todd, J (1996) *The Dynamics of Conflict in Northern Ireland* (Cambridge, Cambridge University Press).

Scheff, T (1994) *Bloody Revenge* (Boulder, Westview).

—— (1997a) 'Honor and shame: local peacemaking through community conferences' wwwsocucsbedu/faculty/scheff/6html.

—— (1997b) 'Deconstructing rage' wwwsocucsbedu/faculty/scheff/7html.

Sennett, R (2002) *The Fall of the Public Man* (London, Penguin).

Shapin, S (1994) *A Social History of Truth* (Chicago, University of Chicago Press).

Shearing, C and Kempa, M (2004) 'A museum of hope: a story of Robben Island' 592 *Annals of the American Academy of Political and Social Science* 62–78.

Smyth, M (2003) 'Truth, partial truth and irreconcilable truths: reflections on the prospects of truth recovery in Northern Ireland' 73 *Smith College Studies in Social Work* 205–20.

Stedman, S, Rothchild, D and Cousens, E (2002) *Ending Civil Wars* (Boulder, Lynne Rienner).

Sykes, G and Matza, D (1957) 'Techniques of neutralisation: a theory of delinquency' 22 *American Sociological Review* 664–70.

Tilly, C (2003) *The Politics of Collective Violence* (Cambridge, Cambridge University Press).

Van Stokkom, B (2002) 'Moral emotions in restorative justice conferences' 6 *Theoretical Criminology* 339–60.

Wilmerding, J (2002) 'Restorative justice and the effects of war' http://csfcoloradoedu/forums/pcacc/nov02/msg00010html.

Wilson, R (2001) *The Politics of Truth and Reconciliation in South Africa* (Cambridge, Cambridge University Press).

Part V

Democracy and Penal Sentiments

15

*Divided Sympathies: David Hume and Contemporary Criminology**

RICHARD SPARKS

I. INTRODUCTION: CRIME, PUNISHMENT
AND THE MORAL SENTIMENTS

WE KNOW THAT crime and punishment can excite powerful and indeed 'wild' emotions, and that these have sometimes been very prominent in recent years in a number of countries. Some observers diagnose a prevalent, even pervasive, 'new punitiveness' (Pratt et al 2005), enjoined in part by the incitements of the popular press and other media (Jewkes 2004) and by the grandstanding populism of contemporary mass politics. The wider reasons for and resonances of this strand of emotionality in our political culture have been extensively and ably debated (see, for example, Garland 2001; Tonry 2004; Simon 1997), and I don't intend to rehearse those arguments here any more than is strictly necessary.[1] It also seems to be the case that these emotional configurations combine closely with varying degrees of mistrust in or disaffection from political processes and institutions (LaFree 1998).

One possible line of interpretation of these dynamics, in severely condensed form, runs roughly as follows. Late modern societies offer somewhat limited opportunities for political involvement and expression, at least in relation to the highly professionalised and managed world of electoral politics. Much of the time we are positioned as audiences and consumers of political rhetoric and events. This suits us well enough in many respects—we have many other things to watch and consume, after all, other things to do with our time, other concerns and priorities. On the other hand, we

---

* This essay grows out of a paper delivered at the XIV World Congress of Criminology, University of Pennsylvania, Philadelphia on 8 August 2005. I am grateful to my co-presenters on that occasion, Lawrence Sherman and Susanne Karstedt, and to members of the audience who offered comments and encouragement.
[1] I have made various attempts to contribute elsewhere, including Sparks 2000, 2001, 2003, 2006.

also sometimes experience ourselves as bystanders—a more disagreeable sensation, and one tinged with powerlessness and a degree of insecurity. Amongst other things this encourages a certain jaded scepticism as to the motives, probity, competence and capacity of our democratic representatives; and the temptation on political actors to offer displays of strength and will results in part from the need to contest this niggardly judgement of their qualities, as well as from the obligation to differentiate themselves from one another, as products in a market-place are compelled to do. Their 'package displays' (Beckett 1997) are produced for a fairly *anti*-political public and one that is mainly fairly comfortable without necessarily being either confident in its apprehension of the future or secure in terms of its estimation of the risks posed by crime, amongst other menaces. Indeed, the public is often quite acutely sensitised to the threats to its comfort and security, even if these are sometimes of rather inchoate character (Tyler and Boeckmann 1997).

Amongst other things, these conditions give rise to a concern that the democratisation of criminal justice may be impossible to achieve without the risk of producing an immoderately punitive system. Certainly there are many obstacles in the way. There is a general sense in which contemporary mass politics can be taken up, at least spasmodically, with the claims of 'redemptive populism', claiming authenticity from direct expressions of popular emotion (Canovan 1999). There is a widespread tendency for criminal justice issues to come to public notice in the form of particular scandals (Fine 1997) and for policy to be produced at least in part through an 'outrage dynamic' (Pettit 2001). There is a suspicion that it often suits political actors to sustain their somewhat tattered legitimacy by prosecuting an endless war, in domestic matters as well as international affairs. Even though the powers of those political actors to affect crime rates may be strictly limited, the behaviour of criminal justice institutions is something on which they can legislate quickly and visibly.

It is tempting under these circumstances, even allowing for the possibility of some degree of overstatement in the interests of concision, to retreat to the view that the emotional palette of crime and justice is entirely gloomy and the social uses of those emotions generally disreputable. Public responses, on this view, are as irrational as they are mean-minded, and riddled through with prejudices and hostility. Political appropriations of the law and order issue are theatrically cynical, covering a chronic incapacity to do much to provide the public with the protection it has been taught to crave with a series of demotic gestures. Of course there is no small number of examples of both these tendencies. Their combined effect would seem to be to exacerbate the mutual distancing and suspicion between people, and to facilitate the production of antagonistic stereotypes. Blame flows easily across the boundaries thus created, and vindictive punishment can be applied with little hesitancy or compunction (*cf* Simon 2001). One of the more worrying possibilities is that although media campaigns, scandals and *causes célèbres* succeed only too well in mobilising the punitive emotions and in bringing them strongly into the domain of politics, this does nothing to assuage the underlying legitimation problems, thereby establishing instead a self-perpetuating demand.

The above is a sketch, even a caricature. Nevertheless, the emotional dispositions that it describes are indeed all significant strains in contemporary public life, as seems now all too well-attested. They represent the strain in current penality that I term, here and elsewhere (Sparks 2001) estrangement. If the sketch were indeed the complete picture, it would be a grim one indeed. However, I suspect that it is plausible to argue that the seeming dominance of these postures of estrangement is not quite as complete as it appears. In the first place I have argued (Sparks 2000) that the eager engagement of the public with mass media narratives of brutal victimisation arises at least in part from a response of intuitive sympathy. This is a partial sympathy, no doubt, and in practice often finds expression in vehement support for vigorous punishment. It thus tends to play into those postures in political rhetoric that would have us *always* see the needs and interests of victims and offenders as diametrically opposed. Yet however much the investment of emotive force in images of victimhood is deployed as a warrant for scaling-up harsh punishment, the readers', viewers' and voters' responses into which it dips for support are not necessarily simply and only vindictive.

Indeed some of those responses are in a certain sense altruistic ones. The media logic depends for its effect upon a capacity for shock and for a certain degree of at least momentary concern for others, and hence an imaginative capacity to see oneself or one's loved ones in the position of the suffering victim. In other words, the sentimentalism of the media narrative seems to offer an opportunity to display solidarity with others' suffering, and thus to express a certain level of civic concern, to people who are provided with a strictly limited range of such opportunities. In our kind of society only certain kinds of events offer much scope for the expression of common emotion—the deaths of princesses, major sporting occasions and shocking crimes have this much in common at least. In this respect it seems that our political culture offers many occasions on which to emote about crime and punishment (*cf* Karstedt 2002), but few on which to take any form of legitimate action to follow up those emotions, beyond endorsing the decisions of the courts to deliver tough and fitting punishment (or to join the chorus of criticism when they 'fail' to do so). Our imaginative capacity to participate in the sufferings of others (if only distantly, if only momentarily) is in this sense part and parcel of the process whereby we are invited to align ourselves with populist campaigns, since we are offered limited opportunity to express our civic involvement, empathy with others' suffering, or indignation in the face of iniquity in any other way.

There are of course also counter-movements that seek to invoke and channel emotions in other ways and it is these on which I wish to focus now. Attempts to generate alternatives to the dominance of estrangement often focus on ways of increasing opportunities for deliberation and participation, on breaking down the social distance and dissociation between victims and offenders or between victims and the system of justice (Loader, this volume). Many of the most promising of these contributions, in practice as well as in theory, are associated with the movement for restorative justice (RJ) (see for example Braithwaite 2000; Ahmed et al 2001; Strang 2002).

My aim in this essay is relatively modest and limited. I want briefly to consider some of the conceptual antecedents for contemporary accounts of the development of empathy (and the withdrawal of empathy, which I am calling estrangement). In this regard I outline the continuing relevance, as I see it, of the views of the philosopher David Hume, especially his account of the mechanism of *sympathy*. I take Hume's account of this issue to anticipate much subsequent social theory, as well as—more obviously—ethical reflection. In particular, Hume's remarks on the generation of sympathy in *conversation* (real, imagined or internal) seem surprisingly contemporary and, I suggest, are of distinct relevance to thinking about some of our current predicaments in handling offending, offenders and victims. For example, I point to some affinity between Hume's conventionalist and dialogical approach to the generation of moral sentiments and recent sociological work that considers how our emotions such as empathy (and estrangement) are *produced* in interaction with others. I briefly consider the relevance here of Collins's discussion of interaction ritual (Collins 2004 and this volume).[2] These resources, I suggest, are quite helpful in thinking about, for example, RJ practices as conversations, or encounters, in which the production of sympathies is a key issue, and a condition of success. But these in turn also assist in grasping why estrangement and dissociation are also among the dominant products of criminal justice. I refer briefly to data from a study of children's conversations about justice and punishment in order to demonstrate some of these dynamics in action.

In this sense RJ is interesting and important, not only because it offers an alternative method of handling offences, addressing the needs of victims and perhaps changing the outlooks of offenders and other direct participants, but also because it holds out some prospect of promoting a different, less exclusionary and more deliberative set of penal sensibilities in the wider public culture. Thus, Ahmed et al suggest that RJ can be seen as an 'opportunity for deliberation' in a context of 'communal moral education'. On this view, 'the deliberation educates the community as to why this particular

---

[2] Something similar could be argued in respect of Layder's (2004) views on 'interpersonal control', the discussion of which he considers to be a missing 'domain' in sociological analysis. However I don't have space in which to develop this point here.

kind of act should be shameful.' One of the attractions of RJ practices in schools, they argue, lies in offering children a chance to listen to 'the moral reasoning of young citizens as they discover for themselves the curriculum of crimes' (Ahmed et al 2002: 25–26).

II. HUME, SYMPATHY AND JUDGEMENT

Perhaps intellectual history is a lot less linear than we tend to assume? Sometimes at least, the ideas that are most provocative to us or most helpful in clarifying our current problems are not the latest, newest, shiniest ones. It is certainly not a question of attempting to claim one's chosen thinker as some sort of undiscovered, proto-criminologist. My aim is simpler (but I hope not so silly): some of our contemporary problems—and more particularly our proposed solutions to those problems—have analogies or antecedents of which we are often less aware than we should be. We will frequently find, as EP Thompson eloquently put it, that 'the mind has walked these cliffs before', sometimes more rigorously and systematically than we have ourselves. It may well not be the case that the answers proposed by our forebears hold good for us now; rather it is the conceptual structure of the *questions*, and perhaps the method of inquiry, that still hold interest.

What I want to suggest here is that my chosen exemplar David Hume (I would like to say hero, but he is such a deliberately non-heroic character) can help in this way in elucidating what is at stake in some of our current dilemmas, especially those concerning when, how much and how to punish, or to refrain from punishing. Hume can help us to understand better what we are *actually doing* when we make moral judgements. He can help us to think about the relationships between our *reasons* (our calculations) and our *feelings* when we do this. So, when we nowadays use terms like 'emotional intelligence', we may be making a distinctively Humean point, without acknowledging, or often knowing, that we are doing so.

It might be the case that Hume can help us to grasp in what ways the making of such judgements *forms* or *defines* us as persons and as members of a certain kind of community. It is for this reason, I am suggesting, that a reading of Hume[3] is so useful in clarifying the extremely topical issue of the respective claims of *restorative justice* (RJ) and *retribution*. And, beyond this, he may also be able to help us get at some more concrete and empirical puzzles (Hume after all was a philosopher deeply convinced of the centrality of the concrete and the empirical) like this one. Students of restorative justice have repeatedly found that a key need of victims in RJ encounters is that of receiving an adequate apology. But why should apologies be so

---

[3] I should acknowledge here that my reading of him is greatly influenced by the feminist one offered by Annette Baier (1995).

central? Why are we seemingly the kind of beings for whom apologies matter so much?

RJ addresses and seeks to manage a certain set of powerful and potentially disruptive emotions. Certain versions of populism in contemporary politics also call upon our moral emotions, again often in extremely potent ways. It seems to me important to begin from the recognition of the inherently and permanently impassioned nature of these topics. The contemporary social sciences—not just criminology and the sociology of punishment as such, but the social analyses of the emotions, of interaction rituals, of political communication and so on—offer many insights into these issues. If we are to think lucidly and reasonably about them, then we need to have a sophisticated view of the curious conjunctions of thinking and feeling, reasoning and emoting, emotional *identification* and emotional *distancing*, that they can involve. Why do many of us now seemingly find the implicit curriculum of RJ so appealing? Conversely, are there sound grounds for finding capital punishment or mass imprisonment objectionable, and for attempting to persuade others that are not already so convinced? I think that some version or extension of Hume's account of the moral sentiments could help us in this matter.

David Hume was born in Edinburgh in 1711 and died there in 1776, spending the greater part of his life in that city and in France. His principal work, *A Treatise of Human Nature* (T), was published in three volumes in 1739–40 when Hume was not yet 30. He revised and extended the views therein in two major subsequent publications, the two 'Inquiries' (the *Inquiry Concerning Human Understanding* (1748) and the *Inquiry Concerning the Principles of Morals* (1752) (2E). (Hume never held an academic post, and was better known during his life and long afterwards as an historian rather than as a philosopher.)

Hume participated in an intense flowering of intellectual activity in Scotland in the middle decades of the eighteenth century, often known as 'the Scottish Enlightenment' (see Buchan 2003). The intellectual culture of that time and place involved the frequent and fluid interaction of scholars of widely varying interests and accomplishments—many of our distinctions between disciplines had no currency at that time. Hume saw himself as contributing to (perhaps even as initiating) a *science* of human nature. He was, notoriously, committed to a strong programme of empiricism in his theory of knowledge and was 'aggressively agnostic' (Baillie 2000) on questions of theology. For these reasons he sought to found his understanding of human moral conduct on a naturalistic view of persons and without reference to any transcendental principle. For Hume, one definition of a wise man is 'one who conforms his behaviour to the evidence before him'.

But here Hume departs from our usual caricature of what 'the Enlightenment' entails. He does not envisage humans as only or primarily rational creatures; neither does he believe that reason must subjugate passion (indeed he famously declared the exact opposite). As Baillie puts it, 'One of Hume's greatest philosophical achievements was to destroy the false opposition between reason and passion, showing passion to penetrate the very heart of the alleged activity of reason' (Baillie 2000: 13). The view of morality characteristic of the *Scottish* Enlightenment (ie not just in Hume, but also his precursor Hutcheson and his younger contemporary Adam Smith) is neither rationalism, nor egoism, but rather an account of the 'moral sentiments', or 'moral sense'. In Hume's hands this account is thoroughly social, inter-subjective, grounded in convention. Morality, for Hume, is less about the discovery of a truth than it is about a series of attempted solutions to problems of peaceful co-existence. As Baier has it, Hume's moral theory understands moral conduct as *social practice* which only 'a cautious observation of human life, of "experiments" gleaned as they occur in the "the common course of the world" can help us really to understand' (1995: 67).

It follows that neither *introspection* nor *rule following* provide the paradigm of morality for Hume. Rather this concerns the cultivation of *character traits* or *virtues* and that make one 'a safe companion' or 'an easy friend', or in one of the numerous senses that he uses of this term, 'good company'. These virtues are social, not solitary and felt, not deduced. The basic capacity that makes a peaceful social life possible is what Hume terms *sympathy*. As Baier clarifies, sympathy is 'not a special emotion but a disposition or principle that spreads emotions from person to person ... a co-ordination or mutual involvement' (1995: 43). We do not, in Hume's view, experience or achieve awareness of our own sentiments in isolation from other people. Thus, Hume argues, 'We can form no wish, which has not a reference to society'. Our passions, he continues, would not have 'any force were we to abstract entirely from the thoughts and sentiments of others' (T: 363). Similarly, he insists, 'men always consider the sentiments of others in their judgements of themselves' (T: 303).

Morality on this view is a 'cognitive-cum-passionate' ensemble—it is fundamentally concerned with our orientation towards other persons and their needs and with the *communication* of these. It is only for this reason, Hume says, that we are capable of feeling indignation at an injustice done to someone else. We have the capacity to 'enter into sentiments that in no way belong to us' (T: 589). Thus one of the recurrent images in Hume's writings on the moral sentiments is that of *reverberation,* or the capacity through the exercise of sympathy to echo in imagination another's fate or experience. The 'minds of men', Hume says,

> are mirrors to one another, not only because they reflect each others' emotions, but also because those rays of passions, sentiments and opinions may be often reverberated, and may decay away by insensible degrees. (T: 365)

Thus MacIntyre glosses the point:

> The passions of each person are therefore inescapably characterized in part as responses to others who are in turn responding to us. So in the reciprocities and mutualities of passion, whether harmonious or antagonistic, each self conceives of itself as part of a community of selves, each with an identity ascribed by others... (MacIntyre 1998: 292–93).

The capacity for some degree of reciprocal understanding is involved whenever we attempt to see the world from beyond the vantage point of simple self-interest and to adopt 'the common point of view' (Blackburn 1998: 201). Hume seems to accept that if a person is genuinely uninterested in the good or bad opinions of others and is essentially focused only on his own immediate interests—Hume calls this being a 'sensible knave'—then we will have few if any grounds in rationality for appealing to him to change his behaviour. However, his point would appear to be that this is relatively unusual and that life lived on such terms would be unsustainable if generalised. Blackburn summarises Hume's views thus:

> It is essentially an ideal of *civility*: the requirement that in a conversation with others we find common ground with them. We do not simply discount their opinion, or still less stay entirely deaf to their voice ... Hume seems to think that we all have an interest in pursuing conversations with others: we need to avoid the 'continual contradictions' which arise if we do not do so. (Blackburn 1998: 210)

Blackburn, Baier and other admirers do not present Hume's views as quaint or as being of merely historical interest, nor indeed as having been superseded by subsequent theory. On the contrary, there is some sense in their work of a Humean revival in ethical theory. It can be argued that Hume's thought finds echoes in the work of a number of leading moralists (see for example, Nussbaum 1996; Blackburn 1998; see generally Wilkinson 2005: ch 5; see also Pinker 2005). Moreover, whilst we often overlook the Scottish thread in the foundation of the social sciences (with the obvious exception of economics), Hume's perspective seems to me strangely premonitory of, for example, aspects of Durkheim's thought, not least in respect of Durkheim's notion of 'collective effervescence'. This notion refers to the sharing or relaying of emotional experience amongst participants in collective activities, especially rituals and ceremonies. Effervescence is for Durkheim 'a sort of electricity' (Durkheim 1912). Thus, in Shilling's summary:

> These processes occur when emotions are structured through various rites to 'fix' themselves to those symbols that are central to people's identity and understanding. This transfer of energy helps a group become conscious of itself as a moral community, binds people together, and structures the inner lives of individuals in accordance with collective symbols. (Shilling 2002: 19)

Perhaps by extension Hume's notion of 'reverberation' is redolent of the ideas of mutual attunement in Randall Collins's account of interaction ritual (2004). Collins argues that one of the most significant, albeit latterly somewhat neglected, legacies of the Durkheimian tradition in sociology and anthropology is (contrary to most commonplace readings) the micro-sociological understanding of the production of solidarities and shared symbols through interaction in small groups. Collins thus construes Goffman as one of Durkheim's most faithful, as well as most creative, successors. For Collins, a key aspect of this inheritance is to focus on the ways in which we are compelled by 'the demands of sociality in the here-and-now'. The situation, as he puts it, 'has its requirements'. Amongst the generic features of ritual actions in Collins's view are that they tend to feature *situational co-presence*, that they *focus* interaction, that they are *entraining* (they include pressures towards conformity and 'thus show one is a member of society'); that they thereby 'do honour to what is socially valued', and that, when ritual proprieties are broken, people feel 'moral uneasiness'. For Collins, rituals are 'the nodes of social structure' in that 'it is in rituals that a group creates its symbols'. Of course, rituals and moments of effervescence can assume darker, more violent forms. One of Hume's concerns is how to capture, so to speak, the capacity for 'rever-beration' in the interests, to borrow Blackburn's term, of civility.

III. JUST TALK?

One of the striking ideas in Hume, taken up by Baier (and associated strongly by her with Gilligan's reinterpretation of moral psychology in *In a Different Voice* (Gilligan 1982)), is that for him the most appropriate image of moral education is not a lecture or a sermon but rather a *conversation*. It is only in communication that we are able to render our inchoate initial feelings into calmer, more settled, 'corrected' standards or principles:

> it is necessary for us, in our calm judgements and discourse concerning the characters of men, to ... render our judgements more public and social ... The intercourse of sentiments, therefore, in society and conversation, makes us form some general standard by which we may approve or disapprove of characters and manners. (2E: 229)

This is where we return to the issue of restorative justice and its retributive competitors. Seen in this neo-Humean light, the peculiar genius of RJ pro-cedures, where they work well, lies in reproducing (in a necessarily artificial and carefully guided, even scripted, context) the density and the demands of everyday conversation.

It may be, my colleagues Evi Girling, Marion Smith and I have suggested in another paper, something about the *structure of conversation itself* that elicits apology, and sometimes demands its acceptance (Girling et al 2006; see also Conley and O'Barr 1998). Similarly, the positioning of the actors as parties to a conversation arguably makes possible, but does not guarantee, the production of sympathy, in either direction, where none previously existed. Certainly Hume felt that the emotion of humility (the opposite of pleasurable pride, and something that shares many of the features that Braithwaite and his co-workers apportion to shame) results from viewing oneself in an unfavourable light, perhaps because we find that disfavour 'seconded' in the responses of others. Consider the following:

> But besides these original causes of pride and humility, there is a secondary one in the opinions of others, which has an equal influence on the affections. Our reputation, our character, our name are considerations of vast weight and importance; and even the other causes of pride; virtue, beauty and riches; have little influence when not seconded by the opinions and sentiments of others. (T: 316)

The recent acknowledgement by Harris, Walgrave and Braithwaite (2004) that RJ conferences entail a complex, sequential, fallible set of emotional dynamics that need, amongst other strategies, to be grasped *in situ* and *as conversations* is a helpful extension of the theoretical prospectus of RJ. Girling, Smith and I have argued in various papers that the tendencies towards distancing and rejection on the one hand versus empathy and re-affiliation on the other are marked at the level of the discourse itself. Certainly we should be alert—as I think Hume would certainly have recognised—to the power of the passions that may be engaged on either side of the duality between *punishment as rejection* and *dialogue as reconciliation*. Consider the following disconcerting example:

> Tim: Tie them to a post ...
>
> Ken: Like in the olden days.
>
> Becky: Tie them to a post and chuck a load of tomatoes at them
>
> Tim: No tie them to the post and set fire to the bottom of the post
>
> [one child laughs].
>
> Becky: No that's killing them.
>
> Ken: Killing them, but that would be a good punishment if they did it.

There are several striking elements here. One is the rather joyous sense of escalation—tying up is not just restraint, but also an opportunity to inflict various revenges on the miscreant. Nevertheless even here someone (often, as in this case, but not always or exclusively, a girl) introduces an objection. Even in moments of high excitement the rebuttal that in punishing to excess you are, as it was put in another group, 'being bad yourself' can always intervene. Another notable point is that in many such cases the persons being punished ('them') and indeed what they have done are very non-specific. This extract is a series of generalised injunctions ('Tie them', 'chuck a load of tomatoes'). This recurs often in our data. It seems that the most forceful and vehement punishments, with all their vivid appeal, are reserved for people who are essentially anonymous and faceless. Things change a lot whenever the conversation develops to include the idea of doing something to *someone* for some particular reason.

A connecting thread throughout many of our conversations with these young people is the idea of 'teaching a lesson'. Teaching lessons is fundamentally what children take punishment to be about. However, 'lesson' is a complex word and can carry a varied freight of meanings (see Smith et al 2000). At one end it means nasty medicine, a deterrent shock, something you would not want to repeat. At other points, it means something very didactic and school-like—you literally 'teach' someone their lessons and check whether they have learned them by giving homework and tests. You can put someone in the 'naughty corner' and 'see' whether they are ready to come out. Sometimes too the children want to go further than this. On occasion 'the lesson' becomes a matter of talking, reasoning, persuading, of encouraging the other person to grasp the effect of their actions on others and to change inwardly. Thus:

> Sally: The more, the more educated people could, erm, go and try and help the person who had like been taken into the corner and try and help them somehow, even though they are like nasty people, I would still like to try and help them as much as possible ... so that he would like become more better and then when he's done that, he might learn a lesson and then he might, erm, that person might start to become like us and try and help other people.

Sally struggles valiantly to articulate a difficult thought about what it would be to deal with an offender with whom you had, or might develop, a relationship. Her conclusion could hardly be more different from those occasions when the conversation becomes dominated by the thrill of violent rejection.

Here I can only scratch the surface of what is a rich, varied and contradictory body of material. The polarities evident in the children's talk seem indicative of some endemic tensions in the realm of punishment and its uses in political culture. Considering these through the prism of conversation helps us to observe them close-up and in the process of formation. The abiding tension between rejection and reconciliation sits deep within our language and the 'vocabularies of penal motive' (Melossi 1993; *cf* Garland 1990) that it contains. The discourse of rejection is 'marked' by signals of distancing, generalising and anonymising. The will towards reconciliation, conversely, uses markers of affiliation and identification.

This tension recalls the one suggested so long ago by Hume and taken up more recently by Baier (1995) between *justice* as 'a cold, jealous virtue' and *sympathy* as the capacity of one's psyche to 'reverberate to another's fate'. Whenever we engage in discourse about crime, wrongdoing, sanctions and punishment, whether in the special conditions of the courtroom or the

RJ conference, or in more everyday settings, we take up, relay, reproduce or transform positions of this kind in our very speech. To consider this aspect of our conduct seriously is to engage in what Hymes (1968) has called 'the ethnography of speaking', defined as the systematic study of the 'situations and uses, patterns and functions of speaking as a social activity'. When we apply this sensibility to legal arenas we begin to investigate what Conley and O'Barr (1998: 9) term 'the linguistic enactment of law's power'. Girling, Smith and I have argued at more length elsewhere (2006) that these methodological recommendations are very much consistent with recent developments in RJ theory which understand RJ procedures as 'communal processes' (Ahmed et al 2001: 11) and stigma and reintegration-work as 'communications' (Ahmed et al 2001: 42).

I have tried in this chapter to suggest some contemporary uses for Hume's notion of sympathy. I have suggested that there is a certain sense in which even some of the more dismaying and seemingly hostile aspects of our penal culture can be read as engaging us through our sympathetic impulses, however perverse the outcome. Sympathies, in this sense, can of course be divisive, partial and exclusionary. But sympathy as Hume understands it is the capacity that provides for the possibility of 'reflexion' and co-ordination: it addresses the otherwise enigmatic question of why we have an interest in one another's interests. Baier argues that amongst the things we take from Hume is the sense that moral reflection 'at its best' consists in 'an emotional response to a fully realised situation' (Baier 1995: 64). This is something very different, as she puts it, from being required to think of morality as 'a nasty, if intellectually intriguing, game of mutual, mutually corrective threats' (1995: 14). Amongst the reasons for taking RJ seriously is that it might be one of the better ways yet devised of exposing ourselves to the 'fully realised situation' rather than to some more schematic or reductive depiction.

REFERENCES

Ahmed, E, Harris, N, Braithwaite, J and Braithwaite, V (2001) *Shame Management Through Reintegration* (London, Cambridge University Press).
Baier, A (1995) *Moral Prejudices* (Boston, Harvard University Press).
Baillie, J (2000) *Hume on Morality* (London, Routledge).
Beckett, K (1997) *Making Crime Pay* (Cambridge, Cambridge University Press).
Blackburn, S (1998) *Ruling Passions: a Theory of Practical Reasoning* (Oxford, Oxford University Press).
Braithwaite, J (2000) 'Repentance rituals and restorative justice' 8(1) *Journal of Political Philosophy* 115–31.
Buchan, J (2003) *Capital of the Mind: How Edinburgh Changed the World* (London, John Murray).
Canovan, M (1999) 'Trust the People! Populism and the Two Faces of Democracy' 47(1) *Political Studies* 2–16.

Collins, R (2004) *Interaction Ritual Chains* (Princeton, Princeton University Press).

Conley, J and O'Barr, W (1998) *Just Words: Law, Language and Power* (Chicago, University of Chicago Press).

Fine, GA (1997) 'Scandals, social conditions and the creation of public attention' 44 *Social Problems* 297–323.

Garland, D (1990) *Punishment and Modern Society* (Oxford, Oxford University Press).

—— (2001) *The Culture of Control* (Oxford, Oxford University Press).

Gilligan, C (1982) *In a Different Voice: Psychological Theory and Women's Development* (Cambridge, Massachusetts, Harvard University Press).

Girling, E, Smith, M and Sparks, R (2006) 'The trial and alternatives as speech situations' in A Duff, L Farmer, S Marshall and V Tadros (eds), *The Trial on Trial* (Oxford, Hart Publishing) vol 2.

Hymes, D (1968) 'The ethnography of speaking', in J Fishman (ed) *Readings in the Sociology of Language* (The Hague, Mouton).

Harris, N, Walgrave, L and Braithwaite, J (2004) 'Emotional dynamics in restorative conferences', *Theoretical Criminology* 8(2) 191–210.

Jewkes, Y (2004) *Media and Crime* (London, Sage).

Karstedt, S (2002) 'Emotions and criminal justice' 6(3) *Theoretical Criminology* 299–318.

LaFree, G (1998) *Losing Legitimacy: Street Crime and the Decline of Social Institutions in the United States* (Boulder, Westview Press).

Layder, D (2004) *Emotion in Social Life: the Lost Heart of Society* (London, Sage).

MacIntyre, A (1988) *Whose Justice? Which Rationality?* (South Bend, Notre Dame University Press).

Melossi, D (1993) 'Gazette of morality and social whip' 2(2) *Social and Legal Studies* 259–79.

Pettit, P (2001) 'Is Criminal Justice Politically Feasible?' 5 *Buffalo Criminal Law Review* 427–50.

Pinker, S (2005) 'Morality arises from shared perspectives, not faith', *The Independent*, 23 March 2005.

Pratt, J Brown, D, Brown, M, Hallsworth, S and Morrison, W (eds) (2005) *The New Punitiveness: Trends, Theories, Perspectives* (Cullompton, Willan Publishing).

Shilling, C (2002) 'The two traditions in the sociology of the emotions' in J Barbalet (ed), *Emotions and Sociology* (Oxford, Blackwell).

Simon, J (1997) 'Governing through crime' in G Fisher and L Friedman (eds) *The Crime Conundrum* (Boulder, Westview Press).

—— (2000) 'Megan's Law: Crime and Democracy in Late Modern America' 25(4) *Law and Social Inquiry* 1111–50.

—— (2001) 'Fear and Loathing in Late Modernity: reflections on the cultural sources of mass imprisonment in the United States' 3(1) *Punishment and Society* 21–33.

Smith, M, Sparks, R and Girling, E (2000) 'Educating sensibilities: the image of "the lesson" in children's talk about punishment' 2(4) *Punishment and Society* 395–415.

Sparks, R (2000) '"Bringin' it all back home": populism, media coverage and the dynamics of locality and globality in the politics of crime control' in K Stenson and R Sullivan (eds), *Crime, Risk and Justice* (Cullompton, Willan Publishing).

—— (2001) 'Degrees of estrangement: cultural theory and comparative penology' 5(2) *Theoretical Criminology* 159–76.

—— (2003) 'Punishment, populism and political culture in late modernity', in S McConville (ed) *The Use of Punishment* (Cullompton, Willan Publishing).

—— (2006) 'Ordinary anxieties and states of emergency' in S Armstrong and L McAra (eds), *Perspectives on Punishment*, (Oxford, Oxford University Press).

——, Girling, E and Smith, M (2001) 'Children talking about justice and punishment' 8 *International Journal of Children's Rights* 191–209.

Strang, H (2002) *Repair or Revenge: Victims and Restorative Justice* (Oxford, Oxford University Press).

Tonry, M (2004) *Thinking About Crime* (New York, Oxford University Press).

Tyler, TR and Boeckmann, R (1997) 'Three strikes and you're out—but why?' 31 *Law and Society Review* 237–65.

Wilkinson, I (2005) *Suffering: a Sociological Introduction* (Cambridge, Polity Press).

16

The Power and Limits of Populism: An Illustration from Recent Penal Developments in New Zealand

JOHN PRATT

I. INTRODUCTION

WHILE RECENT PENAL developments in New Zealand will be the main analytical focus of this chapter, I want to begin by quoting from a speaker in the Canadian federal parliament. In 1975 he proclaimed that 'the cry for law and order has been the cry of nearly every tyrant in history. "Law and order" was the cry of Hitler when he assassinated nearly one million [*sic*] Jews. Law and order has always been the cry of people who want to commit violence against others'.[1] The significance of these comments, I want to suggest, lies not in their graphic contempt for politicians who campaign around law and order issues, but in the way in which they represent a way of thinking about such matters that was then characteristic of modern penal development. For much of the nineteenth and twentieth centuries, penal affairs had been largely addressed and managed 'behind the scenes' by civil servants and bureaucratic organisations working in conjunction with governments, and drawing on advice from academic experts and similar elites (see Loader 2006). The general public were largely excluded from any involvement in such matters. This helped bring about general disinterest in crime and punishment, punctuated only by scandal that periodically emerged from behind the veil that usually covered such matters. As a result, and across modern society as a whole, law and order issues became largely residual matters, marginal to more central concerns of government such as education, health and so on. This explains the indignation of the speaker above at any attempt to move them to the centre of political debate.

---

[1] Hansard 195 vol 1 830 (17 April 1975).

Since that time, however, the disinterest of the public has changed to a demand for greater influence on crime control and penal affairs and governments have increasingly sought to take note of their emotions and mood in policy development (Pratt 2002). Richard Nixon, in his appeal to the emotions and sentiments of the 'great silent majority' of American citizens in the late 1960s, was probably the first politician of stature to break the existing mould. This was then followed by the exploitation of law and order issues in the late 1970s and early 1980s in Britain by Margaret Thatcher and the Conservative Party. Various aspects of penal policy, in particular the (re)introduction of 'short, sharp shock' detention centre regimes, were driven by appeals to the emotive sentiments of the public at large (at least as these were represented by screaming headlines in the tabloid press: Hall 1980), rather than research-led. Today, we find strong relationships between governments and extra-governmental forces which claim to speak on behalf of the public or which in some way represent their feelings about crime and punishment matters and which have become more embedded in policy development. By the same token, government bureaucracies have increasingly had less influence, or uncomfortably share the space previously exclusive to them with such representatives of the public mood and are thereby consigned to roles where they have had to implement the public's rather than their own ideas (Garland 2001; Freiberg 2003; Roberts et al 2003).

It would be possible to trace varying aspects of these elements across many modern societies at the present time. What I want to address in this chapter, however, are issues relating to the particular effectivity of public sentiment and emotion—populism—on penal policy development. While this includes an examination of its power and influence, I also want to examine the limits that there are to this and, indeed, to question the supposed inevitability that commentators such as Ryan (2005: 143; emphasis in original) attribute to this phenomenon: 'politicians are required to *engage* with the public in a manner that a generation ago would have been unheard of in most Western democracies ... the wider public nowadays refuses to be air-brushed out of the policy-making equation.'

II. 'POPULIST PUNITIVENESS'?

Let me begin first by addressing the nature and extent of the relationship between governments and the various channels through which public sentiment is now channelled. Tony Bottoms (1995: 40) coined the phrase 'populist punitiveness' (which has also come to be known as 'penal populism') to capture these trends. Their impact on policy was in the form of 'politicians encourag[ing] punitive laws and sentences and thereby improv[ing] their chances of re-election by making such responses to indicators of the public mood or sentiment' (1995: 40). This, he insisted, was something more than public opinion, since 'we cannot speak in any straightforward fashion about [this] on crime in a way that automatically equates it with a heavily punitive approach.' But there is more to populist punitiveness/penal populism than this. Not only is populism not the same thing as public opinion, in addition it does not represent the voice of the public as a whole, nor is it something which can be measured or surveyed in public opinion polls. Instead, populism represents the voices of significant and distinct segments of the public—those segments which feel that they have not been listened to by governments, unlike more favoured groups; those segments which feel they have been disenfranchised in some way or other by the trajectory of government policy which benefits others but not them. As Shils (1956: 100–01), in one of the first expositions of this concept, observed: 'populism exists wherever there is an ideology of popular resentment against the order imposed on society by a long established, differential ruling class which is believed to have a monopoly of power, property, breeding and fortune.' Populism thus gives a voice to this alienated, dissatisfied section of society. It claims to be their voice, the voice of ordinary people, as it speaks out against the ways in which the government of the day has failed to address their interests. And in addition, it speaks out against those other sectors of society which it judges to have been complicit in this: the government's own bureuacratic organisations; sometimes the entire parliamentary process which is seen as self-serving rather than public-serving; and the various extra-governmental elite groups thought to be tangled up in a loosely fitting coalition of forces that overall represents 'the establishment'.

As such, one way for politicians to re-establish their credentials with the public is for them to make claims to speak on their behalf against the government and the more general 'establishment', translating the simplicity and plain talking of ordinary people into structures that are simple and direct (Taggart 2000: 4), while at the same time distancing themselves from establishment forces. Historically, populist movements have been found on both the right and left of the political spectrum (Taggart 2000), depending on the politics of the existing establishment which they have been reacting against. As such, populist movements are 'of the people but not of the system', as Canovan (1999: 3) puts the matter. There are major differences, then, between populism and the array of new criminal justice social movements and think-tanks and privately funded research organisations that also work outside of the establishment (Downes and Morgan 2002). Populism, unlike these other bodies, claims to represent the aspirations of ordinary people, the general public itself, not the fringe groups or minorities more usually associated with these other extra-establishment organisations, against what is perceived to be a privileged, highly educated, cosmopolitan elite. For these reasons, penal populism today is almost exclusively punitive in direction.

At the same time, this conceptualisation of contemporary public sentiment and mood, unlike the two earlier manifestations of this phenomenon in the Nixon and Thatcher eras, recognises that the public *do* have their own views, which are often forthrightly expressed by them or on their behalf by lobby groups, victims' rights activists, talk back radio hosts and callers, and so on. Importantly then, the public are not mere dummy players, who require political leaders to speak on their behalf; nor are they mere 'dupes', manipulated by the press and exploited by politicians.

In these respects, and well aware of the potential of law and order to bring about electoral success if they are thought to be strong on this, or defeat if thought weak, politicians have been keen to appropriately address these sentiments. Indeed, this matter is no longer the exclusive property of right-wing Conservative (or their equivalent) parties but, since the electoral success of Bill Clinton in the United States, has also become the strategy of liberal and left-leaning parties in Britain, New Zealand and Australia—often leading to a 'bidding war' between the main parties to attract voter support (Newburn 2002). Each is likely to try and appear more punitive than the other to this end (Roberts et al 2003). At the same time, processes of globalisation lend themselves to increasingly swift exchanges of ideas and strategies, while the 'tabloidisation' of the news media shapes them into convenient sound-bites. This has led to the development and popularisation of a new language of punishment, articulated in commonsensical, easily understandable phrases such as 'Three strikes and you're out' (and variations of this, allowing for just two, or even one, strike), 'Life means Life' and 'Truth in Sentencing'. In this way, the general direction of policy is developed not on the basis of evidence-led research but through the fear that politicians have of being trumped by their rivals' ability to latch on to populist aspirations.

In addition, populist influences today are much more broad-based than the manipulation of public sentiment that took place during the Thatcher or Nixon periods. Such has been the growth in the channels through which public sentiments can be expressed, such have been the expectations created by politicians who speak to them, that they are no longer likely to be easily satiated by throwaway gestures such as the short, sharp shock detention centre policies of the first Thatcher government. Instead, they demand more transparency and 'common sense' across the penal system as a whole, not simply longer (and often harsher) prison sentences (*cf* Bottoms 1995). They are likely to be sceptical of parole (which is seen as a subversion of the judicial process by bureaucratic stealth) and also of innovative measures such as home detention (with electronic monitoring) and restorative justice, which seem to undermine the rightful place of prison at the centre of any sentencing spectrum. Again, public emotions frequently insist that communities have the right to know, or to be consulted about the release of particular groups of prisoners, and that the community's own right to security overrides that of individual ex-prisoners to privacy, which politicians have also acknowledged. Bill Clinton, when introducing a federal 'Megan's law' which allowed for community notification of the release of sex offenders, stated that 'we respect people's rights but today America proclaims that there is no greater right than a parent's right to raise a child in safety and love … America warns—if you dare to prey on our children, the law will follow you wherever you go, state to state, town to town' (Office of the Press Secretary 1995).

Even when governments (as in Britain and New Zealand) have been reluctant to go so far and have insisted on keeping notification procedures within the purview of their own bureaucracies, there is still likely to be an onus on them to make gestures of reassurance to public sentiment, once it has been aroused about such matters (often by politicans' own rhetoric). As such, we find provisions in these countries for ever more intrusive and longer periods of surveillance in the community (Nellis 2005). This will almost certainly ensure a greater likelihood of parole violation amongst this group of ex-prisoners, to be then highlighted in the media and thereby increase public insecurities and demands for more protection from them. In addition, public sentiment has an influence and effect at an informal as well as a formal level. In Britain, the murder of eight-year-old Sarah Payne in 2000 prompted widespread *ad hoc* vigilante activities against suspected paedophiles. On a number of occasions recently, local communities have prevented sex offenders from settling in them on release from prison (Pratt 2000)—often after prompting from journalists keen to manufacture a story. In New Zealand, three such ex-prisoners were now living in former prison officer houses next to the prisons they were released from in 2005, as a result of public opposition to their presence beyond these parameters.

What such developments point to is the way in which politicians may actually lose control of events when public emotions are aroused about crime and punishment issues: they are no longer simply 'pulling the strings'—still implicit in the 'populist punitiveness concept—and thereby deleteriously influencing an otherwise benign public. Indeed, rather than trying to find resonance with the public mood when it suits them, in some circumstances politicians may actually be led on by those extra parliamentary forces they find themselves in allegiance with. In these respects, public sentiments are not free-floating phenomena, able to be pounced on by politicians as they choose and then dropped just as quickly. They can often be well organised, channelled and articulated in such a way that they come to assume a life of their own. As such, they provide a set of understandings of crime and punishment through a completely different frame of reference from that which had been available for much of the post-war period (Pratt 2002). These expressions of populism draw on personal experience, common sense and anecdote, rather than social science research. They judge the 'effectiveness' of sanctions on the basis of sentence length, deterrence and satisfaction to victims, rather than financial costs, reconviction rates, humanitarianism and general 'decency' (Loader 2006), the way in which it had previously been judged by civil servants, academics and so on. This can ensure that law and order issues remain central to political agendas, as these representations of public sentiment have the power to override rational argument and analysis in policy development.

III. THE POWER OF POPULISM IN NEW ZEALAND

Furthermore, these sentiments can even become inscribed in the democratic process itself, as recent developments in New Zealand illustrate. Pratt and Clark (2005) provide the following explanation for the particular susceptibility of this country to populist influences. First, it has a unicameral system of government—there is very little by way of institutional blocks to the impact public sentiment can have on politicians—and there is also a strong tradition of public involvement in community affairs. Secondly, there has been a huge disenchantment with the existing political process as a result of both the main parties launching dramatic neo-liberal economic reforms in a country where there had been a strong tradition of egalitarianism and state regulation. Thirdly, there has been the declining authority of established forms of penal expertise, set against the increasing availability and authority of common sense solutions to crime problems put forward by those claiming to speak on behalf of the public in a society where there has always been an emphasis on functional utility and a suspicion of anything resembling intellectualism (Pratt 1992). Fourthly, a range of victims of crime movements with a focus on rape and domestic violence in the 1980s became subsumed into a more general popular movement where every citizen was seen as a potential victim because of their vulnerability to crime. To this we may add a fifth development: the transformation of the local media. In 1989 there were only two, publicly owned, television channels available in New Zealand. Since then, the funding base of state-owned television has been transformed so that it now has to make a profit—and it also has to compete with several private terrestrial channels now available, and with satellite television (to which around 40 per cent of households subscribe). It thus not only gives less space for serious consideration of current affairs, but at the same time, because it seeks to maximise income from advertising during its main news hour, 'dumbs this down' to attract as wide an audience as possible.

Overall, then, in New Zealand in the 1990s the public were increasingly likely to turn away from looking to established institutions for problem-solving, to distrust those in positions of power and authority, and to place great faith in those who spoke a language of common sense and who offered simple solutions to complex (and not easily solvable) problems—which were more readily communicated to them in the transformed media. Such matters are hardly unique to New Zealand. What may be unique to this country, though, in relation to such trends, is the way in which the democratic processes of the country have been dramatically changed in the last 10 years to allow such sentiments to have a formal presence in policy-making. In a bid to offset public disenchantment with the existing electoral system (first past the post), provisions were made for the introduction of non-binding Citizens Initiated Referendum (CIRs) in 1996 (along with a multi-member proportional system of electoral representation).[2]

The CIRs would be indicative but thereby non-binding on government, and would be put before the electorate when petitions were presented to parliament containing the signatures of 10 per cent of registered voters in support of the proposal. One such CIR in 1999—the last of four[3] that have been held since 1996—elicited a 91.75 per cent vote in favour of the following question: 'Should there be a reform of our criminal justice system placing greater emphasis on the needs of victims, providing restitution and compensation for them and imposing minimum sentences and hard labour for all serious violent offences?' It had been the product of the efforts of a Christchurch shopkeeper (Mr Norm Withers), whose mother had been seriously assaulted while minding his premises during his lunch break. In gathering the signatures of 10 per cent of the electorate that was necessary for it to go ahead, he received no help at all from business or any significant political parties. In other words, that he was able to get the requisite signatures was due to highly localised popular support. The massive vote in its favour then seemed to give it an importance over and above the crime and punishment issues it addressed: it became a wave of resentment and discontent against those establishment forces—bureaucrats, civil servants, judges, academics and other liberal elites—who were thought to have somehow conspired together to bring about the plethora of late modern anxieties and insecurities (of which fear of crime had become the most talked about) that weigh on everyday life.

This sense of culpability—of judges at least—seemed to be confirmed, alongside the recognition that the configuration of penal power which had allowed this to happen was no longer sustainable, when in 2000 the Labour-led coalition government introduced a Judicial Complaints process to oversee the appointment, monitoring and disciplining of judges: '[the

---

[2] 'First past the post' essentially refers to the 'winner takes all' electoral process characteristic of the United Kingdom. The political party which wins the most seats, but not necessarily the most votes, forms the government. Multi-member proportionality, characteristic of New Zealand and Germany, gives the electorate two votes: one for the local MP they wish to represent them, the other for the party they wish to see running the country. The party that then gains the most votes ultimately gains the most seats.

[3] The other three were for more pay for firemen; prohibiting battery hen farming; and one to reduce the size of parliament, from 120 members to 99. This one was passed at the same time as the law and order referendum with an 81% vote in favour—and was completely ignored by the government.

Justice Minister] said a worryingly large number of people no longer have full confidence in the justice system' (*The Dominion* 26 February 2000: 3). Earlier, he had warned them to take note of public sentiment and expectations when sentencing. They risked losing their autonomy and discretion if they did not: 'public opinion does not take kindly to being ignored, particularly where there is a suspicion it is being dismissed arrogantly' (*The Press* 26 February 2000: 1).[4]

However, the referendum had been voted on at the end of a decade which had seen levels of imprisonment and sentence lengths significantly increase, while reported crime had declined, with enhancements of already existing restitution for crime victims. In these respects, it was superfluous. In addition (aside from issues relating to its incoherence), it was unworkable. 'Hard labour' in prison would have been completely impractical and in breach of numerous human rights conventions to which New Zealand had been a signatory. And yet the possibilities of challenging the referendum were greatly limited. By now, it had gained the support of the vast majority of MPs across the political spectrum, who frequently referred to it in ensuing debates about law and order, no doubt aware of its vote-winning potential. In contrast, academics and other establishment groups who were critical of it risked being caught up in a maelstrom of populist declamation, having dared to challenge its self-evident righteousness, and where they would find themselves manipulated by sections of the media gorging on the easily digestible feast that reporting law and order issues had become for it. When the Secretary for Justice did publicly express his scepticism, Mr Withers' response was: 'Are they [*sic*] saying the public is thick? [The question] was complex but it was plain English'. It confirmed his view that the only opposition to it was from elite, unrepresentative groups such as 'upper class individuals and a few trendies' (*The Dominion* 12 October 1999: 9).[5] Even the Governor-General and former High Court judge Dame Silvia Cartwright was angrily criticised by prominent opposition MPs for being both anti-populist and indeed for entering the political arena (which was were these matters now firmly belonged), when she made the comment 'prisons don't work' when opening the Crime and Justice Research Centre at Victoria University of Wellington in 2002.

Again, then, public sentiment had become reified and generated new outlets through which it could be addressed: for example, the Sensible Sentencing Trust (SST), a voluntary organisation, came into existence in 2000 to pressure the government to put the referendum into effect. It

---

[4] This is particularly ironic. In a 'mood of the nation' report (UMR Research Ltd 2004), politicians were the least respected of 17 listed occupations; judges came a respectable seventh.

[5] He may well have been right. The two wealthiest constituencies returned the lowest 'yes' votes, albeit 77.5% and 87.33% respectively.

received substantial media coverage as it promoted law and order during the 2002 general election campaign (indeed, unlike most academic experts and civil servants, its spokespeople seemed only too pleased to gain a high media profile). It had its own website and organised two well publicised marches in the run-up to the election. These were intended as remembrance rallies for the victims of violent crime, amidst SST's claim that the murder rate in New Zealand had increased by 1400 per cent over the last 40 years (a figure that was never challenged, even though, so far as can be ascertained, there simply seems to be no substance to this claim[6]). Many of the marchers carried wooden crosses, some bearing the names of murder victims. MPs from all the main political parties as well as government ministers attended the rallies and addressed the marchers in the penal language that was expected of them in these surrounds ('life should mean life, no parole'; 'there's no reason for parole').

The referendum then became a referent against which the contents of the subsequent Sentencing, Parole and Victims' Rights Acts of 2002 could be justified as they passed through parliament. The Ministry of Justice (2002: 1) acknowledged that amongst the objectives of the 2002 legislation was the need 'to respond to the 1999 Referendum which revealed public concern over the sentencing of serious violent offenders. New Zealanders also expressed a desire for better protection from dangerous offenders.' When the Sentencing Act was passed, the Minister of Justice telephoned Mr Withers to congratulate him on his success. Broadly speaking, the legislation significantly increases penalties for violent crime, mandates judges to take into account the gravity of the offending and the culpability of the offender, and exhorts them to make more use of maximum penalties. The Parole Act further restricts parole opportunities for these groups of offenders and makes 'risk to community safety' the sole criterion for parole assessment, with victims having the right to make representations in writing or at parole hearings. The Victims' Rights Act extends the rights of notification of decision-making within the criminal justice process as a whole.

The results of these law changes and the public clamour surrounding them have been predictable. New records have been set for the length of prison terms; the level of imprisonment, 7327 in 2004, was the highest ever; and the rate of imprisonment increased from around 150 per 100,000 of population in 1999 at the time of the referendum to 179 in 2004—indeed, even before the referendum, New Zealand had the second highest imprisonment rate in the OECD; the Ministry of Justice acknowledges that the new legislation will increase the prison population by a further 1000 in the

---

[6] The murder rate in New Zealand has increased since 1960 when it stood at 1.5 per 100,000 of population; in 2002 it stood at 3.1—which would seem to indicate that it has increased by 100% (not 1400%), although even this is rather artificial, since the numbers are still very small: around 40 murders in 1960, 80 in 2002.

next few years (it was initially thought that it would only increase by an extra 300, much to the dismay of opposition MPs who claimed that there should be many more than this); four new prisons are being built at a cost of NZ$800 million (US$550 million; £400 million); even so, there is still likely to be overcrowding in the prisons as a result of the influx caused by the populist-driven legislation—thereby eroding some of the real improvements that have been made in them in the last 10 years. In such ways, the incorporation of public sentiment into the policy-making framework has had the effect of enhancing already existing illiberal trends and strains of intolerance.

It does have to be recognised, though, that by so doing, the public appetite for such matters may have been satiated, or at least appeased, albeit at great social and economic cost—law and order hardly featured in the general election of 2005 as an issue (the election was dominated by taxation and welfare benefits issues). Why should this have been so, when it had been such a major theme in political and public discourse in the late 1990s and at the beginning of the twenty-first century? There would seem to be two main reasons for this. First, once single-issue political concerns have been addressed to at least some satisfaction, then their *raison d'etre* is lost. Here, the public anger and outrage articulated in the referendum had been satiated to some extent by the 2002 law changes—as such, it was difficult to sustain energy and interest beyond this. Second, a period of stable (Labour-led) government between 1999 and 2005, with minimal unemployment and a general rising of living standards, had, it seems, soothed some of the anxieties of the previous 15 years or so that the country seemed to be disintegrating: hence the strong support for punitive measures during that period in a bid to try and provide some measure of cohesion and consensus (Tyler and Boeckmann 1997). This was categorically not, then, a reflection of public opinion 'catching up' with the reality of New Zealand's declining crime rate—most people in this country still believe that crime is increasing (Ministry of Justice 2003).

Be this as it may, it is the victims of crime, so often at the centre of populist discourse, who have gained least from the undoubted influence penal populism has had on sentencing and penal policy-making in New Zealand. They are likely only to have been given false hopes (of compensation or completely unrealistic sentences) and unnecessary fears (fed by completely unrealistic concerns about the parole prospects for murderers, rapists and so on).

IV. LIMITS?

If these developments show the power and force that public emotions may now have on policy-making, it is also clear that there are limits to this.

A repeat attempt, in 2004, to dramatise law and order was a complete failure by the leader of the National Party opposition, Dr Don Brash. His speech to an SST conference (also keen to ensure that law and order remains politically prominent), where he announced his party's policies on crime control, was made within a very clear populist frame of reference. The realities of crime and punishment were discarded in favour of newspaper headlines to understand them:

> I don't intend to recite a lot of statistics to make my case. We all know that New Zealand has a terrible record. It is in front of us each day ... Every day, the media carry stories of horrendous crimes—appalling family violence, resulting in death and disfigurement of women and children; random killings by drug-crazed criminals out on parole; brutal muggings of young tourists visiting our country; dangerous and often drunk drivers, many with numerous previous driving convictions, killing people on the roads. And what is our response? Not much. (Brash 2004: 1)

The response of his own party, he went on to explain, would be to abolish parole and build more prisons (costing around a further NZ$1billion (US$700 million; £500 million)). The prison population, he acknowledged, would then rise by another 50 per cent. His popularity, very high at that point, immediately dropped. He had clearly misjudged the public mood. SST does not represent this. Although that organisation does purport to speak for the public, it only gives *a particular representation* of this which was then shown to be some distance removed from public feelings about these matters. An opinion poll conducted for Television New Zealand the day after the speech showed that 56 per cent of the public favoured parole (with appropriate safeguards). This failure to understand the limits and boundaries of populism is similar to the attempt by the British Conservative Party in 2000 to launch a 'zero tolerance' policy on cannabis use, which then came to nothing (and certainly did not enhance public support for the Conservative Party) after public opinion polls had revealed widespread support for *relaxing* the current legislation (Roberts et al 2003: 52). It would seem, then, that there are clear penal boundaries which public opinion will not cross. Politicians who then march across them are likely to find that they are not being followed. Overall, there seems to be no mass of public support ready to embark on some great, moralistic punishing crusade. Here, penal populism had clearly reached its frontier, for reasons set out above. The coalitions of support that had previously sustained it had fragmented or had fallen into abeyance.

However, they can still be resurrected by high-profile cases which commonsensically highlight travesties of justice, thereby eroding public confidence in the criminal justice system—for example, citizens being prosecuted for defending themselves and their property against burglars; or notorious cases involving the murder or rape of innocents which inflame these sentiments, sometimes making them boil over altogether. In these respects, the New Zealand Labour Government passed the Prisoners and Victims' Claims Act in 2005. This allows crime victims, or their families or other organisations such as SST campaigning on their behalf, to sue ex-prisoners for up to six years on their release for any windfall they might have by then received, such as lotto winnings, earnings from gainful employment or any court-adjudicated damages.[7] Indeed, it was the public consternation and outrage at one such case in 2004, where six prisoners were awarded modest damages for ill-treatment from the prison authorities (over a period of years, in one case), that prompted the legislation. The outrage was not over their ill-treatment—they had been detained in conditions similar to US supermax prisons, for which there was no lawful authority—but their ability to successfully sue the government for this. In explaining the legislation, the Justice Minister emphatically rejected the notion that anyone 'pays their debt to society' while in jail: 'it costs us NZ$50,000 a year to keep someone in prison ... that is a cost to society, not the repayment of a debt ... you don't repay your debt to the victim by being in prison' (*The Dominion Post* 8 January 2005: E3). In his eagerness to respond to the emotions that the case had provoked, he was prepared to imply that going to prison was no longer enough punishment—there had to be some additional penalty, if the public mood on this matter was to be appeased. And while this government may now be wary of expensive additions to the prison estate, there has been no softening of its hostility to the population within it. As such, in addition to the public wrong that the state punishes, individual citizens can also pursue private grievances over the same issue—a remarkable departure from the state's previous monopolistic control of criminal justice disputes.

Strategically (and here I am referring to modern societies other than the USA, where different rules which have led to that country's penal 'exceptionalism' would seem to apply), this legislation illustrates that the way to maintain political popularity is not to propose grandiose and self-evidently expensive plans that will dramatically and obviously expand the boundaries of the penal estate: instead, this can be achieved by seizing and exploiting opportunities for the pursuit of vindictiveness against well-known outsider groups, or for the reassertion of common-sense expectations in the form of 'rights' that might seem periodically under threat. In such ways the boundaries of acceptable levels of punishment can be more discreetly, incrementally and less controversially pushed back—so that the new territories that are reached then become unremarkable and unnoticed, other than as reflections

---

[7] Similar concerns were raised in England over a serial rapist who bought a £7 million lottery ticket while on weekend leave from prison. It was reported that the Government was 'considering extending the six-year limit on lodging a claim, after the High Court ruled [one of his victims] could not sue ... the 76 year old victim of attempted rape is to appeal against the ruling' (http://news.bbc.co.uk/1/hi/uk/4321402.stm).

of the success of government policy and its eagerness to respond to what the public want (and not an example of scandalous or unnecessary excess).

V. INEVITABLE?

These New Zealand developments show the dangers that unleashed public emotions can pose to hard-won rights and liberties, and the way they can further exclude those who are already outsiders, often on the basis of mythical presuppositions. By the same token, though, we can also see from the mirror-image of what made these developments possible in New Zealand that there is no inevitability to them across modern society as a whole. We can see in this mirror ways of counteracting populist influences, or preventing them from surfacing altogether. For example, there are clear cultural barriers to populism. In a country such as Sweden, which demonstrates the value it places on the intelligentsia by awarding Nobel prizes for the highest achievements in literature, science and so on, we would really not expect to find a culture that can tolerate high prison levels or degrading conditions within them; similarly, in the main street of the Norwegian capital, Oslo, which runs from the central railway station to the parliament, the most impressive buildings are those of the Faculty of Law of its university, symbolising the national authority and recognition given to its jurists. Again, in the Scandinavian countries and other low imprisonment societies such as Switzerland it would seem that academic experts still carry considerable respect and prestige and may make a significant impact on policy development (Lappi-Seppala 2000): the law-making process still remains the exclusive prerogative of civil servants and academic experts (Pratt 2008a, 2008b).

Equally, public emotions are unlikely to have much of an effectivity in those societies where there are extensive layers of government which can soak up them up, or which render the seat of power impenetrable to them: thus Canada, with its federal and provincial systems of government, has a rate of imprisonment in decline and has held populism at bay, notwithstanding its proximity to the USA and the ready availability of such influences (Meyer and O'Malley 2005). Even where populist sentiments have been unleashed, as has been happening in the Netherlands in recent years, strong central government bureaucracies may still be able to obstruct these influences (van Swaningen 2005). In other words, bureaucracy can represent a bulwark against the tyranny of populism. Again, there is little by way of a tabloid press in these countries to egg on public sentiment, and state television seems largely unreconstructed. Furthermore, victims of crime in Scandinavia receive financial assistance from the state (which then tries to recover it from the criminal). This brings closure, whereas victims' organisations, law changes and the new government proposals in New Zealand seem calculated to prolong victimisation, to little benefit or gain.

Cultural differences, a strong central state bureaucracy, layer after layer of government which makes policy-making largely impenetrable to populist influences (with the converse being that New Zealand, as a small society with a unicameral system of government, is particularly vulnerable to them), and even language differences, are thus all likely to restrict the influence of populism and allow policy-making to remain largely the domain of governments, civil servants, academics and so on. But outside of those countries which come into this category, then what we have indeed seen taking place elsewhere to varying degrees has been the 'fall of the Platonic guardians'. Loader (2006) rightly suggests, however much some may look on penal developments since then with disdain, it is simply not possible to return to that previous period, since its own conditions of existence have vanished. Indeed, there are no doubt very many who welcome this change, providing as it does an opportunity for a more democratic, more transparent penal politics. However, as an illustration of the form that this new way of penal policy-making might follow, the New Zealand example that has been set out here may help to dispel romantic notions of 'peoplehood' and anti-elitist celebration—at least if long-standing but hard-won fights over human rights and values which can be traced back to the Enlightenment still have any force. But, of course, what has happened in New Zealand is but one example of the form which the reconfiguration of penal power might take. If this chapter has not shared the optimism of Ryan (2003) for such possibilities, then it is nonetheless agreed that such changes pose new challenges for and put new demands on those working in the academy. If penal populism contains within it the menace to human rights and values that have been suggested here, then these have to be defended, and the only way to do this is for those in the academy to actively engage in public and political discourse themselves.

REFERENCES

—— 'Law and Disorder' *The Dominion* (12 October 1999) A9.

—— 'Violent crime referendum cannot be ignored says [Justice Minister] Goff' *The Dominion* (26 February 2000) A3.

—— 'A Punishing Regime' *The Dominion* (8 January 2005) A3.

—— '[Justice Minister] Goff tells judges to get tough' *The Press* (26 February 2000) 1.

Bottoms, A (1995) 'The Philosophy and Politics of Punishment and Sentencing' in C Clarkson and R Morgan (eds), *The Politics of Sentencing Reform* (Oxford, Clarendon Press).

Brash, D (2004) 'Law and Order—A National Priority'. Address to the Sensible Sentencing Trust, 4 July 2004 (Wellington, National Party).

Canovan, M (1999) 'Trust the people! Populism and the two faces of democracy' 47 *Political Studies* 2–16.

Downes, D and Morgan, R (2002) 'The Skeletons in the cupboard: the politics of law and order at the turn of the millenium' in M Maguire et al (eds) *The Oxford Handbook of Criminology* (Oxford, Oxford University Press).

Freiberg, A (2003) 'The Four Pillars of Justice' 36 *Australian and New Zealand Journal of Criminology*.

Garland, D (2001) *The Culture of Control* (New York, Oxford University Press).

Hall, S (1980) *Drifting into the Law and Order Society* (London, Cobden Trust).

Lappi-Seppala, T (2000) 'The fall of the Finnish prison population' 1 *Journal of Scandinavian Studies in Criminology and Crime prevention* 27–40.

Loader, I (2006) 'Fall of the 'Platonic Guardians': Liberalism, Criminology and Political Responses to Crime in England and Wales' 46(4) *British Journal of Criminology* 561–86.

Meyer, J and O'Malley, P (2005) 'Missing the punitive turn? Canadian criminal justice, "balance", and penal modernism' in J Pratt et al (eds), *The New Punitiveness* (Cullompton, Willan Publishing).

Ministry of Justice (2002) *Reforming the Criminal Justice System* (Wellington, Ministry of Justice).

—— (2003) *Attitudes to crime and punishment: A New Zealand study.* (Ministry of Justice, Wellington).

Nellis, M (2005) 'Electronic monitoring, satellite tracking and the new punitiveness in England and Wales' in J Pratt et al (eds), *The New Punitiveness* (Cullompton, Willan Publishing).

Newburn, T (2002) 'Atlantic Crossings' 4 *Punishment and Society* 165–94.

Office of the Press Secretary (1995) Press Release 25 July www.ibiblio.org/.../ whitehouse-papers/1995/Jul/199507-25-Press-Secretary-Statement-onMengans-law-Decision.

Pratt, J (1992) *Punishment in a Perfect Society* (Wellington, Victoria University Press).

—— (2000) 'Sex crimes and the new punitiveness' 18 *Behavioural Sciences and Law* 135–51.

—— (2002) *Punishment and Civilization* (London, Sage).

—— (2008a) 'Scandinavian Exceptionalism in an Era of Penal Excess: Part I—The Nature and Roots of Scandinavian Exceptionalism' *British Journal of Criminology*, doi:10.1093/bjc/azm072.

—— (2008b) 'Scandinavian Exceptionalism in an Era of Penal Excess: Part II—Does Scandinavian Exceptionalism Have a Future' *British Journal of Criminology*, doi:10.1093/bjc/azm073.

—— and Clark, M (2005) 'Penal populism in New Zealand' 7(3) *Punishment and Society* 303–22.

Roberts, J et al (2003) *Penal Populism and Public Opinion* (Oxford, Oxford University Press).

Ryan, M (2003) *Penal Policy and Political Culture in England and Wales* (Winchester, Waterside Press).

—— (2005) 'Engaging with punitive attitudes towards crime and punishment. Some strategic lessons from England and Wales' in J Pratt et al (eds) *The New Punitiveness* (Cullompton, Willan Publishing).

Shils, E (1956) *The Torment of Secrecy* (London, Heinemann).

Taggart, P (2000) *Populism*. (Open University Press, Milton Keynes).

Tyler, T and Boeckmann, R (1997) 'Three strikes and you are out, but why? The psychology of public support for punishing rule breakers' 31 *Law and Society Review* 237–65.

UMR Research Ltd (2004) *Mood of the Nation Report. New Zealand 2004* (Wellington, UMR Research Ltd).

Van Swaningen, R (2005) 'Public safety and the management of fear' 9 *Theoretical Criminology* 289–306.

17

Playing with Fire? Democracy and the Emotions of Crime and Punishment

I. EMOTIONALITY IN CONTEMPORARY POLICING AND PENALITY

S OCIAL ANALYSTS OF punishment have been exercised of late by
what appear to be some significant shifts in the character of contemporary crime control—trends that are most discernible in the USA and
UK, but traces of which have also been apparent in Australia, New Zealand
and several European jurisdictions (Garland 2001; Pratt et al 2005). The
attention of such commentators has focused, in particular, on the at least
partial eclipse of a system administered by experts, working at arm's length
from democratic pressures and pursuing inclusionary goals, by one that has
become more populist in style and punitive in substance (Loader 2006a).
Public discourse on crime has in the process assumed a high emotional
charge, as politicians react to the mass-mediated anger, indignation and
anxieties of the public by promising to 'get tough' with offenders and 'crack
down' on crime. A host of recent crime control developments—spiralling
prison populations, minimum mandatory sentences, controls on sex offenders, zero tolerance policing, anti-social behaviour orders—all attest to a
new political consensus under which governments seek to give voice and
effect to, rather than temper, the impassioned demands of citizens—and
especially victims. In short, the temperature of penal politics has moved
from 'cool' to 'hot' (Garland 2001: 35).

This of course tells only part of the story of the current crime control landscape. Several authors have pointed out that it overlooks important national

* Centre for Criminology, University of Oxford. Email: ian.loader@crim.ox.ac.uk. I would
like to thank Benjamin Goold, David Green, Julian Roberts, Richard Sparks, Lucia Zedner
and my co-editors for their helpful and supportive comments on an earlier version of this
chapter.

differences and trajectories—notably between the US and, say, Germany and France, or Italy, Scandinavia, or Canada (eg, Tonry 2001; Whitman 2003; Pratt et al 2005: Part 3). Others—addressing the US and UK cases—have even argued that this is the wrong story (Matthews 2005). One can point, for instance, to restorative justice initiatives that seek to give institutional effect to human emotions—notably shame, remorse and forgiveness—that are marginalised by standard criminal justice practices. Other social control interventions seek quietly and patiently—outside the purview of the mass media—to foster pragmatic change in ways that neutralise or side-step the passions that crime excites—think of cognitive behaviour programmes, or practices of actuarial justice, or situational crime prevention. Yet these arguably struggle for public acceptance at least in part because they fail to correspond to how people *feel* about crime, or to match-up to the affective investments they have made in 'tough' policing and penal methods of addressing crime. There seems little doubt today that the genie of public emotions is out of the bottle.

This should hardly occasion a great deal of surprise. Passion is after all—as Durkheim has wisely taught us—'the soul of punishment'. Various emotional states—anger, fear, indignation, resentment, disgust, vengeance, guilt, shame, remorse, pity, compassion, pleasure, excitement—are intimately and inescapably tied up with matters of crime and punishment—even though criminology has only sporadically appreciated this. But emotions that the modern penal state once kept in check, held at one remove, or opted not to recognise, seem now to have been unleashed in what many observers regard as illiberal, dangerous ways (Nussbaum 2003; Pratt, this volume). So what should be our response? How, in liberal democratic societies, should governments and crime control institutions seek to handle the individual and collective emotions that crime and punishment arouse?

In addressing this topic we are in fact confronted with a sub-species of a large political conundrum that pre-dates the re-emergence of emotionality in the field of crime control and extends well beyond the penal realm—namely, that of 'the relationship between liberal democracy and the *affective* dimensions of political life' (Markell 2000: 38; emphasis in original). I cannot hope to address this conundrum fully in the space offered by a short paper, so will limit myself instead to the goal of provoking further thought and enquiry on it. My hope is that, by critically comparing three candidate models for resolving the dilemmas which this relationship throws up in the field of crime and punishment, I can cast some valuable light on whether and if so how it is possible—in Markell's (2000) telling phrase—to 'make affect safe for democracy'.

II. THE COGNITIVE DEFICIT MODEL

This first stance that I want to outline and consider one may call the 'cognitive deficit' model. It has been associated in recent years with the important work of academics such as Mike Hough and Julian Roberts (Roberts and Hough 2002a; Roberts et al 2003; Roberts and Hough 2005) and has—in England and Wales—underpinned the recent campaigning efforts of the 'Rethinking Crime and Punishment' Project (Allen 2004). It also often lurks implicitly in the impulse many criminologists have to demystify and demythologise the crime question in a bid to make crime control and penal policy more rational or evidence-based (eg, Wilson and Ashton 1998; Chapman et al 2002; Felson 2002). With this purpose in mind, proponents of this model tend to accord the public emotions that surround crime and punishment little explicit treatment; holding, it would seem, to the belief that the affects are at best irrelevant, at worst inimical, to the pursuit and delivery of reasonable, humane and effective crime control.

The central claim of those who subscribe to the 'deficit' model is that public opinion towards punishment is not uniformly punitive or vengeful, but is rather ambivalent, complex and nuanced—subtleties that the mass media and populist political actors routinely gloss over. The model attributes much of the anger and indignation that people feel towards 'lenient' penal practices to their lack of information about how the criminal justice system works and consequent misunderstanding of it. An extensive body of work on public opinion towards crime and punishment has demonstrated that individuals know little about the extent and distribution of crime, or patterns of sentencing and punishment. The average statistically uninformed citizen continues to believe that volume crime is rising; holds an erroneous view of the relative frequency of violent as against property offences; over-estimates the utility and value of imprisonment; and under-estimates that of community penalties (Indermaur and Hough 2002; Roberts and Hough 2005: ch 1). The political classes have, in turn, embraced such attitudes in ways that articulate and reinforce the ignorance and misunderstandings upon which they rest. The resultant combination of tough-minded policies premised on a motivated presumption of public punitiveness stands, so the argument runs, as a powerful impediment to rational penal reform (Roberts and Hough 2002b).

The public policy goal promoted by advocates of this model is to make good this cognitive deficit by supplying citizens with more robust, independent information about patterns of crime, the purposes and outcomes of sentencing, and the relative use and effects of carceral and community penalties. In this vein, proposals have been made for enhancing the quality of information available to the media and for targeting the provision of reliable knowledge to key sub-audiences. It has been suggested that the legislative proposals of political parties seeking to acquire or retain office are subject to scrutiny in the light of available evidence (Roberts et al 2003: ch 10). Roberts and his co-authors (2003: 167) have, in addition, recommended the establishment of an independent crime information and prevention agency tasked with disseminating reliable knowledge of

what works in reducing crime and disorder—something the Rethinking
Crime and Punishment Project's criminfo.org.uk website has recently
sought to prefigure. The overarching hope—for which there is some
supporting evidence (Hough and Park 2002; Hutton 2005)—is that a
better-informed citizenry will exhibit less punitive, more liberal-minded
attitudes towards crime and punishment, and that it is possible to foster
political responses to crime based on a fuller appreciation of the nuances
of public opinion.

This approach to grasping the meaning and effects of public attitudes
towards crime is intended by its proponents to satisfy the tests of 'realism and pragmatism' (Indermaur and Hough 2002: 200). They appear, in
so doing, to give credence to the 'emotional or dispositional' as well as
the 'informational side' of people's opinions (2002: 201), and argue that
countering 'simplified and tough-minded penal policy' entails a struggle
'not over facts or details but over morals and emotions' (2002: 210;
see also, Allen 2004: 64). Yet these are occasional asides—Roberts and
Hough's (2005) latest book on the topic has not a single index entry on
emotions—and they seem hard to square with the constitutive purposes
and contentions of the deficit model. This model, in the main, effects a
tidy separation of the cognitive from the affective dimensions of public
attitudes, unduly privileging the former over the latter, and consequently
failing to address the emotional and cultural dynamics surrounding the
formation, circulation and reproduction of penal sensibilities (*cf* Girling,
Loader and Sparks 2000; King and Maruna, this volume). Consider in
this regard the key claims made by proponents of the cognitive deficit
approach—namely, that penal policy is 'distorted' by the present interplay
between government, media and popular opinion (Roberts and Hough
2002b: 5), and that public attitudes can be 'corrected' or 'improved'
by better information. These seem to me to be problematic on several
grounds.

The first is signalled by the idea of 'distortion'. This, in my view,
smuggles into the debate on penal policy two claims that stand in need of
greater clarification and defence. First, that 'we' (the experts who admin-
ister, or work in, or research the system) are able broadly to agree on what
a rational crime and penal policy would look like and thus have available
an 'undistorted' counterfactual against which the distortions that result
from public ignorance can be measured and judged. Secondly, that there
is to hand a supply of uncontested politically and culturally neutral information, the dissemination of which would effect the required 'correction'
to current public opinion. There is more than a hint in these claims of a
scholastic frustration that the social world is not designed according to
scientific lights, coupled with a sense that the desired goal is the technocratic one of reconfiguring penal policy so that it is no longer 'inconsistent
with the results of criminological research' (Roberts et al 2003: 160).

Indeed, this motif is sufficiently prominent within the deficit perspective as to warrant a re-issue of the warning that instrumental rationality has also—like emotion—to be made safe for and by democracy (Habermas 1970).

Proponents of the deficit model tend, secondly, to treat the eclipse of liberal penal policy in the decades since 1970 as a huge public relations failure, and urge that the task that stands before us is that of communicating better messages to a poorly informed and superficially severe populace (Allen 2004: 61). It is true that one finds within this perspective much well-intentioned talk of 'improving the quality of public debate' on crime and punishment. But this seems to rest on a monological, top-down dissemination of truths that are already known, rather than a recognition of, and engagement with, the 'fears, frustrations and uncertainties' (Indermaur and Hough 2002: 201) experienced by publics that remain the audience and addressees of crime control institutions and practices, but to whom these practices must be minimally credible (*cf* Green 2006: 147). It is as if, by injecting facts and evidence into public discourse about penal policy, it is possible to force an alteration in the often emotionally compelling dispositions that individuals hold towards crime and punishment—a hope that rests on the felicitous, and optimistic, calculation that the more informed one is about, say, the judicial function or the effects of imprisonment, the more liberal one's orientation towards them becomes.

To voice these concerns is not to gainsay the value of seeking to improve the quality of public discourse on crime and penal policy. Nor is it to decry the worth of making citizens better informed about crime and punishment or to deny that being more informed can have civilising effects. It is however to raise for consideration the limits of one currently influential paradigm within which the cause of penal reform is framed and pursued. These shortcomings flow from a hopeful rationalism which holds that public opinion is best characterised as suffering from a cognitive lack that can and should be rectified. It is, as such, an approach that fails to make sufficient allowance for the fact that such opinion assumes the form of cultural mentalities and sensibilities that are saturated with positive and negative emotions, and shot through with thoughtful feelings and passionate thoughts about crime's entanglement with the social relations and moral condition of the political community one inhabits. The desire that all this can and should somehow be expunged by an increased supply of reliable information about the risks of crime and practices of punishment, and that penal policy would be more legitimate and humane if it were, seems to me to be both sociologically implausible and normatively difficult to sustain. It is for this reason that the cognitive deficit model needs to be supplemented and extended by an approach that is better able to grasp and make sense of the *affects* of punishment.

III. THE INSULATION MODEL

In his recent enquiry into the divergent histories and cultures of punishment found in the US and France and Germany, James Q Whitman (2003: 15) makes the following claim:

> There is an intimate nexus between the politics of mass mobilization, unchecked by bureaucracy, and the making of harshness in criminal punishment; and that is a fact that should raise some uncomfortable questions for any of us who like to think of ourselves as committed to the values of democracy.

It is these 'uncomfortable questions' that proponents of the insulation model urge us to think carefully about. In so doing, they make explicit what remains implicit in the deficit approach—namely, that the public passions aroused by crime and punishment are dangerous, illiberal things. But they also remain less sanguine about the prospects of tempering these passions with greater knowledge, opting instead for an approach that shields the criminal justice and penal system from the democratic political process and the pressure-cooker of public emotion. This position has represented the express or implied response of many liberal commentators to the recent 'punitive turn' in penal politics (Pratt, this volume; Zimring and Johnson 2006; Lacey 2008) where it has underpinned a defensive strategy that moves to shore up those 'buffers' that continue to stand between criminal justice bureaucracies and populist demands, while encouraging professionals to continue to 'do good' by stealth, below the radar screen of electoral politics and newspaper headlines. It is a model that rests on the Platonic fear that democracy in the field of crime and punishment will invariably act as a 'demented solvent of value, decency and good judgement' (Dunn 2005: 45); one that believes that since the affects cannot be made safe for democracy, they must be kept at a distance from, or actively suppressed by, rational public institutions (see, generally, Hall 2005: ch 3).

The grounding for this position lies in the claim that exposing crime control or penal policy to democratic pressures has the practical consequence of making its outcomes harsher and excessive. Pettit (2001), for example, highlights what he calls an 'outrage dynamic' that is operative in this field. Here, exposure of evil is followed by popular outrage which in turn prompts responsive political actors to 'react by showing themselves to be at least as outraged as the general run of people—and to be determined, with the resources at their disposal, to do something about it' (2001: 435). The result, Pettit suggests, is to drive sentences 'towards the cultural maximum' (2001: 437). Others have pinpointed and analysed empirical instances of something like this dynamic at work, most starkly in respect of the citizen-initiated 'three strikes' policy in California (Zimring, Hawkins and Kamin 2001), but also in accounting for penal policy developments in England and Wales since the early 1990s (Windlesham 1997; Faulkner 2006) and recent populist penal trends in New Zealand (Pratt and Clark 2005; Pratt, this volume). In each case, we are advised to absorb essentially the same lesson: that opening penal policy up to democratic pressures unleashes not reasoned deliberation about how societies should punish, but impatient, illiberal emotions that demand harsh penal treatment of offenders.

The policy response promoted by advocates of insulation is to place a series of 'buffers' or 'mediating institutions' (Zimring, Hawkins and Kamin 2001: 172) between public opinion and the operation of the justice system in order that these societal 'leniency vectors', as Zimring and Johnson (2006) have recently termed them, can take precedence over popular opinion, responsive politicians and other 'severity vectors'. Many such mediating practices continue to operate in liberal democracies across the world, precisely in order to protect liberalism from the punitive, majoritarian tyrannies of democracy—think, for example, of unelected, almost irremovable prosecutors and judges, parole boards, doctrines of police independence, criminal justice inspectorates and human rights regimes. The goal of insulationists is thus, minimally, to buttress these actually existing institutional forms and to defend the legitimacy of their functions from those political and social actors who now routinely and carelessly decry their 'remoteness', or 'elitism', or wilful disregard of the 'sturdy common sense and simple virtue' of ordinary people (Canovan 1981: 233). Relatedly, proponents of professional insulation urge that we draw comparative lessons from those places—such as Scandinavia, or Germany, or Canada—where liberal elites have retained a hand on the levers of power within the criminal justice state, where crime policy remains aloof from popular pressures, and where penal outcomes are marked by relative mildness (Pratt 2008a, 2008b). Finally, advocates of insulation commend the discovery and construction of new 'arm's-length' bodies that can entrench professional expertise as the driver of crime control and penal policy—with Sentencing Commissions or Guidelines Councils featuring prominently among the agencies that have been promoted or established in this regard.

In advancing these claims, Pettit (2001: 442) and Zimring, Hawkins and Kamin (2001: 204–09) draw the same revealing analogy between penal policy and the delegation of monetary policy to independent central banks. They argue that sentencing and penal policy-making should—like the setting of interest rates—be given over to expert authorities (Pettit recommends a 'penal policy board'), that are free to determine its direction, away from the heat of popular emotion and political imperatives in ways that make citizens and their elected representatives the 'ultimate arbiter' of policy rather than its 'proximate source' (Pettit 2001: 448). Crime and punishment, in short, are held to be among those matters that liberal democracies—for reasons of good governance and social cohesion—may reasonably seek to remove from the agenda of public debate and electoral politics (*cf* Rawls 1993: 29). Indeed, for Pettit, they stand foremost among the domains of public policy in which there exists a strong case for 'depoliticising' democracy (Pettit 2004).

There can be little doubt that much of what insulationists fear concerning democracy and its relations to the emotions of crime and punishment *are* things that committed democrats have to treat very seriously. My reservations about the model, and suggestion that we navigate an alternative course, are thus intended to *build upon*, rather than jettison, the measures that democratic societies can and should properly take to shield aspects of crime control and penal practice from direct democratic control. But there are nonetheless difficulties with the insulation model that limit its overall value in helping us handle the vexed relationship between politics and affect in this field. Let me cite what I think are the two most noteworthy of these shortcomings. First of all, Zimring and Johnson (2006) import into their analysis what seem to me to be some unwarranted, unhelpful and essentialist claims. The insulation model takes as its point of departure what Shapiro (2003: 94) calls a 'primordialist' account of identity. Its proponents hold that public sensibilities towards crime and punishment exist in a natural and unalterable condition of hostility and punitiveness towards law-breakers (Zimring and Johnson 2006: 270)—a proposition that makes the instrumental strategy of eternal vigilance and damage control seem the only viable one. This is a position that I want, in the next section, to dispute. Zimring and Johnson tend, furthermore, to treat what they call 'leniency' and 'severity vectors' as structural and invariant properties of democratic political systems, rather than contingent and mutable features of the present. Having been both scarred and scared by recent experiences in California and elsewhere in the US, they leap to the conclusion that remote professional actors such as judges, lawyers, police officers and criminologists invariably serve as sober forces of 'moderation' in struggles to determine the course and outcomes of crime control policy, while democratic processes and untutored public sentiment can only ever be emotive sources of penal 'aggravation' (see also, Whitman 2003: 55). This is, in my judgement, an over-generalisation—one which disregards the long history of police and criminal justice actors' involvement in and susceptibility to demands for greater police powers and stiffer punishments on the one hand (eg, Hall et al 1978; Loader and Mulcahy 2003: ch 7) and the capacity of participatory political systems to foster public empathy and penal toleration on the other (eg, Barker 2006).

Secondly, it seems to me that the insulationists' preferred strategy of removing criminal justice and penal policy from the arena of democratic politics, and buttressing the authority and room for manoeuvre of professional expertise, is both problematic in principle, and at risk of proving counter-productive in practice—with the result that the mediating institutions they seek to defend remain planted in some barren cultural soil. Its problem at the level of democratic principle lies in the assumption that deliberation among experts (it is not entirely clearly in what) is better placed than open public dialogue to produce penal policy that is simultane- ously effective, rights-regarding *and* minimally credible to the citizens in whose name it is conducted. It is likely to be counter-productive because seeking by technocratic means to marginalise or suppress the emotions that crime and punishment inescapably arouse, in ways that drain public life of its concern with matters of vital human significance, risks fuelling public resentment and leaving it ripe for demagogic and authoritarian exploita- tion. The remedy may, one fears, end up reproducing the very conditions which breed the malady that insulationists have set themselves the task of neutralising.

IV. THE REDIRECTION MODEL

The third approach to addressing the relationship between politics and affect in the crime control field I wish to discuss is best termed the 'redirec- tion' model. I borrow this term from Markell (2000), who uses it to discuss and dissect the recent efforts of Jürgen Habermas and other liberal nation- alist writers to tame ethnic nationalist sentiments using—in Habermas's case—the device of 'constitutional patriotism' (Habermas 1996; see also, Tamir 1993; Taylor 1996). Markell in fact remains sceptical of what he calls 'the strategy of redirection' arguing that efforts to steer dangerous (ethnic) emotions to safe (civic) institutional harbours founder on the fact that these institutions are never 'quite equivalent to the universal principles they purport to embody' (Markell 2000: 39). This is a salutary warning and much can be learned from Markell's insistence on refusing to erase the tension between concrete political cultures and universal values, and mak- ing 'manifest this failure of equivalence' (2000: 40) between any democratic polity's ideals and aspirations and the messy, compromised, always unfin- ished character of its institutional practices. Yet if democratic theory and politics cannot rest content with simply describing, or swimming with the current of, or seeking to contain, the present pattern of public mentalities and sensibilities towards crime (which it surely cannot), it must engage in some form of 'redirective' practice, however uncertain and incomplete this is destined to remain. It is on this basis that I outline and defend the redirec- tion model as a means of facing up 'to the challenge posed by de-insulated policy making' (Green 2006: 131).

I wish to propose a programme of criminological enquiry and associ- ated practical action that seeks not to wipe the slate and begin again from scratch, but to build upon and extend the nostrums of the cognitive deficit and insulationist perspectives. There is, as mentioned, much to be said for seeking to foster more informed public discourse on crime and punish- ment and, given the practical condition of contemporary penal politics, it is easy to grasp the appeal of standing shoulder to shoulder with advocates of the deficit model distributing factsheets. One can also, in a harsh and illiberal penal climate, feel the importance of backing the insulationists in efforts to defend the realm and legitimacy of those institutions that liberal democracies properly put in place to shield criminal justice and penal practices from unmediated popular influence or control. But, all this having been acknowledged, it seems to me neither possible nor desirable to leave matters there. The deficit and insulationist positions are not without their shortcomings and inadvertent dangers, as I have tried to show. They have also succumbed—in the midst of the fears stirred up by an emotive penal populism—to a conception of democracy that is defensive and 'pragmatic' rather than hopeful and 'redemptive' (Canovan 1999). They are by no means the best that we may reasonably wish or strive for.

The redirection model takes as its starting point the inescapable centrality of the emotions to the question of how societies control crime and punish offenders—whether in settings where the genie of public emotion has been freed from the bottle and cannot easily be put back, and in those societies where state bureaucracies remain strong or resolute enough to keep populist and punitive sentiments at bay. Having done so, it seeks to fashion institutions and institutional practices that mediate between public sensibilities and crime control policy not by mobilising experts in the latter to tutor the former (deficit model), or by establishing and policing a sharp demarcation between the two domains (insulationist model), but by bringing the emotionally laced experiences and demands of citizens in from the shadows and opening them up to the scrutiny of public, communicative reason. The aim is to subject the arbitrary and the irrational to the power of reflection by means of institutional devices that routinely allow voice to, and seek engagement with, the wide range of affects—anger, fear, resentment, disgust, pleasure, but also shame, remorse, pity and compassion—that are aroused or mobilised in social life by problems of crime and punishment (*cf* Stedman Jones 2001: ch 9).

Something approaching this idea has in recent years expressly or implicitly underpinned several attempts to put in place alternative, more participatory means of handling crime problems (or problems that end up as crimes) and penal questions. For all that they differ in the scale and scope of the challenges that they confront, and the practices that are deployed to address them, innovations in local dispute resolution, community courts, restorative justice, and truth and reconciliation commissions share in common this broad purpose (eg, Braithwaite and Strang 2001; Braithwaite 2002). By involving individuals and groups as actors in deliberative processes rather than leaving them as keenly interested but basically impotent spectators, and by deepening their knowledge of individual offenders or of the problems that they have gathered to address, such processes aim to address people's anger, fears and resentments with a view to finding resolutions that depend upon and release the possibilities of remorse, forgiveness and hope. It is clearly important to bring a sober cast of mind towards the claims that are sometimes made on behalf of these emergent institutions and to develop a grounded sociology of their practices and effects (Rossner, this volume). It is also imperative that they are anchored in regulatory frameworks that sustain considerations of human rights and the wider public good (Loader and Walker 2004, 2007: chs 5 and 8). But, while insisting upon this, one must not lose sight of the possibilities that these deliberative processes may hold out for dealing with the emotions of crime and punishment differently.

Such forms of emotion-handling need not and should not, however, be limited to face-to-face dispute-resolving processes, valuable though these may be. Responding to the emotive public demands that crime arouses can also importantly take the form of fostering and sustaining an inclusive civic sphere of public institutions within which crime and penal policy can be formed, monitored and revised. There are several models and practices of citizen engagement and democratic contestation that one may point to and develop in this regard, ranging from citizens juries, panels and assemblies, deliberative polling, experiments in e-consultation and democracy and processes of participatory resource allocation (see, for example, Stoker 2006: ch 11). One can also highlight, in the policing field, proposals for policing boards or policing commissions that would mobilise just these techniques of public will formation (Patten 1999; Loader 2000). But whatever form the institutions of redirection take, and whatever range of techniques they deploy, they share in common the goal of eliciting the social experiences of all those affected by crime control policy with a view not to responding uncritically to public sentiments, but to acknowledging the emotional and moral registers within which these claims are pressed and bringing them, on this basis, into mutual dialogue with one another and with relevant professional constituencies. The aim of such dialogue is to strive after policy outcomes that can be said to rest on some defensible, deliberatively produced conception of the common good. But by enabling people to feel identification with processes that recognise their claims and affirm their sense of belonging to a democratic political community, one can, in so doing, handle public sensibilities towards crime in ways that allow people to see themselves as the authors as well as addressees of crime control practices and thereby feel motivated to consent even when the substantive outcomes do not run their way (see, further, Loader 2006b).

Much conceptual work and institutional experimentation is clearly required in order to flesh out how the strategy of redirection might take shape in the field of crime and punishment—though the resources one might want to draw upon and adapt for this purpose lie plentifully at hand (eg, Young 2000; Hoggett and Thompson 2002; Green 2006). There are also—as Markell rightly insists, on a broader canvas—no guarantees that 'safe' outcomes will derive from this democratic effort to engage and unsettle the passionate identities that crime arouses. We may indeed—as the insulationists fear—be playing with fire. But if the question of how to handle the emotions of crime and punishment and the demands that flow with them is one that can neither be skirted nor wished away, the challenge that confronts us is to find ways of minimising the damage that such emotions can do to individual liberties and social cohesion (tasks that advocates of the deficit and insulation models have set themselves), while at the same time seeking to harness the liberty and solidarity strengthening resources they have potentially to offer (opportunities that these same advocates have left unexploited). The merit of the strategy of redirection in this regard is that it acknowledges the necessity of the former while endeavouring to redeem the promise of the latter. There are two important respects in which this is so.

The redirection model emphasises, first of all, that the rule-governed, rights-regarding crime control and penal systems of the liberal democratic state do not simply require emotional control on the part of individuals— whether of the professionals working in the system or individuals watching from the sidelines. They also rest on an indispensable but often barely noticed emotional substrate. The historical development and contemporary reproduction of such systems depends not only on the enlightened self-interest of individuals, as social contract theorists maintain, but also upon *feelings* of abstract trust and solidarity towards strangers capable of supplying the motivational force necessary to enable people to put and pursue security in common and develop the societal infrastructure required to accomplish it (Loader and Walker 2007: ch 6). Liberal institutions of policing, criminal justice and punishment are, in other words, part products and expressions of the fact that individuals care about how their co-citizens treat each other and are prepared to do something to protect them; wish 'their' state to shield those who are strangers to them from harm while also feeling ashamed if that state abuses its powers, and possess an emotional commitment to a political community that aspires to protect the freedom and security of all its members. Feelings of collective national belonging and solidarity are, in short, important cultural prerequisites for creating *and* constraining the power to police and to punish in liberal societies (Yack 2003; see also Canovan 1996).

Having insisted on this foundational point, the redirection model draws attention, secondly, to the importance of, and possibilities that are generated by, channelling the emotional experiences and claims of citizens into institutional processes of public reason. For if one views public demands for order and security not merely as signs of some primordial state of punitive antipathy towards criminal others (as Zimring and Johnson suggest) but also, in part, as expressions of solidarity towards and compassion for strangers (Sparks 2000), then it becomes possible to invest rather more than insulationists are prepared to do in democracy as a means of simultaneously regulating both criminal justice bureaucracies and an emotionalised policing and penal culture. Public sensibilities towards crime and punishment do, to be sure, often possess a durable, emotionally compelling quality that is not easily shifted by exposure to the so-called facts of the matter. But this is not to say that they are either unambiguously and timelessly punitive, or entirely immune to interaction with the political and institutional contexts which shape them (Shapiro 2003: 95). By designing democratic systems that acknowledge the legitimacy of how people feel towards matters they care deeply about, and enable them to participate in ways that deepen their knowledge of the issues and protagonists involved, one stands a better chance of dispelling lay anxiety, anger and resentment and loosening popular attachment to punitive penal outcomes, than by keeping 'the public' penned in as spectators screaming from the sidelines, or enlisting experts to tell them more about the drama they are watching. This, at any rate, is the prospect that the redirection model invites us to explore.

REFERENCES

Allen, R (2004) 'What Works in Changing Public Attitudes: Lessons from Rethinking Crime and Punishment' 1(3) *Journal for Crime, Conflict and the Media* 55–67.
Barker, V (2006) 'The Politics of Punishing: Building a State Governance Theory of American Imprisonment Variation' 8(1) *Punishment and Society* 5–33.
Braithwaite, J (2002) *Restorative Justice and Responsive Regulation* (Oxford, Oxford University Press).
Braithwaite, J and Strang, H (eds) (2001) *Restorative Justice and Civil Society* (Oxford, Oxford University Press).
Canovan, M (1981) *Populism* (London, Junction Books).
—— (1996) *Nationhood and Political Theory* (Cheltenham, Edward Elgar).
—— (1999) 'Trust the People! Populism and the Two Faces of Democracy' XLVII *Political Studies* 2–16.
Chapman, B, Mirrlees-Black, C and Brawn C (2002) *Improving Public Attitudes to the Criminal Justice System: The Impact of Information* (Research Study 245) (London, Home Office).
Dunn, J (2005) *Setting the People Free: The Story of Democracy* (London, Atlantic Books).
Faulkner, D (2006) *Crime, State and Citizen,* 2nd edn (London, Waterside Press).
Felson, M (2002) *Crime and Everyday Life*, 3rd edn (London, Sage).
Garland, D (2001) *The Culture of Control: Crime and Social Order in Contemporary Society* (Oxford, Oxford University Press).
Girling, E, Loader, I and Sparks, R (2000) *Crime and Social Change in Middle England: Questions of Order in an English Town* (London, Routledge).
Green, D (2006) 'Public Opinion versus Public Judgment: Correcting the "Comedy of Errors"' 46(1) *British Journal of Criminology* 131–54.
Habermas, J (1970) *Towards a Rational Society* (London, Heinemann Books).

—— (1996) 'Citizenship and National Identity' Appendix II to *Between Facts and Norms: Contributions to a Discourse Theory of Law and Democracy* (Cambridge, Polity Press).

Hall, C (2005) *The Trouble with Passion: Political Theory Beyond the Reign of Reason* (London, Routledge).

Hall, S, Clarke, J, Critcher, C, Jefferson, T and Roberts, B (1978). *Policing the Crisis: Mugging, Law and Order and the State* (London, Macmillan).

Hoggett, P and Thompson S (2002) 'Toward a Democracy of the Emotions' 9(1) *Constellations* 106–26.

Hough, M and Park, A (2002) 'How Malleable Are Attitudes to Crime and Punishment?: Findings from a British Deliberative Poll' in JV Roberts and M Hough (eds) *Changing Attitudes to Punishment* (Cullompton, Willan).

Hutton, N (2005) 'Beyond Populist Punitiveness?' 7(3) *Punishment and Society* 243–58.

Indermaur, D and Hough, M (2002) 'Strategies for Changing Public Attitudes to Punishment' in JV Roberts and M Hough (eds) *Changing Attitudes to Punishment* (Cullompton, Willan).

Lacey, N (2008) *The Prisoners' Dilemma: The Political Economy of Punishment in Comparative Perspective.* (Cambridge, Cambridge University Press).

Loader, I (2000) 'Plural Policing and Democratic Governance' 9(3) *Social and Legal Studies* 323–45.

—— (2006a) 'Fall of the "Platonic Guardians": Liberalism, Criminology and Political Responses to Crime in England and Wales' 46(4) *British Journal of Criminology* 561–86.

—— (2006b) 'Policing, Recognition and Belonging' 605(1) *Annals of the American Academy of Social and Political Science* 202–21.

—— and Mulcahy, A (2003) *Policing and the Condition of England: Memory, Politics and Culture* (Oxford, Oxford University Press).

Loader, I and Walker, N (2004) 'State of Denial?: Rethinking the Governance of Security' 6(2) *Punishment and Society* 221–28.

—— (2007) *Civilizing Security* (Cambridge, Cambridge University Press).

Markell, P (2000) 'Making Affect Safe for Democracy? On "Constitutional Patriotism"' 28(1) *Political Theory* 38–63.

Matthews, R (2005) 'The Myth of Punitiveness' 9(2) *Theoretical Criminology* 175–202.

Nussbaum, MC (2003) *Hiding from Humanity: Disgust, Shame and the Law* (Princeton, Princeton University Press).

Patten, C (1999) *A New Beginning for Policing in Northern Ireland: The Report of the Independent Commission on Policing for Northern Ireland* (Belfast, HMSO).

Pettit, P (2001) 'Is Criminal Justice Politically Feasible?' 5 *Buffalo Criminal Law Review* 427–50.

—— (2004) 'Depoliticizing Democracy' 17(1) *Ratio Juris* 52–65.

Pratt, J (2008a) 'Scandinavian Exceptionalism in an Era of Penal Excess: Part I—The Nature and Roots of Scandinavian Exceptionalism' 48(2) *British Journal of Criminology* 119–37.

—— (2008b) 'Scandinavian Exceptionalism in an Era of Penal Excess: Part II—Does Scandinavian Exceptionalism Have a Future' 38(3) *British Journal of Criminology* 275–92.

—— and Clark, M (2005) 'Penal Populism in New Zealand' 7(3) *Punishment and Society* 303–22.

Pratt, J, Brown, D, Brown, M, Hallsworth, S and Morrison, W (eds) (2005) *The New Punitiveness: Trends, Theories, Perspectives* (Cullompton, Willan).

Rawls, J (1993) *Political Liberalism* (New York, Columbia University Press).

Roberts, JV and Hough, M (eds) (2002a) *Changing Attitudes to Punishment* (Cullompton, Willan).

—— (2002b) 'Public Attitudes to Punishment: The Context' in JV Roberts and M Hough (eds) *Changing Attitudes to Punishment* (Cullompton, Willan).

—— (2005) *Understanding Public Attitudes to Criminal Justice* (Buckingham, Open University Press).

Roberts, JV, Stalans, L, Indermaur, D and Hough, M (2003) *Penal Populism and Public Opinion: Lessons from Five Countries* (Oxford, Oxford University Press).

Shapiro, I (2003) *The State of Democratic Theory* (New Haven, Yale University Press).

Sparks, R (2000) '"Bringin' it all Back Home": Populism, Media Coverage and the Dynamics of Locality and Globality in the Politics of Crime Control', in K Stenson and R Sullivan (eds) *Crime, Risk and Justice* (Cullompton, Willan).

Stedman Jones, C (2001) *Durkheim Reconsidered* (Cambridge, Polity Press).

Stoker, G (2006) *Why Politics Matters: Making Democracy Work* (Basingstoke, Palgrave).

Tamir, Y (1993) *Liberal Nationalism* (Princeton, Princeton University Press).

Taylor, C (1996) 'Why Democracy Needs Patriotism' in J Cohen (ed) *For Love of Country: Debating the Limits of Patriotism* (Boston, Beacon Books).

Tonry, M (2001) 'Introduction: Penal Policies at the Beginning of the Twenty-First Century' in M Tonry (ed) *Penal Reform in Overcrowded Times* (Oxford, Oxford University Press).

Whitman, JQ (2003) *Harsh Justice: Criminal Punishment and the Widening Divide Between America and Europe* (Oxford, Oxford University Press).

Wilson, D and Ashton, J (1998) *What Everyone in Britain Should Know about Crime and Punishment* (London, Blackstone Press).

Windlesham, L (1997) *Responses to Crime—Volume 3: Legislating with the Tide* (Oxford, Oxford University Press).

Yack, B (2003) 'Nationalism, Popular Sovereignty and the Liberal Democratic State' in TV Paul, GJ Ikenberry and JA Hall (eds) *The Nation-State in Question* (Princeton, Princeton University Press).

Young, IM (2000) *Inclusion and Democracy* (Oxford, Oxford University Press).

Zimring, FE and Johnson, DT (2006) 'Public Opinion and the Governance of Punishment in Democratic Political Systems' 605(1) *Annals of the American Academy of Social and Political Science* 265–80.

Zimring, FE, Hawkins, G and Kamin, S (2001) *Punishment and Democracy: Three Strikes and You're Out in California* (Oxford, Oxford University Press).

Index

London, restorative justice in 153–5,
  157–9, 164–5
long time frame 147–8
low visibility 147
management 145
natural, as 145–6, 149–52, 165
neighbourhood feuds 160–1
neuroscience 149, 150–2, 165
nurture 145, 149, 151–2, 165
procedural justice 214
property crime 153–4, 157–9, 161–2
rape and near-murder 162
reconciliation 150
restorative justice conference experiments
  152–65
restorative peacemaking 298, 304
sentences, increase in 145
social context 145–6, 165
specific events, focus on 147
status, change in 162–3
suicide bombers 147
symbolic reparations 163
transformation
  evidence of 152–65
  interpretation 162–3
venting of emotions 156–61
victims' rights 150
violent crime 153–4, 158–62
young offenders 153
rituals
  interaction 154, 320, 322
  punitive public attitudes 325
  religion 275
  restorative justice conferences 172–81
  Streetwise policing policy in Amsterdam
    235–6
Roberts, J 349–50
Robinson, J 116
rolling on victims 29
Rossner, M 154
Roy, KG 51
Rubinstein, J 25
Rwanda 299, 301–2
Ryan, M 332, 344

Sappho 281
saving face 245, 251
scapegoating 123, 126, 131, 139
Scheff, Thomas J 38, 40, 41, 56, 69, 163,
  171, 180, 199–200, 287, 299–300, 303
Scheider, M 110
schools *see* education
Scottish Enlightenment 322–3
seductions 41
segregation 101
Seidler, VJ 96
self-awareness 295
self-confidence 59

self-esteem
  collective violence 278
  desistance from crime 87, 94
  elderly male prisoners 268
  meaning 278
  punitive public attitudes and class 126
  restorative justice conferences 182
  restorative peacemaking 305
  senseless violence 41, 47, 50
  shame 55–6
  Streetwise policing policy in Amsterdam
    238–9
self-interest 219–22, 229
self-respect 305
senseless violence 37–52
  affective aspects 39, 40, 43
  alcohol 37–8
  anger 40–1, 44–8
  background factors 39
  bystanders, non-intervention of 38
  case study 43–52
  compulsions 41, 42, 48–9
  crime 37–8
  criminology and study of emotions 39–41
  culture 50–1
  dramatisation of evil 37–8
  emotional experiences 38, 41–52
  emotional process 41
  epidemic of violence 38
  expressive aspects of 39, 40
  habitus 49
  happy hour 38
  heat of the moment 49
  impulsiveness 40, 42, 48, 50–2
  interactive aspect 41
  interpretation of emotions 41, 59–51
  justification for emotions 42, 44–8, 50
  lethal violence 37
  line of interpretation 41
  masculinity 49–51
  media 37
  mental disturbances 37
  moral emotions 41, 48, 50
  moral outrage 38
  narcissistic injury 41
  narrative aspect 43
  needs, satisfaction of basic 39–40
  night-time economy 38
  over-reaction 44
  over-sensitivity 46
  path of action 41
  perpetrators' accounts 41–3
  potentiating reasons 49
  predictability 51
  public nuisance 37–8
  public violence 37
  random attacks 38
  reasons 38–41, 48–9